SHIRLEY JACKSON'S DARK TALES

SHIRLEY JACKSON'S DARK TALES

Reconsidering the Short Fiction

Edited by
Joan Passey and Robert Lloyd

BLOOMSBURY ACADEMIC
LONDON • NEW YORK • OXFORD • NEW DELHI • SYDNEY

BLOOMSBURY ACADEMIC
Bloomsbury Publishing Plc, 50 Bedford Square, London, WC1B 3DP, UK
Bloomsbury Publishing Inc, 1385 Broadway, New York, NY 10018, USA
Bloomsbury Publishing Ireland, 29 Earlsfort Terrace, Dublin 2, D02 AY28, Ireland

BLOOMSBURY, BLOOMSBURY ACADEMIC and the Diana logo are trademarks of
Bloomsbury Publishing Plc

First published in Great Britain 2024
Paperback edition published in 2025

Copyright © Joan Passey, Robert Lloyd and Contributors, 2024

Joan Passey, Robert Lloyd and Contributors have asserted their right under the Copyright,
Designs and Patents Act, 1988, to be identified as Authors of this work.

Cover design: Rebecca Heselton
Cover image © Zoonar GmbH/ Alamy Stock Photo

All rights reserved. No part of this publication may be: i) reproduced or transmitted in any form, electronic or mechanical, including photocopying, recording or by means of any information storage or retrieval system without prior permission in writing from the publishers; or ii) used or reproduced in any way for the training, development or operation of artificial intelligence (AI) technologies, including generative AI technologies. The rights holders expressly reserve this publication from the text and data mining exception as per Article 4(3) of the Digital Single Market Directive (EU) 2019/790.

Bloomsbury Publishing Plc does not have any control over, or responsibility for, any thirdparty websites referred to or in this book. All internet addresses given in this book were correct at the time of going to press. The author and publisher regret any inconvenience caused if addresses have changed or sites have ceased to exist, but can accept no responsibility for any such changes.

A catalogue record for this book is available from the British Library.

Library of Congress Cataloging-in-Publication Data
Names: Passey, Joan, editor. | Lloyd, Robert, Dr., editor.
Title: Shirley Jackson's Dark tales : reconsidering the short fiction /
edited by Joan Passey and Robert Lloyd.
Description: London ; New York : Bloomsbury Academic, 2024. | Includes
bibliographical references and index.
Identifiers: LCCN 2023030764 (print) | LCCN 2023030765 (ebook) | ISBN
9781350361119 (hardcover) | ISBN 9781350361126 (adobe pdf) | ISBN
9781350361133 (epub)
Subjects: LCSH: Jackson, Shirley, 1916-1965–Criticism and interpretation.
| Short stories, American–Women authors–History and criticism. |
American fiction–20th century–History and criticism.
Classification: LCC PS3519.A392 Z895 2024 (print) | LCC PS3519.A392
(ebook) | DDC 813/.54–dc23/eng/20231010
LC record available at https://lccn.loc.gov/2023030764
LC ebook record available at https://lccn.loc.gov/2023030765

ISBN: HB: 978-1-3503-6111-9
PB: 978-1-3503-6115-7
ePDF: 978-1-3503-6112-6
eBook: 978-1-3503-6113-3

Typeset by Deanta Global Publishing Services, Chennai, India

For product safety related questions contact productsafety@bloomsbury.com.

To find out more about our authors and books visit www.bloomsbury.com and
sign up for our newsletters.

CONTENTS

Notes on Contributors   vii

INTRODUCTION   1
    Joan Passey and Robert Lloyd

I
INFLUENCE AND INHERITANCE

Chapter 1
'A RELATOR OF STORIES': SUPERNATURAL PRESENCES IN JOSEPH
GLANVILL'S *SADUCISMUS TRIUMPHATUS* (1681) AND THE SHORT
FICTION OF SHIRLEY JACKSON   9
    Miranda Corcoran

Chapter 2
'THE MOST SEDUCTIVE OF MIRAGES': THE WEIRD AMERICAN
DREAM IN SELECTED SHORT STORIES BY SHIRLEY JACKSON AND
JOYCE CAROL OATES   27
    Joseph S. Norman

Chapter 3
DEMON LOVERS, BLUEBEARD'S WIVES: FOLKLORIC INTERTEXTS
AND HORROR IN SHIRLEY JACKSON AND CARMEN MARIA MACHADO   46
    Erika Kvistad

Chapter 4
NEGOTIATING WITCHCRAFT IN SHIRLEY JACKSON'S SHORT FICTION   64
    Dara Downey

II
BODIES AND MINDS

Chapter 5
NIGHTMARES, NEUROSIS AND CLINICAL PSYCHOLOGY IN THE
SHORT STORIES OF SHIRLEY JACKSON   81
    Alice Vernon

Chapter 6
MEETING THE DEVIL: DIABOLIC INFLUENCE AND DIABOLIC
RESISTANCE IN SHIRLEY JACKSON'S JAMES HARRIS STORIES   97
   Robert Zipser

Chapter 7
'MISSING' WOMEN: SPECTRAL DISPLACEMENT IN SHIRLEY
JACKSON'S SHORT FICTION   113
   Robert Lloyd

III
SPACE AND PLACE

Chapter 8
INTO THE GOTHIC WILDERNESS: THE (UN)NATURAL WORLD IN
'MRS. SPENCER AND THE OBERONS' AND 'THE MAN IN THE WOODS'   135
   Alissa Burger

Chapter 9
THE ANXIOUS CITY IN SHIRLEY JACKSON'S 'PILLAR OF SALT' AND
'THE TOOTH': A PHENOMENOLOGY OF THE UNCANNY   148
   Luke Reid

Chapter 10
ON HER WAY TO THE GROCERY STORE: SHOPPING, ALIENATION
AND THE LOST HOUSEWIFE IN SHIRLEY JACKSON'S SHORT STORIES   162
   Emma Liggins

IV
GENRE AND FORM

Chapter 11
'I COULD DO WITH A CHANGE': SHIRLEY JACKSON'S ENGAGEMENT
WITH POST-WAR SCIENCE FICTION   181
   Janice Lynne Deitner

Chapter 12
'THIS GLOOMY KIND OF STORY': SHIRLEY JACKSON'S *CONTE CRUELS*
AND THE HORROR TALE IN THE POST-PULP ERA   200
   Kevin Knott

Chapter 13
MYTH AND RITUAL IN SHIRLEY JACKSON'S SHORT FICTION   215
   Samantha Landau

Index   229

CONTRIBUTORS

Alissa Burger is Associate Professor of English at Culver-Stockton College, Canton, Missouri, United States. She teaches courses in research, writing and literature, specializing in gender, horror and the Gothic. She is the author of *IT, Chapters One & Two* (Devil's Advocates Series, 2023), *The Quest for the Dark Tower: Genre and Interconnection in the Stephen King Series* (2021), *Teaching Stephen King: Horror, The Supernatural, and New Approaches to Literature* (2016) and *The Wizard of Oz as American Myth: A Critical Study of Six Versions of the Story, 1900-2007* (2012).

Miranda Corcoran is a lecturer in twenty-first-century literature in the Department of English, University College Cork, Cork, Ireland. She is the author of *Teen Witches: Witchcraft and Adolescence in American Popular Culture* (2022) and *The Craft* (2023). She is currently compiling an edited collection on satanic feminism in popular culture.

Janice Lynne Deitner (she/her) is the recipient of the 2019 Trinity College Dublin Provost's PhD Project Award 'Beyond Hill House' which focuses on the critically neglected work of Shirley Jackson. Her thesis, to be submitted September 2023, explores the intersection of physical and communal bodies and minds in Jackson's American contexts. She is also the co-organizer of 'Reading Shirley Jackson in the Twenty-First Century', an online resource and annual event that explores the current state of Shirley Jackson studies.

Dara Downey is Teaching Fellow in American Literature in the School of English, Trinity College Dublin, Dublin, Ireland. She is the author of *American Women's Ghost Stories in the Gilded Age* (2014), editor of *The Irish Journal of Gothic and Horror Studies* and co-editor (with Ian Kinane and Elizabeth Parker) of *Landscapes of Liminality: Between Space and Place* (2016). She is currently writing a literary biography of Shirley Jackson for Palgrave's Literary Lives series.

Kevin Knott is Associate Professor at Frostburg State University, Frostburg, Maryland, United States, where his research interests include Gothic literature and film, particularly during the pulp magazine era. Most recently, he has published on Edgar Allan Poe's influence on pulp-era female horror writers in *Poe and Women: Recognition and Revision* (2023). Currently, he is working on a study of the conte cruel in twentieth-century US and UK popular fiction.

Erika Kvistad is Associate Professor of English at the University of South-East Norway, Norway. Her PhD is on sexual power dynamics in Charlotte Brontë, and she has previously published on haunted spaces on the internet, sexual consent negotiation as a textual and cultural phenomenon, horror webcomics and domestic spaces in Victorian horror. Her most recent work is on digital horror hoaxes.

Samantha Landau is Project Associate Professor at the University of Tokyo, Tokyo, Japan. She is a co-founder of the Gothic in Asia Association (GAA). Her research primarily concerns Gothic fiction. She also researches at the intersection of cultural studies, music and poetry. Shirley Jackson's writing has been one of her main research focuses since 2005 and featured in both her MA and PhD dissertations. In addition to her life as an academic, Samantha has been singing and performing classical music for over thirty years.

Emma Liggins is Reader in English Literature in the Department of English at Manchester Metropolitan University, Manchester, UK. Her publications include *George Gissing, the Working Woman and Urban Culture* (2006), *The British Short Story* (with Andrew Maunder & Ruth Robbins) (2011), *Odd Women? Spinsters, Lesbians and Widows in British Women's Fiction, 1850-1939* (2014), and *The Haunted House in Women's Ghost Stories, 1850-1945: Gender, Space and Modernity* (2020). She also has a chapter on 'The Edwardian Supernatural' in *Twentieth-Century Gothic: An Edinburgh Companion* (2021).

Robert Lloyd lectures in English Literature at Cardiff University, Cardiff, Wales, specializing in women's writing and twentieth-century Gothic fiction. He completed his thesis on figurations of spectrality in Shirley Jackson's writing in 2021, which he is currently developing into a monograph. He has also published on Jackson's life-writing in *Women's Studies*, and is an editorial board member of 'Reading Shirley Jackson in the Twenty-First Century'.

Joseph S. Norman is a creative/critical writer and Lecturer in English & Creative Writing at Brunel University London, London, UK. His research interests include Weird Fiction, Science Fiction, Utopianism, Folk Horror and Heavy Metal. His latest book is *The Culture of "The Culture": Utopian Processes in Iain M. Banks's Space Opera Series* (2021).

Joan Passey is Lecturer in English Literature at the University of Bristol, Bristol, UK, where she specializes in transhistorical Gothic fiction and Victorian literature and culture, with a particular emphasis on environments, coasts and seascapes. She is a BBC/AHRC New Generation Thinker, and her monograph *Cornish Gothic, 1830-1913* was published in 2023.

Luke Reid teaches in the English Department at Dawson College, Montreal, Canada. His research focuses on representations of architecture in the Gothic and horror genres, placing architectural history and theory alongside figures of the haunted house. His publications include work on Shirley Jackson and her

House Trilogy, as well as on depictions of architecture and gothic space in popular television.

Alice Vernon is Lecturer in Creative Writing at Aberystwyth University, Aberystwyth, Wales. Her research examines the intersection between creativity and sleep disorders, the cultural history of paranormal investigations, and horror fiction. Her debut non-fiction book, *Night Terrors* (2022) was BBC Radio 4's Book of the Week.

Robert Zipser is an independent scholar and attorney. His publications include 'The Dangerous Classes: Victorian Moral Rhetoric in Poe's "The Man of the Crowd"' in the spring 2020 issue of the *Edgar Allan Poe Review*, as well as an article on Jackson's novel *Hangsaman* for the inaugural issue of the *Shirley Jackson Studies Journal*. He also delivered a paper on Shirley Jackson's story 'The Witch' at the 2022 American Literature Association Conference.

INTRODUCTION

Joan Passey and Robert Lloyd

Paul Theroux, reviewing *Let Me Tell You*, a collection of Shirley Jackson's previously uncollected works released in 2015, states that 'Jackson remains one of the great practitioners of the literature of the darker impulses'.[1] These darker impulses are a distinct feature of her work, encompassing the perennial dispossession of women within and without the home; the paranoia and suspicion of people's motivations towards their neighbours; the uncanny configuration of the built environment and natural world; in essence, a distillation of what it means to live in a state of psychological instability. Jackson's dark impulses – or recurring themes – are of the anxieties of living in this world, with others, without others. *Dark Tales* refers not just to Jackson's eerie, unsettling themes and prose, but to the way these stories, and Jackson at large, have been kept in the dark for so long. By that we mean the metaphorical dark of critical and popular obfuscation, but also the literal dark of archives, the treasures hidden away in boxes and binders in the Library of Congress, where the remains of Jackson's rich and productive career are housed. These collections, of course, despite popular myths of rediscovery, are cared for and nurtured by archivists, librarians and scholars. One does not uncover something that has not already been cared for, gesturing towards another form of invisible labour, much like the long legacies of great women behind great men, building genres while running households. It is these obfuscating myths about labour, archives, legacy and existing in or being pulled from 'the dark' that we are interested in prying apart here.

Over the years Jackson and her tales have been slowly but steadily 'brought to light', through academic interest, mainstream adaptations and most recently a large-scale republishing project by Penguin. Yet so many of the nooks and crannies of these works and Jackson's life seemingly remain in shadow, and recent acts of partial illumination make these crevices darker still in contrast. Many facets of Jackson's career are cast in dazzling limelight – the attention paid to her 1948 short story 'The Lottery' and novel *The Haunting of Hill House* (1959), for instance, is almost blinding – where others are saturated in a steady, warming glow – *We Have Always Lived in the Castle* (1962), for instance. Chances are, if you know Jackson,

---

1. Paul Theroux, "'Let Me Tell You,' by Shirley Jackson", *New York Times*, 27 July 2015. https://www.nytimes.com/2015/08/02/books/review/let-me-tell-you-by-shirley-jackson.html (accessed 2 September 2022).

these are the three works most likely to trip off your tongue; but to claim they were the tip of the iceberg would be to understate just how much is submerged, and just how little resides on the surface.

It is important to note that many of the studies that do consider Jackson begin this way – obsessed with her absence, documenting her undocumentedness, and this ground feels well-worn enough to raise questions of its own, about the way we justify enquiry into 'lost' and 'uncovered' works, and women's labour in particular. Through considering what has come to the forefront, and what has remained relatively underscrutinized, we can assess what has been valued in Jackson's work over time, and how that might be changing with new readers, discoveries, and twists and turns in culture and society at large. Much like the myths of 'discovering' things in the archives, we might posit that Jackson is not as veiled in darkness as some might think, but rather everywhere, all the time. This collection's existence – as the second academic text to exclusively focus on Jackson's short fiction in thirty years – is proof that she is seen, and that 'occlusion' is one of the ingrained preoccupations of Jackson criticism and reception. This preoccupation has served as an important tool for revivifying Jackson, but it can also be employed as a convenient simplification of her place in literary history. Perhaps it is useful, then, to consider Jackson in terms of abundance rather than lack. As a field we have – correctly – noted Jackson's criminal underestimation, critical neglect, the works that could have been but never were. But this collection works away from those gaps or absences, towards thinking about how she has been received and what she has influenced rather than reflecting on the vacuum where consistent popularity should have been.

Upon Jackson death her husband, Stanley Edgar Hyman, tallied her life's works as 'some short stories', marking the birth of the long tradition of gross underestimations of Jackson's output and impact. In reality these number some 200+ tales, with more being discovered with a regularity alarming for the Jackson completist. *Let Me Tell You* (2016) alone contains fifty-six works – thirty short stories, sixteen essays and reviews, and ten pieces of humorous writing on her family, with only fifteen of the fifty-six previously published. In 2020 'Adventure on a Bad Night' (1944) was seen by the public for the first time when it was published by *The Strand Magazine*. In 2022 'Charlie Roberts' and 'Only Stand and Wait' were brought forth from the Library of Congress, two very brief, previously unreleased vignettes Jackson likely wrote in her twenties when she was developing a daily writing practice that would form the basis of her tremendous productivity. While Jackson died in 1965, aged just forty-eight, leaving us to wonder what wonders could have been, her work is in a constant state of dynamic reanimation and rediscovery. This is a joy as a fan – and a challenge as a critic. Those who read and study Jackson are confronted with multiple hurdles: a relative lack of critical work on Jackson's popular texts, let alone her less well-known work, and then the emergence of new work, still. It is both challenge and opportunity, carving out new spaces for reconsideration and reflection with each addition to the Jacksonian canon.

These reanimations of Jackson take many forms: we are interested here with new critical evaluation and the release of unpublished materials, with collecting the previously uncollected, cinematic and televisual adaptation, and influence, legacy and inheritance: Would there be *The Wicker Man* (1973) without 'The Lottery'? What about *Midsommar* (2019)? Another theme in writing on Jackson, as counter to her absence, is her presence in inspiring generations of celebrated authors, with Stephen King and Neil Gaiman mentioned the most often. Horror author Victor LaValle stated, '[w]hen I meet readers and other writers of my generation, I find that mentioning her is like uttering a holy name'.[2] The Shirley Jackson Awards are the barometer of quality in genre fiction. Winners of those awards often cite Jackson as an explicit inspiration. Ellen Datlow collected a number of these authors, a gaggle of Jackson's monstrous progeny, to contribute to a collection of short stories based on her work, *When Things Get Dark* (2021). There we have the dark again. These stories are, very specifically, not about Jackson, they are not continuations or modernizations to her existing works. Instead, they work to capture that elusive 'Shirley Jackson energy' (2020). Few authors could threaten to become a mode of writing in their own right.

Jackson lives on in Netflix adaptations, fictionalized biographies and innumerable blurbs for new fiction positioned as drawing on her distinctive literary qualities. This collection offers another reanimation, an attempt to capture these dynamic outputs and to think about which parts of Jackson's work are brought from the shadows and which remain in the gloom. Joan Wylie Hall's *Shirley Jackson: A Study of the Short Fiction* was the first and last comprehensive investigation of Jackson's short fiction, and following its publication in 1993 a significant number of short stories have come to light. *Dark Tales* both builds on and departs from Hall's germinal foundations to reconceptualize the character of Jackson's short fiction – which we propose shows her at her most daring, playful and challenging – at a time when she has never been more popular.

Part I, 'Influence and Inheritance', considers the role of short fiction in Jackson's legacy, as a writer still discovered and reread; a presence still actively and implicitly shaping twenty-first-century fiction from beyond the grave. While the relationship between Joyce Carol Oates and Shirley Jackson has been considered before – by Oates herself, even – Joseph Norman offers a new way of framing this influence through national and economic anxieties. Carmen Maria Machado has written extensively about Jackson, and Erika Kvistad's essay is the first to critically engage with the implications of this entanglement, against a backdrop of significantly longer folkloric and fairy-tale histories. Miranda Corcoran extends this chain of influence and inheritance back even further, considering Jackson's own interest in and engagement with seventeenth-century literature. Dara Downey reads the simultaneous denial and foregrounding of the shadowy housewife-as-witch as a significant manoeuvre in a selection of Jackson's short stories, and examines how the subversive potential embodied by the witch figure is circumscribed when set against the demands of maintaining domestic spaces. This section demonstrates the importance of Jackson as reader and Jackson as *read*, unpicking the relationship between author and reader as a productive and generative one.

Francine Prose stated that Jackson 'knows what there is, in this world, to be scared of'.[3] The emphasis there is on Jackson's use of the seeming 'real' world,

---

2. Victor LaValle, 'Prepare to Become the Last of the Human Race', *Slate.com*, 4 March 2014. https://slate.com/culture/2014/03/shirley-jacksons-the-sundial-reviewed.html (accessed 2 September 2022).

3. Francine Prose, 'Foreword', in Shirley Jackson, *Hangsaman* (London: Penguin, 2013).

and horror author Paul Tremblay stated that her appeal lies in the collision of 'realism' with 'ethereal atmosphere'.[4] Criticism of Jackson's work that attempts to sever it from genre fiction (the Gothic, horror, the weird) often focuses on her use of real places, realistic characters and domestic moments. Part II, 'Bodies and Minds', considers the materiality and immateriality of physical forms and the psyche to challenge the rationalist assumptions underpinning the 'real'. While there have been psychoanalytic readings of Jackson's work, Alice Vernon transgresses the disciplinary boundaries of psychoanalysis with a reflection on Jackson's engagement with clinical psychology. Robert Zipser brings Jackson's fractured psyches into dialogue with the diabolic and demonic. Finally, Robert Lloyd considers displacement and spectrality in Jackson's recurrent motif of the 'missing' woman. This section surveys the ways in which Jackson pushes against the tangible and the rational to explore the limits of body, mind and what lies beyond both of these.

Criticism of Jackson's work has been dominated thus far with vital, valuable considerations of gender, the Gothic and, more recently, economics. While the haunted house as location in Jackson's work has been rigorously investigated, beyond this there has been relatively little consideration of space, place, environments and ecologies in her writing, surprising considering the 'green turn' in literary criticism over the last few decades. Part III offers an environmental perspective on Jackson's work. Alissa Burger applies theories of the ecoGothic to Jackson's wildernesses to complicate our understanding of Jackson's use of the Gothic. Luke Reid turns the uncanny towards urban space and the built environment to reflect on Jackson's overlooked cityscapes. Finally, Emma Liggins locates Jackson in a twentieth-century context concerned with the purchasing power of the housewife to consider the grocery store as central to Jackson's critique of gender roles. In this collection we seek to demonstrate the myriad opportunities located in moving away from dominant perspectives, and rereading and reframing Jackson amidst emerging critical frameworks.

Part IV, the final part of this collection, turns towards the question of form – in terms of structure, genre and style. The two most well-known Jackson texts are a short story ('The Lottery') and a novel (*The Haunting of Hill House*), and Jackson's body of work is often conflated in criticism without consideration of the specificities of genre, form and medium. The extent to which Jackson is a Gothic or horror author has been hotly contested. Janice Lynne Deitner complicates the debate even further with an investigation of Jackson's parallels with post-war science fiction. Kevin Knott locates Jackson's work in the 'Conte Cruels' of the twentieth century as a way of offering new nuance and specificity to our understanding of Jackson's influence on and knowledge of contemporaneous genre fiction. Finally, Samantha

---

4. Michael David Wilson, Bob Pastorella and Paul Tremblay, 'TIH 214: Paul Tremblay on Shirley Jackson, Supernatural Turn-Offs, and Ambiguity in Horror Fiction', *This Is Horror*, 12 July 2018. https://www.thisishorror.co.uk/tih-214-paul-tremblay-on-shirley-jackson-supernatural-turn-offs-and-ambiguity-in-horror-fiction

Landau illuminates how mythic and ritualistic structures shape Jackson's form. This section asks how a consciousness of narrative construction and reception shape our reconsideration of her work.

Shirley Jackson's 'The Possibility of Evil' (1965), one of her short, dark tales, is about a woman quietly writing, hidden, in the shadows, and the tremendous evil her words unleash upon the world. In the story Miss Strangeworth circulates poison notes and is stunned (and devastated) one day to receive her own, folded on green paper. While this collection is not so green, and not nearly as fanged, it is similarly haunted by the smaller tales that change our reality. We hope these short essays on short stories will stay with you for a very long time.

References

Anon (2020), 'Eerie, Anxious, Foreboding: No Wonder We Can't get Enough of Shirley Jackson', *Penguin*, 22 July. https://www.penguin.co.uk/articles/2020/07/shirley-jackson-anxious-reading-haunting-hill-house (accessed 2 September 2022).

LaValle, Victor (2014), 'Prepare to Become the Last of the Human Race', *Slate.com*, 4 March. https://slate.com/culture/2014/03/shirley-jacksons-the-sundial-reviewed.html (accessed 2 September 2022).

Prose, Francine (2013), 'Foreword', for *Hangsaman* by Shirley Jackson, London: Penguin.

Theroux, Paul (2015), '"Let Me Tell You," by Shirley Jackson', *New York Times*, 27 July. https://www.nytimes.com/2015/08/02/books/review/let-me-tell-you-by-shirley-jackson.html (accessed 2 September 2022).

Wilson, Michael David, Bob Pastorella and Paul Tremblay (2018), 'TIH 214: Paul Tremblay on Shirley Jackson, Supernatural Turn-Offs, and Ambiguity in Horror Fiction', *This Is Horror*, 12 July. https://www.thisishorror.co.uk/tih-214-paul-tremblay-on-shirley-jackson-supernatural-turn-offs-and-ambiguity-in-horror-fiction

Wylie Hall, Joan (1993), *Shirley Jackson: A Study of the Short Fiction*, Woodbridge: Twayne Publishers.

I

Influence and Inheritance

Chapter 1

'A RELATOR OF STORIES'

SUPERNATURAL PRESENCES IN JOSEPH GLANVILL'S
SADUCISMUS TRIUMPHATUS (1681) AND THE
SHORT FICTION OF SHIRLEY JACKSON

Miranda Corcoran

The supernatural abounds in the stories of Shirley Jackson. Whether it is named, invoked as an otherworldly presence, or simply allowed to linger silently on the periphery of the narrative, the supernatural weaves its way throughout Jackson's considerable body of short fiction. In her recent work on *The Haunting of Hill House*, Melanie R. Anderson explains that while Jackson wrote many tales dealing with explicitly supernatural themes, she also incorporated elements of the supernatural into her more ostensibly realist works.[1] Supernatural forces permeate even Jackson's most mundane tales: characters vanish inexplicably; they change identity or appearance, catch glimpses of doubles or find themselves trapped in uncanny, purgatorial spaces. For many readers, one of the most vexing, yet alluring, aspects of Jackson's work is her tendency to enfold the extramundane within the ordinary. Her stories regularly inculcate a deliberate confusion as to whether the events we are reading about are the product of some otherworldly influence, or else a case of madness, confusion, the powers of the imagination run amuck.

Struggling to categorize the often-imprecise intersection of the supernatural and the everyday that characterizes Jackson's unique approach to storytelling, many readers and critics attempt to situate her work within the realm of the fantastic.[2] As defined by Tzvetan Todorov, the fantastic is essentially the product of uncertainty, an inability on the part of readers, as well as fictional characters,

---

1. Melanie R. Anderson, 'Perception, Supernatural Detection, and Gender in *The Haunting of Hill House*', in *Shirley Jackson, Influences and Confluences*, ed. Melanie R. Anderson and Lisa Kröger (Abingdon: Routledge, 2016), pp. 35–53 (p. 35).

2. The connection between Jackson and the fantastic is discussed by Daryl Hattenhauerin, *Shirley Jackson's American Gothic* (Albany: State University of New York Press, 2003). This is also explored in James Egan's essay 'Comic-Satiric-Fantastic-Gothic: Interactive Modes in Shirley Jackson's Narratives', in *Shirley Jackson: Essays on the Literary Legacy*, ed. Bernice M. Murphy (Jefferson: MacFarland, 2005), pp. 34–51.

to ascribe to an event either natural or preternatural origins. For Todorov, the individual who experiences this event

> must opt for one of two possible solutions: either he is the victim of an illusion of the senses, of a product of the imagination – and the laws of the world then remain what they are; or else the event has indeed taken place, it is an integral part of reality – but then this reality is controlled by laws unknown to us.[3]

The fantastic, as a literary genre, resides within and is defined by the moment of uncertainty that precedes such a choice. According to Todorov's definition, the fantastic appears an ideal generic home for Jackson's work. Her stories and novels more often than not stand on the threshold between the real and supernatural, with the reader frequently struggling to disentangle the two. Consequently, we find ourselves wondering: Has the title character of 'Louisa, Please Come Home' *actually* become another person, or has her family simply forgotten her during her long absence? Has the elderly protagonist of 'The Bus' *really* had a premonition of a strange experience in the town of Ricket's Landing, or is she still dreaming? Has the world *truly* shifted around the unfortunate Ms Morgan in 'Nightmare', or is she merely caught within some kind of all-consuming delusion? Perched on the brink of a decision, still unable to choose, we enter the realm of the fantastic.

While I do not dispute the appropriateness of the fantastic as a generic designation for Jackson's work, I would like to consider how her writing was influenced by the unique understanding of the supernatural presented in early modern demonological studies and witchcraft treatises. As such, this chapter will argue that the unsettling admixture of realism and uncanniness found in Jackson's short fiction draws extensively on conceptions of the supernatural dominant during the sixteenth and seventeenth centuries. At this time, as Bladen and Harmes explain, the natural and the preternatural were not so easily uncoupled: 'Our idea of the supernatural as transcending nature differs from the early modern notion of nature as suffused with signs of the divine.'[4] Consequently, in early modern studies of the supernatural, entities we might now conceive of as manifestations of the paranormal or expressions of superstition – like ghosts, witches and demons – were generally framed as part of the natural world. Spirits and demonic forces were thus an incontrovertible fact, as real as the air we breathe or the earth under our feet. Jackson, an eager student of the occult, would have been very much aware of the early modern vision of the natural world as interpenetrated with spectral forces. This belief that the 'present or visible world' cannot be easily set apart from 'the eternal or spiritual world' is discernible throughout her short fiction, as

---

3. Tzvetan Todorov, *The Fantastic: A Structural Approach to a Literary Genre* (Cleveland: The Press of Case Western Reserve University, 1973), p. 25.
4. Victoria Bladen and Marcus Harmes, 'Introduction: The Intersections of Supernatural and Secular Power', in *Supernatural and Secular Power in Early Modern England*, ed. Victoria Bladen and Marcus Harmes (Farnham: Ashgate, 2015), pp. 1–14 (p. 1).

everyday experiences become increasingly bizarre, and the material world seems beset by unnatural occurrences.⁵

That Jackson's work should reflect a distinctly early modern view of the supernatural is not at all surprising. Although the biographical note appended to her first novel, *The Road Through the Wall* (1948), describing the author as 'a practising amateur witch', was devised by her husband Stanley Hyman,⁶ Jackson had nurtured an abiding interest in the occult from a young age and collected books on subjects such as witchcraft, demonology and fortune telling. When asked to write a children's book on the Salem witch trials in 1953, Jackson responded eagerly, noting that she had 'enough of a library on the subject to get the material easily'.⁷ While critics such as Daryl Hattenhauer are careful to stress that 'Jackson did not literally believe in the supernatural, for example, witchcraft and psychic phenomena',⁸ she was deeply attracted to these subjects. Jackson was particularly fascinated by a study published by the seventeenth-century English clergyman Joseph Glanvill entitled *Saducismus Triumphatus*. In an attempt to counter the increasing scepticism of his age, Glanvill – who frames himself as 'a Relator of Stories'⁹ – collected a range of narratives and proofs in order to demonstrate the veracity of witches, demons and spirits. Significantly, Glanvill, in hopes of appealing to the new scientific attitudes of his ages, marries empirical, rationalist discourse with an exploration of the spiritual realm. It is this very fusion of the everyday, the tangible and the ordinary, with the miraculous and the numinous that would later characterize Shirley Jackson's own writing. As such, this chapter attempts to situate Jackson's short fiction in relation to Glanvill's influential study, demonstrating how she replicates his worldview by interweaving the mundane and the spectacular. Although some work has already been done on Jackson's use of quotations from *Saducismus Triumphatus* in her most famous collection *The Lottery and Other Stories* (1949), the present chapter seeks to move beyond this well-trodden path to explore the influence of Glanvill's work, and the early modern construction of the supernatural as a whole, on Jackson's vast corpus of short fiction.

Although born in 1636 and dead by 1680, the philosopher and clergyman Joseph Glanvill was a lifelong companion of Shirley Jackson's. As a college student in the late 1930s, Jackson – already well versed in occult lore – asked her friend Elizabeth Young to steal a copy of Glanvill's *Saducismus Triumphatus* from the University of Rochester's library. When Young refused, Jackson visited the library herself in order

---

5. Bladen and Harmes, 'Introduction', p. 2.
6. Ruth Franklin, *Shirley Jackson: A Rather Haunted Life* (New York: Liverlight, 2016), p. 217.
7. In Franklin, *Shirley Jackson*, p. 355.
8. Daryl Hattenhauer, *Shirley Jackson's American Gothic* (Albany: State University of New York Press, 2003), p. 8).
9. Joseph Glanvill, *Saducismus Triumphatus, Part the Second* (1681), Preface. https://quod.lib.umich.edu/e/eebo/A42824.0001.001?rgn=main;view=fulltext (accessed 30 April 2021).

to study the book under more legitimate conditions.[10] Upon reading the book, Jackson would have discovered a strange composite of supernatural anecdotes and scientific reasoning. First published in 1666 as *A Philosophical Endeavour towards the Defence of the Being of Witches and Apparitions*, Glanvill's book caused a significant stir in contemporary English intellectual circles. It was republished in a second edition in 1667 and in an expanded edition, entitled *A Blow at Modern Sadducism*, in 1668. A number of other editions were printed before 1681, when a 600-page posthumous version of the book, now bearing the name *Saducismus Triumphatus: OR, Full and Plain Evidence Concerning Witches and Apparitions*, was printed under the editorship of the philosopher Henry More.[11] In keeping with the early modern view of the supernatural as existing within, rather than transcending, nature, Glanvill's book 'sought to disprove the claim that witchcraft was impossible by putting forward various naturalistic theories to explain witchcraft phenomena and the nature of spirits'.[12] *Saducismus Triumphatus* therefore incorporates a 'selection of rigorously investigated testimonial accounts of recent supernatural events involving spirits, apparitions, demons and witchcraft'.[13] Building on newly developed scientific ideas, contemporary metaphysics and innovative medical paradigms, the book was intended to both 'support Glanvill's belief in witchcraft and provide a basis for the development of testable hypotheses about how demons and witches interacted with the material world'.[14] In short, *Saducismus Triumphatus* would function as a 'scientific study of "super"-natural phenomena'.[15] As Glanvill himself elucidates, the testimonies he collected function as empirical, verifiable evidence of supernatural occurrences:

> I have no humour nor delight in telling Stories, and do not publish *these* for the gratification of those that have; but I record them as *Arguments* for the *confirmation* of a Truth which hath indeed been attested by multitudes of the like Evidences in all places and times.[16]

Moreover, Glanvill, who felt that growing scepticism about the existence of witches was the first step towards atheism, attempted to work within the intellectual structures laid out by new scientific bodies like the Royal Society (founded in 1660).

---

10. Franklin, *Shirley Jackson*, p. 106.

11. Julie A. Davies, 'Poisonous Vapours: Joseph Glanvill's Science of Witchcraft', *Intellectual History Review* 22 (2012): 163–79 (pp. 163–4).

12. Davies, 'Vapours', p. 163.

13. Julie A. Davies, *Science in an Enchanted World: Philosophy and Witchcraft in the Work of Joseph Glanvill* (Abingdon: Routledge, 2018), p. 1.

14. Davies, *Science*, p. 1.

15. Davies, *Science*, p. 1.

16. Joseph Glanvill, *Saducismus Triumphatus, First Part* (1681), Preface. https://quod.lib.umich.edu/e/eebo/A42824.0001.001?rgn=main;view=fulltext (accessed 30 April 2021), emphasis in original.

Julie A. Davies explains that while carefully documented, replicable experiments were the primary method through which the Royal Society endeavoured to verify new scientific claims, 'in the face of limited scientific capability, *the consistent testimony of individuals or groups* was considered an alternative means through which experience and knowledge could be confirmed'.[17] Glanvill's collection of 'Stories' about preternatural activity is therefore intended to serve as this kind of 'consistent testimony,' providing reliable and verifiable evidence of how the supernatural interacted with the mundane world.

From early in her career as a writer, Shirley Jackson was both fascinated and profoundly influenced by Glanvill's 'Stories'. Despite claiming that 'I have always been interested in witchcraft and superstition, but have never had much traffic with ghosts',[18] Jackson's most famous novel *The Haunting of Hill House* (1959) appears deeply indebted to her early encounters with Glanvill. The strange nocturnal rappings that so terrify Eleanor and Theodora in that book seem directly drawn from Glanvill's description of the Drummer of Tedworth, a poltergeist that tormented the Mompesson family with loud night-time knockings. Indeed, Glanvill's description of Mr John Mompesson's affliction by 'a very great knocking at his Doors, and the outsides of his House' that 'continued a good space, and then by degrees went off into the Air'[19] is clearly echoed in Eleanor and Theodora's terrifying assault by a strange knocking that pounds 'regularly for a minute, and then suddenly more softly, and then again in a quick flurry, seeming to be going methodically from door to door at the end of the hall'.[20] However, other, lesser-known works also draw explicitly on the contents of *Saducismus Triumphatus*. In *Life among the Savages* (1953), a memoir comprising light, domestic pieces previously published in women's magazines, Jackson reproduces a humorous document composed by her husband testifying to the haunting of their own home. The document, entitled 'Some Poltergeist Incidents in the Residence of S.E.H., Esquire',[21] not only parodies Glanvill's language, right down to the early modern typographical convention of using the letter 'f' in place of 's', but it also adopts the same rationalist approach employed throughout *Saducismus Triumphatus*. Jackson (and Hyman's) capacity to so astutely parody the form and content of early modern demonological treatises clearly indicates a profound understanding of the genre's conventions.

Jackson's most overt deployment of *Saducismus Triumphatus* appears in her collection *The Lottery and Other Stories*, originally subtitled 'The Adventures of James Harris'. The seemingly innocuous name James Harris refers to Child Ballad 243, a folk song known in Scotland as 'The Demon Lover' and in North America

---

17. Davies, 'Vapours', p. 165, emphasis added.
18. Shirley Jackson, 'Experience and Fiction', in *Come Along with Me* (London: Penguin, 2013), pp. 204–14 (p. 211).
19. Glanvill, *Saducismus Triumphatus, Part the Second*, p. 91.
20. Shirley Jackson, *The Haunting of Hill House* (London: Penguin, 2006), p. 36.
21. Shirley Jackson, *Life Among the Savages* (London: Penguin, 2019), appendix.

as 'The House-Carpenter'. Anthologized in the nineteenth century by folklorist Francis James Child, 'The Demon Lover' tells of a woman who, believing her lover dead, marries another man. After a number of years, her previous lover returns and lures the woman away to sea. Far from the coast, the lover reveals himself to be a demonic entity:

> They had not sailed a league, a league,
> A league but barely three,
> Until she espied his cloven foot,
> And she wept most bitterly.[22]

In most versions of the ballad, the demon lover sinks the ship and drowns the woman for her perceived faithlessness. Samantha Landau observes that contemporary scholarship on the ballad tends to position it as a conservative injunction that women adhere to dominant social norms of chastity and obedience.[23] However, as Landau also notes, some versions of the ballad function more as a general warning to women about placing their trust in men, a key theme in *The Lottery*.[24] Versions of the Demon Lover, or James Harris, manifest throughout the collection in various forms, and the ballad itself is reproduced in its entirety in the appendix. In his most overt guise, Harris is described but never actually seen in a tale aptly titled 'The Daemon Lover'. In this unsettling story, a young woman is abandoned on her wedding day by her fiancé Jamie. She searches the city for him, asking everyone she meets for a man dressed in blue and carrying a bunch of flowers. When she finally traces him to an apartment she hears 'low voices and sometimes laughter' inside, yet despite returning every day for a week, no one answers her frantic knocks.[25] The figure of James Harris weaves his way through the various stories collected in *The Lottery*: a cruel farmer in 'The Renegade' is named Harris, while in 'The Tooth', we meet a strange man in a blue suit bearing the name Jim. In many of these tales, the Demon Lover exerts an uncanny power over female protagonists who often follow him into madness or despair. An alluring, satanic figure, James Harris embodies 'the intrusion of the demonic as a force that breaks the bonds of matrimony, family, and the socially acceptable dreams of women, replacing them with madness, dreams of adventure, or loneliness'.[26]

---

22. in Alisoun Gardner-Medwin, 'The Ancestry of "The House-Carpenter": A Study of the Family History of the American Forms of Child 243', *The Journal of American Folklore* 84 (1971): 414–27 (p. 416).

23. Samantha Landau, 'Occult Influences in Shirley Jackson's "The Lottery"', *Gauken* 11 (2018): 1–21 (p. 14).

24. Landau, 'Occult Influences in Shirley Jackson's "The Lottery"', p. 15.

25. Shirley Jackson, 'The Daemon Lover', in *The Lottery and Other Stories* (London: Penguin, 2009), pp. 9–28 (p. 28).

26. Landau, 'Occult Influences in Shirley Jackson's "The Lottery"', p. 16.

As such, it is appropriate that Jackson peppers the collection with quotations drawn from *Saducismus Triumphatus* that deal specifically with the deceptive power of the Devil and his minions. Three of the four sections that comprise *The Lottery* are prefaced by epigraphs taken from Glanvill's study. The first of these, marking the beginning of Section II, reads in part: 'We are in the dark to *one anothers* purposes and intendments; and there are a thousand intrigues in our little matters, which will not presently confess their design even to *sagacious inquisitors*.'[27] The quotation, placed within the context of Glanvill's book, is derived from a passage where the author discusses the inscrutability of supernatural forces, explaining that we human beings are fundamentally incapable of understanding the motivations of other people, never mind those of the *other* world. The next epigraph is one that characterizes the other worldly as not merely inscrutable but actively deceptive. Prefacing Section III, we find a passage from *Saducismus Triumphatus* that recounts the confession of one Margaret Jackson (presumably, no relation), who 'did give herself unto the black Man, from the top of her head to the sole of her foot'.[28] Shortly after doing so, Margaret awoke to find a man lying beside her in bed, 'whom she supposed to be her Husband; though her Husband had been dead twenty years, or thereby'. The man, we are told, promptly disappeared, and so Margaret supposed him to be the Devil. Echoing the tale of the Demon Lover, Margaret's confession not only suggests the power of the other world to impinge on and deceive the inhabitants of this one but also alludes to the deceitful power of men. The final epigraph taken from Glanvill begins the fourth and final section. This quotation is borrowed from a passage in *Saducismus Triumphatus* wherein the author explains why it is the case that diabolic forces should prey only upon a select few human souls. Here, Glanvill explains that the diabolic can only exert power over those individuals whose greed, envy or hatefulness is such that they have been abandoned by the good spirits sent by God to watch over them:

> we are never liable to be so betrayed and abused, till by our *vile dispositions* and *tendencies* we have forfeited the *tutelary* care, and *oversight* of the better Spirits; who, though generally they are our guard and defence against the malice and violence of *evil Angels*, yet it may well enough be thought, that sometimes they may take their leave of such as are swallowed up by *Malice, Envie,* and *desire* of *Revenge,* qualities most contrary to their *Life* and *Nature;* and leave them exposed to the *invasion* and *solicitations* of those *wicked Spirits,* to whom such hateful *Attributes* make them very *suitable*.[29]

In this section of his study, Glanvill appears to be offering a rational justification for how the supernatural acts upon the natural realm, a hypothesis grounded in

---

27. Jackson, *The Lottery*, emphasis in original.
28. Jackson, *The Lottery*.
29. Glanvill, *Saducismus Triumphatus, First Part*, p. 21.

'an emerging awareness of psychological illness'.[30] In contrast to early modern sceptics, Reginald Scot (*c.* 1538–99) for instance, who blamed witchcraft beliefs on the melancholic proclivities of elderly women prone to fantasy, Glanvill considered negative mental states to be a prerequisite for demonic encounters. Indeed, Glanvill ardently believed that excessive melancholy could 'leave one vulnerable to spiritual attack and allows a variety of *demonically inspired* delusions to take hold'.[31] In a similar manner, Jackson's stories marry an interest in the psychological with the occult, as depression, loneliness and frustration appear to leave ordinary middle-class women open to paranormal encounters. However, in as much as the supernatural appears as a deceptive, predatory force throughout *The Lottery*, Jackson also entertains the possibility that the other worldly might represent an escape from the oppressive strictures of mid-century American life. Håvard Nørjordet notes that while American editions of *The Lottery* present the first section without an epigraph, the first British edition includes another epigraph derived from *Saducismus Triumphatus*:

> She saith, That after their Meetings, they all make very low Obeyances to the Devil, who appears in black Cloaths, and a little Band. He bids them Welcome at their coming, and brings Wine or Beer, Cakes, Meat, or the like. He sits at the higher end. . . . They eat, Drink, Dance and have Musick. At their parting they use to say, *Merry meet, merry part.*[32]

This description of a witch's sabbath appears in the confession of one Elizabeth Style, who was examined in late January and early February of 1664, and whose name Jackson borrows for the protagonist of 'Elizabeth', a story in the third section of *The Lottery*. This quotation, however, differs from the other extracts incorporated into *The Lottery*'s paratexts in its representation of witchcraft and the demonic encounter as pleasurable, even desirable. The sabbath is framed like a 'merry' party, complete with food and music. Indeed, the emphasis on the presence of wine or beer, cakes and meat at the encounter mirrors Jackson's tendency to accentuate 'the sensory richness of food' in her own writings.[33] Later, in her final completed novel, *We Have Always Lived in the Castle* (1962), the lavish detail with which Jackson describes her heroines' preparation and consumption of 'little tiny hot' pancakes,

---

30. Davies, *Science*, p. 111.
31. Davies, *Science*, p. 19, emphasis added.
32. In Håvard Nørjordet, 'The Tall Man in the Blue Suit: Witchcraft, Folklore, and Reality in Shirley Jackson's *The Lottery or, the Adventures of James Harris*', unpublished MA thesis, University of Oslo, pp. 49–50. https://www.duo.uio.no/bitstream/handle/10852/25403/Norjordet.pdf?sequence=1&isAllowed=y (accessed 30 April 2021).
33. Shelley Ingram and Willow G. Mullins, 'Would You Like a Cup of Tea?: Food, Home, and Mid-Century Anxiety in the Later Novels of Shirley Jackson', in *The Routledge Companion to Literature and Food*, ed. Lorna Piatti-Farnell and Donna Lee Brien (Abingdon: Routledge, 2018), pp. 342–50 (p. 250).

'scrambled eggs and toasted biscuits and blackberry jam', and 'very special rum cakes'[34] bespeaks the pleasure they take in existing, self-sufficiently, outside of the standard, patriarchal family structure. Consequently, if this epigraph had remained in later editions of the collection, it might have suggested an ambivalence about the supernatural, indicating that while the Demon Lover may be a dangerous and deceptive creature, he is also enticing, erotic and potentially liberating.

Although the possibility for such an ambivalent reading of the supernatural is largely absent from *The Lottery* due to the excision of the first epigraph, many of Jackson's other tales present the occult as suffused with deep ambiguities. In some stories, it is a menacing force, leading characters to madness and despair, while in others it takes on a more alluring aspect. Moreover, while Jackson's other short stories and (posthumously published) short story collections do not allude directly to either Joseph Glanvill or *Saducismus Triumphatus*, as *The Lottery* with its rich paratexts does, they nevertheless display a deep indebtedness to Glanvill's work and the early modern conception of the supernatural. Melanie R. Anderson is adamant that the paranormal 'peppers Jackson's creative work, even those stories ostensibly received as humorous sketches of family life,' and that this pervasive supernatural presence attests to the propensity of evil to lurk 'in the most ordinary of circumstances'.[35] In a number of Jackson's posthumously collected tales, the Devil makes an appearance as a sometimes charming, sometimes malevolent figure, whose representation owes much to early modern demonology. Explicit representations of the Devil, complete with horns and cloven hooves that may or may not be concealed by 'pointed patent leather shoes',[36] appear in 'Devil of a Tale' and 'The Smoking Room,' while more covert allusions to the Prince of Darkness can be discerned in characters like the 'lady of the fire' who manifests in 'Lord of the Castle'.[37] In all of these stories, the Devil, whether appearing as a stereotyped horned figure or in a more alluring guise, enters into some sort of pact with a human agent. In 'Devil of a Tale,' the wise Lady Katherine agrees to bear the Devil's son in exchange for a 'throne on earth' and 'the wealth of the world'.[38] In 'The Smoking Room' the Devil and a college student sign a written contract, while in 'Lord of the Castle' the narrator believes that a beautiful, yet diabolic, woman has entered his service. The foregrounding of contracts and pacts in all of those stories sets them in clear relation to early modern ideas about witchcraft and the Devil.

---

34. Shirley Jackson, *We Have Always Lived in the Castle* (London: Penguin, 2019), p. 24, 55, 10.

35. Anderson, 'Perception, Supernatural Detection, and Gender', p. 36, 35.

36. Shirley Jackson, 'The Smoking Room', in *Just an Ordinary Day* (London: Penguin, 2017), pp. 3–8 (p. 3).

37. Shirley Jackson, 'Lord of the Castle', in *Just an Ordinary Day* (London: Penguin, 2017), pp. 199–209 (p. 206).

38. Shirley Jackson, 'Devil of a Tale', in *Just an Ordinary Day* (London: Penguin, 2017), pp. 158–9 (p. 158).

Indeed, it is the notion of a unique, quasi-legalistic relationship between the witch and Satan that distinguishes the early modern witch from her precursors.

Witches, sorcerers and analogous figures have a lineage stretching back far into antiquity. However, the witch as commonly imagined – a broomstick-riding servant of the Devil, who worships him at a collective meeting called a sabbath – is very much an early modern construction, born in the early years of the fifteenth century. This image of the witch was defined by two main characteristics. First, a witch was one who employed evil magic, or *maleficium*; and second, and perhaps most significantly, the witch had entered into a pact with the Devil, agreeing to serve him in exchange for the power to work this harmful magic.[39] The precise nature of the diabolic pact was a matter of great interest to theologians, demonologists and philosophers of the early modern period, and Joseph Glanvill was no exception. *Saducismus Triumphatus* is filled with lengthy ruminations on the precise nature of the pact, which he – like many of his contemporaries – understood as the source of the witch's power:

> The Witch *occasions*, but is not the *Principal* Efficient, she seems to do it, but the *Spirit* performs the wonder, sometimes immediately, as in *Transportations* and *Possessions*, sometimes by applying other Natural Causes, as in raising *Storms*, and inflicting *Diseases*, sometimes using the *Witch* as an *Instrument*, and either by the Eyes or Touch, conveying Malign Influences: And these things are done by vertue of a *Covenant*, or *Compact* betwixt the *Witch* and an *Evil Spirit*.[40]

In keeping with the dominant intellectual rhetoric of his era, Glanvill was particularly interested in the mechanics of the satanic pact because such interactions between witches and demons had the potential to affirm the existence of the supernatural.[41] As Walter Stephens argues in his study of witchcraft and sexuality, interactions between witches and demons – whether contractual or, as was often the case, sexual in nature – were seen to provide empirical proof that physical contact with the diabolic is possible.[42]

The pact motif is represented most explicitly, and indeed most playfully, in 'The Smoking Room', a short story that was unpublished in Jackson's lifetime, but which later appeared in the 1996 collection *Just an Ordinary Day*. 'The Smoking Room' is a tale defined by the interweaving of the fantastic and the mundane. It opens with a young college girl struggling to finish a paper in her dormitory smoking room when she is interrupted by a 'terrific crash and sort of sizzle'.[43] The sudden

---

39. Brian C. Levack, *The Witch Hunt in Early Modern Europe* (Abingdon: Routledge, 2006), p. 29.

40. Glanvill, *Saducismus Triumphatus, Part the Second*, p. 5, emphasis in original.

41. Davies, *Science*, p. 5.

42. Walter Stephens, *Demon Lovers: Witchcraft, Sex, and the Crisis of Belief* (Chicago: University of Chicago Press, 2002), p. 35.

43. Jackson, 'Smoking Room', p. 3.

conflagration, it is soon revealed, is the result of the Devil manifesting, unbidden, in the smoking room. The narrator describes him as 'taller that I imagined. And noisier', with 'barely noticeable horns'.[44] He asks, in a rather embarrassed tone, for a cigarette, and then explains that he has come to take the girl's soul. However, when she surveys the contract giving Satan possession of her soul, the clever young woman decries the document as not 'awfully legal' and suggests drawing up an alternative document.[45] The new contract, laden with complex legal rhetoric, confuses the Devil and he ends up accidentally selling his soul to the girl *and* gifting her with 'an A in Chemistry 186, the power to be invisible when I come in after hours, a date with the captain of the football team for senior ball –' and a 'date with that blond guy' for her friend Bobbie.[46] This story, where the Devil manifests in the ordinary world of a 1930s college dormitory, thus recalls the early modern belief that the Devil was abroad on earth, a real and tangible figure of menace.

However, Jackson's story deviates from Glanvill's and many other early modern accounts of the satanic pact in one crucial way: the narrator *benefits* from the exchange, keeping her soul and increasing her material wealth. In *Saducismus Triumphatus*, the demonic pact is generally characterized by deception, as the Devil takes the witch's soul without giving her the promised reward in exchange. In the confession of Elizabeth Style, for example, the accused witch explains that the Devil

> promised her Mony, and that she should live gallantly, and have the pleasure of the World for Twelve years, if she would with her Blood sign his Paper, which was to give her Soul to him, and observe his Laws, and that he might suck her Blood.[47]

When Style agreed and signed the contract, 'the Devil gave her Sixpence, and vanished with the Paper'.[48] The disingenuous nature of the Devil is also alluded to in other contemporary accounts. Less than thirty years later, Abigail Hobbs of Salem explained that while she had agreed to enter the service of the diabolic for a period of two years in exchange for 'fine cloths', she was bitterly disappointed not to receive this compensation.[49] Accounts such as these follow an oft-repeated script (usually the result of leading questions on the part of examiners) and are intended to show that while the Devil may offer women power and wealth in exchange of their souls, he is a deceptive creature and will gladly cheat his subjects.

---

44. Jackson, 'Smoking Room', p. 3.
45. Jackson, 'Smoking Room', p. 4.
46. Jackson, 'Smoking Room', p. 7.
47. Glanvill, *Saducismus Triumphatus, Part the Second*, p. 136.
48. Glanvill, *Saducismus Triumphatus, Part the Second*, p. 136.
49. 'Examination of Abigail Hobbs, April 19, 1692', *Salem Witch Trials: Documentary Archive and Transcription Project*. http://salem.lib.virginia.edu/n69.html (accessed 30 April 2021).

'The Smoking Room' deftly undermines such moralistic uses of the Devil's pact, as the unnamed narrator employs her quick wits and knowledge of the law to trick Satan into pledging her *his* soul. Consequently, if we are to read the various demon lovers who weave their way through *The Lottery* as emblematic of men's capacity to deceive and abuse women, then 'The Smoking Room' complicates this motif by having a young woman seize power from a demonic male figure. Indeed, in the closing moments of the story, the narrator has become increasingly authoritative, while the Devil, failing to conjure a puff of smoke, is forced to depart with a 'weak sizzle'.[50] Similarly, in 'Devil of a Tale', the wise Lady Katherine is shrewd enough to keep the Devil's right eye hostage in a box bearing a cross on the lid, thus ensuring that he will uphold their bargain fully. These stories lack the punitive outcomes of the early modern confessions upon which they are based, allowing intelligent women to carefully negotiate their own terms and thus profit from the satanic pact. The narrator of 'The Smoking Room' thrives, while Lady Katherine similarly benefits from her own diabolical arrangement, at least until her son thwarts her carefully laid plans. Both of these stories also suggest a sexual, or at least an erotic, encounter with the Devil that leads not to ruin but pleasure and material gain. Agreeing to bear the Devil's child, Lady Katherine is rewarded with wealth, happiness and a long life. The narrator of 'The Smoking Room', although she does not engage in sexual intercourse with her Devil, does appear to find him sexually attractive. Upon his initial appearance, she describes him as 'a charming young man', and later stresses that 'He was a good-looking guy'.[51] The manner in which the narrator and the Devil sit back and smoke for a minute, 'looking at each other', alongside their flirty banter, also suggests an attraction.[52] As noted earlier, sexual interaction with the Devil or his minions was a cornerstone of early modern demonology. While Glanvill himself disputes the possibility of '*carnal Copulation* with the *Devil*',[53] for many thinkers of the time, accounts of demonic copulation provided irrefutable evidence that the supernatural was a tangible reality.

At the same time, copulation with demonic bodies was viewed as an expression of the witch's devotion to the Devil. Demonic sex was the most common expression of demonolatry, or 'the intentional worship of and subservience to demons'.[54] Furthermore, as Walter Stephens elucidates, 'sexual submission to demons was defined as a ritual act, demonstrating the witch's servitude in both body and soul to the demonic familiar and to Satan, the archenemy of God'.[55] Concomitantly, demonic sexual relationships were regularly framed, in demonological literature, as deeply unpleasant, even torturous experiences. Early witchcraft theorists may have quoted accused witches who described demonic sex as intensely pleasurable,

---

50. Jackson, 'Smoking Room', p. 8.
51. Jackson, 'Smoking Room', p. 3, 4.
52. Jackson, 'Smoking Room', p. 4.
53. Glanvill, *Saducismus Triumphatus, Part the Second*, p. 8.
54. Stephens, *Demon Lovers*, p. 13.
55. Stephens, *Demon Lovers*, p. 13.

but by the late sixteenth century, the majority of continental European accounts portrayed the act as painful and devoid of pleasure.[56] Jackson's stories, although eliding any description of actual demonic intercourse, do present women who take pleasure in their attraction to and interaction with the Devil. In 'The Smoking Room' and 'Devil of a Tale' we find scenarios more akin to those detailed later, in seventeenth-century English pamphlets, which, according to Charlotte-Rose Millar, centred on women who were 'willing participants in pleasurable sexual relationships with devils'.[57] Jackson therefore modifies the standard early modern conception of demonic sex by framing erotic encounters with the diabolical as neither an act of submission nor as a painful, punishing ordeal. Rather, these women find pleasure, both intellectual and erotic, in flirting and verbally sparring with the Prince of Darkness.

The appearance of the Devil in a number of Jackson's stories naturally aligns her work with an early modern worldview in which most 'Christians accepted the possibility of the Devil's preternatural intervention in the world and were assured of God's supernatural presence'.[58] However, the subtler penetration of the supernatural into her fiction, its capacity to merge with and become indistinguishable from the natural, also echoes the ontology of Glanvill and his contemporaries. Bladen and Harmes observe that although early modern thought shared our conception of the supernatural 'in so far as it distinguished the divine from the mortal, and the ghostly from the physical', it did not position the supernatural as inimical to the natural.[59] Consequently, early modern thinkers readily imagined our world to be filled with what Glanvill terms *'Intelligent Creature*[s] *of the Invisible World'*.[60] There was, within this framework, no meaningful division between the realm of the supernatural and that of mundane, because the 'visible world was nevertheless under surveillance from, and accessible to, the spiritual world'.[61] The dualistic conception that there must necessarily exist some sort of separation between the tangible, physical plane and the spiritual plane is a much later ideal, one that would characterize a subsequent push towards modernity.[62] Jackson's fiction – and particularly her short fiction – likewise refuses to separate the physical world from the spiritual, nor does she draw any kind of clear line between fantasy/delusion and actual supernatural intervention. In this way, Jackson troubles the binary dualisms that characterize modernity and engages with an ontological fluidity closer to that of the early modern period.

---

56. Stephens, *Demon Lovers*, p. 19.
57. Charlotte-Rose Millar, 'Sleeping with Devils: The Sexual Witch in Seventeenth-century England', in *Supernatural and Secular Power in Early Modern England*, ed. Victoria Bladen and Marcus Harmes (Farnham: Ashgate, 2015), pp. 207–31 (p. 208).
58. Bladen and Harmes, 'Introduction', p. 1.
59. Bladen and Harmes, 'Introduction', p. 1.
60. Glanvill, *Saducismus Triumphatus, Part the Second*, p. 5.
61. Bladen and Harmes, 'Introduction', p. 3.
62. Bladen and Harmes, 'Introduction', p. 3.

Many of her stories describe elaborate delusions or fantasies that could also, potentially, be supernatural in nature. In the deeply anxious tale 'Nightmare', secretary Toni Morgan is tasked with delivering a cumbersome package to a Mr Shax, a moniker Jackson frequently used to denote demonic figures, though it was, in actuality, the name of her cat.[63] As she ventures out into the streets of New York, Ms Morgan observes posters prevailing upon passers-by to 'Find Miss X', and win an array of wonderful prizes, from 'twelve thousand dollars, a trip to Tahiti' to, more implausibly, 'a Thoroughbred horse and a castle on the Rhine'.[64] Ms Morgan is initially perturbed to discover that the description of Miss X, as relayed by a passing sound truck, matches her appearance exactly:

'Miss X is walking the streets of city, completely alone. She is wearing a blue hat with a red feather, blue gloves, and dark blue shoes.'

Good heavens, Miss Morgan thought; she stopped and looked down at her shoes; she was certainly wearing her blue ones.[65]

What begins as a mildly annoying competition in which the quarry vaguely resembles Ms Morgan swiftly transforms into a nightmare of anxiety, as reality appears to shift around her so that she is repeatedly, unmistakably identified as the errant Miss X. When Ms Morgan removes her gloves and buttons up her coat in order to less closely resemble the description of Miss X, the sound truck announces, 'I'll tell you, folks, Miss X is now wearing her coat buttoned up so you can't see her blue suit, and she's taken off her gloves.'[66] When she buys a new hat and acquires a second parcel, the sound truck announcer is careful to inform the public that 'Miss X is now wearing a gray and red hat, and is carrying *two* packages'.[67] More unsettling still, not only do posters appealing to the public to 'Find Miss X' proliferate across the city, but the unfortunate Ms Morgan even stumbles upon a parade complete with Boy Scouts, majorettes and twelve elephants, all set up to draw further attention to Miss X.

The exact nature of the events described does, of course, remain elusive. As in Todorov's formulation of the fantastic, we are left caught between the possibility that Ms Morgan is delusional – and the familiar laws of our reality remain unviolated – and the possibility that she has fallen under some wicked spell – and so the laws governing our reality are fundamentally upended. Jackson does not provide us with an answer to this conundrum. The story ends ambiguously when Ms Morgan is approached by a 'man in a blue suit' who asks if she is Miss X.[68] Exhausted, Ms

---

63. Hattenhauer, *Shirley Jackson's American Gothic*, p. 70.
64. Shirley Jackson, 'Nightmare', in *Just an Ordinary Day* (London: Penguin, 2017), pp. 42–59 (p. 44, 52).
65. Jackson, 'Nightmare', p. 46.
66. Jackson, 'Nightmare', p. 49.
67. Jackson, 'Nightmare', p. 52.
68. Jackson, 'Nightmare', p. 57.

Morgan responds that she is, and the man reveals that he is in some way connected to the competition, telling her that 'this town's no good. No one spotted you. [. . .] We'll have to do it again tomorrow in Chicago'.[69] In the closing paragraph of the story we find Ms Morgan sleeping comfortably in 'the big hotel', suggesting that she has followed the blue-suited man to Chicago.[70] 'Nightmare' has parallels with a number of Jackson's other stories, such as 'Louisa, Please Come Home', that feature ordinary, middle-class women suddenly losing their identity or sense of self and becoming someone else entirely. Jackson generally remains silent as to whether such transformations are psychological or supernatural in nature. 'Nightmare' certainly courts both interpretations. Ms Morgan's belief that she is the victim of an elaborate conspiracy could easily be the product of psychosis, but it could also have been brought about by supernatural means. The young man who appears to take 'Miss X' to Chicago for another leg of the competition is, significantly, dressed in a blue suit, a sartorial choice that aligns him with the figure of James Harris from *The Lottery and Other Stories*.[71] We could, therefore, read him as yet another demonic figure, who, in the tradition of the Demon Lover, lures a young woman to her doom.

An equally vexing hesitation between the natural and preternatural characterizes 'A Visit', an eerie tale originally published as 'The Lovely House' in 1950. The story concerns a young woman called Margaret – a common name in Jackson's oeuvre, which may or may not harken back to the accused witch Margaret Jackson described by Glanvill – who spends the summer visiting the home of her wealthy friend, Carla. Upon first arriving at Carla's house, Margaret is immediately enchanted by the building, which she anthropomorphizes as an elegant woman, with a 'long-boned structure', 'curving staircases' and 'arched doorways'.[72] Once she begins to explore the house, however, it becomes apparent that the building is a cornucopia of potentially supernatural wonders. As in a fairy tale, Margaret and Carla enter, first, a room that is 'all gold, with gilt on the window frames and on the legs of the chairs and tables', and then, a room that is 'silver', with 'small chairs of silver brocade'.[73] Lastly, Margaret and Carla find themselves in a room where their image is captured in a seeming infinite mise en abyme:

> The mirrors on both sides of the room showed the door opening and Margaret and Carla coming through, and then, reflected, a smaller door opening and a small Margaret and a smaller Carla coming through, and then, reflected again, a still smaller door and Margaret and Carla, and so on, endlessly, Margaret and Carla diminishing and reflecting.[74]

---

69. Jackson, 'Nightmare', p. 57.
70. Jackson, 'Nightmare', p. 58.
71. Hattenhauer, *Shirley Jackson's American Gothic*, p. 70.
72. Shirley Jackson, 'A Visit', in *Come Along with Me* (London: Penguin, 2013), pp. 93–116 (p. 93).
73. Jackson, 'A Visit', p. 95.
74. Jackson, 'A Visit', p. 95.

This wondrous sequence, in which the girls find themselves trapped within an endlessly proliferating series of reflections, foreshadows later images of entrapment that will proliferate throughout the text. Investigating the house's tower room, Margaret encounters Carla's great aunt – uncannily, also named Margaret – a witchlike figure who possesses a 'huge old cat' and is reputed to practise alchemy.[75] The elder Margaret resides alone in her tower, keeping the windows open 'to the winds' and delighting in the volatility of nature, which she terms her 'tapestries'.[76] While serving as a reflection or double of the younger Margaret, the appearance of the older woman also seems to prefigure the girl's eventual fate, to be trapped forever within the house. This possibility is seemingly affirmed by Margaret's earlier discovery of a mosaic of a beautiful girl with the words 'Here was Margaret, who died for love' set in the floor beside it.[77]

Later, Margaret meets Paul, yet another Demon Lover figure, who she takes to be Carla's brother.[78] Although vaguely delineated, the story implies that Paul is an immortal being – retaining his youth and vigour – while the elderly Margaret, presumably a past love, has been left to age in the tower. Again, Jackson remains equivocal about the role of the supernatural within the text. The closing lines of the story indicate that Margaret, like her elderly double, will be trapped for eternity within the house, as Carla's mother promises to weave her and the rest of the family into one of her tapestries, forever to adorn the walls of the lovely house. The ambiguity here is challenging, and as with Todorov's fantastic, the reader is frozen by indecision: Are we to ascribe a supernatural source to Margaret's strange experiences, or can we explain them as a dream, delusion or fantasy? My contention here is that, for Jackson, there is no need to choose. Her work not only exemplifies the fantastic, defined, as it often is, by 'the reader's hesitation',[79] but it is also emblematic of an early modern ontology in which late modernity's distinction between the natural and the supernatural simply does not hold true. *Saducismus Triumphatus*, a text that wielded immense influence over Jackson's life and work, sees no contradiction in proffering a 'science of witchcraft' because it was written at a time when the natural was easily reconcilable with numinous.[80] Likewise, Glanvill's work, and that of his contemporaries, rarely imagined a need to choose between psychological and supernatural explanations for events. In *Saducismus Triumphatus* Glanvill explicitly rejects the creeping scepticism that sought to explain witchcraft beliefs as a delusion of unstable elderly women. Rather than discarding the psychological in favour of the supernatural, Glanvill makes room for both possibilities by arguing that witches are susceptible to 'melancholic humours' and that this predisposition makes them vulnerable to the influence

75. Jackson, 'A Visit', p. 104.
76. Jackson, 'A Visit', p. 106.
77. Jackson, 'A Visit', p. 99.
78. Hattenhauer, *Shirley Jackson's American Gothic*, p. 53.
79. Todorov, *The Fantastic*, p. 31.
80. Davies, 'Vapours', p. 168.

of spirits and demonic familiars.[81] Similarly, it could be argued that in Jackson's stories, the frustration, alienation and insecurity that afflicted so many middle-class American women in the middle decades of the twentieth century invites supernatural interference. After all, it is the desperation of the titular housewife in 'Mrs Spencer and the Oberons' that causes her to be haunted by untraceable voices and music. Equally, in 'The Beautiful Stranger', it is another Margaret's loneliness that causes her to imagine, or discover, that her husband has been replaced by an infinitely more thoughtful doppelgänger. More whimsically, it seems that it is precisely Dimity Baxter's frustration with being belittled by arrogant male co-workers that summons Mallie and her magical cookbook in 'Dinner for a Gentleman'. For Jackson, as for Glanvill, the psychological and supernatural are not irreconcilable but, rather, composite parts of a complex, multifaceted reality.

In her study of occult influences in Shirley Jackson's fiction, Landau observes that in many of Jackson's stories 'lack of superstition and inability to attach deep meaning to traditions cause the modern mind to interpret demonic and magical presences through logic. These attempts ultimately fail – for Jackson, superstition and belief in the supernatural are powerful and irreplaceable'.[82] The contentious relationship between the occult and modern logic that Landau identifies here is, I believe, central to the interpretative frustrations experienced by many readers who attempt to determine whether the fantastic occurrences that populate Jackson's work are natural or supernatural in origin. Such readers are looking at Jackson's work through the lens of modern logic, which hinges upon a dualistic divide between the physical and spiritual planes. Though Jackson's interest in the occult appears to have been intellectual rather than devotional, much of her fiction was shaped by her interest in early modern witchcraft treatises and demonological studies. Glanvill's *Saducismus Triumphatus*, with its rigorous attempts to situate the supernatural within an observable naturalistic schema, appears to have been a powerful influence on Jackson's work. Like Glanvill, Jackson does not separate the mystical from the mundane, the spiritual from the physical. Instead, she imagines a world in which these forces are inextricable, and the natural world is permeated by supernatural forces.

References

Anderson, Melanie R. (2016), 'Perception, Supernatural Detection, and Gender in *The Haunting of Hill House*', in Melanie R. Anderson and Lisa Kröger (eds), *Shirley Jackson, Influences and Confluences*, 35–53, Abingdon: Routledge.

Bladen, Victoria and Marcus Harmes (2015), 'Introduction: The Intersections of Supernatural and Secular Power', in Victoria Bladen and Marcus Harmes (eds), *Supernatural and Secular Power in Early Modern England*, 1–14, Farnham: Ashgate.

---

81. Davies, 'Vapours', p. 171.
82. Landau, 'Occult Influences in Shirley Jackson's "The Lottery"', p. 11.

Davies, Julie A. (2012), 'Poisonous Vapours: Joseph Glanvill's Science of Witchcraft', *Intellectual History Review* 22: 163–79.
Davies, Julie A. (2018), *Science in an Enchanted World: Philosophy and Witchcraft in the Work of Joseph Glanvill*, Abingdon: Routledge.
'Examination of Abigail Hobbs, April 19, 1692', *Salem Witch Trials: Documentary Archive and Transcription Project*. http://salem.lib.virginia.edu/n69.html (accessed 30 April 2021).
Franklin, Ruth (2016), *Shirley Jackson: A Rather Haunted Life*, New York: Liverlight.
Gardner-Medwin, Alisoun (1971), 'The Ancestry of "The House-Carpenter": A Study of the Family History of the American Forms of Child 243', *The Journal of American Folklore* 84: 414–27.
Glanvill, Joseph (1681), *Saducismus Triumphatus, Part the Second*, Preface. https://quod.lib.umich.edu/e/eebo/A42824.0001.001?rgn=main;view=fulltext (accessed 30 April 2021).
Hattenhauer, Daryl (2003), *Shirley Jackson's American Gothic*, Albany: State University of New York Press.
Ingram, Shelley and Willow G. Mullins (2018), 'Would you Like a Cup of Tea?: Food, Home, and Mid-Century Anxiety in the Later Novels of Shirley Jackson', in Lorna Piatti-Farnell and Donna Lee Brien (eds), *The Routledge Companion to Literature and Food*, 342–50, Abingdon: Routledge.
Jackson, Shirley (2006), *The Haunting of Hill House*, London: Penguin.
Jackson, Shirley (2009), 'The Daemon Lover', in *The Lottery and Other Stories*, 9–28, London: Penguin.
Jackson, Shirley (2009), *The Lottery and Other Stories*, London: Penguin.
Jackson, Shirley (2013), 'A Visit', in *Come Along with Me*, 93–116, London: Penguin.
Jackson, Shirley (2013), 'Experience and Fiction', in *Come Along with Me*, 204–14, London: Penguin.
Jackson, Shirley (2017), 'Devil of a Tale', in *Just an Ordinary Day*, London: Penguin.
Jackson, Shirley (2017), 'Lord of the Castle', in *Just an Ordinary Day*, 199–209, London: Penguin.
Jackson, Shirley (2017), 'Nightmare', in *Just an Ordinary Day*, 42–59, London: Penguin.
Jackson, Shirley (2017), 'The Smoking Room', in *Just an Ordinary Day*, 3–8, London: Penguin.
Jackson, Shirley (2019), *Life Among the Savages*, London: Penguin.
Jackson, Shirley (2019), *We Have Always Lived in the Castle*, London: Penguin.
Landau, Samantha (2018), 'Occult Influences in Shirley Jackson's "The Lottery"', *Gauken* 11: 1–21.
Levack, Brian C. (2006), *The Witch Hunt in Early Modern Europe*, Abingdon: Routledge.
Millar, Charlotte-Rose (2015), 'Sleeping with Devils: The Sexual Witch in Seventeenth-century England', in Victoria Bladen and Marcus Harmes (eds), *Supernatural and Secular Power in Early Modern England*, 207–31, Farnham: Ashgate.
Nørjordet, Håvard, 'The Tall Man in the Blue Suit: Witchcraft, Folklore, and Reality in Shirley Jackson's *The Lottery or, the Adventures of James Harris*', unpublished MA thesis, University of Oslo, 49–50. https://www.duo.uio.no/bitstream/handle/10852/25403/Norjordet.pdf?sequence=1&isAllowed=y (accessed 30 April 2021).
Stephens, Walter (2002), *Demon Lovers: Witchcraft, Sex, and the Crisis of Belief*, Chicago: University of Chicago Press.
Todorov, Tzvetan (1973), *The Fantastic: A Structural Approach to a Literary Genre*, Cleveland: The Press of Case Western Reserve University.

Chapter 2

'THE MOST SEDUCTIVE OF MIRAGES'

THE WEIRD AMERICAN DREAM IN SELECTED SHORT STORIES BY SHIRLEY JACKSON AND JOYCE CAROL OATES

Joseph S. Norman

American Weird Fiction perturbs everyday life in the United States, uniquely exposing the nation's once meaningful 'national motto'[1] – the American Dream – as a seductive mass-delusion, a pernicious myth, a nightmare. This chapter develops this notion of the Weird American Dream through selected short stories by Shirley Jackson and Joyce Carol Oates (1938–), drawing primarily from Jackson's posthumous collections: *Let Me Tell You* (2015) and *Dark Tales* (2017), and Oates's recent collections, especially *High Crime Area* (2014) and *Night-Gaunts and Other Tales of Suspense* (2018). It continues the process of exploring the various correspondences between the work of both authors begun by Patten[2] and Kokkinou.[3] This chapter further cements Jackson's reputation as innovative writer of the Weird while recognizing Oates's under-appreciated contribution to this tradition. Ultimately it argues that, in the stories of Oates and Jackson, life in America in characterized by inequality, anxiety and fear, and that both writers use their distinct, yet similar, styles of Weird Fiction to subvert and reveal the changing landscape of America's self-conception. Written throughout the late twentieth and early twentieth centuries, these stories demonstrate how the Puritan Dream of Social Democracy has changed – especially during the damaging economic policies of the Reagan era – and they pre-empt the era of the Trump administration, which would attempt to change the meaning of the American Dream forever.

---

1. Jim Cullen, *The American Dream: A Short History of an Idea That Shaped a* Nation (New York: Oxford University Press, 2004), p. 5.

2. Andromachi Kokkinou, 'The Performance of Normality: Changing Norms in the American Gothic of Shirley Jackson and Joyce Carol Oates' (dissertation, Leiden University (The Netherlands), Faculty of Humanities, 2014).

3. Ann Lucille Patten, 'The Female Uncanny?: A Historicized Reading of the Uncanny Fiction of Edith Wharton, Shirley Jackson & Joyce Carol Oates' (thesis, Trinity College (Dublin, Ireland), School of English, 2008).

The Weird Tales Tradition in America

Weird Fiction is, like America itself, characterized by great diversity and hybridity: it encompasses and frequently combines many styles, tones, forms and genres (Gothic, horror, science fiction and/or fantasy).[4] And the defining feature of The Weird is, like the elusive, nebulous concept of the American Dream, often identified as an effect or sensation: a 'particular kind of perturbation'.[5] While it is now a global, cross-media phenomenon with strong antecedents in Britain,[6] Weird Fiction is a mode closely associated with America from its outset: Edgar Allen Poe is retrospectively acknowledged as the original writer of Weird Tales.[7] To Darnall, 'the strange visions of Poe are deeply rooted in the life of the American people',[8] and Murphy locates Poe's work in the American Transcendental tradition, whose principles of self-reliance and rugged individualism provided the foundations for the American Dream. The US pulp magazine *Weird Tales* popularized its titular term during the 1920s and 1930s, launching the careers of major writers in the field like Robert Howard, Clarke Ashton Smith and the first self-consciously Weird writer H. P. Lovecraft. Famously basing his work in a strange, fictionalized yet highly realistic version of his home region, Providence, Rhode Island, Lovecraft was inspired by the 'dark elements of strength, solitude, grotesqueness, and ignorance', which he saw in backwoods New England,[9] sometimes referred to as 'Lovecraft country'.[10] His tombstone in Rhode Island famously reads, 'I AM PROVIDENCE'. Around the turn of the millennium, writers of the 'New Weird' sought to radically reimagine the mode's frequent Pulp trappings and reactionary tendencies,[11] including prominent author Jeff Vandermeer whose eco-conscious works, such as his Southern Reach Trilogy (2014) and *Borne* (2017), often portray a post-apocalyptic America rendered bizarrely dystopian by climate change, heavily inspired by the St. Marks National Wildlife Refuge in Florida.

---

4. China Miéville, 'Weird Fiction', in *The Routledge Companion to Science Fiction*, ed. M. Bould, A. M. Butler, A. Roberts and S. Vint (London: Routledge, 2009), pp. 510–15.

5. Mark Fisher, *The Weird and The Eerie* (London: Repeater Books, 2016), p. 15.

6. James Machin, *Weird Fiction in Britain 1880–1939* (Palgrave Gothic, 2018).

7. S. T. Joshi, 'Poe, Lovecraft, and the Revolution in Weird Fiction', Ninth Annual Commemoration Program of the Poe Society, 7 October 2012, https://www.eapoe.org/papers/psblctrs/pl20121.htm

8. F. M. Darnall, 'The Americanism of Edgar Allan Poe', *The English Journal* 16, no. 3 (1927): 185–92. doi:10.2307/803600. Accessed 12 July 2021.

9. H. P. Lovecraft, 'The Picture in the House', *The H. P. Lovecraft Archive*, 1920; 2009.

10. See Matt Ruff's novel *Lovecraft Country* (2016) for a fictionalized engagement with the relationship between Lovecraft and New England (as well as the legacy of his racism).

11. See Jeffrey Andrew Weinstock, 'The New Weird', in *New Directions in Popular Fiction*, ed. Ken Gelder (London: Palgrave Macmillan, 2016), p. 16; and Timothy S. Murphy and Benjamin Noys, 'Introduction: Old and New Weird', *Genre: Forms of Discourse and Closure* 49, no. 2 (2016): 117–34.

Women of the Weird: Shirley Jackson and Joyce Carol Oates

Jackson became a notorious household name in America for 'The Lottery' (1948) at the age of twenty-four, while Oates received national acclaim with *The Wheel of Love* (1970) aged thirty-two. 'The Lottery', a Weird Folk Horror tale of an ancient murderous rite lingering in modern, rural America, perfectly exemplifies the Weird American Dream – shockingly dismantling the modern nation's core principles – as well as the style of 'quiet Weird tale' which S. T. Joshi uses to distinguish Jackson from earlier writers of the Pulp Weird.[12] Oates wrote a glowing appraisal of 'The Lottery',[13] and there are thematic parallels in her own story 'The Corn Maiden', where sadistic teenager Jude manipulates a pair of her naive friends into the cult-like kidnapping and abuse of a mentally disabled classmate, aiming to make her the victim of ritual sacrifice.[14] Writing in 2001, Joshi declared Shirley Jackson one of 'the two leading writers of weird fiction since Lovecraft' alongside British writer Ramsey Campbell,[15] an assertion corroborated by the inclusion of Jackson's 'The Summer People' in the prominent anthology *The Weird* (2012), edited by Jeff and Anne Vandermeer. Described as 'a chilling yet subtle tour de force of the weird',[16] 'The Summer People' is – like 'The Lottery' – one of several stories by Jackson that depicts menace behind the fade of a happy, harmonious rural town: the threat of a local, tribal collective against the outsider minority.

Oates and her extensive oeuvre maintain a complex relationship with the life and work of Shirley Jackson, and there is much evidence to suggest Jackson's influence on Oates. *The Weird* anthology also includes Oates's 'Family', as discussed herein, and explicitly compares the story's style to Jackson. Both writers share Syracuse University as their alma mater: Jackson graduated with a BA in Journalism in 1940,[17] and Oates with a BA in English in 1960.[18] Both married men with whom they had attended university and were also involved in literary arts, Jackson's husband the critic Stanley Edgar Hyman and Oates's husband Raymond J. Smith a professor of eighteenth-century poetry. Various publishers, anthologizers and

---

12. S. T. Joshi, *The Modern Weird Tale: A Critique of Horror Fiction* (Jefferson: McFarland & Co., 2001), Kindle edition. [n.p.].

13. Joyce Carol Oates, 'Editor Joyce Carol Oates on the Enduring Spell of Shirley Jackson', *The Library of America Interviews*, 14 May 2010, https://www.loa.org/news-and-views/508-editor-joyce-carol-oates-on-the-enduring-spell-of-shirley-jackson

14. Oates, 'Library of America Interviews'.

15. Joshi, *The Modern Weird Tale*.

16. Jeff Vandermeer and Anne Vandermeer, *The Weird: A Compendium of Strange Stories* (Tor Books, 2012), Kindle Edition [n.p.].

17. Britannica, The Editors of Encyclopaedia, 'Shirley Jackson', *Encyclopedia Britannica*, 27 March 2021, https://www.britannica.com/biography/Shirley-Jackson (accessed 7 June 2021).

18. Leo Robson, 'The Unruly Genius of Joyce Carol Oates', *The New Yorker*, 29 June 2020. Accessed 6 October 2020.

critics have compared Oates's work to that of Jackson throughout her career.[19] Oates edited the *Library of America* collection *Shirley Jackson: Novels and Stories* in 2020, having previously reprinted Jackson's 'A Visit' in the anthology *American Gothic Tales* (1996). Both writers' works have been compared with the same authors, including Poe, Kafka, Plath and Hawthorne.[20] Oates's short story 'Accomplished Desires' (*Esquire*, 1968) is a loose, fictionalized reworking of Jackson's notoriously complex relationship with Hyman, and told in a somewhat Jackson-like manner.[21] It provides a tragic account of a young student's successful attempt to seduce her university professor (Hyman), leading to the suicide of his wife (Jackson), a Pulitzer Prize–winning poet. Yet Oates sees Jackson as 'too quirkily original' to be influential,[22] although she admits being held under the 'enduring spell' of Jackson's work.[23]

The Weirdness of Jackson's oeuvre has been more readily acknowledged and charted: Wylie Hall, Nasrullah, Patten and Darryl Hattenhauer have worked to pinpoint what Joshi calls the 'pervasive atmosphere of the odd' – the Weirdness – in Jackson's work. To Nasrullah, 'Almost every story is about a protagonist's discovering or failing to discover or successfully ignoring an alternate way of perceiving a set of circumstances or the world',[24] as is the case in 'The Possibility of Evil, 'The Summer People' and 'The Lottery'. If Jackson, therefore, 'seems especially interested in how characters order their worlds and how they perceive themselves in the world', then, I deduce from Nasrullah's comments, the Weird perturbation of her work derives from the frequent 'change in a character's perspective' which 'leads to anxiety, terror, neurosis, or even a loss of identity'.[25] Jackson's are tales of 'individual loneliness',[26] as with 'Home' and 'The Possibility of Evil', although often told in an unsympathetic manner, even demonstrating what Joshi calls

---

19. The *New York Times* compared Oates's debut novel *With Shuddering Fall* (1965) to Jackson's classic 'The Lottery', as does the blurb for the 2018 HarperCollins paperback of *With Shuddering Fall*. Jeff and Anne Vandermeer draw such parallels in *The Weird*. Anne Lucille Patten's PhD thesis from Trinity College Dublin on the short fiction of the 'female uncanny' discusses both Oates and Jackson alongside Edith Wharton.

20. See: Scott Hales's '"All is Poe": Reading Poe in Joyce Carol Oates' "Poe Posthumous; or, The Light-House"', *The Edgar Allen Poe Review* 11, no. 2 (Fall 2010): 85–108.

21. See Ruth Franklin's biography *Shirley Jackson: A Rather Haunted Life* (Liveright Publishing Corporation, 2016). Josephine Decker's Jackson biopic *Shirley* (2020) and Susan Scarf Merrell's eponymous 2014 novel on which it was based explore a similar fictionalized account to Oates's story, following a student from one of Hyman's classes who comes to live with the couple, causing a rift in their relationship.

22. Oates, *The Library of America Interviews*.

23. Oates, *The Library of America Interviews*.

24. Nasrullah Mambrol, 'Analysis of Joyce Carol Oates's Stories', 19 June 2020, https://literariness.org/2020/06/19/analysis-of-joyce-carol-oatess-stories/

25. Mambrol, 'Analysis of Shirley Jackson's Stories'.

26. Joshi, *The Modern Weird Tale*, p. 36.

'utterly refreshing glee at the exhibition of human greed, misery, and evil'.[27] Even Jackson's semi-autobiographical 'domestic' stories, often distinguished from her more clearly fictional work, cannot be easily separated from this pervasive sense of oddness.[28]

Oates's engagement with the Weird is less pervasive, more sporadic, than Jackson's. It is more difficult to make generalizations about Oates's extensive oeuvre, and Weird Fiction, in its strictest sense, appears there in a minority relative to other modes and styles. As John Barth observes, 'Joyce Carol Oates writes all over the aesthetical map.'[29] Yet Greg Johnson provides one exception, making the broad claim that Oates's 'larger endeavor in fiction [. . .] is to probe relentlessly the complex mysteries of human personality and identity'.[30] And the majority of Oates's story collections, spanning over forty volumes, are published with Weird-adjacent descriptions – tales of darkness, horror, suspense and so on – and her work is frequently located within the Southern Gothic tradition.[31]

For the purposes of this chapter, the most pertinent stylistic parallels between Jackson and Oates include the following. Murphy's identification of Jackson's Poe-like 'mastery of atmosphere and eerie effects'[32] and interest in the 'fictional possibilities of the disturbed psyche'[33] are equally applicable to Oates. Yet, in the stories discussed herein as in Poe, the atmosphere is never *merely* that of eeriness, the disturbed psyche never reducible to straightforwardly Gothic tropes. Instead, Jackson and Oates destabilize the American quest for self-determination by writing characters affected by a profound sense of anxiety and dread, often ambient and difficult to identify, suggesting the onset of madness. Following Patten's observations, this effect is achieved when 'Jackson and Oates individually create their own gaps in the texts, which a reader is free to fill with their own set of perspectives, preintentions and recollections, and thereby creating their own version of an unsettling or deeply frightening story'.[34] To Patten, 'In Jackson, the uncanny becomes a weird tale, where the author communicates unease over mass movements and the elemental nature of evil in man', while the uncanny in Oates is linked to her complex position in relation to mainstream feminist discourse: 'In Oates, the uncanny utilizes tropes of the grotesque to relate the problems that remain inside the Feminist movement as well as those that stem from diminished

---

27. Joshi, *The Modern Weird Tale*, pp. 48–9.
28. Joshi, *The Modern Weird Tale*.
29. Mambrol, 'Analysis of Shirley Jackson's Stories'.
30. Greg Johnson, *Joyce Carol Oates: A Study of the Short Fiction* (New York: Twayne Publishers, 1994), p. 93.
31. See Kokkinou, 'The Performance of Normality'.
32. Mambrol, 'Analysis of Shirley Jackson's Stories'.
33. Bernice M. Murphy, *Shirley Jackson: Essays on the Literary Legacy* (Jefferson: McFarland & Co., 2005), p. 9.
34. Patten, 'The Female Uncanny?', p. 22.

levels of social capital.'[35] In the stories by Oates and Jackson herein, this subversive operation of the uncanny, the Weird and the grotesque certainly operate in the way Patten explains, combining to enact a broader level of sociopolitical critique.

The Weird American Dream

The phrase 'The American Dream' can be traced back at least as far as James Truslow Adams's one-volume history *The Epic of America* published in 1932, who spoke of 'that American dream of a better, richer, and happier life for all or citizens of every rank' which galvanized the nation's foundation.[36] Jim Cullen outlines the Dream's three basic manifestations: the Dream of the Good Life (the colonization of the so-called New World by the Puritan Founding Fathers, and the Declaration of Independence); the middle-class Dream of Upward Mobility, Equality and Homeownership, with which many stories by Jackson and Oates are concerned; and the Dream of the Coast, symbolized by literary characters like Jay Gatsby, Hunter Thompson's alter-ego Raul Duke and Nathanael West's Tod Hackett, and embodied in the lure of materialist gain woven into the history of the California Gold Rush, Las Vegas casino culture and Hollywood itself.

Shirley Jackson's family lived what Ruth Franklin describes as the 'classic American up-by-the-bootstraps saga',[37] or Cullen's Dream of Upward Mobility. A wealthy English family suddenly loses all of its money 'under mysterious circumstances [. . .] they change their name, burying all traces of the past, and travel across an ocean and a continent to San Francisco'.[38] Shirley's great-great-grandfather rebuilt the family's wealth by working to build the first mansions in California, which were inhabited by the 'robber barons' who made their fortune in the aftermath of the Gold Rush by investing in railroads.[39] This prosperity was passed down the generations, with Shirley's father rising to chairman of the board at the Traung Label and Lithograph Company.[40] As a teenager, Shirley's life followed a trajectory opposite to that of Dream of the (West) Coast: As Franklin explains, 'As desperate migrants from the Dust Bowl journeyed west overland in search of work and sustenance, the well-to-do Jackson's, unscathed by the Depression, were heading east.'[41] The family's move from California to Rochester, New York, was 'motivated by a desire for material wealth'[42] enabled Leslie Jackson to accept a promotion. Yet, while the young Shirley would miss her family's life

35. Patten, 'The Female Uncanny?', p. 326.
36. Cullen, *The American Dream*, p. 4.
37. Franklin, *Shirley Jackson*, p. 21.
38. Franklin, *Shirley Jackson*, p. 21.
39. Franklin, *Shirley Jackson*, p. 14.
40. Franklin, *Shirley Jackson*, p. 13.
41. Franklin, *Shirley Jackson*, p. 13.
42. Franklin, *Shirley Jackson*, p. 22.

on the West Coast, she would eventually settle out East in North Bennington, Vermont, with her own family, where she died in 1965, providing for her family through her successful writing.

Oates's great-grandparents were Hungarian migrants to the United States, who came to own a small farm, also in Rochester, on which Oates's father 'hated' to work, eventually working for General Motors.[43] Yet, while Oates grew up in the same region in which Jackson lived for many years, nearby in Millersport, her life in this working-class, farming community, which Oates describes as a 'daily scramble for existence',[44] contrasts sharply with Jackson's comfortable if peripatetic upbringing. Now firmly established as one of the great American literary figures, Oates's own life represents, as with Jackson's family, the Dream of Upward Mobility, as well as a feminist-creative Dream of a self-sufficient female artist – an achievement which Jackson shared.

Developed from Jackson and Oates's own experiences, we shall see herein how the selected stories discussed here chart the reshaping of the American Dream from the Social Democracy of the Puritans towards the libertarian ultra-capitalist version of the Dream of the Coast that prevails in contemporary America.

The Dream of Home Ownership: 'Night-Gaunts', Joyce Carol Oates (2017)

As Jim Cullen explains, 'the United States was never a "free," "open," or "virgin" land. It has, nevertheless, afforded opportunities for a great many people (including some black and Latino people, among others) to do something that was previously difficult if not impossible: acquire a place they could call their own'.[45] Here Cullen articulates the 'resilient and versatile' yet 'imperfect, even fatally flawed' 'Dream of owning a house';[46] and the ownership of a house (if not a *home*) is central to many of Oates and Jackson's stories. As Franklin observes, 'Houses – one of her lifetime obsessions and the gravitational centre of much of her fiction – were in Jackson's blood.'[47] While she 'never saw any of her great-great-grandfather's creations, except in pictures', Franklin suggests that Jackson was inspired by 'eerie tales' that surrounded the Old New England houses which he helped to build.[48] Similarly, while the farmhouse in which Oates grew up was more modest, she describes it as 'the site of reoccurring dreams', featuring 'human faces' with blurred

---

43. Joyce Carol Oates, *The Lost Landscape: A Writer's Coming of Age* (St Ives: 4th Estate, 2016), pp. 5–9.
44. Darkecho.com, 'Author Focus: Joyce Carol Oates', 10 June 2011, https://web.archive.org/web/20110610030614/http://www.darkecho.com/darkecho/horroronline/oates.html
45. Cullen, *The American Dream*, p. 136.
46. Cullen, *The American Dream*, p. 136.
47. Franklin, *Shirley Jackson*, p. 13.
48. Franklin, *Shirley Jackson*, p. 17.

features that are 'laced with a kind of visceral dread'.[49] Houses feature as prominent symbols in Jackson's most popular novels, *The Haunting of Hill House* (1959) and *We Have Always Lived In The Castle* (1962), as they do in the stories discussed herein: 'Home' and 'The Possibility of Evil'. In her tales 'The Bus' and 'The Summer People', it is *going away from home* which instigates the story's problems.

Both eerie houses and dreadful faces feature prominently in the titular story from Oates's collection *Night-Gaunts and Other Tales of Suspense*, the opening and concluding image of which is a ghostly apparition in the window of a Colonial mansion, belonging to the family of protagonist, sensitive young writer Horace Phineas Love, Jr.: 'In a high, small, octagonal window of the (vacant) house he sees the face he is not prepared to see.'[50] The face is that of his long-deceased father, 'gaunt, narrow, grave as a face carved in granite',[51] the first of several 'hauntings' Love experiences, which mirror his own writing, and are linked to his father. Just as Oates fictionalized Shirley Jackson's life in 'Accomplished Desires', her 'Night-Gaunts' is a roman-à-clef, providing a loose, thinly veiled account of the life of H. P. Lovecraft. Both the story's title and the collection's epigraph are drawn from Lovecraft's 1938 poem 'Night-Gaunts'. Here, using the Petrarchan sonnet form, Lovecraft develops a bizarre, impressionistic picture of 'rubbery things [. . .] with membranous wings', withholding until the final couplet their Weirdest aspect: 'If only they would make some sound, \Or wear a face where faces should be found!' Oates's tale centres on Horace, charting the effect these gaunts have upon his life, his understanding of his family history and his development as a writer. Outlining the decline of the Love/craft family, Oates portrays Love/craft himself in a largely sympathetic light, making his life story into a kind of tragic Künstlerroman, both concerned with, and *in the form of*, the Weird tale. Oates emphasizes the ways in which Love/craft's personality was ironically shaped by a *lack* of love and affection at home, his acceptance of corporal punishment, and the constant advocation of racism and social Darwinism by his father. It is in the final section '4. Weird Love' that the tormented Love finally achieves inner peace, spending long hours writing weird tales in the library. Here, Love makes a crucial admission, that '*How otherwise can I speak of my love. My writing, my books, my weird tales are my love. It is weird love I offer you. And who? – because I love you.*'[52] As someone renowned for her utter dedication to the craft of writing, Oates clearly empathizes with Love/craft, despite his lifelong, unrepentant racism. Alan Moore emphasizes the importance of Lovecraft's fiction entirely *because* of the writer's flaws, calling him 'an almost unbearably sensitive barometer of American dread' for capturing the fears of

---

49. Oates, *The Lost Landscape: A Writer's Coming of Age*, p. 7.
50. Oates, *The Lost Landscape: A Writer's Coming of Age*, p. 277.
51. Joyce Carol Oates, *Night-Gaunts and Other Tales of* Suspense (Croydon: Head of Zeus Ltd, 2018), p. 277.
52. Oates, *Night*-Gaunts, p. 277.

'white, middle-class, heterosexual, Protestant-descended males'.[53] Therefore the psyche of Horace Love also operates as barometer for the quintessential New England colonial gentleman. Here the legacy of colonial racism persists through the attitudes of Horace's father, which he passes down to the next generation, just as the father's alcoholism is linked to the sexual abuse of his son. The ghostly (or ghost-*like*) night-gaunts, therefore, seem to be psychological manifestations of the intergenerational trauma which Horace endures.

In Lovecraft's stories, the Weird effect is often linked to the ways in which his descriptions of such creatures cannot be accounted for simply through either aberrant psychology, science fiction, or the supernatural. Oates's gaunts are rationalized to an extent, as the result of the syphilis from which Horace is revealed to be dying, and the trauma experienced at the hands of his father: 'a sort of optical imprint in the child's brain'.[54] Yet they become stranger over time, acquiring 'more definition, as if, rooted in the child's brain, like actual roots, or rapacious parasites, they had now the power to grow',[55] as well as taking sonic and olfactory forms. Intrinsically linked to his father's death, the gaunts 'descend in a fine greenish toxic froth into his nostrils, like the froth that had shone about his father's lips in the coffin, if the eyelids drooped shut',[56] and they resemble the facial birthmarks that both father and son share, often likened to a hand or a mass of tendrils.[57] Using a quintessentially Lovecraftian device, however, Oates has Horace trace similar creatures through the culture of the Gothic and macabre, noting likenesses in works by Ovid, Dante, Bosch, Goya and of course Lovecraft's own fictional, mythopoeic tome, the Necronomicon. It is through this combination of strange details and references suggesting the supernatural, yet without fully undermining the rational, psychological explanation for Horace's experiences, that Oates effectively achieves her pastiche of the Lovecraftian Weird.

By the end of the tale, Oates suggests that Horace himself has become a gaunt through his realization that he now haunts the library, and – returning to the story's opening image – sees again the strange face in the window of the family house. In America, the dream of owning one's own home – even of finding a home there at all – has been tarnished by the process by which such a dream claims to be enabled; and even Love finds himself 'locked out of his own house' at the story's conclusion. The Dream is, as Cullen suggests, quite literally 'fatally flawed'.

---

53. Philip Eli, 'The Unlikely Reanimation of H.P. Lovecraft', *The Atlantic*, 20 August 2015, https://www.theatlantic.com/entertainment/archive/2015/08/hp-lovecraft-125/401471/
54. Oates, *Night-Gaunts*, p. 289.
55. Oates, *Night-Gaunts*, p. 290.
56. Oates, *Night-Gaunts*, p. 290.
57. Oates previously used a birthmark as the controlling motif in a horror tale, 'Bloodstains' (1971), from the *Nightside* collection (1977).

Shirley Jackson 'Home' (1965)

Jackson's story 'Home', originally published in the *Ladies' Home Journal*, August 1965 and anthologized in *Dark Tales*, also takes a haunted manor, working to keep new inhabitants out, as its central motif. It is a ghost story that moves away from the Gothic mode, combining Jackson's trademark sense of small-town America with a satirical irony, to create its Weird effect. Ethel Sloane and husband leave the city and buy an old house[58] which, perched atop a steep hill, affords a commanding presence over a small village. The village-folk treat Ethel civilly yet with remove, issuing frequent warnings about the dangers of taking 'the Old Sanderson road',[59] suggesting a safer route *home* instead. Upon hearing the villagers' warnings about the road, Ethel starts to imagine herself as the landed gentry, an educated elite who preside benevolently over a local superstitious populace: 'the Sanderson place, she thought, and felt oddly feudal with pride. We're the lords of the manor'.[60] Ethel ignores the locals' advice, of course, and regularly uses the road. Soon she sees a barefooted child and old woman there and drives them up to her house. Ethel is certainly affected by the realization that she has encountered ghosts, with the skin on her neck 'crawling as though some wet thing walked there'.[61] As Joshi comments, 'The house controls its inhabitants, not the inhabitants the house. It is on its sufferance that they are there at all.'[62]

Yet, brushing aside this frisson of Weirdness, she still seems more concerned with lauding her superiority over the folk of the village. 'Two ghosts of our very own', Ethel remarks to her husband; '*My* very own', she said. 'I just can't wait to see their faces in the village.'[63] When, on an especially wet and muddy night, Ethel again takes the road and picks up the ghosts, she swerves off the road and narrowly survives. While Ethel is naturally shaken by the ordeal – 'Crying, breathless, Ethel put her hand down on the steering wheel, weak and exhausted'[64] – her response is hardly the customary Gothic terror of confrontation with the supernatural. She acknowledges the ghosts' intentions ('I was almost killed, she told herself, they almost took me with them'[65]) yet returns to the hardware store the next morning, seemingly unaffected.

This encounter with the supernatural is significant for her, less for confirming the continuation of the human soul after death, or casting doubt over her own sanity, but for the way in which it confirms her status in the village: The ghostly

---

58. Shirley Jackson, 'Home', in *Dark Tales* (St Ives: Penguin Random House, 2017), p. 171.
59. Jackson, 'Home', p. 171.
60. Jackson, 'Home', p. 175.
61. Jackson, 'Home', p. 178.
62. Jackson, 'Home', p. 21.
63. Jackson, 'Home', p. 178, emphasis added.
64. Jackson, 'Home', p. 179.
65. Jackson, 'Home', p. 179.

duo were headed *home*, to her home which used to be their own, a fact which seems to affirm Ethel's sense of belonging to, and superiority over, the villagers, whose fears and history she can *claim* as her own. The story concludes as it began, with Ethel sharing mundane conversation with the clerk in the hardware store. Ethel reveals the fact of her accident to him and starts to probe further into the villagers' concerns over the Old Sanderson road once more, but cannot bring herself to formulate a specific question. It is not clear if Ethel will continue to risk the road and, therefore, her life. Yet, the clerk's final question to Ethel, 'will you and the mister be coming to the PTA social tomorrow night?',[66] comes after implying his knowledge of her clash with the local ghosts and therefore marks a rite of passage in village life, affirming the villagers' acceptance of Ethel's place within it.

Again, owning a *house* in America does not necessarily provide one with a *home*. As Joshi observes, 'this story could be a model of Jackson's ability to transform the events of her own life into weird fiction',[67] and the motif of city folk struggling to fit in with small town society and the persecution they face reoccurs in Jackson's work, echoing her own family's struggles to fit in while living in North Bennington during the late 1940s, where their lifestyle, friends and her husband Stanley's Jewish identity mean that they 'could never truly integrate themselves into the community'.[68] With Jackson's American Dream, homeownership is rigidly enforced by conservative and patriarchal norms – even, as in 'Night-gaunts', from beyond the grave.

'Home' exemplifies Franklin's observation that 'One of the ironies of Jackson' fiction is the essential role that women play in enforcing the standards of the community – standards that hurt them most'.[69] This is certainly also true of the story 'The Possibility of Evil', which, published in 1965, it was to be Jackson's last. Mrs Strangeworth, moral crusader in a small American town, realizes that her fellow townsfolk, sick of the mean-spirited letters she sends them, have turned against her, destroying the precious 'red and pink and white roses' which 'massed along' her 'narrow lawn'.[70] Mrs Strangeworth's perfect house and garden (with its American Beauty roses) symbolize the American Dream, just as their destruction reveals its inverse: the nightmare beneath the tale's seemingly idyllic unnamed town. Jackson's tale is imbued with unease, dread and a sense of perturbation, yet no traces of the supernatural are present, and nothing tangible seems immediately wrong. The story's Weird effect is, following Patten, achieved by the gaps which Jackson deliberately leaves in the story, enabling the reader to speculate on the nature of the titular evil – Are Mrs Strangeworth and her cruel letters to blame for the bad atmosphere in the town? Or are the suggestions of teenage abuse founded?

66. Jackson, 'Home'.
67. Joshi, *The Modern Weird Tale*, p. 21.
68. Franklin, *Shirley Jackson*, p. 202.
69. Franklin, *Shirley Jackson*, p. 213.
70. Shirley Jackson, 'The Possibility of Evil', *Dark Tales* (St Ives: Penguin Books, 2017), p. 5.

– in a similar manner to the nature of the titular 'Night-Gaunts' in Oates's story, a question left deliberately unresolved and therefore made Weird.

Joyce Carol Oates 'Family' (1989)

Oates's tale 'Family' – first published in December, 1989, in *Omni* magazine and anthologized in *The Weird* – was described by the Vandermeer's as 'a tale of weird science fiction and strange ritual that reads like the love-child of Shirley Jackson and China Miéville'.[71] A brief synopsis of Oates's tale, however, seems in many ways a different kind of Weird Tale than those told by Jackson: 'Family' depicts a grim and desolate post-apocalyptic, future America, characterized by recession, power failures, famine, 'unmarked bombers'[72] and gang violence. To a certain extent, the tale moves away from the realism with which Oates is regularly associated, striking a more Jackson-esque tone with its allegorical approach to characters and locations, which are sketched out in less detail than is usual for Oates, allowing for a broader, symbolic resonance. It is a tale of the rural outskirts of the American continent, where failing 'model communities' (The Valley, The Wheel, The Mirror Tower) and declining colonial families rub along together, maintained under an oppressive Martial Law: 'only within compounds maintained by government-registered property owners and heads of families were civil rights, to a degree, still operative'.[73]

As Werlock observes, 'Oates concerns herself with the formulation of the American Dream and how it has changed and even soured through the decades of American prosperity and preeminence.'[74] Similarly to the Love family in the later 'Night-Gaunts', 'Family' details the decline of a once-respectable family into decadence and decay, in this case peaking with revelations of incest and infanticide. And, in its depiction of their transformation by a bizarre reptilian condition in an obscure US backwater location, it also bears many similarities with Lovecraft's classic Weird science fiction tale, 'The Colour Out Of Space' (1941), regarded by Oates as among his best.[75] Narrated by the unnamed youngest daughter from this central family, they debate making 'an attempt to feed starving men, women, and children who gathered outside'[76] the fence of their property. Living

---

71. Joyce Carol Oates, 'Family', in Jeff Vandermeer and Anne Vandermeer, *The Weird: A Compendium of Strange Stories* (Tor Books, 2012), Kindle Edition.
72. Oates, 'Family', p. 759.
73. Oates, 'Family', p. 760.
74. Abby H. P. Werlock, *Encyclopedia of the American Novel* (New York: Facts on File, 2015), [n.p.] Online.
75. Oates edited the anthology *Tales of H.P. Lovecraft. By H.P. Lovecraft, Selected and Introduced by Joyce Carol Oates* (Hopewell: The Ecco Press, 1997), which included 'The Colour out of Space' and nine other classic tales of the 'Cthulhu' Mythos.
76. Oates, 'Family', p. 763.

in 'mysterious encampments' in the foothills, compared to 'villages like those once displayed in museums as being the habitations of Native American peoples', these desperate people are rumoured to have 'fled their cities at the time of the general urban collapse, as well as their former ranchers and their descendants, and various wanderers and evicted persons, criminals, the mentally ill, and victims of contagious diseases'.[77]

Again, literally looming large in the tale is a family house: 'made of stone, stucco, and clapboard; the newer wings, designed by a big-city architect, had a good deal of glass, and looked out into the Valley'.[78] While neighbouring families had sold off their properties years ago, 'before the market had begun to realize its full potential', and become 'landless, and their investments were shaky', the tale's titular family had survived by only 'selling all but a few of the acres of land surrounding our house',[79] and 'nearly all of our servants'.[80] Any semblance of a healthy household begins to fail once its members catching a mysterious flu-like illness which also causes disturbing bodily deformity: the tale's Weirdest aspects involves the Father's replacement of the ill Mother with 'New Mother', and he too eventually becoming replaced with 'New Father'; here, the children's fears of monstrous step-parents become literalized when the New Parents are revealed to bear the appearance of bizarre crocodile-like creatures.[81] Instigating one of several moments of visceral body horror, the eldest daughter, Cory, gives birth to a deformed child, whose father is unknown, and causes a rift in the family. Cory eventually dies from a violent attack – clearly perpetuated by her own, now monstrous baby – in which her 'breasts had been partly devoured, and her chest cavity exposed; she must have been attacked in the night by rats'.[82] Like 'The Lottery' and 'The Corn-Maiden', the tale' concludes with a sacrifice: the Family eventually lowers Cory's deformed child into a barrel of rats ('There – it is entirely out of our hands'[83]), enabling the family to make a new start by 'abolishing the calendar and declaring it the year 1'.[84]

'Family' is a grotesque parody of the American Dream of Self-Realization: the continuation of this old family, from respectable colonial stock, may be threatened by the emergence of planned communities, which, once again, experiment with radically new ways of arranging society; but there is a rot within them that runs deeper than economic struggle or changing cultural conditions. This dystopian world of Oates's tale, ostensibly located somewhere in an unnamed state in the near future, operates allegorically as America under Neoliberal capitalism. The family itself forms a parody of the Founding Fathers, with 'New' Father and 'New'

77. Oates, 'Family', p. 760.
78. Oates, 'Family', p. 756.
79. Oates, 'Family', p. 756.
80. Oates, 'Family', p. 757.
81. Oates, 'Family', p. 758.
82. Oates, 'Family', p. 762.
83. Oates, 'Family', p. 764.
84. Oates, 'Family', p. 764.

Mother named like New England and New York. Published at the conclusion of Ronald Reagan's presidency, it is possible to read Oates's dystopian America – with its poverty, recession, martial law and hostility to outsiders – as Reaganomics – with its rising poverty rate, 'stagflation', increased military spending and anti-immigration policies – in microcosm. And if America still leads the way for globalization, then, as the prophetic seventeen-year-old Eileen in Jackson's 'The Intoxicated' bleakly responds to the question, 'What are you saying about the future of the world?': 'I don't really think it's got much future [. . .] at least the way we've got it now.'[85]

The Dream of the Coast: Joyce Carol Oates, 'The Rescuer' (2012)

As with Jackson's 'The Summer People' and 'The Bus', Oates's 'The Rescuer' (2012) is concerned with a vulnerable woman leaving a comfortable home for an unfamiliar, dangerous location, and, drawing on Jackson's quietly Weird style, gradually develops an atmosphere of rising anxiety and menace. As such, it confirms Werlock's observation that 'In her [Oates's] short stories, the naïveté is often the innocence of youth; many stories focus on adolescent girls becoming aware of the potential of their own sexuality and the dangers of the adult world.'[86] Told in the first person, 'The Rescuer' begins with protagonist Lydia receiving a call 'from home. Your brother, they said'.[87] Her brother Harvey resides in a 'scuffed' and 'soiled' 'English Tudor House'.[88] Lydia – ostensibly the titular rescuer – is a sheltered early-career academic, reconnecting with Harvey who has dropped out of his seminary college and become embroiled in drugs and debt in a squalid area of Trenton, New Jersey, with an ethnically diverse population. In this way, the tale shows the reality of the Dream of Homeownership, away from the white-picket-fenced lawns of middle-class white prosperity. There is the sense that the Tudor House, even decades after the Civil War, will never easily be occupied by Black American families, instead 'partitioned into apartments' to accommodate communities pushed into poverty.

As well as the general sense of Jackson-esque brooding menace which Oates develops as Lydia tries to restore her brother back to health, the tale is made Weird by a seemingly tangential sub-narrative of Lydia's research, translating ancient manuscripts in the obscure, fictional language of Eweian (unrelated to the Ewe language spoken in Togo and parts of Ghana). Lydia's research often converges with the interests of her brother, who has continued his fascination with Christian

---

85. Shirley Jackson, 'The Intoxicated', in *The Lottery and Other Stories* (London: Penguin, 2009), p. 5.
86. Werlock, *Encyclopedia of the American Novel*.
87. Joyce Carol Oates, 'The Rescuer', in *High Crime Area* (St Ives: Head of Zeus Ltd, 2015), p. 97.
88. Oates, 'The Rescuer', p. 104.

mysticism and ancient mysteries, despite his addiction. In this manner, a Weird sensibility, akin to Lovecraft's fictional grimoire or M. R. James's antiquarian obsessions with ancient manuscripts, is woven into Oates's tale – subtly, through minor details.

Reading 'half a dozen pages of the Eweian manuscript', Lydia realizes that 'there were other aspects of the text in which the author's meaning was less clear. I was beginning to see that the ancient text contained another, secret text inside it. The surface text was just a patina, the truth lay beneath'.[89] In the same way that Oates does not provide a conclusion to many strands of her complex tale, Lydia does not resolve the ancient text's secret, and her research forms little more than a welcome distraction from the grim reality of her life with her brother in Trenton. Yet, this tantalizing promise of a secret beneath the surface of the ancient text suggests a similar sub-layer of meaning within Oates's story 'The Rescuer' itself; and there is one particular scene which allows this broader message to become apparent. Lydia drives her exploitative new friends (Maralena, Mercedes, Salaman) to Atlantic City – the New Jersey coastal resort famous for its casinos and boardwalks – and funds their night out gambling and drinking, naively expecting to be repaid. Having been plied into drinking too much, Lydia becomes confused and starts to lose control. Eventually she stands at the top of an escalator in the Trump Taj Mahal (with the collection published in 2014, Donald Trump was little more than a 'crude American entrepreneur'[90] at this stage), and shouts, '"How scale walls of Hades"? Plato says this is a veil of illusion! A cave of illusions! Delusions! The casino is the cave! You must wake yourself – save your souls!'[91] No one seems to hear, of course, save the security guard who escorts Lydia back to her friends.

Quoting an obscure line from her own research ('How scale walls of Hades?'), Lydia offers a critique of American Capitalism with echoes of Susan Strange's famous indictment of financial markets as 'Casino Capitalism',[92] where people gather in the casino 'like entranced spirits of Hades – nothing could wake them from their trance except a sudden *win*'.[93] Stunned by the diversity of Americans who are entranced in such a way – 'so many were elderly, walking with difficulty, with canes, or walkers', 'So many were African-American [. . .] Asian-American'[94] – Lydia's higher learning seems to enable her to see through such folly, and, after all, she does cry out from a literally elevated position.

Yet Lydia is also one of these 'entranced spirits', for, while she sees through the logic of the casino ('Most players were losers, in fact. Otherwise, how could a casino

---

89. Oates, 'The Rescuer', p. 170.
90. Oates, 'The Rescuer', p. 174.
91. Oates, 'The Rescuer', p. 174.
92. See Susan Strange, *Casino Capitalism* (Manchester: Manchester University Press, 1986).
93. Oates, 'The Rescuer', p. 172.
94. Oates, 'The Rescuer', p. 172.

keep in business?'),[95] she cannot escape her own personal Hades: her life with her brother in Trenton. When she does try to drive away, to return to 'the idyllic University campus that floated like a fairy-world just slightly above the polluted soil and waters of New Jersey', Lydia feels 'a powerful yearning' rising within her, 'to exit the same highway at Camden Avenue, and make my way home'.[96] While Lydia should be the rescuer of the story's title, come to drag Harvey away from his self-destructive lifestyle and violent friends, there seems little hope of rescue for either. Given Lydia's initially 'God-besotted brother',[97] the title raises the prospect of a spiritual rescue through Jesus. Yet no divine intervention seems possible in Oates's narrative, the potential for revelation suggested through Lydia's academic pursuits seems doomed, and Harvey's new obsession with poetry offers little more than a distraction from his desperate situation. Even at the beginning of the story, when Lydia's future as a successful scholar seems assured, her future is 'the most seductive of mirages',[98] a refracted vision of an oasis that leads her further into the desert.

The story has no resolution, and its final scene offers little in the way of hope. The discovery of a recently murdered body in Harvey's apartment – hastily removed by Lydia and Harvey during the night – confirms the extent of the criminality of Harvey's friends; and the apathy which Harvey expresses towards this discovery seems fatalistic, resigned towards doom. Lydia reflects a similar sense of doom when, in the final sentences, she cannot resist her most sensible impulses. Seeing Harvey's 'friend' Leander, as jocular as he is sinister, flagging down her car, thumbing a lift, Lydia's actions betray her thoughts: '*Oh no! Not a chance* even as my car braked to stop.'[99]

'The Rescuer' is an excellent example of the style of Weird Realism that Oates's stories develop, acting as a snapshot into the lives of Harvey and Lydia, and providing a portrait of the poverty and deprivation of small American towns, as well as the faded glamour and desperation of Atlantic City. By the end of the tale, we realize that the Eweian manuscript that Lydia has been translating, which seemed tangential initially, actually enacts a Weird unravelling of late capitalist, neoliberal America: the process of translation and the application of its ideas to Lydia's current situation is symbolic of the realization that the American Dream has been corrupted and this corruption is endemic.

Conclusion

Few writers have expressed in such a subtle and evocative manner the nature of living in contemporary America, where unease and anxiety threaten to overwhelm

---

95. Oates, 'The Rescuer', p. 172.
96. Oates, 'The Rescuer', p. 187.
97. Oates, 'The Rescuer', p. 98.
98. Oates, 'The Rescuer', p. 100.
99. Oates, 'The Rescuer', p. 193.

those who believe in its central dream-myth. Through their deeply individualistic styles, both writers showcase the importance and the endurance of the Weird Tale, reimagining it for the critical-feminist viewpoint of the New Weird. Jackson is one of several literary writers of the strange and macabre – alongside Poe, Lovecraft, Kafka and many others – to whom Oates's work is indebted, and in which the style and themes of this earlier writer are present, yet rarely in a straightforward or explicit manner; and Jackson's legacy continues in the work of contemporary women writers of the Weird and the Gothic, such as Carmen Maria Merchado (1986–) and Sarah Waters (1966–).

Through her bitterly satirical and Quietly Weird fiction, Jackson captured the rise of a specific sense of American uncertainty during the late 1940s, 1950s and 1960s, and which continues in the Weird Realism, Dystopian Allegory and careful pastiche of Oates's work, throughout the following decades and into the present. It is the 'America First' policies promoted by the Trump administration which form the most extreme catalyst for Cullen's observation that 'In the twenty-first century, the American Dream remains a major element of our national identity, and yet national identity is itself marked by a sense of uncertainty that may well be greater than ever before.'[100] 'The American Dream is dead', declared Donald Trump, upon announcing his presidential candidacy in 2015, yet, as Sarah Churchwell argues, Trump's ambitions were 'exactly the reverse of the ideas the "American Dream" was coined to advance'.[101] By the time Joyce Carol Oates published 'The Rescuer' in 2012, the Dream of social mobility through hard work that helped establish families like those of Oates and Jackson in America had largely been replaced by the purely Neoliberal Dream of the Coast. The Trump administration would work hard to end it once and for all.

The emergence of European imperialists into the lands of the First Nations civilization constituted, for the colonized, a radically new and radically destructive entity. Through their fictional visions of a twentieth- and twenty-first-century America, where the Dreams of equality and mobility which the colonizers sought to foster have become distorted and unfeasible, Jackson and Oates work to reveal the process of colonization *as Weird* and to demonstrate that a new conception of history is necessary. Following Fisher, 'if the entity *is* here, then the categories which we have up until now used to make sense of the world cannot be valid. [. . .] it is our conception of the world that must be inadequate'.[102] And it is through tales of the Weird American Dream such as those written by Jackson and Oates that Fisher's new conception of the world can begin.

---

100. Cullen, *The American Dream*, p. 6.
101. Sarah Churchwell, *Behold America: A History of America First and the American Dream* (Croydon: Bloomsbury Publishing Plc, 2019), p. 3.
102. Fisher, *The Weird and The Eerie*, p. 15.

References

Anderson, Melanie R. and Lisa Kröger, eds (2016), *Shirley Jackson, Influences and Confluences*, New York: Routledge.

Anderson, Jill E. and Melanie R. Anderson (2020), *Shirley Jackson and Domesticity: Beyond the Haunted House*, London: Bloomsbury Academic.

Bastian, Katherine (1983), *Joyce Carol Oates's Short Stories: Between Tradition and Innovation*, Frankfurt: Burn, Lang.

Britannica, The Editors of Encyclopaedia Britannica (2021), 'Shirley Jackson', Encyclopedia Britannica, 27 March. https://www.britannica.com/biography/Shirley-Jackson

Churchwell, Sarah (2019), *Behold America: A History of America First and the American Dream*, Croydon: Bloomsbury Publishing Plc.

Cullen, Jim (2004), *The American Dream: A Short History of an Idea that Shaped a Nation*, New York: Oxford University Press.

Darkecho.com (2011), 'Author Focus: Joyce Carol Oates', 10 June. https://web.archive.org/web/20110610030614/http://www.darkecho.com/darkecho/horroronline/oates.html

Darnall, F. M. (1927), 'The Americanism of Edgar Allan Poe', *The English Journal* 16 (3): 185–92. https://doi.org/10.2307/803600

Di Iorio Sandín, L. (2007), 'The Latino Scapegoat: Knowledge through Death in Short Stories by Joyce Carol Oates and Junot Díaz', in L. Di Iorio Sandín and R. Perez (eds), *Contemporary U.S. Latino/ A Literary Criticism. American Literature Readings in the 21st Century*, New York: Palgrave Macmillan. https://doi.org/10.1057/9780230609266_2

Fisher, Mark (2016), *The Weird and The Eerie*, London: Repeater Books.

Franklin, Ruth (2016), *Shirley Jackson: A Rather Haunted Life*, New York: Liverlight Publishing Corporation.

Hales, Scott (2010), '"All is Poe": Reading Poe in Joyce Carol Oates' "Poe Posthumous; or, The Light-House"', *The Edgar Allen Poe Review* 11, no. 2 (Fall): 85–108.

HarperCollins Canada (n.d), 'About the Book: *With Shuddering Fall* By Joyce Carol Oates'. https://www.harpercollins.ca/9780062795694/with-shuddering-fall/

Hattenhauer, Darryl (2003), *Shirley Jackson's American Gothic*, Albany: State University of New York Press.

Jackson, Shirley (2009), *The Lottery and Other Stories*, St Ives: Penguin Books.

Jackson, Shirley (2017), *Dark Tales*, St Ives: Penguin Random House.

Johnson, Greg (1994), *Joyce Carol Oates: A Study of the Short Fiction*, New York: Twayne Publishers.

Joshi, S. T. (1990), *The Weird Tale*, Holicong: Wildeside Press.

Joshi, S. T. (2001), *The Modern Weird Tale*, Kindle edition, Jefferson: McFarland & Co.

Joshi, S. T. (2012), 'Poe, Lovecraft, and the Revolution in Weird Fiction', Nineth Annual Commemoration Program of the Poe Society, 7 October. https://www.eapoe.org/papers/psblctrs/pl20121.htm

Kokkinou, Andromachi (2014), 'The Performance of Normality: Changing Norms in the American Gothic of Shirley Jackson and Joyce Carol Oates', [dissertation], Leiden University (The Netherlands), Faculty of Humanities.

Library of America (2010), 'The Library of America Interviews Joyce Carol Oates about Shirley Jackson', 4 May. https://www.loa.org/news-and-views/508-editor-joyce-carol-oates-on-the-enduring-spell-of-shirley-jackson

Loeb, Monica (2001), *Literary Marriages: A Study of Intertextuality in a Series of Short Stories by Joyce Carol Oates*, Bern: Verlag Peter Lang.

Lovecraft, H. P. (1920; 2009), 'The Picture in the House', *The H. P. Lovecraft Archive*.
Machin, James (2018), *Weird Fiction in Britain 1880 –1939*, London: Palgrave Gothic.
Mambrol, Nasrullah (2020), 'Analysis of Shirley Jackson's Stories', literariness.org, 24 April. https://literariness.org/2020/04/24/analysis-of-shirley-jacksons-stories/
Mayer, Sigrid and Martha Hanscom (1998), *Critical Reception of the Short Fiction by Joyce Carol Oates and Gabriele Wohmann*, Columbia: Camden House.
Miéville, China (2009), 'Weird Fiction', in M. Bould, A. M. Butler, Adam Roberts and Sherryl Vint (eds), *The Routledge Companion to Science Fiction*, 510–15, London: Routledge.
Murphy, Bernice M. (2005), *Shirley Jackson: Essays on the Literary Legacy*, Jefferson: McFarland & Co.
Murphy, Timothy S. and Benjamin Noys (2016), 'Introduction: Old and New Weird', *Genre: Forms of Discourse and Closure* 49 (2): 117–34.
Norman, K. and M. Torborg (1984), *Isolation and Contact: A Study of Character Relationships in Joyce Carol Oates's Short Stories, 1963–1980*, Goteborg: Acta Universitatis Gothoburgensis.
Oates, Joyce Carol, ed. (2010), 'Joyce Carol Oates on the Enduring Spell of Shirley Jackson', 'The Library of America Interviews', 14 May. https://www.loa.org/news-and-views/508 -editor-joyce-carol-oates-on-the-enduring-spell-of-shirley-jackson
Oates, Joyce Carol (2012), *The Corn Maiden: And Other Nightmares*, St Ives: Head of Zeus.
Oates, Joyce Carol (2015), *High Crime Area*, St Ives: Head of Zeus Ltd.
Oates, Joyce Carol (2016), *The Lost Landscape: A Writer's Coming of Age*, St Ives: 4th Estate.
Oates, Joyce Carol (2018), *Night-Gaunts and Other Tales of Suspense*, Croydon: Head of Zeus Ltd.
Patten, Ann Lucille (2008), 'The Female Uncanny?: A Historicized Reading of The Uncanny Fiction of Edith Wharton, Shirley Jackson & Joyce Carol Oates', [thesis], Trinity College (Dublin, Ireland), School of English.
Pickering, Samuel F. (1974), 'The Short Stories of Joyce Carol Oates', *The Georgia Review* 28 (2): 218–26. http://www.jstor.org/stable/41397080 (accessed 11 November 2020).
Robson, Leo (2020), 'The Unruly Genius of Joyce Carol Oates', *The New Yorker*, 29 June. https://www.newyorker.com/magazine/2020/07/06/the-unruly-genius-of-joyce-carol -oates
Ruff, Matt (2016), *Lovecraft Country*, New York: HarperCollins.
Severin, Hermann (1986), *The Image of the Intellectual in the Short Stories of Joyce Carol Oates*, Frankfurt: Peter Lang.
Sreelakshmi, P. (1996), *Elective Affinities: A Study in the Sources and Intertexts of Joyce Carol Oates's Short Fiction*, Madras: T.R. Publications.
Vandermeer, Jeff and Anne Vandermeer (2012), *The Weird: A Compendium of Strange Stories*, Kindle Edition, Tor Books.
Werlock, Abby H. P. (2015), *Encyclopedia of the American Novel, Companion to* Literature, New York: Facts on File.
Weinstock, Jeffrey Andrew (2016), 'The New Weird', in Ken Gelder (ed.), *New Directions in Popular Fiction*, London: Palgrave Macmillan.

Chapter 3

DEMON LOVERS, BLUEBEARD'S WIVES

FOLKLORIC INTERTEXTS AND HORROR IN SHIRLEY JACKSON AND CARMEN MARIA MACHADO

Erika Kvistad

In 'The Daemon Lover', a Scottish ballad whose earliest versions date from the 1600s, a woman is enticed into leaving her husband and child by her former lover, the sea captain James Harris. Once they are out at sea, she finds that they are not sailing to 'the banks of Italy' after all, but to 'the mountain of hell'. In the final stanza, Harris, apparently grown monstrously tall, breaks the ship apart and sinks it.[1] Shirley Jackson encountered 'The Daemon Lover', which goes by a variety of other names including 'James Harris', 'The House-Carpenter', and 'A Warning to Married Women', in Francis James Child's *The English and Scottish Popular Ballads* (1860), an anthology of traditional ballads that she first read in childhood.[2] The epilogue to her collection *The Lottery, or the Adventures of James Harris* (1949) is the final half of a version of it, Child 243 F, from the point where the heroine boards James Harris's ship to her betrayal and drowning.

In this chapter, I explore how deeply this folkloric intertext is embedded in the horror elements of Jackson's short fiction. I read Jackson's stories alongside the work of Carmen Maria Machado, a contemporary author whose horror stories both explicitly and implicitly echo Jackson, and examine how Machado's 'The Husband Stitch' draws on Jackson's use of 'The Daemon Lover' while reworking it into a different folkloric form: the Bluebeard story. I argue that this shift in folkloric structure, even in stories with very similar themes and preoccupations, fundamentally changes the nature of horror in the two writers' work. In this way, the chapter argues that 'The Daemon Lover' is not only a central intertext for Jackson's short fiction, it also structures much of her work's conception of horror. Folkloric form, here, shapes the kind of story it is possible to tell.

---

1. This version of 'The Daemon Lover' is the one excerpted in Jackson's *The Lottery*, Child Ballad 243.
2. Ruth Franklin, *Shirley Jackson: A Rather Haunted Life* (New York City: W. W. Norton, 2016), p. 30.

Critical attention to Jackson's use of the 'Daemon Lover' ballad often focuses on the role of James Harris, a character who takes his name from the ballad and appears recurrently, in a variety of forms and roles, throughout *The Lottery*. Joan Wylie Hall's study of Jackson's short fiction discusses *The Lottery* in its entirety and describes it as a semi-connected story cycle, dividing it into thematic subgroups and explicating the ways in which the figure of James Harris recurs in the stories. In her reading, a 'motif of menace [. . .] radiates from the James Harris tales to infect most of the relationships in the book'.[3] Håvard Nørjordet follows Hall in reading *The Lottery* as a cohesive single work centred on Harris, seeing Harris as a single, but intentionally inconsistent figure: he argues against Lenemaja Friedman's assertion that 'none of the in-name-only Harris characters has any relationship or likeness to the others', noting that 'If Harris had been a stable and consistent character, he would not make a credible demon; demons embody ambiguity and dreamy logic, not consistency'.[4] While Nørjordet sees Harris primarily as a supernatural folklore figure, Wyatt Bonikowski reads the demon lover in Lacanian terms, 'suggesting that the demon lover is for the feminine subject what the Lady of courtly love is for the masculine subject – that is, a representation of the Thing and of the impingement of the Real on the subject'.[5] Edwina Keown and Bernice M. Murphy's 'Uncanny Irish-American Relations' also addresses Harris and the demon lover in a comparison of Elizabeth Bowen and Jackson's demon lover stories.[6]

This chapter's reading of 'The Daemon Lover' in Jackson, however, shifts the focus from Harris as a figure to the structure of the ballad as a whole. I read the 'Daemon Lover' ballad as an instantiation of what I describe here as the Demon Lover theme in Jackson: the theme of a woman's growing isolation as she realizes that those around her do not recognize or share her perception of reality and that she has been betrayed by someone she believed loved her. (Both Jackson and the ballad, of course, use the spelling 'daemon'; I use 'demon' here to make it easier to distinguish between the concept of the Demon Lover theme and the titles of the two texts.) The horror of the ballad protagonist's lonely death is, I argue, the horror at the heart of much of Jackson's work: what you thought was intimacy with another person turns out to be something very different.

I go on to explore how Jackson's Demon Lover theme is reworked in Carmen Maria Machado's 'The Husband Stitch'. Like Jackson's stories, 'The Husband

---

3. Joan Wylie Hall, *Shirley Jackson: A Study of the Short Fiction* (Woodbridge: Twayne, 1993), p. 9.

4. Lenemaja Friedman, *Shirley Jackson* (Bobbs-Merrill, 1975), p. 67; Håvard Nørjordet, 'The Tall Man in the Blue Suit: Witchcraft, Folklore, and Reality in Shirley Jackson's *The Lottery, or the Adventures of James Harris*' (Oslo: University of Oslo, 2005), p. 15.

5. Wyatt Bonikowski, '"Only One Antagonist": The Demon Lover and the Feminine Experience in the Work of Shirley Jackson', *Gothic Studies* 15, no. 2 (2013): 66–88, p. 71.

6. Edwina Keown and Bernice M. Murphy, 'Uncanny Irish-American Relations', in *The Green Book: Writings on Irish Gothic, Supernatural and Fantastic Literature*, No. 9 (Bealtaine 2017), pp. 57–84.

Stitch' draws heavily on folklore, here primarily in the more contemporary form of urban legends: the narrator tells versions of a number of well-known urban legends throughout the story, and the frame narrative itself is a version of a folk story, 'The Green Ribbon'. But through this range of folklore retellings, Machado also continually draws on and re-examines the themes of Jackson's work, in particular the Demon Lover theme. I do not read 'The Husband Stitch' as an explicit and intentional take on Jackson; considering how clearly Machado refers to Jackson elsewhere in her work, I think any purposeful references here would have been more obvious. Machado says that she began to read Jackson early in the process of working on the collection *Her Body and Other Parties* (2017), in which 'The Husband Stitch' appears. She submitted an early draft of a story to a writers' workshop and found that everyone agreed that it reminded them of Jackson, who Machado had never read; she went on to read 'everything [. . .] Jackson ever wrote'.[7] Machado herself attributes this to 'the second-hand influence you get when the authors you have read have already internalized the work of someone like Jackson'.[8] In addition to the effects of this second-hand influence, 'The Husband Stitch' and much of Jackson's short fiction draw from the shared well of a folkloric story tradition: repeated, echoing stories of abandoned, isolated, disempowered, threatened, hurt women. 'The Husband Stitch' both makes use of and thematizes this story tradition: the stories that '[e]veryone knows [. . .] but no one ever believes'.[9] In doing so, Machado shapes the Demon Lover theme into a different folkloric structure. Drawing on Casie Hermansson's work on Bluebeard and feminist intertextuality, I argue that Machado's story becomes a Bluebeard narrative, a story in which repeated, individual narratives of solitary horror and betrayal are strung together, contextualized and interpreted, creating the possibility of meaning, connection and change.

But while there is a note of hope to this reworking of the theme from one folkloric structure into another, both variants remain, fundamentally, horror stories. Examining Machado's intertextual work as a horror story about connection, vulnerability and complicity, I argue, gives us a clearer sense of Jackson as a horror writer centred on the experience of isolation. Where Machado's use of familiar folkloric intertexts, the stories 'everyone knows', has an aspect of both warning and potential connection and solidarity, for Jackson the continual return of the Demon Lover narrative functions neither as a warning nor as a possibility for common ground, only as a bleak confirmation of what we should already have known.

---

7. Joe Fassler, 'How Surrealism Enriches Storytelling about Women', *The Atlantic*, 12 October 2017. https://www.theatlantic.com/entertainment/archive/2017/10/how-surrealism-enriches-storytelling-about-women/542496/ (accessed 14 September 2022).

8. Fassler, 'How Surrealism Enriches Storytelling about Women'.

9. Carmen Maria Machado, 'The Husband Stitch', 2014, in *Her Body and Other Parties* (Minneapolis: Graywolf Press, 2017), pp. 5–6.

One Long Documentation of Anxiety: Jackson and the Demon Lover

The 'Daemon Lover' ballad has a long tradition of reworkings in ballad form, although adaptations into other modes and explicit uses of the ballad as an intertext seem rarer, with a major exception – Elizabeth Bowen's short story 'The Demon Lover' (1941), which is semi-contemporary with Jackson's work.[10] While Toni Reed's *Demon-Lovers and Their Victims in British Fiction* (1988) finds echoes of the ballad throughout literary history in texts like *Dracula*, *Tess of the D'Urbervilles* and *Wuthering Heights,* it does so primarily by abstracting the ballad into the broader motif or archetype of 'an aggressive man's attempts to dominate and destroy a naive impressionable woman'.[11] Reed's summary of the basic ballad plot, 'a demonic figure tempts, seduces, betrays, and victimizes women', immediately suggests how idiosyncratic Jackson's own use of the ballad is.[12] In Jackson's versions, the key aspect of the ballad is not the seduction, or even the demonic figure himself – rather, it is the protagonist's slow realization that what she experienced as connection and intimacy was not real, or at least that only she experienced it as real, and that she is alone with her perception of reality. This theme – a woman's increasing isolation as she becomes aware that there is a mismatch between her own perception of reality and others', and that her experience of connection with someone else has been a delusion – is what I describe as the Demon Lover theme. While this chapter focuses on Jackson's short fiction, this theme appears throughout her work – we might think of the scene in *The Haunting of Hill House* where Eleanor is in bed clutching Theo's hand in the dark, only to discover, when the lights come on, that Theo is on the other side of the room: 'God God – whose hand was I holding?'[13] For Jackson, the emotional effect of the moment when the lights come on is what the 'Daemon Lover' ballad is about.

As noted earlier, the figure of James Harris makes appearances throughout *The Lottery*, in or out of focus. He is sometimes nameless but usually called Jim or Mr Harris or James Harris; when his clothes are mentioned it is always a blue suit (this makes him recognizable when unnamed, as in 'The Intoxicated'); when his occupation is mentioned he is always a writer; when his height is mentioned he is always tall.[14] He is sometimes central to the plot, as in 'The Daemon Lover',

---

10. See, for instance, John Burrison, '"James Harris" in Britain since Child', *The Journal of American Folklore* 80, no. 317 (1967): 271–84.

11. Toni Reed, *Demon Lovers and Their Victims in British Fiction* (Lexington: University Press of Kentucky, 1988), p. 8.

12. Reed, *Demon Lovers*, p. 8.

13. Shirley Jackson, *The Haunting of Hill House* (London: Penguin, 2006), p. 120.

14. By my count, James Harris appears in seven or eight of the stories in *The Lottery*. He appears in 'The Daemon Lover' as 'Jamie' and 'James Harris'; in 'Like Mother Used to Make' as 'Mr. Harris' (possibly James – the protagonist overhears another character tell him that 'My *father's* name was James' (38)); in 'The Villager' as 'Harris'; in 'Elizabeth' as 'Jim Harris';

and sometimes incidental, as in 'The Intoxicated', but he is always in some way unknowable – absent or blurred, seen in outline rather than in detail. The protagonist of 'The Daemon Lover' has difficulty remembering his face, and in the one story where someone has an in-depth conversation with him, 'The Tooth', she is heavily drugged at the time.

The omnipresence of James Harris in the collection is, however, at least in part a retrospective move by Jackson: some of the Harris characters in stories published elsewhere originally had other names, and Jackson changed them for inclusion in *The Lottery*. Mr Harris, the invasive co-worker in 'Like Mother Used to Make', was originally Mr Lang, and Jim, the man on the bus in 'The Tooth', is named Ray in the version of the story published in the *Hudson Review*.[15] She also changed the name of a story originally published as 'The Phantom Lover' in 1949, to 'The Daemon Lover'. I would suggest that the overwriting of earlier antagonists with Harris's name suggests that we can see Harris as an *instance* of the Demon Lover and that Jackson's use of Harris's name only underscores a pattern that was already there in her work. Not every story with a James Harris appearance is actually a Demon Lover story (like 'The Intoxicated', one of Jackson's stories of a predicted apocalypse, in which the man in the blue suit appears to just be there to observe), and not every story with Demon Lover themes mentions James Harris (this is particularly a tendency for stories published outside *The Lottery*, like 'The Beautiful Stranger', 'The Good Wife', and 'The Honeymoon of Mrs Smith'). Even 'The Tooth', arguably the Jackson story that follows the ballad plot most closely, originally had an antagonist with a different name. The Demon Lover theme in Jackson's work, then, does not necessarily always spring from the single mythical figure of James Harris – rather, Harris appears as an *instance* of the Demon Lover, and the theme itself runs deeper.

While the Demon Lover theme is pervasive in Jackson's work, the two stories that illustrate it most clearly are both from *The Lottery*: 'The Daemon Lover' and 'The Tooth'. In 'The Daemon Lover', an unnamed woman wakes on what is meant to be her wedding day, apparently to a man she has not known for very long. Her fiancé, of course, is James Harris. She spends the morning nervously preparing to meet him, feeling painfully unsure of herself: 'she thought with revulsion, It's as though I was trying to make myself look prettier than I am'.[16] When the appointed time passes and he does not arrive, she eventually goes to his apartment to look for him, but finds that he has moved out. Finally, she traces him back to another

---

in 'Seven Types of Ambiguity' and 'Of Course' as 'Mr Harris'; and in 'The Tooth' as 'Jim'. In 'The Witch' and 'The Intoxicated', he is nameless, but appears as a man in a blue suit. 'Got a Letter from Jimmy' is ambiguous – we learn so little about Jimmy that it is difficult to clearly categorize him as a James Harris instance.

15. Franklin, *Shirley Jackson*, p. 243; Shirley Jackson, 'The Tooth', *The Hudson Review* 1, no. 4 (Winter 1949): 503–21.

16. Shirley Jackson, 'The Daemon Lover', in *The Lottery and Other Stories* (London: Penguin, 2009), p. 11.

apartment building, where according to a passer-by he was 'going to see his girl', but although 'she was sure she could hear low voices and sometimes laughter', no one answers the door.[17]

As in the ballad, a heroine pledges herself to a man who she believes loves her, only to find that he is not what she thought.[18] In the ballad, James Harris appears to be demonic in nature: he reveals cloven feet, promises to take the heroine to 'the hills of Hell', and is able to physically break their ship into pieces. In the story, he is ambiguously supernatural – as is often the case in Jackson, nothing definitively supernatural ever happens, but there is certainly something weird not only about Harris's complete disappearance, but about the way other people behave in his wake. His landlords appear to have allowed him to stay with them without having any idea who he is ('"He's one of Dottie's friends." "Not *my* friends," Mrs Royster said'), and the people the heroine seeks help from are consistently unhelpful and mocking.[19] Part of the effect of the abandonment, of course, is that everyone *seems* to be deliberately playing along with Harris to torment her, but the heroine is denied the relief of knowing for sure that this is the case and thus gaining a clear view of her enemy and his abilities.

In the version Jackson quotes, the 'Daemon Lover' ballad begins with the heroine asking: 'O where have you been, my long, long love, / This long seven years and mair?'[20] Prior to the start of the ballad, the heroine is abandoned by James Harris. They get engaged, and then apparently he leaves her without a word; the heroine has to ask him where he has been. The heroine is now married to another man and has children, and Harris responds to learning this by telling her angrily about the other romantic prospects he has missed out on in order to court her a second time: 'I might hae had a king's daughter, / Far, far beyond the sea; / I might have had a king's daughter, / Had it not been for love o thee.'[21] Comparing the two narratives in terms of plot, then, we could read Jackson's 'The Daemon Lover' as taking place before the ballad begins: the two are engaged, their wedding day has come, and the demon lover has inexplicably disappeared.

This parallel implies the possibility of a hopeful continuation to Jackson's story, if not a hopeful end: the ballad heroine gets married and has a family in the period where the demon lover is away. But the end of the story seems to remove even this hope for some kind of connection. From the moment the heroine wakes up, the narrative follows her thoughts and actions closely, emphasizing her sense that time

17. Jackson, 'The Daemon Lover', pp. 25–8.
18. To echo the folkloric elements of these stories, I refer to the unnamed protagonist here as 'the heroine'; since Machado's protagonist tells her story in the first person, I refer to her as 'the narrator'.
19. Jackson, 'The Daemon Lover', p. 17.
20. 'James Harris (The Daemon Lover)', Child 243F. Available on *Internet Sacred Text Archive*. https://www.sacred-texts.com/neu/eng/child/ch243.htm (accessed 14 September 2022).
21. 'James Harris (The Daemon Lover)', Child 243F.

is passing slowly and painfully; there are only occasional disruptions, as when she falls asleep accidentally and loses an hour. The final paragraph, though, telescopes an indefinite, maybe interminable stretch of time: 'She came back many times, every day for the first week. She came on her way to work, in the mornings; in the evenings, on her way to dinner alone, but no matter how often or how firmly she knocked, no one ever came to the door'.[22] This suggests that Jackson has simply cut out the interim marriage, leaving the rest of the ballad plot intact: vows, abandonment, the lover's possible transformation into a beast (in the apartment building where the heroine looks for him, she instead finds a rat, 'its evil face alert, bright eyes watching her'), and the heroine's condemnation – to the hills of Hell in the ballad, and here to unending loneliness.[23]

'The Tooth' picks up on other aspects of the ballad plot, and again, what Jackson emphasizes and alters is telling. The heroine, Clara, leaves her husband and children for the day and boards a bus to the city to visit the dentist. While she is in a codeine and whisky haze on the bus, a strange man, Jim, starts to talk to her, telling her about a dreamlike landscape where 'the stars are as big as the moon and the moon is as big as a lake'.[24] Clara has her tooth extracted under anaesthesia, and, when she wakes, gradually discovers that she no longer remembers who she is. At the end of the story, Jim comes to fetch her. Here there is apparently no previous relationship with the demon lover, but in fact Clara's aching tooth seems to fill this role, functioning as a source of unease in her marriage and isolating her from her husband. Her husband mentions that her tooth has been troubling her 'on and off for years', and adds, 'accusingly', that she had a toothache on their honeymoon.[25] As in the ballad, the heroine in 'The Tooth' sets out on a journey, but here she does so without any intention to leave her family permanently; she leaves her husband with a series of guilty, worried instructions for their care. This aspect of the story reads like a lower-key, more insidious version of Elizabeth Bowen's 1945 story 'The Demon Lover', in which the heroine's former lover kidnaps her in a car. The demon lover does not steal Clara from her family, but nor does he seduce her into abandoning them; he just disconnects her from them.

In Toni Reed's reading, the cultural recurrence of the demon lover motif has to do with the way it 'reflects a social reality' for women – it both dramatizes the social control of women and acts as a warning against female transgression.[26] But the elements and themes that Reed sees as central in demon lover narratives – temptation, seduction, power, innocence and corruption – are oddly absent from Jackson's versions. Both 'The Tooth' and 'The Daemon Lover' cut the ballad's moment of seduction, where the heroine makes the choice (which I think can

---

22. Jackson, 'The Daemon Lover', p. 28.
23. Jackson, 'The Daemon Lover', p. 27.
24. Shirley Jackson, 'The Tooth', in *The Lottery and Other Stories* (London: Penguin, 2009), p. 271.
25. Jackson, 'The Tooth', p. 267.
26. Reed, *Demon Lovers*, p. 2, p. vii.

be interpreted as either coerced or relatively free) to board James Harris's ship. In 'The Daemon Lover' the whole mid-part of the ballad is missing, while in 'The Tooth' Clara has no idea that she is making a fateful decision when she gets on the bus. Even Harris himself is a nebulous, almost absent figure rather than, in Reed's terms, an 'aggressively dominant' one. He is never present on the page in 'The Daemon Lover' and only occasionally turns up in 'The Tooth', and most of what actually happens to the heroines of the two stories is enacted by someone other than him, as if by proxy – the people the heroine meets on the street in 'The Daemon Lover'; the dentist in 'The Tooth'. While he does seem to have some kind of supernatural power, it is never quite clear how much agency he is exercising over the heroines' fates. In this way, Jim or James Harris himself is deemphasized; it is as if, rather than being unfortunate enough to encounter a supernatural being, the heroine has just run into a basic law of nature.

In Jackson's interpretation of the ballad, then, the horror does not centre on sexual threat, but on the inescapability of the heroines' drift into isolation. But although Jackson's versions of the ballad do not quite follow Reed's sexually aggressive man/innocent and naive woman pattern, they are still gendered in significant ways. Jackson does have Demon Lover stories with men as victims: in 'Like Mother Used to Make' James Harris takes over a man's apartment like a cuckoo, and 'Paranoia' has hints of a gender-swapped Demon Lover pattern, with a female aggressor and a male victim. But in the same way that it matters that the ballad has a female victim, it matters that the Demon Lover stories are usually about women. The Demon Lover stories pick up on and exploit the mid-century, middle-class American woman's relative economic precarity, as in 'Elizabeth', where the heroine is troubled by the dinginess of her apartment while preparing to entertain a male caller, or 'The Daemon Lover', where the heroine is similarly troubled by her shabby wedding outfit. They pick up on her frequent need to rely on men (as in 'The Honeymoon of Mrs Smith', where the heroine's life falls apart after the death of her father), her subjection to others' decisions (as in 'The Tooth', where Clara is put on the bus by her husband), and her forced passivity in romantic relationships (which is central in 'The Daemon Lover'). The experience of horror in these stories – the sense of claustrophobic restriction, the vulnerability to violence and abandonment, the dread of not being understood or listened to – is built from elements of this gender role. 'I think all my books laid end to end would be one long documentation of anxiety', Jackson wrote in her diary, and in the Demon Lover stories it is a primarily female anxiety, documented over and over again.[27]

Convincing Each Other of Some Horrible Notion: Jackson and Bluebeard

The other well-known folk narrative that appears in Jackson's work is also one of female vulnerability and romantic betrayal: the Bluebeard story. Bluebeard

27. Shirley Jackson, diary entry, 1963, quoted in Franklin, *Shirley Jackson*, p. 477.

is a much slighter presence in her work than the Demon Lover – she uses the story structure once, in 'The Honeymoon of Mrs Smith' – but it is a striking one. This section and the next reads the Bluebeard narrative in terms of feminist intertextuality, arguing that this folkloric structure allows for the transformation of narratives of victimization into solidarity and, ultimately, change. The Bluebeard story is about how women are betrayed, suffer and die repeatedly, but it is also about how, when these disparate narratives of suffering are brought together and connected, the cycle can be broken. Machado draws on these aspects of Bluebeard in 'The Husband Stitch'. What Jackson does with the story, though, is almost the reverse of this.

Bluebeard, Aarne-Thompson type 312, is a French folktale that first appears in print in Charles Perrault's 1697 collection of fairy tales. In this story, a young woman gets married, her husband tells her that there is one room in the house she may never enter, and she does so anyway, only to discover the murdered bodies of all his previous wives. She then has to try to avoid becoming his next victim once he discovers what she knows. At the end of most versions, the heroine's brothers rescue her and kill her husband.

There is a long and varied tradition of Bluebeard retellings: Casie Hermansson's study of feminist intertextuality and Bluebeard describes the story as 'astonishingly prevalent', particularly in women's writing, and Maria Tatar, Cristina Bacchilega, and Rose Lovell-Smith, among others, have written extensive explorations of the story's afterlives.[28] Hermansson argues that the Bluebeard story is meta-intertextual, in the sense that the story is a frequent source of material for feminist retellings, but also itself enacts what she describes as feminist intertextuality. For Hermansson, 'the surviving heroine performs feminist intertextuality' by rewriting Bluebeard's plot: 'In changing the terms of the story, the heroine extricates herself from the plot that was to enclose her'.[29] The Bluebeard story, then, has two strands: there is Bluebeard's plot, the way Bluebeard himself expects things to go, which is a plot about male power, control and violence, and there is the heroine's plot, the heroine's revision of Bluebeard's plans, which is a plot about women's stories as a source of power and liberation. In the first strand women suffer repeatedly and repetitively; in the second strand, an interpretable record of repeated, repetitive suffering brings change and justice. The horror the heroine experiences – the recognition that she is no different from the earlier wives, but just another in a long chain of victims – turns into the power to break this chain. Deindividualization ('metonymy is used by Bluebeard to make all his wives the same wife', writes

---

28. Casie Hermansson, *Reading Feminist Intertextuality Through Bluebeard Stories* (Lewiston: Edwin Mellen Press, 2001), p. 1. See also Maria Tatar, *Secrets Beyond the Door: The Story of Bluebeard and His Wives* (Philadelphia: Princeton University Press, 2004), Cristina Bacchilega, *Postmodern Fairy Tales: Gender and Narrative Strategies* (Philadelphia: University of Pennsylvania Press, 2010), and Rose Lovell-Smith, 'Feminism and Bluebeard', *ELO*, no. 5 (1999): 43–53.

29. Hermansson, *Reading Feminist Intertextuality*, p. 6.

Hermansson) becomes connection; connection becomes solidarity.[30] Here is the heroine's discovery of the previous wives in Perrault: 'At first she could not see anything plainly, because the windows were shut. After some moments she began to perceive that the floor was all covered over with clotted blood, on which lay the bodies of several dead women, ranged against the walls. (These were all the wives whom Bluebeard had married and murdered, one after another.)'[31]

The heroine's perception moves from darkness, to sight, to witnessing the bodies, to a full chronological narrative of what Bluebeard has done. Her ability to witness, interpret, and contextualize the deaths of the previous wives leads to her liberation, the death of Bluebeard, and the breaking of Bluebeard's cycle of marriage and death. It is also worth noticing that she does not do this alone: she is accompanied by her sister, a character with no obvious role in the narrative, which in itself makes her seem oddly significant (the fact that she is the only character with a given name, Anne, adds to this). The sister does not rescue the heroine or even really comfort her, she is just there – a witness to the heroine's suffering, just as the heroine witnessed the suffering of the earlier wives.

What happens to the Bluebeard theme in Jackson's hands? Jackson wrote two versions of 'The Honeymoon of Mrs Smith', neither of which was published in her lifetime; both are reprinted in *Just an Ordinary Day* (1996).[32] The major difference between the two is Mrs Smith's awareness of her new husband's reputation in version 2, which means that while version 1 is a Roald Dahl-esque black comedy, version 2, though still occasionally funny, is profoundly bleak. Version 2, the version I will focus on in this reading, begins with a newly married woman realizing that the other people in the grocery store are talking about her and her husband behind her back. She buys only a few things for the weekend, telling the clerk that she 'may be going away'.[33] On reflection, she adds a pound of coffee: 'I can probably drink up a pound before.'[34] Over the course of the story, it becomes apparent that her neighbours all strongly suspect that Mrs Smith's husband has killed several previous wives in order to collect their life insurance. One of them, Mrs Jones, tries to tell her about this and offer help: 'if you ever *ever* need help – of *any* kind – just open your mouth and scream, see?'[35] But Mrs Smith, it turns out, was fully aware of these rumours when she married him. The story ends with Mr

---

30. Hermansson, *Reading Feminist Intertextuality*, p. 58.

31. Charles Perrault, 'Blue Beard', 1697, in *The Blue Fairy Book*, ed. Andrew Lang (London: Longmans, Green, and Company, *c*. 1889), pp. 290–5. Available on *Folklore and Mythology Electronic Texts*, ed. D. L. Ashliman. https://www.pitt.edu/~dash/perrault03.html (accessed 14 September 2022).

32. References to the story in this chapter are, from here on, to version 2 as reprinted in Shirley Jackson, *Dark Tales* (London: Penguin, 2016).

33. Shirley Jackson, 'The Honeymoon of Mrs Smith', in *Dark Tales* (London: Penguin, 2016), p. 41.

34. Jackson, 'The Honeymoon of Mrs Smith', p. 42.

35. Jackson, 'The Honeymoon of Mrs Smith', p. 49.

Smith returning home and his wife waiting impatiently for him to murder her, thinking: 'Why does it take so long, why *does* it take so long?'[36]

'The Honeymoon of Mrs Smith' acts almost as a meta-commentary on other feminist intertextual uses of the Bluebeard story, draining the story of the potential that other writers have found in it. Like Jackson's uses of 'The Daemon Lover', her use of Bluebeard has none of the uneasy, ambivalent sexual elements of many other retellings. The heroine chooses to marry Mr Smith, in the almost-certain knowledge that he will kill her, because she hopes it will give her life a sense of narrative meaning that has been missing since her father's death; accepting his proposal, she sees 'the repeated design which made the complete pattern'.[37] Her neighbours, too, seem to see her marriage and coming death in these fairy-tale terms: 'If the dreadful fact *were* true (and they all hoped it was), Mrs Smith was, for them, a salvation and a heroine, a fragile, lovely creature whose preservation was in hands other than theirs'.[38] But she is constantly aware that the next element of the plot has been delayed a little too long: 'Everyone is waiting; it will spoil everything if it is not soon.'[39] When it finally comes, the scene of her approaching death is an anticlimax: Mr Smith gets up 'wearily' from the couch to kill her, as if this has become, by now, a drab routine to him.[40]

Moreover, in Jackson's hands, the Bluebeard story is stripped of the potential for female fellowship and solidarity. Mrs Smith imagines herself and Mrs Jones not as distinct individuals, but, as their surnames suggest, as similar variations on a generic type: 'Here we are, Helen Smith was thinking, two women of the singular type woman [. . .] differing, actually, in no essential, although we would both deny indignantly that we were the same person, seeking the same destiny.'[41] But in contrast to the Perrault story, similarity here does not lead to connection. Mrs Smith does not just refuse Mrs Jones's help, she also refuses to share her perception of reality. Both women are fairly sure that Mr Smith really is a murderer, and even Mrs Smith occasionally lets this slip: when Mrs Jones says that dying by stabbing might be preferable to drowning, she replies, 'It's not our choice'.[42] But she also repeatedly undercuts this certainty, specifically by comparing it to folklore: 'You see how silly we sound? Here we are, talking as though we were children telling ghost stories. We'll end up convincing each other of some horrible notion.'[43]

In the fairy tale Sister Anne is not a saviour figure, just as here, too, Mrs Jones offers her husband's help rather than her own. But Anne is the other woman who shares the heroine's narrative, her perception of reality. This role, which Mrs Smith

36. Jackson, 'The Honeymoon of Mrs Smith', p. 52.
37. Jackson, 'The Honeymoon of Mrs Smith', p. 50.
38. Jackson, 'The Honeymoon of Mrs Smith', p. 43.
39. Jackson, 'The Honeymoon of Mrs Smith', p. 51.
40. Jackson, 'The Honeymoon of Mrs Smith', p. 52.
41. Jackson, 'The Honeymoon of Mrs Smith', p. 46.
42. Jackson, 'The Honeymoon of Mrs Smith', p. 49.
43. Jackson, 'The Honeymoon of Mrs Smith', p. 49.

refuses to allow Mrs Jones to take on, is explicitly evoked at one other point in Jackson's work. At the start of 'The Daemon Lover', the heroine is writing a letter to her sister, 'dearest Anne', to tell her about her engagement: 'I can hardly believe it myself, but when I tell you how it happened, you'll see it's even stranger than that'.[44] But the letter is never finished, and the heroine remains alone with her strange story.

As Lonely as I Have Ever Been: 'The Husband Stitch', Jackson, Bluebeard, and the Demon Lover

In 'The Honeymoon of Mrs Smith', the heroine uses a comparison to folk narrative to discredit what both she and Mrs Jones know is true. This sounds like a ghost story, she argues, so it cannot be real – though at the same time she obliquely suggests that these kinds of stories do have the power to make people share an understanding of reality: 'We'll end up convincing each other of some horrible notion.' In Carmen Maria Machado's 'The Husband Stitch', the repeated patterns of folk narrative become exactly this: a way of recognizing and sharing a horrible truth.

'The Husband Stitch' is not Machado's most obviously Jacksonian work. Her story 'Blur' (2017), in which a woman loses her glasses during a road trip, strongly echoes 'The Tooth' – the unreality and vulnerability of transit, the experience of being misunderstood or ignored by everyone around you, and the perceptual blurriness suggested by the title (which here operates on different levels and with different causes: nearsightedness, a Xanax haze and gaslighting by a romantic partner). This is not just a Demon Lover story but a Jackson Demon Lover story, in which a mysterious man in a blue suit appears to lead the protagonist into unknown territory. 'Blur' makes compelling use of Jacksonian elements to explore an abusive relationship between two women. The dynamic between the protagonist and her girlfriend is a clear precursor to *In the Dream House* (2019), Machado's intertextual memoir of an abusive relationship. The memoir flickers through genres, forms, pastiches, and textual references as the narrator takes repeated runs at finding a way to tell this difficult story: 'Dream House as Picaresque', 'Dream House as Romance Novel', 'Dream House as Folktale Taxonomy'. 'Blur' feels as if it might be a beginning to this project: Dream House as Shirley Jackson Story.

But where 'Blur' is so close to Jackson that it almost functions as a pastiche, 'The Husband Stitch' in my reading is a full-scale reworking of Jackson that shapes Jackson's thematic elements, in particular her Demon Lover theme, into a different folkloric form. This brings out both the similarities in themes and emphasis and the differences in final effect between Jackson's horror and Machado's. Reading 'The Husband Stitch' alongside Jackson allows us to contrast how the two authors use intertextuality not just as a technique, but as a concept: the recollection and

---

44. Jackson, 'The Daemon Lover', p. 9.

repetition of an old story means something completely different in Machado and in Jackson.

'The Husband Stitch' is a deeply intertextual story, and most strikingly it is full of references to a specific kind of folklore: the urban legend, a contemporary folkloric sub-genre made up of stories, often though not always with some sort of horror element, that are told and retold as though they were true and either self-experienced or, more commonly, experienced by a friend or relative of the teller. The plot of the story itself is a version of another frequently recirculated story, sometimes titled 'The Green Ribbon', although this one cannot be described as an urban legend, since for reasons that will become obvious it is never told as though it were true.[45] In this story, a young man marries a woman who always wears a ribbon around her neck. He keeps asking her about the ribbon and suggesting that she should take it off, but she never does, and she refuses to answer questions about it. Finally, on her deathbed, the woman relents and unties the ribbon, and her head falls off.

'The Husband Stitch' follows a woman as she has her first sexual experiences, gets married, gets pregnant, raises her son and finally dies. She has a green ribbon around her throat, and her husband is somewhat invasively interested in it, but she refuses to discuss it or let him touch it. Finally she allows him to untie it, and the story ends, like 'The Green Ribbon', with her head falling off. The fact that Machado's heroine's ribbon is green ties it specifically to the version many American Millennial readers will know from childhood: the version of the story in Alvin Schwartz's *In a Dark, Dark Room* (1984), a horror story collection for child readers. In an interview, Machado says that she had thought about this story since she first read it as a child: 'When I went back and actually re-read it, I was struck by the quiet, persistent violence of the story'.[46]

In 'The Husband Stitch', the process of retelling stories itself becomes quietly, persistently violent. The heroine's narrative is shot through with pre-existing stories, some in brief allusions and some told in full. They are stories that readers might be expected to know from *somewhere*, though we may not quite remember where, so that the narrator only needs to allude to them for us to know the one she means: 'A hook-handed man. A ghostly hitch-hiker repeating her journey. An old woman summoned from the rest of her mirror by the chants of children.'[47] She

---

45. This basic plot is at least 200 years old; it appears in short stories by Alexandre Dumas and Washington Irving, and Irving described it as inspired by an older French story tradition. See 'The Adventure of the German Student', *Library of America*, 2016. https://storyoftheweek.loa.org/2016/03/the-adventure-of-german-student.html (accessed 12 September 2022).

46. Alyssa Greene, 'Carmen Maria Machado: On the Dark Power of Urban Legends', *Lambda Literary*, 13 November 2017. https://www.lambdaliterary.org/2017/11/carmen-maria-machado-on-the-dark-power-of-urban-legends/ (accessed 14 September 2022).

47. Machado, 'The Husband Stitch', p. 5.

adds: 'Everyone knows these stories – that is, everyone tells them – but no one ever believes them.'[48]

A distinguishing feature of urban legends is that they are told as though they were true – or, as Jean E. Fox Tree and Mary Susan Weldon note in their 2007 study of urban legend retellings, as though the risk that they may be true means they should be passed on just in case, to disseminate the warnings they hold: 'The story may be false, but the risk of not heeding the advice is greater than the embarrassment of passing on a falsehood.'[49] These stories are never fully taken seriously – 'no one ever believes them' – but nor do they ever really go away. They continue to circulate as half-disavowed warnings, and in this story they are specifically warnings to women. As Jane Dykema argues in 'What I Don't Tell My Students About "The Husband Stitch"' (2017), the surgical procedure of the story's title is also exactly this, a piece of half-knowledge that never reaches official status, a warning that can neither be taken seriously nor put fully out of one's mind: 'Reliable information about, or even an official definition of, the husband stitch is conspicuously missing from the internet. No entry in Wikipedia, nothing in WebMD. Instead there are pages and pages of message board entries and forum discussions on pregnancy websites, and a pretty good definition on Urban Dictionary.'[50]

In Jackson's stories death usually waits outside the final scene, sometimes just outside, and the inset urban legends in 'The Husband Stitch' are overall more explicitly violent: a girl dying of fear in a cemetery; a woman dying from exposure to embalming fluid after wearing a wedding dress stolen from a corpse; a girl faced with a hook-handed killer; woman after woman cut open in childbirth and sewn together again. Still, these legends are in the same vein of cautionary folklore as the 'Daemon Lover' ballad, and they continually echo the Demon Lover theme, emphasizing female isolation and vulnerability, betrayals of trust, and the sense that one's perception of reality is misaligned with the rest of the world. The Demon Lover theme appears not only in the pre-existing urban legends, but in the stories the narrator tells about her own life. Here, attempts at trust and intimacy with a romantic partner always lead to betrayal and greater isolation – the end of the story, in which the narrator finally lets her husband cross her long-held boundary and untie her ribbon, is the final and most dramatic instance of this.

The longest of the embedded stories is a retelling of an urban legend about a young woman whose mother becomes ill while they are travelling. She goes out to find a doctor and leaves her mother in their hotel room; on her return, her mother is gone and the hotel clerk claims to never have seen either of them before.

---

48. Machado, 'The Husband Stitch', pp. 5–6.
49. Jean E. Fox Tree and Mary Susan Weldon, 'Retelling Urban Legends', *American Journal of Psychology* 120, no. 3 (Fall 2007): 459–76, p. 459.
50. Jane Dykema, 'What I Don't Tell My Students About "The Husband Stitch"', *Electronic Literature*, 10 October 2017. https://electricliterature.com/what-i-dont-tell-my-students-about-the-husband-stitch/ (accessed 14 September 2022).

She then 'wanders the streets of Paris for years, believing that she is mad, that she invented her mother and her life with her mother in her own diseased mind. The daughter stumbles from hotel to hotel, confused and grieving, though for whom she cannot say.'[51] The narrator tells us that she does not need to tell us the moral of this story: 'I think you already know what it is'.[52] In Machado's retelling, then, this legend becomes an echo of Jackson's 'The Daemon Lover', and the unspoken moral or warning is the same: that women are always at risk of losing their connections to those around them and their ability to trust their own perception of reality. A story from the narrator's childhood speaks to the same idea – as a child she is terrified at the sight of disembodied toes in the produce aisle of the supermarket, until her father manages to convince her that what she actually saw were *potatoes*: 'I had seen them with my own eyes. But beneath the sunbeams of my father's logic, I felt my doubt unfurling [. . .] As a grown woman, I would have said to my father that there are true things in this world only observed by a single set of eyes.'[53]

But in the world of this story and its embedded narratives, things observed only by a single set of eyes are always shadowed by doubt, and the women who observe them are always fundamentally isolated. At the end of the story, the narrator, like the heroines of Jackson's 'The Daemon Lover' or 'The Honeymoon of Mrs Smith', feels a profound sense of loneliness as she realizes the truth about her marriage and what her husband wants from her: 'As my lopped head tips backward off my neck and rolls off the bed, I feel as lonely as I have ever been.'[54]

If 'The Husband Stitch' is full of Demon Lover themes, full of all these lonely endings, what does it mean to say that it is also a Bluebeard narrative? In Hermansson's terms, the Bluebeard story is one in which the stitching-together of individual stories of suffering creates something different to the sum of its parts. When the heroine discovers her predecessors and understands what happened to them, she reads it, correctly, as a warning: unless she does something, this will be her fate too. This recognition turns into solidarity with the preceding wives: she breaks the cycle of marriage and murder, and avenges the other women as well as herself. 'The Husband Stitch', then, becomes oddly hopeful for a paradoxical reason: because it brings together *so many* stories that all have the same bleak moral. The intertextual pattern of the narrative, of so many different sets of eyes observing the same thing, becomes a way of counteracting the self-doubt and isolation in each individual story.

Jane Dykema describes the experience of teaching 'The Husband Stitch', a story she says she has a strong impulse to share with others – like an urban legend – but does not quite know how to talk about. 'There is a truth in the tales that I recognize viscerally but have never been taught,' she writes.[55] In the classroom,

---

51. Machado, 'The Husband Stitch', p. 19.
52. Machado, 'The Husband Stitch', p. 19.
53. Machado, 'The Husband Stitch', pp. 8–9.
54. Machado, 'The Husband Stitch', p. 31.
55. Dykema, 'What I Don't Tell My Students'.

she struggles with the sense that this story describes something that feels true but unprovable, exemplified by the husband stitch itself, a concept that has no place in official medical discourse but that lives on in 'women's chatter'.[56] The story and the process of reading it communally becomes a way of connecting these disparate, disbelieved narratives, putting them into context with each other, letting them corroborate each other: 'Once, after class, a student approached me urgently. "That happened to my mother," she said. "I didn't want to say it in class, but they did that to her. The husband stitch." Her eyes were wet, unblinking. "It's real," she said.'[57]

'The Husband Stitch' is still a horror story, but one about the horror of connection: hearing these stories puts the reader themselves in a vulnerable position, emphasized by the narrator's increasingly invasive and upsetting instructions for reading the story aloud ('give a paring knife to the listener and ask them to cut the tender flap of skin between your index finger and thumb'). In the final scene the narrator dies, and the reader is left with her headless body. The reader of the story, then, is cast as Bluebeard's final wife, the one who makes sense of all these dead bodies, who sees what the moral of the story is, and who must use what she knows to try to survive. The story insistently asks the question Dykema imagines asking her students: 'Do you feel it, too?'[58] In Jackson's take on Bluebeard, by contrast, there is no possibility of this kind of solidarity through shared pain: here, the stories of the earlier wives do not act as warnings to the protagonist, but only as a confirmation of what she in some way already knew.

Conclusion: You Already Know

This chapter has explored how a well-established folkloric structure in Jackson's short fiction, the Demon Lover theme, might appear in a different light when seen alongside the work of a later horror author who responds to and reworks this theme. As suggested by the appearance of the theme in stories that either make no explicit references to the ballad, or that were rewritten in retrospect to include these references, Jackson's use of the Demon Lover theme goes beyond the ballad itself. It could be fruitful to see the Demon Lover not just as an explicit folkloric intertext that ties together the *Lottery* stories, but as a thematic keynote of almost all of Jackson's horror.

Considering that Jackson writes horror, there is actually very little room in her work for the experience of *being horrified*, which implies surprise. The defining emotional experience of fear in her work is, instead, *sinking realization* – the growing awareness of something you should have known all along, or that you in some way already did know. (The short story 'The Lottery' does contain an experience of surprised horror, but part of the effect of the story is our awareness

---

56. Dykema, 'What I Don't Tell My Students'.
57. Dykema, 'What I Don't Tell My Students'.
58. Dykema, 'What I Don't Tell My Students'.

that the character knew what was going to happen, that she should not have been surprised.) Jackson's specific use of the 'Daemon Lover' ballad as an intertext is an important part of this construction of fear. Machado's intertextual use of earlier folklore, as well as of Jackson's own themes, echoes Hermansson's concept of feminist intertextuality in that it is fundamentally about the possibility of change through the telling of stories. The narrator's continual reminders that we already know these stories, that we already know what they mean, function as warnings and exhortations. Like Bluebeard's last wife examining the bodies of her predecessors, the reader is asked to recognize that these stories implicate us, too.

Jackson's use of intertextuality is very different. In her work, the recurrence of an often-retold story does not create the possibility of changing it; instead it establishes the story as a fundamental truth that we should already have known. The protagonists' experiences of betrayal is compounded by a sense of inevitability – this was always going to happen, and the protagonist should have realized that. The 'Daemon Lover' ballad, if it is a warning, is one that is never recognized in time, and its repetitions only create 'one long documentation', one isolated incident after another.

References

'The Adventure of the German Student' (2016), *Library of America*. https://storyoftheweek.loa.org/2016/03/the-adventure-of-german-student.html

Bacchilega, Cristina (2010), *Postmodern Fairy Tales: Gender and Narrative Strategies*, Philadelphia: University of Pennsylvania Press.

Bonikowski, Wyatt (2013), '"Only One Antagonist": The Demon Lover and the Feminine Experience in the Work of Shirley Jackson', *Gothic Studies* 15 (2): 66–88.

Burrison, John (1967), '"James Harris" in Britain since Child', *The Journal of American Folklore* 80 (317): 271–84.

Dykema, Jane (2017), 'What I Don't Tell My Students About "The Husband Stitch"', *Electronic Literature*, 10 October. https://electricliterature.com/what-i-dont-tell-my-students-about-the-husband-stitch/

Fassler, Joe (2017), 'How Surrealism Enriches Storytelling about Women', *The Atlantic*, 12 October. https://www.theatlantic.com/entertainment/archive/2017/10/how-surrealism-enriches-storytelling-about-women/542496/

Faucheux, Amandine (2016), 'Her Body and Other Parties: An Interview with Carmen Maria Machado', *NDR*, Issue 6.2, May. http://ndrmag.org/interviews/2016/05/her-body-and-other-parties-an-interview-with-carmen-maria-machado/

Fox Tree, Jean E. and Mary Susan Weldon (2007), 'Retelling Urban Legends', *American Journal of Psychology* 120, no. 3 (Fall): 459–76.

Franklin, Ruth (2016), *Shirley Jackson: A Rather Haunted Life*, New York City: W. W. Norton.

Greene, Alyssa (2017), 'Carmen Maria Machado: On the Dark Power of Urban Legends', *Lambda Literary*, 13 November. https://www.lambdaliterary.org/2017/11/carmen-maria-machado-on-the-dark-power-of-urban-legends/

Hall, Joan Wylie (1993), *Shirley Jackson: A Study of the Short Fiction*, Woodbridge: Twayne.

Hermansson, Casie (2001), *Reading Feminist Intertextuality through Bluebeard Stories*, Lewiston: Edwin Mellen Press.
Jackson, Shirley (1949), 'The Tooth', *The Hudson Review* 1, no. 4 (Winter): 503–21.
Jackson, Shirley (1963), 'Diary Entry', Quoted in Ruth Franklin, *Shirley Jackson: A Rather Haunted Life*, New York City: W. W. Norton.
Jackson, Shirley (2006), *The Haunting of Hill House*. 1959, London: Penguin.
Jackson, Shirley (2009), 'The Daemon Lover', in *The Lottery and Other Stories*. 1949, London: Penguin.
Jackson, Shirley (2009), 'The Tooth', in *The Lottery and Other Stories*. 1949, London: Penguin.
Jackson, Shirley (2016), 'The Honeymoon of Mrs Smith', in *Dark Tales*, London: Penguin.
'James Harris (The Daemon Lover)', Child 243F. Available on *Internet Sacred Text Archive*. https://www.sacred-texts.com/neu/eng/child/ch243.htm
Keown, Edwina and Bernice M. Murphy (2017), 'Uncanny Irish-American Relations', *The Green Book: Writings on Irish Gothic, Supernatural and Fantastic Literature*, No. 9, Bealtaine, 57–84.
Lovell-Smith, Rose (1999), 'Feminism and Bluebeard', *ELO*, no. 5: 43–53.
Machado, Carmen Maria (2017), 'The Husband Stitch'. 2014, in *Her Body and Other Parties*, Minneapolis: Graywolf Press.
Nørjordet, Håvard (2005), 'The Tall Man in the Blue Suit: Witchcraft, Folklore, and Reality in Shirley Jackson's *The Lottery, or the Adventures of James Harris*', Oslo: University of Oslo.
Perrault, Charles. 'Blue Beard'. 1697, in Andrew Lang (ed.), *The Blue Fairy Book*, 290–5, London: Longmans, Green, and Company, ca. 1889. Available on *Folklore and Mythology Electronic Texts,* ed. D. L. Ashliman. https://www.pitt.edu/~dash/perrault03.html
Reed, Toni (1988), *Demon Lovers and their Victims in British Fiction*, Lexington: University Press of Kentucky.
Tatar, Maria (2004), *Secrets Beyond the Door: The Story of Bluebeard and His Wives*, Princeton: Princeton University Press.

Chapter 4

NEGOTIATING WITCHCRAFT IN SHIRLEY JACKSON'S SHORT FICTION

Dara Downey

In Shirley Jackson's 1950 story 'A Visit' (sometimes reprinted as 'The Lovely House'), the protagonist Margaret finds herself overwhelmed by the strange hospitality of her friend Carla Rhodes' family, with whom she is staying for the summer, in the family's large and eccentrically decorated mansion. Mrs Rhodes spends her days completing a needlepoint image of the house, which will be the latest in the vast collection of tapestries and other works of art, all of which depict the house itself, in a bewildering *mise en abŷme* that testifies to the work of generations of women. When Carla's brother and a friend come to visit, the two young women find themselves drawn into a whirl of dances, dinners and lingering walks in the extensive grounds. A significant moment comes when, as Margaret stands watching Mrs Rhodes' embroidery, Carla insists she hurry up to join the two men (referred to as Paul and the captain) for a picnic, as 'Mother is always at her work, but my brother is rarely home.'[1]

As I argue in this chapter, in Jackson's stories 'The Man in the Woods' and 'Lord of the Castle' (both unpublished until the twenty-first century), as well as in 'A Visit', female characters are repeatedly positioned as constantly engaged in the running and upkeep of domestic spaces dominated by largely absent men, to whom they are subordinated. However, the dutiful, diligent domestic woman who (as Carla acknowledges) upholds the household while men rule it from afar is shadowed in these stories by another, very different female figure – that of the witch. In the case of 'A Visit', this position is occupied by an older woman, also called Margaret, who lives in a wind-swept tower, who may potentially be a ghost, and who Carla's family strongly discourage the younger Margaret from seeking out. Here, then, as well as in the other stories mentioned above, the witch figure is a barely acknowledged element of the domestic arrangements, though a central element of the narratives. As I outline later, this vacillation between denying and

---

1. Shirley Jackson, 'A Visit (For Dylan Thomas)', in S. E. Hyman (ed.), *Come Along With Me: Classic Short Stories and an Unfinished Novel* (New York and London: Penguin, 2013 [1950]), p. 110.

foregrounding the witch who is the Other to the domestic housewife is something of a commonplace in mid-century literature and culture, from anthropology and folklore to film and television. Indeed, the figure of the witch becomes, in these discourses, a means of navigating gender relations within domestic space. What the stories by Jackson discussed here help to highlight is the extent to which the housewife role serves to obscure and delimit the subversive potential opened up by a trope that laminates domestic work and witchcraft onto one another. Specifically, Jackson's stories often narrate a process whereby heterosexual marital and familial structures both co-opt and stifle that potential.

In order to elucidate the ways in which this scenario plays out in Jackson's short fiction, this chapter begins by situating the stories examined here within contemporary ideas around gendered domestic labour, and anthropological thinking on witchcraft and goddesses, particularly Margaret Murray's notion of 'witch cults', in which covens of female witches are imagined as worshipping a male god or devil. Murray's thesis, with which Jackson's academic husband, Stanley Edgar Hyman, was most likely familiar, rose in popularity around the middle of the twentieth century, just as the witch emerged as a resonant figurative counterpart to the American housewife in literature and popular culture. In examining her stories within this wider context, I argue that Jackson's writing repeatedly portrays women's combined skills in housework and witchcraft as rendering them simultaneously indispensable and threatening to the patriarchal domestic order. As the association with witchcraft implies, housework was often coded in twentieth-century American culture as an inconveniently premodern, inefficient and ultimately suspect necessity that gave rise to a host of variations on the housewife/witch opposition, producing a tension that, as Jackson's stories highlight, the patriarchy works hard to contain.

The Housewife as Witch

As gender boundaries were realigned in the post-war years, and as the availability of paid domestic labour rapidly dwindled in the United States, middle-class women were increasingly burdened with the direct running and care of the household. Just as the housewife gained control over the work conducted in the home, however, the opinions of a legion of psychoanalysts, sociologists and home-economics specialists swept in to tell her that she was doing it wrong and needed a professional to guide her in the vital work of keeping house for men and children.[2] As Glenna Matthews argues, the insistent theorizing and codifying of housework

---

2. See Emily-Jane Cohen, 'Kitschen Witches: Martha Stewart: Gothic Housewife, Corporate CEO', *Journal of Popular Culture* 38, no. 4 (2005): 650–77; R. S. Cowan, *More Work for Mother: The Ironies of Household Technology from the Open Hearth to the Microwave* (New York: Basic, 1983); and M. Horsfield, *Biting the Dust: The Joys of Housework* (London: Fourth Estate, 1997).

in the 1950s and early 1960s took the work of passing on domestic skills out of the hands of older women and placed it firmly in those of commercially motivated, generally male 'experts'.[3] The scientific usurpation of housework also served to drive a deeper wedge between the sexes, as men were excluded from receiving such training themselves.[4] As Mary Sanders points out, '[d]ifferences between the sexes were [. . .] emphasized by the idea that men and women were not suited to the same activities, particularly in the workplace'.[5] Housework therefore became women's work, and women's work alone, but work that they did under the aegis of the male control of knowledge.

Indeed, one of the ways in which this gendered division was discursively maintained was through the insistence that housework was not in fact work. As Kathleen M. Kirby argues, '[m]en's work tends to be localized, attached to particular places and time periods. That is, when men are "off work", they are not working. Women [. . .] are rarely "off work" when at home.'[6] Because housework bleeds into what men would consider to be 'leisure time',

> Men who had to accept time-discipline and specialized occupations may have begun to observe differences between their own work and that of their wives. Perhaps they focused on the remaining 'premodern' aspects of women's household work: it was reassuringly comprehensible, because it responded to immediate needs; it represented not strictly 'work' but 'life,' a way of being; and it also looked unsystematized, inefficient, nonurgent.[7]

This movement was coterminous with popular discourses that suggested that the housewife did all of the work needed to maintain a home as if by magic, with no effort on her part whatsoever. According to Margaret Horsfield, in order to ensure that 'her social standing was intact despite having to do housework', the housewife was constantly reassured by advertising agencies and domestic advice books alike that 'housework, correctly pursued, is not really *work* at all'. Consequently, she 'should not be tired, she should not be a mere overworked housecleaner. Her job is to be a ladylike homemaker: with all the new advice and devices available to her this should be perfectly possible, with little effort on her part'.[8] This vision of housewifely effortlessness both undermined the notion that women's work

---

3. Glenna Matthews, *'Just a Housewife': The Rise and Fall of Domesticity in America* (New York and Oxford: Oxford University Press, 1987), 154–5.

4. Matthews, *'Just a Housewife'*, p. 162.

5. Mary Sanders, 'Was Friedan Right: The Feminine Mystique in Newspapers, 1958-1959', *Fides et Historia* 39, no. 2 (2007): 45.

6. Kathleen M. Kirby, *Indifferent Boundaries: Spatial Concepts of Human Subjectivity* (New York and London: Guilford Press, 1996), p. 63.

7. Nancy F. Cott, The Bonds of Womanhood: 'Woman's Sphere' in New England, 1780–1835 (New Haven and London: Yale University Press, 1997), p. 61.

8. Horsfield, *Biting the Dust*, pp. 56–7.

was actually work and denied her any sense that she was in fact responsible for the effects she produced in the home. Indeed, if any work has been put it, the implication ran, it was by male scientists and the producers of commercial goods. As Jessamyn Neuhuas demonstrates, earlier in the century, advertisements for household cleaning products often featured cartoon elves or imps, suggesting that you got yourself a supernatural familiar in the bargain when you bought the latest vacuum cleaner or laundry detergent.[9] These had disappeared by mid-century, perhaps implying that the housewife had now absorbed those powers into herself, or that magic had been replaced by science.

A version of the former shows up in Jackson's 'The Very Strange House Next Door' (1959). The narrator, Addie, a local gossip, is appalled when the West family moves into her insular small town, failing as they do to fit into her rigid sense of how women should run their households. The Wests employ a maid called Mallie, who claims quite openly to have magical powers that help her to speed through housework, cobbling dinner together out of a few acorns, and fashioning beautiful curtains from wild plants and feathers. The story suggests that only a witch could get all the housework done in the time available, and with what appear to be limited resources. It becomes clear that the story is critiquing censorious contemporary attitudes towards domestic labour when Addie remarks that Mallie does all of the shopping for the family, and buys nothing except a single chicken every day for the cat, who is clearly her familiar. Addie remarks that she and the other local gossips 'finally decided that [the husband] must bring food home from the city, although why Mr Honeywell's store wasn't good enough for them, I couldn't tell you'.[10] The Wests are, inevitably, run out of town by the sheer force of Addie's vitriol and social influence: Mallie's crime, it would seem, is that she doesn't shop, and Mrs West's is that she employs a maid in the first place. Moreover, Mallie's witchcraft allows her to repurpose what she finds in the garden, turning directly to nature for her raw materials, bypassing production and economic relations entirely. There is evidently no place in this world for housework that doesn't follow the rules.

What is merely implied here – that witchcraft is incompatible with patriarchal capitalism, but also that it can contribute to the smooth running of the nuclear family that supports precisely that capitalist system – becomes more overt in 'A Visit', 'Lord of the Castle' and 'Man of the Woods'. In order to understand what is happening in these stories, it is useful to explore briefly another set of discourses that set out in the first half of the twentieth century to examine gendered power relations – that is, anthropology and folklore studies focused on witchcraft. In particular, the influential work of Margaret Murray effectively bound witchcraft within a structure that sought to elevate it to the position of a religion, while simultaneously subordinating the witch's power to that of a male priest or god

---

9. Jessamyn Neuhuas, *Housework and Housewives in Modern American Advertising: Married to the Mop* (New York: Palgrave Macmillan, 2011), pp. 15–51.

10. Shirley Jackson, 'The Very Strange House Next Door', in *Just an Ordinary Day*, ed. Laurence Jackson Hyman and Sarah Hyman Stewart (New York: Bantam Books, 1998), p. 372.

figure, producing a structural inequality that Jackson's stories dramatize and critique. During the early decades of the 1900s, Murray's work offered a new understanding of the figure of the witch as integrated within a persecuted and previously unknown religious cult uncovered by Murray herself.

In *The Witch-Cult in Western Europe: A Study in Anthropology* (1921), its follow-up, *The God of the Witches* (1931), and numerous later publications, even when women appeared to rank more highly than men in the Old Religion, as Murray calls it, she is adamant that they remained 'without executive power'.[11] In other words, while men could be *both* politically and symbolically important in such cults, women's ceremonial and imaginative power remained curtailed by their lack of any power in relation to decision-making and organizational issues. What is interesting about her writing is the degree to which Murray often seems to figure the witch-cult as a proto-feminist or at least egalitarian religious movement, and then quickly reverts to asserting the greater importance of male members, with no suggestion that she might be critical of this arrangement. For example, she asserts in *The God of the Witches* that '[w]hether man or woman, the witch was consulted by all, for relief in sickness, for counsel in trouble, and for foreknowledge of coming events'.[12] However, she goes on to state that '[i]n practice, it seems that women-witches were most frequently consulted on personal matters, men-witches on affairs of political importance'.[13] Indeed, she presents a narrative in which women initially ruled the cult but were replaced by men, only to continue in a sort of curatorial role when the movement was driven underground:

> Early priesthoods appear to have been largely composed of women; as the religion changed, men gradually took over the practice of the ritual. [. . .] But when a religion is decaying and a new one taking its place the women often remain faithful and carry on the old rites, being then obliged to act as priestesses.[14]

Murray further asserts that the leader of the cult was sometimes female, but that the role never passed from woman to woman, only man to man or woman to man – in other words, it wasn't matrilineal.[15] However, this is a point on which she was somewhat ambivalent:

> The position of the chief woman in the cult is still somewhat obscure. Professor Pearson sees in her the Mother-Goddess worshipped chiefly by women. This is very probable, but at the time when the cult is recorded the worship of the

---

11. Margaret Murray, *The God of the Witches* (Oxford: Oxford University Press, 1970 [1931]), p. 69.
12. Murray, *The God of the Witches*, p. 45.
13. Murray, *The God of the Witches*, p. 146.
14. Murray, *The God of the Witches*, p. 65.
15. Margaret Murray, *The Witch-Cult in Western Europe* (Oxford: Oxford University Press, 1971 [1921]), pp. 38–9.

male deity appears to have superseded that of the female, and it is only on rare occasions that the God appears in female form to receive the homage of the worshippers. As a general rule the woman's position, when divine, is that of the familiar or substitute for the male god. There remains, however, the curious fact that the chief woman was often identified with the Queen of Faerie, or the Elfin Queen as she is sometimes called.[16]

Here, she insists that the very pinnacle of the hierarchy, the God of the Witches, was incontrovertibly male, while acknowledging that he occasionally appears in female form. Thus, while the wider implication of Murray's argument is that women were important to the witch cult, both imaginatively and as leaders, it is as if she can't quite bring herself to assert that the cult actually worshipped a goddess, or that it included high-ranking female priests. Jackson's writing often depicts an identical gendered hierarchy, but, I argue, does so in a way that critiques the power structures that leave women confined and relatively powerless, even when the entire domestic system is dependent upon both their labour and their presence in the home.

The Witch at Home

This is precisely what happens in 'The Man in the Woods', which builds an imagined scenario around the ritual killing of a priest-king described by James Frazer in *The Golden Bough*.[17] The protagonist is Christopher, a young man who seems to have dropped out of college, and finds himself walking through the countryside, apparently without purpose. Like the speaker in Robert Frost's 'The Road Not Taken' (1916), when the road he is following splits in two, he takes the darker, lonelier path through the woods; he finds himself at a small stone house, and is invited in by two welcoming but rather taciturn women, Phyllis and Aunt Cissy (short for Circe). When 'the host', Mr Oakes, makes an appearance in the kitchen, the two women move immediately to stand by the door, and Aunt Cissy silently prepares and then serves food. The next morning, Mr Oakes takes Christopher out into the hall to show him the house and to talk, as if this would not be possible in the presence of the women. He notes that Christopher must not yet have seen the rest of the house, as

> 'Our handmaidens keep to the kitchen unless called to this hall.'
> 'Where do they sleep?' Christopher asked. 'In the kitchen?' He was immediately embarrassed by his own question, [. . .] but Mr Oakes shook his head in amusement and put his hand on Christopher's shoulder.

---

16. Murray, *The Witch-Cult in Western Europe*, p. 13. See also Catherine Noble, 'From Fact to Fallacy: The Evolution of Margaret Alice Murray's Witch-Cult', *The Pomegranate* 7, no. 1 (2005): 18–19.

17. James Frazer, *The Golden Bough: A Study in Magic and Religion* (Ware, Herts: Wordsworth Reference, 1921), pp. 1–3.

'On the kitchen floor', he said. And then he turned his head away, but Christopher could see that he was laughing. 'Circe', he said, 'sleeps nearer to the door from the hall.'[18]

The women are not part of the conversations between the two men, for whose comfort and shelter the house exists as they bide their time between ritual battles with the next would-be contender for the position of ruler of the woods. In typical Jackson fashion, the story never reveals whether the protagonist wins and replaces Mr Oakes, or is killed by him; however, since, following Frazer's formulation, one must kill the other, the men are essentially replaceable. It is the women who permanently occupy the heart of the house, dealing with all upkeep and hospitality, but they remain (at best) secondary to the 'host', existing merely to feed and offer ambiguous guidance to the next challenger. They cannot be done without, but even Circe (the name of a powerful sorceress from Greek myth, who can turn men into animals) is here made to sleep on the kitchen floor near the door, in case she is needed to serve the man who is dependent upon her skills.

The figure of the powerful domestic witch who exists merely to serve male power structures was in fact a relatively commonplace trope in popular culture before and during Jackson's stories were written and published, potentially drawing on Murray's influential thesis. Fritz Leiber's novel *Conjure Wife* (1943), for example, transforms the everyday activities and rivalries of a group of faculty wives into witchcraft employed purely to advance their husbands' careers. Leiber claimed that one of the sources for the novel was 'John W. Campbell's remark in a letter that "the modern woman carries so much in her purse that they might easily include the paraphernalia of witchcraft"'.[19] In other words, the inspiration for the book was precisely the idea that women's daily domestic duties and possessions were mysterious and, by extension, occult. The suggestion is that men were wilfully ignorant of the practical details of how women in mid-century America arranged their lives, assuming women's activities to be arcane and unknowable, but also not worth knowing, despite the fact that many of the men of the novel have dedicated their lives the pursing arcane knowledge. The novel focuses on Normal Saylor, the protagonist, who lectures on 'primitive' myth and folklore in a small liberal-arts college. Early on, he discovers that his wife Tansey has been using spells to prop up his academic career, and forces her to stop, because he believes her to be dangerously delusional. The result is that he is no longer protected from the spells that the other wives cast to help their husbands and hinder their competitors, and neither is Tansy, placing the couple in grave danger.

Conjure Wife therefore, like 'The Man in the Woods', imagines a world in which women wield considerable power behind the scenes. However, they do so only

---

18. Shirley Jackson, 'The Man in the Woods', in *Let Me Tell You: New Stories, Essays, and Other Writings*, ed. Laurence Jackson Hyman and Sarah Hyman DeWitt (New York: Random House, 2015), p. 183.

19. Bruce Byfield, '"Sister Picture of Dorian Grey": The Image of the Female in Fritz Leiber's Conjure Wife', *Mythlore* 17, no. 4/66 (1991): 24.

in order to prop up wider forms of political, professional and economic power wielded by men, power that actively expropriates and objectifies the methods employed by women. Indeed, Leiber's novel insists that women are happy with this situation; Tansy tells Norman that '[w]omen might be able to rule the world openly, but they do not want the work or the responsibility', again suggesting that women's work is not in fact work.[20] In this, she is echoed by Robert Graves, who asserted in *The White Goddess* (1948) that

> woman has of late become virtual head of the household in most parts of the Western world, and holds the purse-strings, and can take up almost any career or position she pleases; but she is unlikely to repudiate the present system, despite its patriarchal framework. With all its disadvantages, she enjoys greater liberty of action under it than man has retained for himself; and though she may know, intuitively, that the system is due for a revolutionary change, she does not care to hasten or anticipate this. It is easier for her to play man's game a little while longer, until the situation grows too absurd and uncomfortable for complaisance. The Vatican waits watchfully.[21]

While this is effectively how Graves ends *The White Goddess*, with a somewhat smug assertion that the patriarchy won't be overturned anytime soon, because women couldn't be bothered with world domination, Norman is unconvinced by Tansy's statement. Uncovering this wellspring of feminine power supporting the life he thought he was living has overturned his deeply held belief system about the fundamental rational nature of existence. As the novel puts it,

> It was almost impossible to take at one gulp the realisation that in the mind of this trim modern creature he had known in completest intimacy, there was a whole great area he had never dreamed of, an area that was part and parcel of the dead practice he analysed in books, an area that belonged to the Stone Age and never to his, an area plunged in darkness, acrouch with fear, blown by giant winds.[22]

Both the source of and the solution to Norman's discomfort here is made somewhat more explicit in the 'witch comedy' films from around this time, including *I Married a Witch* (1942) and *Bell, Book, and Candle* (1958). Both films feature malevolent, attractive witches who ultimately give up their powers to be with men they love, becoming softer and more domesticated in the process, just as Tansy does at the end of *Conjure Wife*.[23] Perhaps the best-known example of this trope is the long-running

---

20. Fritz Leiber, *Conjure Wife* (London and New York: Penguin, 1969 [1943]), pp. 131–2.
21. Robert Graves, *The White Goddess*, ed. Grevel Lindop (New York: Farrar, Straus, and Giroux, 1997 [1948]), p. 473.
22. Leiber, *Conjure Wife*, p. 17.
23. See Marion Gibson, 'Retelling Salem Stories: Gender Politics and Witches in American Culture', *European Journal of American Culture* 25, no. 2 (2006): 92–3; and

television series *Bewitched* (1964–72), which revolves around a witch named Samantha, who falls in love with a mortal called Darrin, and 'comes out' to him as a witch shortly after they marry. Darrin reacts badly, and 'immediately demands that she cease using her powers at once', which Bernice M. Murphy attributes to his 'horror [...] that his wife is considerably more talented and powerful than himself', a horror also felt by Leiber's Norman Saylor.[24] Here, Samantha dutifully does what she is told, and almost never uses 'magic to clean her house or whip up meals. Instead, she exemplifie[s] the housewife's version of the American frontier virtues of making do and working hard, without magical advantages *or* expensive gadgets'.[25] As Marion Gibson puts it, '[s]afely domesticated, Samantha decisively reversed the stereotype of the home-wrecking witch, and in doing so suggested that all was well with the heavily gendered ideals of American family life'.[26]

Conjure Wife is less extreme in this regard, and the book ends without necessarily asserting that Tansy will no longer practice magic – if anything, their ordeal, as Tansy's soul is stolen from her body, convinces Norman that her protections are necessary, since the other wives are revealed to be actively malevolent, jealous of Tansy's beauty and Norman's success. At the same time, their attempts to take over Tansy's body are only foiled because he applies science and reason to the practice of magic and saves the day, successfully re-establishing a more normative gendered power dynamic in his marriage and in the narrative. The book, just like the films and *Bewitched*, therefore transforms the witch wife from an unpredictable threat to a useful partner, safely containing her and the subversive potential she represents. For folklorists and anthropologists, as well as fiction writers and makers of film and television, depictions of witchcraft at mid-century in America therefore facilitate the negotiation of gender relations within the capitalist patriarchal system of the home and the family. As I argue in the rest of this chapter, the portrayal of domestic women with supernatural powers in Jackson's short stories functions as a form of protest against patriarchal control of that power, even as they similarly acknowledge that patriarchal structures still hold sway – for now. Indeed, these stories can be read as critical dramatizations of precisely the process described in both *Conjure Wife* and *Bewitched*, as women's domestic and supernatural powers are consistently confined within and sacrificed to systems controlled by men.

Binding and Unleashing Female Power in Jackson's Stories

This sacrifice is, I argue, central to an understanding of what happens in Jackson's story 'A Visit', with which I began this chapter. As Paul and the captain's visit to the

---

Bernice M. Murphy, *The Suburban Gothic in American Popular Culture* (Basingstoke and New York: Palgrave Macmillan, 2009), pp. 41–3.
 24. Murphy, *The Suburban Gothic in American Popular Culture*, p. 49.
 25. Gibson, 'Retelling Salem Stories', p. 95.
 26. Gibson, 'Retelling Salem Stories', p. 95.

family home draws to an end, the latter berates Mrs Rhodes for the fact that the carpets are becoming threadbare, statues and mosaics are chipped and broken, fish and plants are beginning to die. At the same time, Margaret (a namesake of Murray) becomes curious about the house's tower, which the family seem reluctant to discuss. She is fascinated by one particular mosaic, depicting a girl looking out of the same tower, with the inscription 'Here was Margaret, who died for love'.[27] She eventually learns that the tower is the refuge (or prison) of

> an aunt, or a great-aunt, or perhaps even a great-great-great-aunt. She doesn't live there, at all, but goes there because she cannot *endure* the sight of tapestry. [...] She has filled the tower with books, and a huge old cat, and she may practice alchemy there, for all anyone knows. The reason you never see her would be that she has one of her spells of hiding away. Sometimes she's downstairs daily.[28]

Margaret is told this by Paul, who she assumes is Carla's brother, though it seems later on that only she and the aunt can see him. Margaret finally enters the tower and speaks to the aunt, who is also named Margaret, and who may be a ghost: the tower has no glass in the windows, yet she appears to be unperturbed by a sudden storm that lashes in through the openings; later, when she appears at a ball, only Paul and young Margaret acknowledge her presence. Paul's description implies that the older woman is also a witch, but she equally appears to be a victim of the house and those who inhabit it, and apparently tries to warn the younger Margaret that the same fate is in store for her. We are given hints that the coming days might be less than pleasant for the younger Margaret, as the older woman continually states that it would be better if the whole thing were over and done with, and that she cannot help her young namesake. Paul is positioned as a sort of demon lover, a figure who appears frequently in Jackson's work, there to lure Margaret into staying in the house.[29] A conversation between Paul and the older Margaret during the ball implies that they had a dalliance at some point in the past, possibly helping to explain the inscription below the mosaic. The younger Margaret will, presumably, also be induced to die for love, becoming the house's resident ghostly witch, helping to halt the decay of the house by replacing the older woman whose influence is presumably waning. As the summer draws to an end, and the family refuse to discuss Margaret's departure, it would seem that the older Margaret's warnings were in vain, and the younger will now join a long line of women who have been absorbed into the house.

What we have is this story is a system in which the house is kept clean and new by the work of two quite different women – by the crafting and handiwork of the delicate, stylish Mrs Rhodes, and the spells and arcane arts of the hardier, more

---

27. Jackson, 'A Visit', p. 113.
28. Jackson, 'A Visit', p. 112.
29. See Wyatt Bonikowski, '"Only One Antagonist": The Demon Lover and the Feminine Experience in the Work of Shirley Jackson', *Gothic Studies* 15, no. 2 (2013): 66–88.

brusque Margaret, who, like the protagonist, seems to be a non-family member brought in as a sacrifice. Presiding over them, as in Murray's formulation, is the figure of Paul, who is, as a potential suitor, responsible for keeping the system going, without actually inhabiting the house as the women do. The system therefore requires the constant presence of a domestic woman and a witchlike one, but the absence of a powerful, possibly demonic man who nonetheless looms over the life of the house. When the men leave, Carla is already breathlessly anticipating her brother's next visit and all the exciting things that she and Margaret will do when he returns, as if the rest of the family exist in a kind of stasis in the interim. Like Murray's witches and erstwhile priestesses, the women in the story are given meaning only by men, to whom they must yield up their time, their work and their very lives.

The System Overturned

What happens when this structural inequality is flouted is dramatized – and critiqued – in Jackson's story 'Lord of the Castle'. The story opens as the male narrator's father, the eponymous lord of the castle, is hanged for witchcraft by a crowd of superstitious villagers who are, in the narrator's mind, delighted to see him brought low. We are later told that the villagers

> believe that a demon haunts the castle, and makes the land dark and blood-thickened, and that so long as the lord is under this demon's claw, there will be death and destruction along the land. My father was good and kind, but he sought this demon on the hill to defeat it, and was defeated himself.[30]

The narrator explains this to his half-brother, the ominously named Nicholas, who appears out of nowhere after their father is executed. Nick persuades the narrator not to seek revenge on the demon directly, as he will surely be killed, and the narrator instead decides to marry, presumably to produce an heir who he can train to wreak revenge for him. He rides down into the village, and pauses by the house of the man 'who stopped before my father and challenged the demon of the hill. When my father's sword had taken the man's life, it was witchcraft that helped him, they cried; not all the strength of my father's arm nor the power of his voice could avail against their cries' (185). It is clear that at least some of the villagers see the lord of the castle as himself the demon, but at the same time, the suggestion here is that he was not powerful enough, and therefore had no sway over the villagers, having relinquished his control of the castle and domain to a demon. Using witchcraft for men is, in this schema, giving power to another, and this is how the story plays out for the narrator as well.

30. Shirley Jackson, 'Lord of the Castle', in *Just an Ordinary Day*, ed. Laurence Jackson Hyman and Sarah Hyman Stewart (New York: Bantam Books, 1998), p. 184.

When he stops before the house, he meets the man's daughter, Elizabeth, and decides to marry her whether she wants it or not, ordering Nicholas to conduct her to the castle. Understandably, Elizabeth is incensed, vowing that her new position will finally allow her to take vengeance for her father's death. The narrator, becoming more arrogant and tyrannical by the minute, locks her up in a tower until she repents, but Nick points out that this situation will most likely speed along the confrontation with the demon, stating that "nothing will bring him more quickly than the defiance of a beautiful woman."[31] In other words, the demon that the men in the story cannot control and are destroyed by is directly aligned with female rage and insubordination, as becomes clear when the narrator, who has been struggling to understand his father's books, experiences a breakthrough and decides to summon the demon that very night. A woman emerges from the fire in front of which he has laid his potions and spoken his incantations; he immediately forgets both Elizabeth and that he was supposed to be seeking vengeance for his father's death, instead summoning the entrancing demon again and again, neglecting all else.

When Nick tells him that he had ordered Elizabeth released, because she has transferred her affections to him, the narrator realizes that his half-brother 'had stolen my life while I had lain idly under the curse of my spells', and that 'my fair lady had held me bound in witchcraft', a phrase that could equally apply to the demon or to Elizabeth.[32] This ambiguity is extended when he confronts the demon and learns that Nicholas and she have betrayed him together, repeating the pattern that occurred with his father. In his rage, he runs 'into the darkness of the night outside, and knew only that there was a flaming torch in my hand, but the castle was old and trees were dry, and there was more wood than stone that had gone to make up my home'.[33] He too is therefore doomed to be executed, like his father, 'for the crimes of witchcraft and murder, for Elizabeth lay in the ruins of the ruins of the castle'.[34] On the scaffold, Nick tells him that the demon is his mother, who rescued him from the flames, and that he is now the lord in the narrator's place. As the angry villagers push the narrator up the steps to his death, he sees Nick 'ride along, up the long road to the smoldering [sic] embers of my house', and realizes that 'now, indeed, the devil held the hill'.[35] As suggested earlier, the story implies that this has always been the case, and that this is ample punishment for the narrator's quick temper and patronizing attitude towards the villagers and his intended wife. Like the host in 'The Man in the Woods', the men here are ultimately replaceable and interchangeable, but while they wield 'executive power', in Murray's terms, the story suggests that the real power in the home is held by women, and that the virtuous, wifely Elizabeth and the seductive, treacherous demon are two aspects of the same feminine force.

31. Jackson, 'Lord of the Castle', p. 186.
32. Jackson, 'Lord of the Castle', p. 188.
33. Jackson, 'Lord of the Castle', p. 189.
34. Jackson, 'Lord of the Castle', p. 189.
35. Jackson, 'Lord of the Castle'. p. 190.

What this story presents is therefore a complex reversal of the situation set out in the other stories. Here, the magic user is male and dabbles in the occult for power and domination rather than for home-making purposes; meanwhile, the female demon, who wields her supernatural powers in a far more overt way than the older women in the other stories discussed here, is the one who rules the home rather than meekly sleeping in the doorway. Moreover, as in 'A Visit', Elizabeth is sacrificed, but no renewal of the domestic space takes place – instead, the castle is burnt to the ground, along with the potential wife, and no human being lives there. The story, which is even more ambiguous than 'A Visit', can therefore be read as a criticism either of overtly supernatural women who work against rather than in the service of the domestic realm and usurp male control, or (perhaps more satisfyingly) of men's usurpation of women's role as purveyors of the supernatural within the home. This latter reading might therefore be extended to suggest that Jackson's stories situate the witch-in-the-house as an underappreciated but central aspect of domestic harmony, helping to bolster the implicit critique of the host's dismissive attitude in 'The Man in the Woods'.

What 'Lord of the Castle' and 'The Very Strange House Next Door' also dramatize, however, is the violent nature of society's suspicion of all forms of magic, especially when it is wielded by a woman. As Silvia Federici asserts,

> The witch-hunt [. . .] was a war against women; it was a concerted attempt to degrade them, demonize them, and destroy their social power. At the same time, it was in the torture chambers and on the stakes on which the witches perished that the bourgeois ideals of womanhood and domesticity were forged.[36]

By 'the end of the 17th century, after women had been subjected for more than two centuries to state terrorism', she argues, 'a new model of femininity [had] emerged: the ideal woman and wife – passive, obedient, thrifty, of few words, always busy at work, and chaste'.[37] This model of tamed, obedient femininity facilitated the emergence of 'the type of family the contemporary bourgeois wisdom demanded – modelled on the state, with the husband as the king, and the wife subordinate to his will, selflessly devoted to the management of the household'.[38] As Federici implies, however, and as Jackson's stories also suggest, this process also ensures that the domestic woman as an idea was effectively built upon the very witchiness and power that it is defined against and that this constitutive ambiguity continues to exercise imaginative social influence in twentieth-century America. Indeed, the stories discussed here suggest that a balance must be maintained between conventional domestic femininity and the supernatural skills and knowledge without which, it seems, no house can remain in good repair. The devoted,

---

36. Silvia Frederici, *Caliban and the Witch: Women, the Body, and Primitive Accumulation* (London: Penguin, 2004), p. 204.
37. Frederici, *Caliban and the Witch*, p. 118.
38. Frederici, *Caliban and the Witch*, p. 210.

domestic woman is, as in Elizabeth's case, thus never far from the figure of the witch. The housewife is therefore a kind of 'enemy within', haunting the very house that she ostensibly makes unhaunted by her care and cleaning. The haunting is gestured towards but contained when, as in *Bewitched*, the woman is made into a wife and subordinated to her husband. Nevertheless, the depiction of the housewife-as-witch remains a means to acknowledge the patriarchal discomfort with the necessity of the presence of women within the home.

References

Bonikowski, Wyatt (2013), '"Only One Antagonist": The Demon Lover and the Feminine Experience in the Work of Shirley Jackson', *Gothic Studies* 15 (2): 66–88.

Byfield, Bruce (1991), '"Sister Picture of Dorian Grey": The Image of the Female in Fritz Leiber's *Conjure Wife*', *Mythlore* 17 (4/66): 24–8.

Cohen, Emily-Jane (2005), 'Kitschen Witches: Martha Stewart: Gothic Housewife, Corporate CEO', *Journal of Popular Culture* 38 (4): 650–77.

Cott, Nancy F. (1997), *The Bonds of Womanhood: 'Woman's Sphere' in New England, 1780–1835*, New Haven and London: Yale University Press.

Cowan, Ruth S. (1983), *More Work for Mother: The Ironies of Household Technology from the Open Hearth to the Microwave*, New York: Basic.

Federici, Silvia (2004), *Caliban and the Witch: Women, the Body, and Primitive Accumulation*, London: Penguin.

Frazer, James George (1993), *The Golden Bough: A Study in Magic and Religion*, Ware, Herts: Wordsworth Reference.

Gibson, Marion (2006), 'Retelling Salem Stories: Gender Politics and Witches in American Culture', *European Journal of American Culture* 25 (2): 85–107.

Graves, Robert ([1948] 1997), *The White Goddess*, ed. Grevel Lindop, New York: Farrar, Strauss, and Giroux.

Horsfield, Margaret (1997), *Biting the Dust: The Joys of Housework*, London: Fourth Estate.

Jackson, Shirley (1998), 'Lord of the Castle', in L. J. Hyman and S. H. Stewart (eds), *Just an Ordinary Day*, 181–90, New York: Bantam Books.

Jackson, Shirley (1998), 'The Very Strange House Next Door', in L. J. Hyman and S. H. Stewart (eds), *Just an Ordinary Day*, 365–77, New York: Bantam Books.

Jackson, Shirley ([1950] 2013), 'A Visit (For Dylan Thomas)', in S. E. Hyman (ed.), *Come Along With Me: Classic Short Stories and an Unfinished Novel*, 101–25, New York and London: Penguin.

Jackson, Shirley (2015), 'The Man in the Woods', in L. J. Hyman and S. H. DeWitt (eds), *Let Me Tell You: New Stories, Essays, and Other Writings*, 173–87, New York: Random House, 2015.

Kirby, Kathleen M. (1996), *Indifferent Boundaries: Spatial Concepts of Human Subjectivity*, New York and London: Guilford Press.

Matthews, Glenna (1987), *'Just a Housewife': The Rise and Fall of Domesticity in America*, New York and Oxford: Oxford University Press.

Murphy, Bernice M. (2009), *The Suburban Gothic in American Popular Culture*, Basingstoke and New York: Palgrave Macmillan.

Murray, Margaret A. ([1931] 1970), *The God of the Witches*, Oxford: Oxford University Press.

Murray, Margaret A. ([1921] 1971), *The Witch-Cult in Western Europe*, Oxford: Oxford University Press.
Neuhaus, Jessamyn (2011), *Housework and Housewives in Modern American Advertising: Married to the Mop*, New York: Palgrave Macmillan.
Noble, Catherine (2005), 'From Fact to Fallacy: The Evolution of Margaret Alice Murray's Witch-Cult', *The Pomegranate* 7 (1): 5–26.
Sanders, Mary (2007), 'Was Friedan Right: The Feminine Mystique in Newspapers, 1958–1959', *Fides et Historia* 39 (2): 39–58.

II

BODIES AND MINDS

Chapter 5

NIGHTMARES, NEUROSIS AND CLINICAL PSYCHOLOGY IN THE SHORT STORIES OF SHIRLEY JACKSON

Alice Vernon

Introduction

America in the 1950s was the site of a medical revolution. Pharmacology, neuroscience and psychiatry saw numerous developments and innovation using the technological advancements of the Second World War. Groundbreaking research into the functions of the brain, neurosurgery, psychotherapy and the nervous system was being undertaken on an international scale, but it was particularly in America that this research pervaded the lives of the general public. In the post-war era, there was a cultural emphasis placed on the idea of social recovery and a return to happiness and comfort. This was largely centred on consumer goods – new cars, refrigerators, recreational activities – but it also involved a discourse between medicine, therapy and emotional well-being. The 1950s brought mood-changing medicines such as tranquilizers, sedatives and antidepressants from the doctor's cabinet to the drug-store window display.

Alongside this cultural shift in discussions of medicine and the mind, Shirley Jackson was producing some of her most well-known pieces of writing. Her short stories and works of fiction have often been scrutinized under the lens of psychoanalysis, but this chapter seeks to go further and compare some of her short stories to specific trends and ideas in pharmacology and neuroscience. It aims to take her stories off the therapist's couch and instead place them in the pharmacy, the sleep laboratory and the doctor's clinic. In doing so, this chapter will show that Jackson's work, while being a populous landscape for psychoanalytical criticism, is also intrinsically linked to 1950s healthcare. Her own struggles with mental and physical illness, and her subsequent consumption of now-banned prescription drugs, are examined in her short stories against the context of contemporary medical practice. It is not simply about her experiences, then, but also the American public's experience of the clinic.

This chapter will begin with an examination into Jackson's presentation of sleep in comparison to the advent of sleep laboratories and the understanding of dreams in the mid-twentieth century. In 1953 Nathaniel Kleitman and Eugene Aserinsky tracked the journey of the sleeping brain, coining the term Rapid Eye Movement

(REM) to describe a key sign of the stage of sleep in which dreams are experienced. This discovery, combined with the continuing interest in dream analysis sparked by Sigmund Freud's *The Interpretation of Dreams* (1899), made sleep a popular subject of discussion in the 1950s. Using Jackson's story 'Nightmare', I will demonstrate the ways in which contemporary ideas of sleep and sleep disorders are presented in these stories.

The following section moves from troubled sleep to a troubled waking life. Rollo May's influential text, *The Meaning of Anxiety* (1950), brings together and attempts to explain the reason for instances of unfounded and general fear that seemed to seep into every corner of American culture. Stories such as 'The Daemon Lover' demonstrate acutely the anxiety that Jackson experienced in her own life. It is a story rife with panic, second-guessing and self-consciousness, and reflects popular discussion by psychologists and magazine journalists alike of the anxiety surrounding the unsettled housewife.

In the final part of the chapter, I will explore the 1950s clinic and its influence on Jackson's writing. Exploring the changing environment of medical examination, Michel Foucault, in his 1963 text *The Birth of the Clinic*, describes the way in which the 'space of the body and the space of the disease possess enough latitude to slide away from one another'.[1] This 'sliding away' is a recurring theme in some of Jackson's stories that take disease, doctors and self-medication as their focus. Stories such as 'The Tooth' and 'Colloquy' will demonstrate how clinical discourse and the rise in popular prescription medicines infiltrated both Jackson's life and work. Together, these sections will explore a selection of themes in Jackson's short work that are reflective of wider socio-medical contexts, but with a particular focus on 1950s interventions in mental health and illness.

As the subsequent analysis will demonstrate, the medical literature, clinical advancements and newly formed medical associations in the mid-twentieth century sought to clarify and quantify some of the brain's stranger functions and processes. These ideas and discoveries reformed the American clinic, which in turn made large-scale changes to the accessibility and commodification of mood-altering drugs. Shirley Jackson, experiencing these changes first-hand, demonstrates in her stories how the cold objectivity of the doctor's gaze often worsened the very ailments it tried to treat. Despite the intrinsic connection Jackson had to contemporary clinical treatment and pharmaceutical interventions, analysis of her work in relation to medical history has been relatively sparse.

Nightmares

Dreams, nightmares and other strange sleep phenomena were an important part of Shirley Jackson's life. They reflected her moods, her current crises or

---

1. Michael Foucault, *The Birth of the Clinic*, trans. A. M. Sheridan (London: Routledge, 1997 [1963]), p. 10.

physical complaints, and they also represented an unknowable part of herself that influenced many of her stories. In one of her lectures, 'How I Write', she describes an episode of sleepwalking. On waking up, she found a piece of paper, on which was written, "'oh no oh no Shirley not dead Theodora Theodora." It was written in my own handwriting, but as though it had been written in the dark'.[2] Theodora is the name of a protagonist in Jackson's 1959 novel, *The Haunting of Hill House*, suggesting that aspects of this book emerged through her own troubled sleep. She then expresses her fear of writing in her sleep, and describes how she continued to work on the manuscript 'as though something were chasing me, which I kind of think something was'.[3] The notion of being pursued, of undertaking long, rambling journeys through the city, is a key feature of many of Jackson's short stories. A prime example is 'Nightmare', which will be the focus of this section of the chapter.

In 1899, Sigmund Freud first published his infamous analysis on the images of sleep, *The Interpretation of Dreams*. This text sought to apply psychoanalytic theory to the narratives, characters and recurring tropes not only of the dreams of Freud's patients, but of his family, his friends, and of Freud himself. An interesting aspect of *The Interpretation of Dreams* is the narrative quality Freud applies to the anecdotes recorded by himself and his participants. They are structured like a short story, and their tangling, surprising and disorientating subjects are reminiscent of Jackson's fiction. While sleep and dreams feature in numerous stories by Jackson, 'Nightmare' particularly seems to reflect the dialogue between the supernatural and the clinical. This is a peculiar, anxious story in which Toni Morgan, running an errand for her boss, appears to be unknowingly at the centre of a city-wide advertising campaign. While its title suggests the nature of the story, it is dream-like and nightmarish in terms of its content: Toni is pursued for reasons she doesn't understand, and each time she changes her appearance, so too does the description of 'Miss X' being blared across the city through loudspeakers. The more she tries to escape, the more frantic the chase becomes, until the story ends with a bizarre suggestion that she was involved in the competition after all. It is simultaneously lucid and nonsensical in much the same way as a dream, but the paranoid flight from the strange advertising campaign is perhaps what makes this story most resemble the nightmare for which it is titled. Comparing 'Nightmare' side-by-side with *The Interpretation of Dreams*, it seems to mimic the patterns, symbols and curiosities of Freud's anecdotes – almost as though it has fallen out of his notebook.

One of the most prominent motifs in 'Nightmare' is Jackson's emphasis on colour. The world of this story is dazzlingly bright and vivid; colour, especially the colour of clothing, seems to be a way that the protagonist clings to reality, even though the story descends into something wholly unreal. For example, in the opening to the story Jackson describes Toni as follows:

---

2. Shirley Jackson, 'How I Write', in *Let Me Tell You* (London: Penguin Classics, 2015), p. 393.
3. Jackson, 'How I Write', p. 393.

> She was wearing a royal blue hat with a waggish red feather in it, and her suit was blue and her topcoat a red and grey tweed, and her shoes were thin and pointed and ungraceful when she walked; they were dark blue, with the faintest line of red edging the sole. She carried a blue pocketbook with her initials in gold, and she wore dark blue gloves with red buttons.[4]

There is an obsessive focus on describing the colour of clothes, yet the adjectives themselves are very simple, with frequent repetition of 'red' and 'blue'. In writing the scene this way, Jackson seems to want to defy the ethereal, imagistic representation of dreams in literature; Toni is not experiencing a nightmare that is hazy and indescribable but, rather, something tangible, life-like and detailed. In doing so, the anxiety is all the more palpable – it is difficult to pin down the unreality of Toni's situation.

Colour features in one of Freud's anecdotes in particular. It is the dream, Freud describes, of a 'non-neurotic girl of a rather prudish and reserved type'.[5] The dream involves the girl arranging flowers, and Freud focuses on psychoanalysing the colours she mentions. More specifically, he aligns her description of colour with the overarching theme he applies to the dream as a whole: that she nervously anticipates her loss of virginity on her forthcoming wedding night. For example, Freud writes:

> In association with pinks, which she then calls carnations, I think of carnal. But her association is colour, to which she adds that carnations are the flowers which her fiancé gives her frequently and in large quantities. At the end of the conversation she suddenly admits, spontaneously, that she has not told me the truth; the word that occurred to her was not colour, but incarnation, the very word I expected. Moreover, even the word 'colour' is not a remote association; it was determined by the meaning of carnation (i.e., flesh-colour) – that is, by the complex.[6]

This excerpt demonstrates Freud's tendency to focus intensely on small, seemingly insignificant details related within a dream, as seen here in the long analysis of one type of flower mentioned by the girl. It attaches meaning to even the most minor of aspects in a dream. Similarly, in 'Nightmare', Jackson writes with a compulsive attention to detail. The description of colour in the story suggests that it is being related and reflected on; her use of colour emphasizes that the dream was incredibly vivid, but also suggests a need to relate as much detail, no matter how trivial, as possible to allow for the kind of investigation carried out by Freud. This repetition

---

4. Shirley Jackson, 'Nightmare', in *Just an Ordinary Day* (London: Penguin Classics, 2017), p. 42.

5. Sigmund Freud, *The Interpretation of Dreams*, trans. A. A. Brill (London: George Allen & Unwin Ltd., 1913 [1899]), p. 352.

6. Freud, *The Interpretation of Dreams*, p. 353. Original emphasis.

of colour warps 'Nightmare' into something other than a formulaic short story: it becomes a clinical document that consciously presents itself for psychoanalysis.

In her biography of Shirley Jackson's life, Ruth Franklin writes of Jackson's troubled sleep. She illustrates how Jackson 'suffered throughout her life from dreams in which the devil appeared to her in various guises and tried to lure her into his trap; these became more frequent during periods of psychological stress'.[7] Jackson was fascinated by the occult and the spiritual, but it is clear that, for Jackson, sleep was also a site of Gothic phantoms and a sense of disorientation and dissociation. While Jackson dreamt of the devil and unconsciously scribbled the beginnings of ghost stories, however, sleep researchers in the 1950s found ways to shine a clinical light on one of the strangest of the brain's functions. These developments were helped considerably by the invention in the mid-1930s of the electroencephalogram (EEG). This was a machine that could chart the brain's electrical activity using electrodes fitted to a patient's head. As Kroker describes, the advent of the EEG meant that 'sleep no longer was as it was experienced; sleep was as it had been inscribed by a machine'.[8] It led researchers to discover that the functions of the sleeping brain could be tracked throughout the night, showing that sleep was not a mysterious void into which one fell, but a progression of stages with different characteristics and electrical impulses. One of the most prominent sleep researchers during this period was Nathaniel Kleitman. Combining data provided by the EEG with older observations on the phenomenon of fluttering eyelids during sleep, he and his assistant, Eugene Aserinsky, defined the process of REM.

The vivid and curious narratives of dreams could now be simplified into an erratic zigzag on a ream of paper. Kenton Kroker aptly describes the conflicting attitudes to sleep and dreams in this era: 'Both dreaming and sleeping were found, in different configurations, within the spheres of the personal and the public, of the visible and the invisible, of the animal and the human, of the clinical and the experimental, and even of the sacred and the profane'.[9] Jackson's 'Nightmare' seems to cling to the idea of the dream as 'sacred', as something that should be recorded in a narrative, in creative prose, rather than an erratic line on a ream of paper.

'Nightmare' seems to resist clinical understandings of dreams, instead returning to a Freudian practice of turning the dream into a cohesive narrative and translating the strange imagery of sleep into words, rather than quantifiable lines. Moreover, 'Nightmare' is an archetypal stress-dream: one of inescapable pursuit, of being lost and humiliated. Towards the end of the story, having convinced herself that, without her prior knowledge or consent, she is the 'Miss X' of the city-wide competition, Jackson writes: 'She decided that whatever else,

---

7. Ruth Franklin, *Shirley Jackson: A Rather Haunted Life* (New York and London: Liveright Publishing Corporation, 2016), pp. 211-12.

8. K. Kroker, *The Sleep of Others and the Transformation of Sleep Research* (Toronto: University of Toronto Press, 2015 [2007]), p. 257.

9. Kroker, *The Sleep of Others*, pp. 7-8.

she must get as far from the neighbourhood as she could.'[10] To apply a Freudian analysis to its content, it emphasizes a palpable sense of anxiety in relation to Toni's association to consumer goods. To catch Toni is to win – a hyperbolic reflection of the relationship between the wife, the home and the 'good life' as symbolized by vacations, home décor and the best car model. These prizes intensify in their grandiosity alongside Toni's increasing stress, from a 'mink coat' to 'a castle on the Rhine'.[11] While trying to complete a simple errand, she finds herself trying to escape the advertising van – to escape being caught. It is a dream of anxiety, a condition that quickly became a kind of crisis in 1950s America. Where 'Nightmare' translates anxiety into a distorted, darkly humorous story, the next section will demonstrate Jackson's more intense examination of generalized panic in accordance with contemporary discourse.

The Age of Anxiety

In his influential 1950 text, *The Meaning of Anxiety*, Rollo May draws attention to the pervasive fears experienced on a vast scale within American society. The weight of post-war recovery, trauma and myriad other reasons, he claims, are to blame for such general discomfort. May explains:

> The alert citizen, we may assume, would be aware not only of the more obvious anxiety-creating situations in our day, such as the threats of war, of the uncontrolled atom bomb, and of radical political and economic upheaval; but also of the less obvious, deeper, and more personal sources of anxiety in himself as well as in fellow-men – namely the inner confusion, psychological disorientation, and uncertainty with respect to values and acceptable standards of conduct.[12]

May's text was part of a wave of investigations and psychoanalysis into the unhappiness that was thought to have gripped the majority of American citizens. As people tried to rebuild their lives following the Second World War, it was often with the spectre of shell-shock, post-war anxiety, bereavement or, for both men and women, loss of income or sense of purpose through employment necessitated by (and exclusive to) the war effort.

May defines anxiety in terms of its relationship to fear. In fear, he says, there is an object – a real, tangible target that does represent some direct threat to the observer. In anxiety, however, 'the individual's efforts to flee generally amount to frantic behaviour because he does not experience the threat as coming from a

---

10. Jackson, 'Nightmare', pp. 53–4.
11. Jackson, 'Nightmare', p. 44, p. 52.
12. Rollo May, *The Meaning of Anxiety* (Auckland: Pickle Partners Publishing, 2015 [1950]), p. 19.

particular place, and hence he does not know where to flee'.¹³ This description of anxiety seems to closely reflect some of Jackson's stories – in particular, it relates to stories that feature a rambling, frantic walk that seems to worsen the protagonist's condition the further they go. As previously discussed, 'Nightmare' is a dream of anxiety – the panic of being pursued, the self-consciousness of being a solitary woman in the city, and the anxiety of being bombarded by – or even associated with – household consumer goods.

Another of Jackson's short stories, 'The Daemon Lover', involves a similarly panicked journey. This story features the recurring character of Jim (or Jamie, or James) Harris – a strange, sometimes hallucinated, man who occasionally appears in Jackson's fiction to taunt or tempt the vulnerable female protagonist. In 'The Daemon Lover', the situation involves the former; the protagonist searches aimlessly through the city to find Jamie, who is missing on the morning she claims they agreed to be married. The more she asks about him, the less certain she is that she knows him at all. Throughout the story, the protagonist is embarrassed and self-conscious at her pursuit of her missing lover, constantly imagining what people must think of her; her anxiety is rooted in social expectations, and the fear of seeming different or transgressive for factors beyond her control.

'The Daemon Lover', in particular, seems to embody the cultural crisis of anxiety in middle-class American women. Indeed, Joan Wylie Hall calls Jackson 'an eloquent voice of the Age of Anxiety' whose female protagonists 'lead narrow lives, circumscribed by the walls of the house or office, yet they are even more susceptible than the men and children to huge losses: of love, identity and existence itself'.¹⁴ For the protagonist in 'The Daemon Lover', this idea of loss – or the anxiety of loss – is palpable. Even before Jamie's non-arrival at the apartment, the protagonist is shown to be in a distressed state of mind. Jackson begins the story with the phrase, 'She had not slept well', and alludes to a few hours of fragmented, fitful dreams.¹⁵ There is an increasing sense in the opening paragraphs that the protagonist is suffering from more than 'pre-wedding jitters'; she appears to be stuck, indecisive, even self-destructive. She begins to write a letter to her sister, Anne, but second-guesses herself. Jackson writes: 'Sitting, pen in hand, she hesitated over what to say next, read the lines already written, and tore up the letter.'¹⁶ A possible reading of this sentence precludes what is to come: at the heart of everything the protagonist does, or does not do, in the story is the fear of what other people will think of her. Throughout 'The Daemon Lover', there are references to the protagonist's frustration, worry and self-consciousness over the way she believes she appears to the rest of society.

---

13. May, *The Meaning of Anxiety*, p. 52.

14. Joan Wylie Hall, *Shirley Jackson: A Study of the Short Fiction* (New York: Twayne Publishers, 1993), p. 90.

15. Shirley Jackson, 'The Daemon Lover', in *The Lottery and Other Stories* (London: Penguin Classics, 2009b [1949]), p. 9.

16. Jackson, 'The Daemon Lover', p. 8.

When Jamie does not arrive at her apartment at the agreed time, she decides to go and look for him. This increasingly anxious walk through the city only serves to call her sanity into question; she projects onto other people a delusion that she is being mocked for her dilemma, that 'everyone thinks it's so funny'.[17] At the same time, however, she expresses worry at how she is perceived – a lone woman asking after her absent lover – by the people she asks for help. This seems to reach a particular climax when she briefly considers going to the police. Jackson writes:

> And then [she] thought, What a fool I'd look like. She had a quick picture of herself standing in a police station, saying, 'Yes, we were going to be married today, but he didn't come,' and the policemen, three or four of them standing around listening, looking at her, at the print dress, at her too-bright make-up, smiling at one another. She couldn't tell them any more than that, could not say, 'Yes, it looks silly, doesn't it, me all dressed up and trying to find the young man who promised to marry me, but what about all of it you don't know? I have more than this, more than you can see: talent, perhaps, and humour of a sort, and I'm a lady and I have pride and affection and delicacy and a certain clear view of life that might make a man satisfied and productive and happy; there's more than you think when you look at me'.[18]

This imagined outburst reveals a large part of the protagonist's inner trouble. She is at her most anxious when she is in the public eye, a place she has found herself because of her supposed abandonment by her fiancé. She feels pressed to defend herself, to encourage the people she speaks to not to misjudge her for something a man has (or has not) done. Over the course of the story, there is a growing sense of unease that her identity is tied to Jamie's infidelity. The recurrent self-loathing is a result of her association to James; she at once resents having to look for him, but is also frantically compelled to continue the search. Wyatt Bonikowski, discussing Jackson's James Harris stories, writes, 'Women in these stories are offered an impossible choice: either to conform to a passive position within rigidly defined gender roles or be abjected into a permanent state of anxiety, insecurity, and even madness outside the Symbolic order.'[19] What is at stake, in other words, is not only the protagonist's marriage but her wider social standing and security – it is James who, already, controls her sense of self-worth.

At the end of 'The Daemon Lover', the protagonist narrows her search to a single flat; it is only through deludedly believing the words of a young boy that she settles on the address. As the reader has come to expect, there is no answer to her knock, but here Jackson presents a sad compulsion: 'She came back many times, every day for the first week. She came on her way to work, in the mornings; in the evenings,

17. Jackson, 'The Daemon Lover', p. 23. Original emphasis.
18. Jackson, 'The Daemon Lover', p. 23.
19.. Shirley Jackson, '"Only One Antagonist": The Demon Lover and the Feminine Experience in the Work of Shirley Jackson', *Gothic Studies* 15, no. 2 (2013): 69.

on her way to dinner alone, but no matter how often or how firmly she knocked, no one ever came to the door' (2009b [1949]: 28). There is a phantom-like emptiness to the protagonist; without James, without the social respectability of marriage, she wanders like a ghost. 'The Daemon Lover' represents the contemporary fear, then, that to be a woman alone is to be a woman forgotten, existing only on the fringes of society.

Jackson was certainly aware of the contemporary discussions in psychology and psychoanalysis. Indeed, she moved in the same circles as some of the era's most prominent psychologists. In 1952, Shirley and her husband, Stanley, took a year's lease on a house that belonged to the German psychoanalyst, Erich Fromm. Fromm taught at Bennington College, and thus was a colleague of Stanley. As Ruth Franklin notes:

> The fact that the house belonged to Fromm also intrigued [Shirley]. To her amazement, he had left all his files and notebooks out in plain view in the wing of the house he had used as his office. Even though she was sorely tempted to peek, she packed them up and put them discreetly in the attic. [. . .] In typically contrarian fashion, Stanley would use Fromm's library to write a polemic against his theories for Parisian Review.[20]

Jackson, then, would have had an understanding of Fromm's theories; it is likely that Fromm, too, knew of Jackson's fiction. One of Fromm's texts, *The Art of Loving*, written after the Jackson's tenancy in 1956, seems to be particularly connected to the disorientation and anxiety that feature in Jackson's work. In discussing anxiety, Fromm writes:

> The experience of separateness arouses anxiety; it is, indeed, the source of all anxiety. Being separate means being cut off, without any capacity to use my human powers. Hence to be separate means to be helpless, unable to grasp the world – things and people – actively; it means that the world can invade me without my ability to react. Thus, separateness is the source of intense anxiety. (2013 [1956]: 24–5)

This sense of being 'unable to grasp the world' is a prominent aspect of Jackson's writing, particularly in the stories discussed here; each features a sense of wandering, either mentally or physically, or both, without ever seeming to reach safety or a specific goal. In this respect, then, the relationship between Jackson and Fromm's theories is prominent.

The cultural crisis of anxiety was not limited to the psychoanalyst's couch, however. The first section demonstrated the advancements in recording and understanding brain function, which in turn led to developments in creating medicines to treat certain problems. The sinister side to these new treatments

---

20. Franklin, *Shirley Jackson*, p. 321.

was the commercialization of the pharmacy. Anxiety, because of its vague, all-encompassing symptoms, and the way in which it was seen to be so pervasive in society, provided fertile ground for advertising the milder forms of medicines used to treat severe mental illnesses. And as the next section will show, the rise of such easily purchasable, mood-altering drugs often caused more problems than they solved. For Shirley Jackson, these problems were worthy of interrogating in her fiction.

The Clinic, Psychosurgery and the Rise of Miltown

The doctor's clinic was reshaped in the 1950s. One of the biggest changes was the way in which patients accessed medicine. Consumer goods had become an important part of American middle-class life, and medication was suddenly embroiled in the cultural phenomenon of buying happiness. As David Herzberg describes, 'Like suburban houses, new cars, and washing machines, medicine became part of a new consumerist "American dream" that reconfigured conceptions of what a good middle-class life – what happiness itself – ought to be like.'[21] The rise of drug stores commercialized medication, vitamins and supplements until they were as easy to obtain as a pair of stockings or a handkerchief. In this way, as Herzberg illustrates earlier, the miracle cures and vitality boasted by pharmaceutical advertising quite literally prescribed the ideal American quality of life.

Through the development of neurosurgery and EEG impulse-monitoring, scientists were better understanding different mental states and conditions. Alongside this, they could also measure the effects of certain drugs on the brain with the intention of treating serious illnesses such as epilepsy and schizophrenia. One such drug was Thorazine, introduced in the United States in 1955. According to Gordon M. Shepherd, Thorazine had an 'immediate and dramatic' effect on psychiatry, making mentally ill patients 'quiet, cooperative, and able to begin to function normally.'[22] Thorazine was known as a 'major tranquilizer' because of its rather drastic change in the behaviour of the patient. But such a powerful medicine did not have mass-market appeal. The same year as Thorazine was introduced to the United States, another drug was developed – a 'minor tranquilizer' – that rapidly dominated American culture: Miltown. This drug was long-lasting, and was believed to be a completely safe medicine free from side effects. It became a common feature in 1950s lifestyle magazines, both in advertisements and in articles and testimonials that demonstrated the wonders Miltown could do for the American public. As Herzberg describes, one feature in *Cosmopolitan* 'praised Miltown for relieving stomach distress, skin problems, "the blues" and depression,

---

21. David Herzberg, *Happy Pills in America: From Miltown to Prozac* (Baltimore: Johns Hopkins University Press, 2009), p. 4.

22. George Shepherd, *Creating Modern Neuroscience: The Revolutionary 1950s* (Oxford: Oxford University Press, 2010), p. 208.

oversensitivity to summer heat, fatigue, inability to concentrate, lack of "social ease", behaviour problems in children, and insomnia'.[23] With such a wide array of vague symptoms, there were very few people to whom Miltown did not promise a cure.

Towards the end of her life, Shirley Jackson was prescribed a dangerous mix of now-regulated medicines that likely did more harm than good to her body and mind. As Ruth Franklin notes:

> Shirley became one of the many 1950s housewives to diet with Dexamyl, a combination pill that included both amphetamines and barbiturates and was also used to treat depression and anxiety. [...] Over the years other prescriptions would be added to the cocktail: Miltown, the spectacularly popular 'mother's little helper' introduced to the market in 1955; later Valium and Seconal, and eventually the antipsychotic Thorazine, which may have exacerbated Shirley's anxiety rather than alleviating it.[24]

Jackson, then, was an active recipient of the prescription medicines that flooded American homes. This awareness and personal experience of anxiety, hypersensitivity of symptoms and increased frequency in trips to the doctor's office left an impression on several of Jackson's stories. 'The Tooth' is perhaps the most obvious example of this. It follows the strange, somnambulistic journey of Clara as she makes her way to the dentist to have her toothache treated. From the opening paragraphs of the story, we learn that Clara has self-medicated with what seems like a practised hand to combine and accumulate the effects of codeine, whisky and sleeping pills. As Robert Haas notes, 'Her rationale here must be purely from experience (Jackson herself took a lot of medicines). For only recently has neuroscience explained how these modalities are all distinct, hence additive (e.g., aspirin blocks pain in a different way than does whisky, hence aspirin plus whisky does more than either alone).'[25]

The story becomes increasingly more frantic and fragmented as it progresses. Especially in regard to Clara's disorientation and distress, which rises to a crescendo at the dentist's office and then seems to become something else entirely, there is an increasing sense that the procedure represents more than an extreme case of dentist-anxiety. After enduring a strange, hallucinatory bus journey, she arrives at the dentist's office and has her tooth X-rayed. Jackson writes:

> She felt, while they were taking an X-ray, that there was nothing in her head to stop the malicious eye of the camera would look through her and photograph the nails in the wall next to her, or the dentist's cuff buttons, or the small thin

---

23. Shepherd, *Creating Modern Neuroscience*, p. 43.
24. Franklin, *Shirley Jackson*, pp. 285–6.
25. Robert Haas, 'Shirley Jackson's "The Tooth": Dentistry as Horror, the Imagination as a Shield', *Literature and Medicine* 33, no. 1 (2015): 138–9.

bones of the dentist's instruments; the dentist said, 'Extraction,' regretfully to the nurse, and the nurse said, 'Yes, doctor, I'll call them right away'.[26]

This is one of the first moments where the image of the dentist seems to split; on one hand, it is simply a dentist X-raying a rotten tooth, and on the other it is an act of surveillance and interrogation. Clara's fear of the 'malicious camera', of having a hidden or repressed side to her revealed to strangers, occurs again in the story. The dentist is not equipped to extract the tooth, and sends Clara to a dental surgeon. Here, the horror truly begins, and the narrative becomes so abstract as to represent something else entirely. For example, after her tooth is pulled and Clara regains consciousness, Jackson writes: 'There was no blood anywhere around except in her mouth; everything was as clean as before. The dentist was gone, suddenly, and the nurse put out her arm and helped her out of the chair. "Did I talk?" she asked suddenly, anxiously. "Did I say anything?"'[27] The ordeal of Clara's tooth extraction and the hazy, disoriented events that follow seem particularly reminiscent of the rise in psychosurgery. Surgery of the temporal lobe to treat epilepsy became a widespread practice in the 1950s, but brain surgery was also used as one of the only forms of therapy for mental illnesses such as severe depression. According to Gordon M. Shepherd, 'Between 1946 and 1956, 60,000 – 80,000 psychosurgery operations were performed worldwide.'[28] One of the most famous examples (although it was hidden from public knowledge until the 1980s) was the disastrous lobotomy performed on Rosemary Kennedy, sister of President John F. Kennedy, in 1941 to cure her severe mood swings. Instead, it left her with severe and irreversible brain damage.

Viewing 'The Tooth' as a metaphor for lobotomy and other psychosurgical procedures allows a clearer understanding of some of the more cryptic lines and moments in the story. At the beginning of the story, for instance, Clara and her husband are discussing the tooth as a recurring issue. Jackson writes, '"You had a toothache on our honeymoon," he said, accusingly.'[29] Clara abruptly changes the subject. Later, after she is subjected to an X-ray, Jackson describes how the tooth 'seemed now to be the only part of her to have any identity'.[30] Just before Clara succumbs to the surgeon's dose of what is presumably nitrous oxide, her final stab of emotion is not one of pain or relief to finally be rid of the tooth, but of 'outrage'.[31] The tooth is not simply a tooth, but a problem in Clara's marriage. It is part of the mouth; part of intimacy, consumption and conversation. The tooth has cast a shadow over Clara's honeymoon, reveals Clara's keen awareness for

---

26. Shirley Jackson, 'The Tooth', in *The Lottery and Other Stories* (London: Penguin Classics, 2009 [1949]), pp. 275–6.
27. Jackson, 'The Tooth', p. 281.
28. Shepherd, *Creating Modern Neuroscience*, p. 203.
29. Jackson, 'The Tooth', p. 267.
30. Jackson, 'The Tooth', p. 276.
31. Jackson, 'The Tooth', p. 280.

self-medication and makes Clara worried about revealing a hidden part of herself through the X-ray or a drug-induced soliloquy. The toothache is thus representative of Clara's discomfort in her marriage; it is the only way for her to have a sense of individuality. It must be removed. As Darryl Hattenhauer describes, '[Jackson's] characters rarely win, succeed, or transcend. They do not grow as much as they disintegrate.'[32] Indeed, in no way does Jackson present Clara as being 'cured' once her tooth is pulled; the story ends with a strange, ambiguous hallucination. This is the horror at the root of the story: in using dental surgery to symbolize psychosurgery, Jackson demonstrates that while the procedures are, in essence, the same, there is a gulf between them in terms of their efficacy and that emotional disorder is not the same as a rotten tooth despite how it might be interpreted through the clinical gaze.

The psychosurgical procedures of the 1950s could inflict brain damage just as much as they claimed to cure other disorders. It is this idea of losing something by way of a cure that pervades 'The Tooth'. In a moment of dark humour typical of Jackson's fiction, Clara notes the signs above the doors in the surgeon's office: 'Some of them said "DDS," some of them said "Clinic," some of them said "X-Ray." One of them, looking wholesome and friendly and somehow most comprehensible, said "Ladies".'[33] This seems to be a rather pointed association between women and the 'malicious eye' of the clinical gaze. After the extraction, Clara enters the 'wholesome and friendly' realm of the 'Ladies' room, and is shocked to discover that she has 'no idea which face was hers'.[34] From then until the end of the story, Clara struggles to associate herself with any sort of self-identity. Her face, her belongings and her clothes are a mystery to her. When she looks in her pocketbook, it reads almost like an autopsy or dissection of someone else: 'Handkerchief, plain, white, uninitialed. Compact, square and brown tortoise-shell plastic, with a powder compartment and a rouge compartment; the rouge compartment had obviously never been used, although the powder cake was half-gone.'[35] The problem tooth and its subsequent extraction can thus be read as a metaphor for more serious medical procedures. Robert Haas aptly defines this aspect of the story: 'Becoming a patient is a strange, profound, and terrifying change for Clara, the pain and fear sweeping away most ordinary human concerns, and her personhood being lost as she became "all tooth", subject to the arcane procedures and absolute control of medical personnel focused exclusively upon it.'[36] Indeed, Clara's sense of self-alienation is reminiscent of one infamous psychosurgical procedure in 1953. American neuroscientist William Scoville, Shepherd notes, performed a 'bilateral temporal lobe resection in one patient for relief of debilitating epilepsy, producing

---

32. Darryl Hattenhauer, *Shirley Jackson's American Gothic* (Albany: State University of New York Press, 2003), p. 3.
33. Jackson, 'The Tooth', p. 278.
34. Jackson, 'The Tooth', p. 283.
35. Jackson, 'The Tooth', p. 284.
36. Haas, 'Shirley Jackson's "The Tooth"', p. 144.

a profound loss of recent memory'.[37] While this event took place several years after 'The Tooth' was published in *The Lottery and Other Stories* (1949), Jackson's story reflects the notion of a 'profound loss' caused by such invasive surgery.

Another story that takes the medical professional as its antagonist is 'Colloquy'. This very short story demonstrates a troubled conversation between Mrs Arnold and 'the doctor'. Mrs Arnold, wanting to keep her concerns private, visits someone other than her '"regular doctor" as "Doctor Murphy would probably feel it was necessary to tell [her husband]"'.[38] This anxiety to share her problems with her husband reflects one of the key discussions behind the cultural push to return women to domestic roles in the 1950s. During the Second World War, women were employed in a vast array of jobs, including as engineers, factory workers and scientists. As Jonathan M. Metzl notes, however:

> Often-overwhelming social pressure sought to have women give up their jobs and return to their positions as happy, reproductive home-makers, in order to ensure jobs for returning veterans. Popular culture extolled a 'new femininity' – really an old maternity – not by a picture of a woman in rolled-up, working sleeves, but rather by a mother at home with her children.[39]

This closing-off of socially acceptable roles led to anxiety and depression in women, which magazines and pharmaceutical companies warped into the idea that the unhappy housewife caused an unhappy husband and children. Indeed, in Metzl's assessment of contemporary popular magazines, he notices how 'mothers in these magazines are overtly assumed to reject their maternal duties, and spread a pathology that threatens to disrupt the well-being of their male husbands, sons and doctors'.[40]

This section has demonstrated that 'The Tooth' and 'Colloquy' can be grouped together as examples of Jackson's work that reflects the clinical and pharmaceutical shaping of cultural gender roles. The doctor became an extension of the family, a kind of twin to the husband, whose discretion only extended as far as matters that did not ultimately affect the husband's mental or physical health. These two stories show Jackson's own critical analysis of the ways in which the clinic pervaded the middle-class home, including her own. 'The Tooth' shows the protagonist's adeptness at self-medication – a possible parallel to Jackson's own routine – and reflects an unsettling comparability between psychiatric interventions and surgery to remove diseased or decaying parts of the body. 'Colloquy', on the other hand, demonstrates anxiety in confessing symptoms to a doctor, for fear of it reaching

---

37. Shepherd, *Creating Modern Neuroscience*, p. 202.
38. Shirley Jackson, 'Colloquy', in *The Lottery and Other Stories* (London: Penguin Classics, 2009 [1949]), p. 145.
39. Jonathan M. Metzl, '"Mother's Little Helper": The Crisis of Psychoanalysis and the Miltown Resolution', *Gender and Identity* 15, no. 2 (2003): 235.
40. Metzl, '"Mother's Little Helper"', p. 230.

the husband's ear. In a culture where the clinic was not private for women, and where unhappiness was aligned with neglect of the family, it is no wonder that the simple solution of taking Miltown became so pervasive. Jackson's stories, then, exist as a fictional parallel to this phenomenon.

Conclusion

Post-war America saw a revolution both in the clinic and in the home. Advances in technology developed during the Second World War were used to image and quantify brain processes, particularly in relation to sleep research. As medical understanding of the brain developed, so too did pharmacology in regard to creating drugs to soothe or attempt to cure mental illness. At the same time, the American domestic environment was in upheaval. Women were being socially pressured back into the home and away from their wartime employment, to fulfil a more conservative role and allow returning soldiers to resume work. This crisis of gender was a contributing factor to what was considered to be 'The Age of Anxiety'. The clinic and the home thus converged; minor tranquilizers advertised to ease women's domestic worries were sold as a consumer good rather than a brain-altering chemical. The anxious housewife became a symbol of American culture but seemed rather to symbolize the wonders of American medicine and pharmaceutical companies. There was no problem in the home that could not be solved by Miltown. Commercialism and consumer goods, self-medication and a confession in the doctor's office could restore domestic bliss.

Much of Shirley Jackson's short fiction reflects these social attitudes and phenomena, but almost always presents these ideas from the perspective of the restless housewife. She examines the prevalent social expectations – being the perfect secretary, fiancée or wife – and imbues them with evil, anxiety and pain. Having acute experience herself of psychotherapy and the clinic, Jackson brings a personal, cynical understanding to her stories. Additionally, Jackson's social circle included prominent psychologists such as Erich Fromm, and she maintained a keen interest in dream analysis and other aspects of psychology and psychoanalysis. This chapter, then, has sought to examine some of her stories in relation to the clinical discourse of the era. 'Nightmare' seems to come straight from the pages of Freud's *The Interpretation of Dreams*, whereas 'The Daemon Lover' embodies the discussion of the crisis of anxiety – the perpetual fear that has no particular or realistic focus. In 'The Tooth' and 'Colloquy', anxiety is brought into the clinic. The former can be read as a reflection of the frequent psychosurgical operations conducted on patients throughout the era, often with catastrophic memory loss or drastic personality change. 'Colloquy' is more simple, but no less horrifying – it represents the monitoring of housewives within the doctor's office but also alludes to a paranoia and miscommunication borne of the clinical setting.

Jackson experienced and consumed – and ultimately suffered from – contemporary trends and advances in psychoanalysis and pharmacology. The drugs prescribed to Jackson – Miltown, barbiturates – were eventually deemed to be harmful and regulated. Indeed, it is with a touch of sad irony that 1965, the year of Jackson's death, saw a new law implemented for the control of barbiturates, as well as 'investigation and control over tranquilizers like Miltown and Valium'.[41] The stories that most explicitly take a clinical theme, 'The Tooth' in particular, also seem to be acutely aware of the harmful effects of psychotherapy and medication. The antagonist in these stories, then, is not the advertising van, the absent Jamie Harris or the rotten tooth; it is the clinical gaze that pursues and reduces the anxious woman.

References

Bonikowski, Wyatt (2013), '"Only One Antagonist": The Demon Lover and the Feminine Experience in the Work of Shirley Jackson', *Gothic Studies* 15 (2): 66-88.

Foucault, Michel ([1963] 1997), *The Birth of the Clinic*, trans. A. M. Sheridan, London: Routledge.

Franklin, Ruth (2016), *Shirley Jackson: A Rather Haunted Life*, New York and London: Liveright Publishing Corporation.

Freud, Sigmund ([1899] 1913), *The Interpretation of Dreams*, trans. A. A. Brill, London: George Allen & Unwin Ltd.

Fromm, Erich ([1956] 2013), *The Art of Loving*, New York: Open Road Media.

Haas, Robert (2015), 'Shirley Jackson's "The Tooth": Dentistry as Horror, the Imagination as a Shield', *Literature and Medicine* 33 (1): 132-56.

Hall, Joan Wylie (1993), *Shirley Jackson: A Study of the Short Fiction*, New York: Twayne Publishers.

Hattenhauer, Darryl (2003), *Shirley Jackson's American Gothic*, Albany: State University of New York Press.

Herzberg, David (2009), *Happy Pills in America: From Miltown to Prozac*, Baltimore: Johns Hopkins University Press.

Jackson, Shirley ([1949] 2009a), 'Colloquy', in *The Lottery and Other Stories*, 145-7, London: Penguin Classics.

Jackson, Shirley ([1949] 2009b), 'The Daemon Lover', in *The Lottery and Other Stories*, 9-28, London: Penguin Classics.

Jackson, Shirley ([1949] 2009c), 'The Tooth', in *The Lottery and Other Stories*, 265-86, London: Penguin Classics.

Jackson, Shirley (2015), 'How I Write', in *Let Me Tell You*, 389-93, London: Penguin Classics.

Jackson, Shirley (2017), 'Nightmare', in *Just an Ordinary Day*, 42-58, London: Penguin Classics.

Kroker, Kenton ([2007] 2015), *The Sleep of Others and the Transformation of Sleep Research*, Toronto: University of Toronto Press.

May, Roll ([1950] 2015), *The Meaning of Anxiety*, Auckland: Pickle Partners Publishing.

Metzl, Jonathan M. (2003), '"Mother's Little Helper": The Crisis of Psychoanalysis and the Miltown Resolution', *Gender and Identity* 15 (2): 228-55.

Shepherd, Gordon M. (2010), *Creating Modern Neuroscience: The Revolutionary 1950s*, Oxford: Oxford University Press.

---

41. Herzberg, *Happy Pills in America*, p. 96.

Chapter 6

MEETING THE DEVIL

DIABOLIC INFLUENCE AND DIABOLIC RESISTANCE IN SHIRLEY JACKSON'S JAMES HARRIS STORIES

Robert Zipser

Shirley Jackson's short story collection, *The Lottery and Other Stories* (1949) ('*The Lottery*'), was originally subtitled *The Adventures of James Harris*.[1] This subtitle was dropped in more recent editions of the anthology such as Farrar, Strauss and Giroux's 2005 paperback edition, likely because Jackson's identification with her most famous story 'The Lottery' makes any subtitle commercially unnecessary. However, the subtitle was highly significant because stories such as 'The Daemon Lover', 'Like Mother Used to Make', 'Elizabeth', 'The Tooth' and 'The Witch' are linked by Harris's recurrent diabolic presence, in differing forms, and his efforts to malignantly influence the lives of the female protagonists or, in the case of 'The Witch', the protagonist's child.

An interpretation of James Harris as the Devil is not new to Jackson criticism; however, little critical attention has been paid to Jackson's use of the seventeenth-century Protestant concepts that certain emotional states such as yearning, melancholy, shame, and anger, present in the stories 'The Daemon Lover', 'Like Mother Used to Make', 'Elizabeth' and 'The Tooth', invited and permitted diabolic temptation. Nor have critics correctly addressed the contrast that Jackson presents in the often-misinterpreted story 'The Witch' which provides a countervailing model of diabolic resistance and alludes to the Wilderness Temptation of Christ.

Jackson separates the sections of *The Lottery* with four epigraphs from seventeenth-century English Puritan theologian and philosopher Joseph Glanvill's work *Saducismus Triumphatis* (1683), Glanvill's defence of the belief in witchcraft against sceptics. Each epigraph refers in some way to the Devil. Jackson's use of a seventeenth-century work as a backdrop to her twentieth-century stories suggests that we should look to seventeenth-century Protestant theological concepts to understand Harris's exploits in *The Lottery* and how he is able to negatively impact

---

1. Shirley Jackson, *Shirley Jackson Novels and Stories*, ed. Joyce Carol Oates (New York: The Library of America, 2010). Subsequent references shall appear parenthetically in the text.

the lives of the female protagonists in 'The Daemon Lover', 'Like Mother Used to Make', 'Elizabeth' and 'The Tooth' but is unable to do so in 'The Witch'.

Seventeenth-century Protestantism, with its focus on sin, the Fall of Man and damnation, elevated the biblical role of the Devil as tempter, as Nathan Johnstone notes, 'into the single most important aspect of his agency, which virtually eclipsed all others'.[2] This occupation of the Devil formed a crucial element of Calvinism, the dominant Protestant faith in both seventeenth-century England and New England. Calvinism taught that men and women were engaged throughout their lives in constant spiritual warfare against Satan. The Devil continually assaulted them in his effort to lead them into sinful activity. Man's ongoing fight against Satan mirrored the battle that Christ waged against the Devil in the desert. As John Calvin stated, 'That we daily must fight the same imposture, is the experience of individual Christians.'[3]

It was commonly believed that the Devil could tempt men and women in two ways: first, by physical seduction of the flesh, and second, by influence upon the spirit through the injection of sinful worldly thoughts into the mind. These thoughts and fantasies heightened negative emotions and sinful tendencies that were already present due to man's inherent corrupt nature. Of course, these two methods were not mutually exclusive; the Devil could sometimes employ both at the same time.

The method of physical seduction was primarily believed to be directed at women. Unfortunately, this belief arose from the stereotype of women accepted by both the English and New England Puritans which formed one of the bases of the witchcraft persecutions in New England and Europe. Women were viewed as being weaker than men not only physically but, more importantly, spiritually and morally. They were constantly unsatisfied and yearning for more than they had, both emotionally and sexually, and weak-willed, and therefore unable to withstand the sexual seductions of the Devil. Furthermore, they were viewed as passive actors in respect to sex who were acted upon by male aggressors. As Elizabeth Reis notes in her study of the female soul and body in Puritan New England: 'Women were in a double bind during witchcraft episodes. Their souls, strictly speaking, were no more evil than those of men, but the representation of the vulnerable, unsatisfied, and yearning female soul, *passively waiting* for Christ but *always ready to succumb to the devil*, inadvertently implicated corporeal women themselves.'[4]

Given this stereotype of female vulnerability, and the Puritan belief that the Devil assumed human form as a man, it is not surprising that the accusation and the admission (sometimes under coercion) of sexual intercourse with the Devil

---

2. Nathan Johnstone, 'The Protestant Devil: The Experience of Temptation in Early Modern England', *Journal of British Studies* 43 (2004): 173–205.

3. Adrian Hallett, 'The Theology of John Calvin. Part Three: The Christian's Conflict with the Devil', *Churchman* 105, no. 4 (1991): 293–325.

4. Elizabeth Reis, 'The Devil, the Body, and the Feminine Soul in Puritan New England', *The Journal of American History* 82, no. 1 (1995): 15–36 (emphasis mine).

was not unusual in seventeenth-century witchcraft persecutions in England, New England (less so) and Europe. Indeed, this practice is suggested by the third interstitial quotation from *Saducismus Triumphatis* that Jackson inserts into the collection: 'when she awaked, she found a Man to be in bed with her, whom she supposed to be her Husband; though her Husband had been dead twenty years, or thereby, and that the Man immediately disappeared: And declares, That this Man who disappeared was the Devil' (115). This epigraph both reinforces the concept of the Devil as a male seducer and foreshadows James Harris's seductions of female protagonists in *The Lottery*.

In the Appendix to *Saducismus Triumphatis*, which contains confessions of witches from Sweden, not cited by Jackson, one of the accused witches states that

> the Devil used to play upon an Harp before them, and afterwards to go with them that he liked best, into a Chamber, where he committed Venerous Acts with them; and this indeed all confessed, That he had carnal knowledge of them, and that the Devil had Sons and Daughters by them, which he did Marry together, and they did couple together, and brought forth Toads and Serpents.[5]

A reference to sex with the Devil also appears in the New England Puritan minister and theologian Increase Mather's work *An Essay for the Recording of Illustrious Providences* (1684). Mather cites the confession of Rebecca Greensmith, an accused witch who was executed in Connecticut during an outbreak of witchcraft in that colony that preceded the more famous Salem trials. After being charged with witchcraft, Greensmith confessed that 'the devil had frequently the carnal knowledge of her body'.[6]

In her biography of Shirley Jackson, Ruth Franklin describes Jackson's lifelong interest in both the history and social causes of seventeenth-century witchcraft that began as early as her undergraduate years at the University of Rochester, where she first read *Saducismus Triumphatis* and learned of its major influence on Cotton Mather.[7] Jackson continued to intently study this field, and in 1956, she published *The Witchcraft of Salem Village*, a history of the Salem trials written for children. Franklin points out that although the book was primarily a chronological factual history of the trials, it also described some of the social biases against women in the colony which underlay the accusations.[8]

---

5. Joseph Glanvill, *Saducismus Triumphatis: Or, Full and Plain Evidence Concerning Witches and Apparitions* (London: Printed by A.L., 1683), Appendix A.

6. Increase Mather, *An Essay for the Recording of illustrious Providences: Wherein an Account is given of Many Remarkable and Very Memorable Events which have Hapned [sic] this Last Age, Especially in New England* (Boston: Printed by Samuel Green for Joseph Browning, 1684), p. 138.

7. Ruth Franklin, *Shirley Jackson: A Rather Haunted Life* (New York: Liveright Publishing Corporation, 2017), p. 106.

8. Franklin, *Shirley Jackson*, pp. 356–8.

Lynette Carpenter, in her feminist reading of *We Have Always Lived in the Castle*, has described Jackson's incorporation of the male–female dynamics of the witchcraft persecutions into her work, although focusing more on female power than on female passivity.[9] Wyatt Bonikowski, however, has recognized Jackson's indirect allusions to the historical Christian link between women with evil and her recurrent theme of 'passivity in the face of demonic repetition ... particular to feminine subjectivity'.[10] Similarly, Samantha Landau, in her discussion of Jackson's stories, including 'The Daemon Lover', has suggested Jackson's awareness of the Puritan stereotype that women were morally and intellectually inferior to men and easy prey for the Devil.[11]

In addition to temptation of the flesh, seventeenth-century Protestants and Anglicans believed that the Devil, as his essence was spiritual, would invisibly work upon the spirits of men and women by injecting into their minds sinful thoughts and ideas in order to encourage transgressions. As Anglican theologian Robert Burton stated in his famous treatise *The Anatomy of Melancholy* (1621): 'for the devil he is a spirit, and hath means and opportunities to mingle himself with our spirits, and sometimes more slyly, sometimes more abruptly and openly, to suggest such devilish thoughts into our hearts.'[12] This concept was echoed in the writings of the English Puritan minister Richard Capel: 'to trouble the spirits potently, to raise the humours, to proceed by presenting matter immediately to the phantasie of man, is within his reach; that the divell can doe, and therefore (halving leave) hee is able to put those acts into a man, and to worke with power in the children of disobedience.'[13]

Although all men and women, due to their 'fallen' corrupt natures, could be tempted by the Devil, those persons who were naturally prone to sadness, discontent, anger or bitterness were especially vulnerable to the Devil's predations. It was believed that the Devil had a special affinity for these emotions because they resonated with his own anguish. Burton wrote: 'he insults and domineers in melancholy distempered fantasies and persons especially; melancholy is *balneum*

---

9. Lynette Carpenter, 'The Establishment and Preservation of Female Power in Shirley Jackson's *We Have Always Lived in the Castle*', *Frontiers: A Journal of Women Studies* 8, no. 1 (1984): 32–8.

10. Wyatt Bonikowski, '"Only One Antagonist": The Daemon Lover and the Feminine Experience in the Work of Shirley Jackson', *Gothic Studies* 15, no. 2 (2013): 66–88.

11. Samantha Landau, 'Occult Influences in Shirley Jackson's "The Lottery"', *Gakuen* 936 (2018): 11–21.

12. Robert Burton, *The Anatomy of Melancholy, What It Is, with All the Kinds, Causes, Symptoms, Prognostics and Several Cures of It* (London: Printed for Thomas McLean Haymarket, 1826), p. 587.
This work was first published in 1621.

13. Richard Capel, *Tentations their Nature, Danger and Cure* (London: Printed by R. Badger, 1633), p. 32.

diaboli, as Serapio holds, the devil's bath, and invites him to come to it'.[14] The Lutheran theologian Jacob Boehme similarly preached that the melancholy spirit would attract Satan because '[F]or where it is dark, there he freely enters in; he maketh Representations or Images before the Soul, and terrifieth it with his *Wiles*, or abominable *Thoughts* that it should *despair* of GOD's Grace'.[15]

Melancholy could arise from numerous causes, but two of the chief ones were solitude and loneliness. It was also linked with self-doubt. Seventeenth-century Protestant theologians were not familiar with the terms 'self-esteem' or 'self-identity', but they were very familiar with congregants who, partly because Protestantism required its followers to engage in continuous self-examination, were tormented by feelings of sinfulness, failure and worthlessness which modern psychologists would call *shame*. Protestant theologians believed that when the Devil saw these torments, he sought to magnify them so that the sufferer would lose hope and forget the promise of salvation. Thus, the English Non-Conformist Puritan preacher and author Thomas Brooks wrote that 'in order to accomplish his design, he [Satan] keeps the believer's eye upon his sins, unworthiness, short comings, and daily omissions that he is so taken up with his sinfulness as to lose sight of Christ'.[16] This quotation from Brooks also aligns with the corresponding Puritan concept that the ultimate goal of the Devil was to drive his victims into a state of despair. Despair (a form of extreme melancholy) was deemed a sin because it effectively alienated the sinner from God. In this way, it mirrored and recapitulated the Devil's own existential torment.

Another emotional state believed in the seventeenth century to be a 'doorway' to diabolic temptation was anger, sometimes called the 'cholerick' humour. In the broad sense, 'anger' also included envy, pride, spite, jealousy and bitterness. Boehme wrote of the cholerick personality that

> There is great *Danger*, with, or in, this Complexion, if the Soul liveth according to the *outward* Imagination; it hath a hard Bond, when one Fire-source or Quality is bound or tied to the *other*: The fierce wrathful *Devil* hath a powerful Access to it; for the fiery Property is useful for him: He is also Proud, Stately and Envious; and so also is THIS *Complexion*.[17]

Significantly, this same emotional state is referred to in the fourth interstitial quotation from Glanvill used by Jackson in *The Lottery* which refers to persons whose '*Malice, Envy,* and *Desire* of *Revenge* [. . .] leave them exposed to the *Invasion*

---

14. Burton, *Anatomy of Melancholy*, p. 587.

15. Jacob Boehme, *The Four Complexions Or, A Treatise of Consolatory Instruction Against the Time of Temptation For a Sad and Assaulted Heart* (London: Printed for J. Scott at the Black Swan in Pater-Noster, 1701), p. 35. This work was first published in 1621.

16. Thomas Brooks, *The Precious Remedies against Satan's Devices* (New Haven: Nathan Whiting, 1832), p. 143. This work was first published in 1652.

17. Boehme, *The Four Complexions*, p. 35.

and *Solicitations* of those *wicked Spirits*, to whom such hateful *Attributes* make them very suitable' (177). Jackson's use of this theme foreshadows the interactions between James Harris and the female protagonists of 'Like Mother Used to Make' and 'Elizabeth' (discussed herein) who are respectively envious and jealous and bitter.

However, all hope was not lost. For John Calvin, the model for resistance to the Devil had been laid out for man in the Wilderness Temptation of Jesus, Mt. 4.1-11. In the book of Matthew, Jesus is led out by the Spirit to the desert where he fasts for forty days and forty nights. He then encounters Satan in human form, referred to as 'the tempter'. The Devil presents Christ with three temptations, including – in keeping with Satan's role as Prince of the World – the offer of 'all the kingdoms of the world in their magnificence', designed to tempt Jesus to forsake God's plan for him. Christ, relying on his faith in God, refuses each temptation and then banishes Satan from him with a simple command: 'Get away, Satan!' The Gospel then states that 'the devil left him'. Calvin and the Puritans believed that the faithful Christian, who armed himself with the faith and prayer that Paul called 'the armor of God', Eph. 6.11, a term frequently invoked by Puritan ministers, could similarly repel the temptations of Satan. Thus, resistance to Satan required active rebellion, the opposite of passive acquiescence.

Shirley Jackson applies these same seventeenth-century Protestant concepts concerning the Devil and diabolic temptation to twentieth-century New York women in 'The Daemon Lover', 'Like Mother Used to Make', 'Elizabeth' and 'The Tooth'. James Harris enters the lives of each of these women, and they each become involved with him on both mental and (at least implicitly) physical levels.

In 'The Daemon Lover' we see the after-effect of diabolic temptation rather than the seduction itself (which Jackson will later portray in 'The Tooth'). At the start of the story, we learn that Harris, in corporeal form, has already acted in the diabolic capacity of physical tempter. He has already physically seduced the unnamed female protagonist into committing to marry him, itself a sinful transgression.

In Jackson's descriptions of the woman's preparation for Harris's scheduled arrival to her apartment, and in her later search for Harris, we see the sadness, self-doubt, anxiety, guilt over sin and shame historically thought to invite the Devil. Like several other women in *The Lottery*, the woman in 'The Daemon Lover' lives alone in a one-bedroom apartment, suggesting the solitary loneliness associated with melancholy. Moreover, she is ridden with shame over her age and attractiveness: 'Anxiously she pulled through the dresses in the closet, and hesitated over a print she had worn the summer before; it was too young for her' (10). Putting on her make-up, it occurs to her that

> She could not try to disguise the sallowness of her skin, or the lines around her eyes, today, when it might look as though she were only doing it for her wedding, and yet she could not bear the thought of Jamie's bringing to marriage anyone who looked haggard and lined. You're thirty-four years old after *all*, she told herself cruelly in the bathroom mirror. Thirty, it said on the license. (12)

These passages link the protagonist to other of Jackson's female characters in *The Lottery* whose very fragile senses of self-identity allow them to be easily influenced by outside forces.

When the woman suddenly realizes that she has forgotten to put clean sheets on the bed, she hurries to do so 'working quickly to avoid thinking consciously of why she was changing the sheets' (11). Jackson leaves ambiguous whether the woman has already had sex with Harris or is planning to have sex with Harris to consummate the wedding. What is more important is her sense of guilt over a perceived sin.

While waiting for Harris to arrive, the woman muses on the fantasy future she has discussed with Harris: 'the golden house-in-the-country future they had been preparing for the last week' (12). The passage implies that, in addition to physical intimacy, Harris has injected *worldly* fantasies into her mind, aligning with the seventeenth-century concept of the Devil as both a physical and spiritual tempter.

Of course, Harris never shows up and the woman goes out onto the street looking for him. In her questioning of people in the neighbourhood whom she hopes might have seen Harris, such as a florist and a magazine-stand owner, she betrays the same feeling of shame and fragile self-esteem seen in the earlier passages: 'She was suddenly horribly aware of her over-young print dress, and pulled her coat around her quickly' (19). She thinks of asking the police to help her find Harris but imagines them looking at her judgmentally and tries to mentally reassure herself: 'I have more than this, more than you can see: talent, perhaps, and humor of a sort, and I'm a lady and I have pride and affection and delicacy' (21). The reference to 'talent' suggests that she may have at one time aspired to be some type of artist, perhaps a writer, but that her youthful dream was never realized. This links her to the protagonists of the subsequent stories 'The Villager' (a failed dancer) and 'Elizabeth' (a failed writer) (discussed later) who suffer from a sense of shame over their past artistic failures.

Finally, she is told by a demonic young boy that he has seen Harris enter an apartment building and go upstairs. The woman enters the building and climbs the stairs to find two apartments: one with the door locked and one with the door open. She also sees a discarded ribbon of the type that might have held flowers on the ground which she takes as proof that Harris has been there. As she will do in 'The Tooth', Jackson here is likely alluding to a Nathaniel Hawthorne work which discusses the Devil. In 'Young Goodman Brown', Brown sees a pink ribbon in the woods which he immediately interprets as concrete proof that his wife has gone into the woods with the Devil; in fact, it is a spectral illusion (a form of spectral evidence) created by Satan. Jackson's allusion to Hawthorne's story reinforces the link between the modern events of 'The Daemon Lover' and seventeenth-century Puritanism and reveals that, like Brown, this character is vulnerable to diabolic deception.

The protagonist knocks on the locked door. There is no answer but she hears 'something that might have been laughter far away' (24). This invisible laughter suggests that, at this point, Harris may have assumed the invisible spiritual form of the Devil. When she enters the other unlocked apartment, she finds a desolate and somewhat hellish scene: 'the empty attic room [. . .] floorboards unpainted' (24). She sees 'bags of plaster, piles of old newspapers, a broken trunk' and then a rat, 'its evil face alert' (24).

Jackson reveals that this protagonist's fate, at least during her life, will be one of damnation to repeated frustration and lonely misery: 'She came back many times, every day for the first week. She came on her way to work, in the mornings; in the evenings, on her way to dinner alone, but no matter how often or how firmly she knocked, no one ever came to the door' (25). The victim here is condemned to despair, and it is implied that this despair was Harris's goal. Contextually, this scene foreshadows *James Harris, the Daemon Lover*, the ballad that Jackson inserts as her Epilogue in which the Devil punishes the woman who accompanies him by depriving her of ever knowing the joys of heaven. At the same time, it recalls the Puritan belief that the Devil sought to drive the sinner into a state of despair and alienation from God.

In the story 'Like Mother Used to Make', which immediately follows 'The Daemon Lover' in the collection, we meet another woman living alone in New York in a one-bedroom apartment. The young woman, Marcia, lives down the hall from her friend and opposite personality-type, David, who is fastidious, reserved and disciplined while Marcia is unkempt, loud and disorganized. David has invited her for dinner and, concerned that she might forget, he leaves his own immaculate apartment and walks down the hall to Marcia's messy apartment to leave her a note. Letting himself into her apartment with a key, David sees disorder and chaos: 'Marcia's bed was unmade and a pile of dirty laundry lay on the floor. The window had been open all day and papers had blown wildly around the floor' (28). The disorder of Marcia's room suggests an apathetic indifference to life and a generalized sadness, two symptoms associated with classical melancholy and modern depression.

David returns to his own apartment to carefully prepare dinner for himself and Marcia. In keeping with her general disorganization, Marcia arrives late. Jackson describes her as a 'tall handsome girl with a loud voice, wearing a dirty raincoat' (29).

In Marcia, in addition to melancholy, we first see one of the categories of anger linked by seventeenth-century writers to diabolic temptation: envy. Marcia is painfully aware of the great difference between her disordered world and David's pristine world, mournfully admitting that she doesn't know how to live David's disciplined life: 'Someone should teach me, I guess' (30). She tells David: 'Everything's beautiful [. . .] I mean everything [. . .] furniture, and nice place you have here, and dinner, and everything' (30).

Marcia and David are having dessert when James Harris arrives. Significantly, Harris has come to visit Marcia and not David as Marcia represents another flawed female character who is the preferred target of the Devil's temptation. Harris's initial influence on Marcia is subtle and invisible, in accordance with Protestant concepts of spiritual temptation. His very presence seems to heighten Marcia's shame about her life and her envy of David. These feelings prompt her to lie to Harris, claiming, in a betrayal of David, that David's meal and apartment are in fact hers (32).

The deception continues as Marcia, at Harris's suggestion, goes with Harris into David's living room and sits with him on the couch. Having adopted the false role of the hostess and assigned David the role of the guest, she says to David: 'Sit down, Davie, won't you?' (33). David recognizes her tone as one that a hostess uses to address a party guest who has overstayed his welcome. Marcia and Harris then effectively push David out of his own apartment, with David timidly accepting the role of a visitor who realizes that it is time to go. 'I'm sorry you have to leave so soon', Marcia tells David (34). In a reversal of their actual roles, David leaves Marcia occupying his warm beautiful apartment and he goes to her cold dirty apartment.

The story ends with the strong indication that Harris has switched from spiritual tempter to the role of physical tempter that he employed in 'The Daemon Lover'. As he cleans up Marcia's apartment, David hears 'faintly down the hall the sound of laughter', which recalls 'The Daemon Lover', and 'the scrape of a chair being moved' and then 'the sound of his radio' (34). We assume that Marcia, due to her envy, melancholy and shame, will be unable to resist the Devil's seduction. Jackson leaves Marcia's actual fate ambiguous. But we know from other stories in the collection such as 'The Daemon Lover' and 'The Tooth', and the Epilogue, that romantic relationships with James Harris result only in despair, madness or destruction. Marcia approximates a younger version of the woman in 'The Daemon Lover' whose romantic hopes will be dashed.

Like the aforementioned two women, Elizabeth Style in the story 'Elizabeth' is a 'rather unhappy and desperate young woman' (150) who lives alone in a one-bedroom apartment where she experiences 'lonely ugly evenings in one chair with one book' (150). Moreover, she too suffers from a sense of shame; in her case both about her failed aspirations and her looks. We are told that she came to New York eleven years ago with 'moderate ambition' (124) to be a writer. Instead, she has ended up working in a third-rate literary agency as a fiction editor for a mediocre and duplicitous agent with whom she is having a sexual relationship. Now, at the age of thirty-one, she compares herself unfavourably with younger prettier women such as Daphne Hill, the innocent young receptionist that her partner/boyfriend hires.

In addition, Elizabeth is a vicious human being. If Marcia possesses one of the cholerick personality traits thought by seventeenth-century Protestants to invite diabolic temptation, Elizabeth possesses all of them. She is spiteful, vengeful, bitter and jealous. We see this early in the story when, angry that a young soda jerk has not submitted his play to her agency, she pushes her way onto a city bus and vengefully elbows another passenger in the ribs in order to get on the bus first (123).

At work, her nastiness continues. She lies to prospective clients and steals their material, and she is dismissive of well-meaning relatives who have come to town and want to see her. Her jealousy boils over when the younger prettier Daphne Hill shows up at the agency and Elizabeth realizes that Robert Shax has hired Daphne without telling her.

In this story James Harris is an adult writer, of some success, who was once a client of the agency. He never appears physically; he is just a photo on the wall and a voice on the telephone. Like the woman in 'The Daemon Lover' and Marcia in 'Like Mother Used to Make', Elizabeth is tempted by Harris, if at a distance. She envisions a romantic relationship with Harris that will allow her to escape her petty life. Accordingly, she calls Harris and makes a date with him for the same night (144). As with Marcia, Elizabeth's interaction with Harris seems to only increase her angry emotions. It is immediately after her interaction with Harris that Elizabeth commits her own particular sin – one much more serious than Marcia's transgression – by firing the innocent and harmless Daphne.

Elizabeth returns to her apartment that night to wait for Harris. Essentially, she is now in the same position as the woman at the end of 'The Daemon Lover'. While waiting for Harris, Elizabeth too fantasizes about the worldly rewards that her relationship with Harris, whom she now imagines as a 'stranger, a gallant dark man with knowing eyes who watched her across a room', will bring her: 'a job and a sunny apartment [. . .] a warm garden, green lawns' (152). At the end, she is left to wait for a man who may never show up and for a blissful escape that will never happen. Elizabeth's position at the end of the story is also ironic and evokes the Puritan concept of vulnerable women. Although Elizabeth believes herself to be the active orchestrator of her future, she is left in a passive role – waiting and yearning for her date with the Devil.

With 'The Tooth' Jackson presents us with a somewhat different type of character but with a similar outcome. Clara Spencer does not live alone in a one-bedroom apartment. She is married with children. Nor does she exhibit many traits associated with anger. Nonetheless, she suffers from her own lonely melancholy. She is stuck in a stagnant marriage. She has long ago lost her own identity; it has been swallowed up by her role of dutiful caretaking wife and mother.

Clara suffers from a bad tooth which must be extracted, and her husband puts her on a bus to New York to see a better dentist than they have in town. The tooth, at least on one level, represents her unsatisfying marriage and has been with her since her wedding day. Her husband tells her that '[I]t's about time something was done. You had a toothache on our honeymoon' (208). Although initially unaware of it, Clara yearns for escape and romantic fulfilment, a return to an earlier freer self. This state of discontent and yearning for emotional and sexual satisfaction aligns with the state of the female soul believed by the Puritans; accordingly, it makes Clara a prime candidate for the seduction of the Devil.

In this story James Harris, who appears to have reassumed the same guise he used in 'The Daemon Lover', is more overtly the diabolic tempter than in any other story in *The Lottery*. Clara first sees him when he touches her arm in an all-night café at a rest stop. Clara, who throughout the journey is half-asleep from codeine, looks up and sees only a man in a blue suit who looks tall (211). Harris then accompanies Clara on the bus all the way to New York. As Richard Capel and Robert Burton observed in the seventeenth century, the Devil can present 'matter immediately to the phantasie of man' and suggest 'devilish thoughts into our hearts'. Throughout the bus ride, Harris intermittently seduces Clara with descriptions of a distant and exotic oriental paradise. The descriptions have a dream-like quality: 'Even farther than Samarkand', he was saying, 'and the waves ringing on the shore like bells' (211). Then later, '[T]he flutes play all night', the strange man said, 'and the stars are as big as the moon and the moon is as big as a lake' (211). As they approach New York, he tells her: '[T]he sand is so white it looks like snow, but it's hot, even at night it's hot under your feet' (213). These fantasies recall the 'golden house-in-the-country future' imagined by the protagonist of 'The Daemon Lover' and the 'warm garden, green lawn' mused on by Elizabeth. In line with the Devil's reputed ability to read minds, these fantasies are tailored to Clara's own subconscious desires which are not for a secure future but for a romantic escape from her stagnant life.

When they get to New York, Harris promises Clara that he will be there waiting for her after she finishes with the dentist. He then appears to vanish into thin air: 'She thought to watch for his blue suit going through the door, but there was nothing' (213).

Jackson portrays the actual extraction of Clara's tooth as a surreal experience. Under the ether, Clara has a dreamy vision, filled with 'ringing confusedly loud music' in which she is running down a long clear hallway and 'at the end of the hallway was Jim, holding out his hands and laughing' (219). When Clara emerges from the ether, she regrets that she was not able to reach Jim in the dream. The rotten tooth is gone and there is blood in her mouth. 'God has given me blood to drink', she tells the nurse (220). This line of dialogue is very revealing. Jackson here again references a scene from a Nathaniel Hawthorne work – here, *The House of the Seven Gables* (1851). In that scene, a man wrongly convicted of witchcraft in Salem warns his accusers from the scaffold that God will give them blood to drink as their punishment. This line further ties this story, and indeed the entire collection, to seventeenth-century New England Puritanism and witchcraft and, by association, to the Devil.

After the extraction, Clara goes into a bathroom in the building, where other women are applying make-up. Angela Hague has noted that Clara enters a new hallucinatory state that involves 'a loss of self and will, a casting away of identity'.[18] She looks into the mirror only to realize that she doesn't know which reflection is hers. She removes her stockings and shoes and lets her hair down and goes out of the building to meet Jim. Apparently taking Jim's hand, she imagines herself running along the white sands past Samarkand with Jim (224). At first glance, we might be tempted to think that Clara has finally been freed from the prison of her stagnant life. But this ending must be read in comparison to the other endings of the stories discussed above. The Devil is a liar. Clara is only running, in a sort of deluded madness, down a New York street. There will be no real escape for her.

'The Witch' is one of the shorter stories in *The Lottery*. It has not received anywhere near the level of critical attention of 'The Daemon Lover', 'The Tooth' or the title story 'The Lottery'. However, I believe that this lack of critical attention is an oversight. I interpret 'The Witch' as being one of the most significant and

---

18. Angela Hague, "'A Faithful Anatomy of Our Times': Reassessing Shirley Jackson", *Frontiers: A Journal of Women Studies* 26, no. 2 (2005): 78.

pivotal stories in the collection because it serves as a counterpoint to the plots of the aforementioned stories and to the type of female vulnerability portrayed in those stories. The plot of 'The Witch' is simple enough: a young mother is travelling by train with her imaginative four-year-old son and infant daughter who is strapped into her seat. The boy is entertaining himself by looking out the window and naming everything he sees: a river, a bridge, a cow (53). His mother, patient and composed, humours him by nodding and occasionally saying, 'Fine' (53).

When the boy claims to have seen a 'big old ugly old bad old witch', James Harris, as if on cue, enters the train car. He is again wearing his trademark blue suit but is this time an elderly man with white hair. He begins talking to the boy in at first a benign manner. When he asks the boy his name, the suspicious boy answers: 'Mr. Jesus'. The mother's reaction here is telling. Clearly displeased with the boy's statement, she admonishes him: '"*Johnny*," the little boy's mother said. She caught the little boy's eye and frowned deeply' (54). James Harris then begins telling a story about his own little sister. Harris's motivation here is ambiguous, although clearly malicious. He is not tempting the mother but is more likely attempting to corrupt the child. His story begins innocently enough, relating his memory of his little sister whom he loved more than anything else in the world, but it soon turns completely Satanic as Harris tells the boy that he pinched and pinched the girl 'until she was dead', and then 'cut off her head and her hands and her feet and her hair and her nose' (55). The mother is caught off guard for a moment. Her smile fades and '[S]he opened her mouth, and then closed it again' (55).

At this point, Joan Wylie Hall, in her leading work on Jackson's short stories, *Shirley Jackson: A Study of the Short Fiction*, which offers excellent observations on other tales, completely misinterprets 'The Witch' because she fails to recognize the biblical subtext. She claims that the mother becomes helpless and 'distressed' and is 'deprived of control', even the control of her own voice.[19] In fact, nothing could be further from the truth. Indeed, the mother is the only character in *The Lottery* who is able to banish Harris from her presence, likely because she seemingly does not possess any of the traits such as melancholy, shame, doubt or envy that make the female characters discussed above vulnerable to Harris. The mother has a very clear sense of who she is and what she must do to protect her son. After recovering from her initial shock, she tells Harris: '[J]ust what do you think you're doing? [...] Get out of here' (56). When Harris does not immediately leave, she warns him that she can easily call the conductor. As Harris gets up to go, the mother firmly tells him: 'Don't ever come back in this car.' Harris, now defeated, simply says, 'Excuse me' and leaves. The little boy, unfazed, goes back to looking out the window.

Other critical readings of the story have also missed the point. Hague, in her very brief mention of the story, focuses only on the boy's nature. In a more recent reading of the story, L. N. Rosales, following Hall, also claims that the

---

19. Joan Wylie Hall, *Shirley Jackson: A Study of the Short Fiction* (New York: Twayne Publishers, 1993), p. 22.

mother has been rendered powerless by Harris and stripped of her agency, going so far as to assert that '[I]t does not matter that the man left the carriage at her prompting, because the interaction still haunts her'.[20] Putting aside the issue that there is no proof that the mother is haunted by the encounter, this reading also fails to recognize the biblical subtext, and further fails to acknowledge the difference between the mother's active response to Harris's sinister overtures and the passive yielding to Harris that we have seen in the other stories discussed earlier. In comparison to the female protagonists in those stories, the mother in 'The Witch' appears to be the only female who *does* assert her agency in the face of James Harris.

The interaction between the mother and Harris must be read in conjunction with the earlier reference to the mother's strong reaction to the boy's mild blasphemy. That scene is perhaps the only place in the collection where religion becomes part of the plot. The likely reason for Jackson to insert that anomalous exchange is to imply that the mother is a believing Christian and to contrast the mother with the other vulnerable female characters discussed above. Her exercise of will to banish Harris then may, on one level, be interpreted in light of the New Testament and seventeenth-century Protestant theology. Effectively, the mother's firm and unambiguous banishment of Harris recapitulates Christ's banishment of Satan in the wilderness. An awareness of this biblical subtext enriches our understanding of Jackson's continued engagement throughout the collection with the Calvinist themes of diabolic temptation and diabolic resistance. It allows us to place 'The Witch' within the greater context of the collection and to give it greater prominence than previous critics have allowed.

The collection ends with the Epilogue taken directly from *James Harris, The Daemon Lover (Child Ballad No. 243)*, a Scottish ballad. A young woman is lured by Harris to leave her husband with apparent promises of worldly riches and a romantic destination. However, shortly after boarding Harris's ship, she sees his cloven foot and realizes he is the Devil. She then sees their true destination: the desolate icy mountains of Hell (239). James Harris then sinks the ship, drowning her. This vision of Hell as cold and desolate rather than a place of fire and brimstone also draws on seventeenth-century Protestant concepts. The New Testament described a physical Hell that was a place of 'wailing and grinding of teeth', Mt. 8.12, as well as a place of 'unquenchable fire', Mt. 3.12. This vision of Hell as a place of physical pain and torture continued into the Middle Ages and on into the Renaissance as with Dante's *Inferno*. However, in the seventeenth century Protestant concepts of Hell became more complex. Physical torment remained a feature of Hell but became mixed with spiritual torment. It came to be understood that damnation was also existential in nature, and that the damned would also suffer the potentially greater

---

20. L. N. Rosales, '"Sharp Points Closing in on Her Throat": The Domestic Gothic in Shirley Jackson's Short Fiction', in *Shirley Jackson and Domesticity: Beyond the Haunted House*, ed. Jill E. Anderson and Melanie R. Anderson (London: Bloomsbury Academic, 2020), pp. 86–9.

torture of being eternally cut off and isolated from God's grace. As William C. Creasy notes: 'The image so solidly established during the Middle Ages and early Renaissance of Dante's burning fires and eternal, unbearable physical torment had slowly shifted to focus on a hell of isolation and despair. The fires still burned in the Pit, but in the seventeenth century it was primarily spiritual suffering – the *poena damni* – on which eternal damnation rested.'[21] This concept is perhaps nowhere more powerfully expressed than in Christopher Marlowe's *The Tragical History of Dr. Faustus* (1601) in which Mephistopheles explains to Faustus that Hell is not located in one specific physical place of fire and brimstone but, for those angels who fell with Satan, is an existential state of spiritual despair at being cut off from God which follows them wherever they go: 'where we are is hell, And where hell is there must we ever be.'[22]

This concept of Hell as an existential state of isolation and despair sheds light on the fates of the women of Jackson's 'The Daemon Lover', 'Elizabeth', 'The Tooth' and possibly 'Like Mother Used to Make.' As a state of mind, Hell can exist not only after life but during life. Indeed, seventeenth-century Protestants saw the Devil as driving victims to earthly despair. Jackson suggests that their relationships with James Harris have condemned, or will condemn, the above women to loneliness, frustration and sorrow while they are alive and, if we take the Epilogue as being prophetic, perhaps to a journey to the mountains of Hell after they are dead.

In the stories discussed earlier, Shirley Jackson suggests that the Devil is real and that those emotional weaknesses of melancholy, self-doubt, discontent, shame, and anger which were thought to make women vulnerable to the Devil in the seventeenth century could pose the same danger to women in the twentieth century. However, this should not be construed to mean that Jackson thought that all women were weak, sad, envious, and unconfident and therefore prey for the Devil, but rather that women who did not overcome those traits in themselves were at risk. At the same time, strong women, who were sure of their identities and their worth, like the woman in 'The Witch', whether such assurance came through faith or through simple self-confidence, could, as Capel and Boehme also promised centuries ago, assert their inherent willpower to repel the evil that opposed them. In this sense, the mother in 'The Witch' also aligns with such active Jackson women as Natalie Waite and Merricat Blackwood who are ultimately able to assert their will against diabolic figures.

This analysis of the characters of the female protagonists in 'The Daemon Lover', 'Like Mother Used to Make', 'Elizabeth', 'The Tooth' and 'The Witch' in light of seventeenth-century concepts of diabolic temptation, diabolic resistance, and Hell, which have not been heretofore greatly discussed, can provide the reader

---

21. William C. Creasy, 'The Shifting Landscape of Hell', *Comitatus: A Journal of Medieval and Renaissance Studies* 11, no. 1 (1980): 40–64.

22. Christopher Marlowe, *Dr. Faustus*, ed. Sylvan Barnet (New York: Signet Classics, 2010), p. 65.

of Jackson with a greater understanding of the interactions and endings of those stories which might otherwise appear murky and ambiguous. It can add resonance to the stories through their link with history and reveal for the reader the true importance – and perhaps the necessary reinclusion – of Jackson's choice of subtitle for the collection: *The Adventures of James Harris*.

References

Barnet, Sylvan, ed. (2010), *Dr. Faustus*, New York: Signet Classics.
Boehme, Jacob (1701), *The Four Complexions Or, A Treatise of Consolatory Instruction Against the Time of Temptation For A Sad And Assaulted Heart*, London: Printed for J. Scott at the Black Swan in Pater-Noster.
Bonikowski, Wyatt (2013), '"Only One Antagonist": The Daemon Lover and the Feminine Experience', *Gothic Studies* 15 (2): 66–88.
Brooks, Thomas (1832), *The Precious Remedies Against Satan's Devices*, New Haven: Nathan Whiting.
Burton, Robert (1826), *The Anatomy of Melancholy, What It Is, with All the Kinds, Causes, Symptoms, Prognostics and Several Cures of It*, London: Printed for Thomas MacLean, Haymarket.
Capel, Richard (1633), *Tentations their Nature, Danger, and Cure*, London: Printed by R. Badger.
Carpenter, Lynette (1984), 'The Establishment and Preservation of Female Power in Shirley Jackson's *We Have Always Lived in the Castle*', *Frontiers: A Journal of Women Studies* 8 (1): 32–8.
Creasy, William C. (1980), 'The Shifting Landscape of Hell', *Comitatus: A Journal of Medieval and Renaissance Studies* 11 (1): 40–64.
Franklin, Ruth (2017), *Shirley Jackson: A Rather Haunted Life*, New York: Liveright Publishing Corporation.
Glanvill, Joseph (1683), *Saducismus Triumphatis: Or, full and plain Evidence Concerning Witches and Apparitions*, London: Printed by A.L.
Hague, Angela (2005), '"A Faithful Anatomy of Our Times": Reassessing Shirley Jackson', *Frontiers: A Journal of Women Studies* 26 (2): 73–96.
Hall, Joan Wylie (1993), *Shirley Jackson: A Study of the Short Fiction*, New York: Twayne Publishers.
Hallett, Adrian (1991), 'The Theology of John Calvin. Part Three: The Christians Conflict with the Devil', *Churchman* 105: 293–325.
Johnstone, Nathan (2004), 'The Protestant Devil: The Experience of Temptation in Early Modern England', *Journal of British Studies* 43: 173–205.
Landau, Samantha (2018), 'Occult Influences in Shirley Jackson's "The Lottery"', *Gakuen* 936: 11–21.
Mather, Increase (1684), *An Essay for the Recording of Illustrious Providences: Wherein an Account is given of Many Remarkable and Very Memorable Events which have hapned [sic] this Last Age, Especially in New England*, Boston: Printed by Samuel Green for Joseph Browning.
Oates, Joyce Carol, ed. (2010), *Shirley Jackson Novels and Stories*, New York: The Library of America.

Reis, Elizabeth (1995), 'The Devil, the Body, and the Feminine Soul in Puritan New England', *The Journal of American History* 82 (1): 15–36.
Rosales, L. N. (2020), '"Sharp Points Closing in on Her Throat": Shirley Jackson's Short Fiction', in J. Anderson and M. Anderson (eds), *Shirley Jackson and Domesticity: Beyond the Haunted House*, 86–9, London: Bloomsbury Academic.

Chapter 7

'MISSING' WOMEN

SPECTRAL DISPLACEMENT IN SHIRLEY JACKSON'S SHORT FICTION

Robert Lloyd

In her 1993 study of Shirley Jackson's then-published short fiction, Joan Wylie Hall observes how her stories deal with characters who 'become enmeshed in extraordinary situations that either free them or, more often, trap them'.[1] These women – 'typically in their twenties and thirties' – are just one example of the various orders of female protagonists Hall identifies in Jackson's oeuvre (along with 'the unmarried urban woman' and 'the country housewife'), all of whom are 'subject to anxiety and crisis' in one form or another.[2] In a similar vein, Melanie R. Anderson suggests in her introduction to *Shirley Jackson and Domesticity* (2020) that a characteristic feature of Jackson's writing is 'her penchant for linking the position of women in 1950s America to gothic themes of the uncanny and entrapment'.[3] These two assessments, published twenty-seven years apart, underline the degree to which Jackson deals with what might be termed femininity-in-crisis: through her fiction, the gendered experience of everyday life is transformed into a gothic drama which stages the threat of women's entrapment and diminished presence within their own lives, to the point where the viability of their autonomy and agency begins to break down. Nowhere is this process seen more clearly than in Jackson's figuration of the 'missing' or 'lost' woman. The missing woman is the attenuation of identity taken to its logical extreme, and one which serves as a pronounced inscription of the inescapably spectral character of femininity in 1950s America.

Missing women are, so to speak, everywhere in Jackson's texts. Indeed, it can be argued that they constitute the most significant category of female characters in her short fiction because they are the victims of a process which affects all of the

---

1. Joan Wylie Hall, *Shirley Jackson: A Study of the Short Fiction* (New York: Twayne, 1993), p. xii.

2. Hall, *Shirley Jackson*, p. xii, p. xiii.

3. Melanie R. Anderson, 'Introduction', in *Shirley Jackson and Domesticity: Beyond the Haunted House*, ed. Jill E. Anderson and Melanie R. Anderson (New York and London: Bloomsbury, 2020), pp. 1–6 (p. 2).

women who populate these stories, as summarized by Hall. In *A Study of the Short Fiction*, she suggests that the female characters depicted in these texts 'struggle to declare their selfhood' because there are always 'obstacles to attaining a secure sense of identity'.[4] Although she does not explicitly invoke the idea of women who are missing in this observation, Hall's description of characters who are denied a clear expression of identity points to a situation in which women are never quite 'present' in their stories; in this struggle for finding and securing a clear sense of self, they are only part successful. As a result, women in Jackson's stories can be said to 'embody a postwar sensibility of dislocation and loss'.[5] It is suitably ironic that the 'missing women' of these stories serve as the most visible (dis)embodiments of a wider cultural displacement of femininity, a configuration which haunts the domestic and urban milieux from which these women disappear.

Almost all of Jackson's protagonists express concern over their capacity to be noticed or listened to: one can think of Natalie's inability to speak to her family about her sexual assault and subsequent trauma in *Hangsaman* (1951), and Toni's negotiation of the complex dynamic between recognition and anonymity that animates 'Nightmare' (1996). These experiences result from, and therefore reflect, a wider cultural anxiety surrounding women's social visibility and what should be done about it, which characterized both popular and political discourse in the immediate aftermath of the Second World War.[6] The subsequent (re)codification of female gender roles as coextensive with the domestic sphere paralleled the diminished visibility and presence of women within the most public arrangements of space. It is perhaps no accident that the feminist discourse which emerges out of this culture and its immediate aftermath is deeply invested in the gothicized language of spectral conditioning, so that 'one of the most powerful metaphors in feminist theory [has been] the idea of the woman as "dead" or "buried (alive)" within male power structures which render her "ghostly"'.[7] Diana Wallace's parenthetical '(alive)' is significant, because it maintains the possibility of reading ghostliness and haunting beyond the narrow confines of the dead returned to life. Instead, ghostliness becomes a condition by which women are made to live *in the first place*, rather than as a belated *return* to living after or beyond death.

The selection of short stories analysed in this chapter – all of which were published in the posthumous collection *Just an Ordinary Day* (1996) – demonstrate how 'missing' is a polyvalent term. Although there are characters who physically disappear, there are equally significant configurations of metaphorical

---

4. Hall, *Shirley Jackson*, p. xiii.

5. Hall, *Shirley Jackson*, p. xiv.

6. William H. Chaffe describes this dynamic in detail in *The Paradox of Change: American Women in the 20th Century*. See in particular the chapter 'The Debate on Woman's Place', pp. 174–93.

7. Diana Wallace, '"The Haunting Idea": Female Gothic Metaphors and Feminist Theory', in *The Female Gothic: New Directions*, ed. Diana Wallace and Andrew Smith (Basingstoke: Palgrave Macmillan, 2009), pp. 26–41 (p. 26).

disappearance or erasure at work. A number of Jackson's short stories address the phenomenon of substitution, wherein one identity is swapped or exchanged for another (or, sometimes, for no alternative at all). This figuration of substitution operates through a spectral dynamic of presence-absence, and so my analysis draws upon Esther Peeren's conceptualization of missing persons as 'living ghosts' in *The Spectral Metaphor*. While a missing person might be assumed to be simply 'absent' (since this is the very condition which first invites attention), Peeren argues instead that 'the elusive fate of the missing, even when their death is virtually certain, works to preserve and extend their lives in the minds of those left behind [. . .] While they cannot be seen, they remain present; those looking for them know that they, or their remains, must be somewhere.'[8] Peeren is careful to note the differences between more substantial forms of apparitionality – such as the spirits conjured by a medium – and the ghostliness of the missing: this latter group are not attended by a 'surplus of signification' but, rather, 'mark a lack of meaning and knowledge'.[9] Although substitution and disappearance are not perfect synonyms, both participate in the operations of displacement or dislocation, particularly with regards to the consequent conditions of expressing agency. As Peeren notes:

> The association between missing persons and victimhood indicates the degree to which the missing are deprived of agency. Their vanishing is seen as something that happens or is done to them and, after disappearing, they can no longer speak for themselves but have to be spoken for and imagined by others.[10]

Passivity becomes the hallmark of the missing person, and this is a recurring element in Jackson's short stories. In 'The Good Wife', a jealous and paranoid husband incarcerates his wife while he writes letters which appropriate her voice and character. In 'The Missing Girl', the disappearance of a teenager from a summer camp is resolved when the adults responsible for her safety collude to deny her existence in the first place – she cannot be 'missing', because there is no 'she' to miss. The forced erasure of these characters is perpetrated on an expectation of unarticulated agency, and in so doing, brings into existence that same passivity.

This diminishment of the female subject is also what defines the function of spectral displacement: the (ultimately unsuccessful) struggle to find a secure

---

8. Esther Peeren, *The Spectral Metaphor: Living Ghosts and the Agency of Invisibility* (Basingstoke and New York: Palgrave Macmillan, 2014), p. 144.

9. Peeren, *The Spectral Metaphor*, p. 144.

This dynamic between a 'profusion' and 'lack' of signification also maps onto the different modalities of spectral subjectivity between Jackson's novels and short stories, particularly the feminine multiplicity of *The Bird's Nest*. Part of the apparatus which defines Elizabeth Richmond as spectral is that her plurality exceeds the reader's capacity to understand her as an individual, whereas it is the inability to signify sufficiently which constitutes the spectral 'lack' of the various female characters in the short stories discussed in this chapter.

10. Peeren, *The Spectral Metaphor*, p. 145.

localization (in time and/or place) that enables the women of these stories to signify as fully present individuals. This displacement is not uniform, affecting characters to different degrees depending on their situation. However, each of the stories I analyse in this chapter evinces a shared preoccupation with women's experience of being in the world, and the tension between this and the conditions that attenuate their presence, thereby rendering them spectral within their particular environments. This evanescence of individuality, of a secure sense of self that is continually displaced, is evidence for what I read as a seam of figurative spectralization that runs through the centre of Jackson's short fiction, one that has been underappreciated in previous scholarship, and which makes a claim on Jackson as a writer of unexpectedly spectral stories.

Aberrant Adolescence: 'The Missing Girl'

Appearing in the December 1957 issue of *The Magazine of Fantasy and Science Fiction*, 'The Missing Girl' offers the most literal instantiation of the vanished or erased woman in Jackson's short fiction. Martha Alexander disappears from Phillips Education Camp for Girls Twelve to Sixteen, having told her roommate Betsy, in a rather cryptic manner, that she has 'something to do' that night.[11] When she fails to return after three days, Betsy informs the Camp Mother – Old Jane – about her disappearance, whereupon the police are called in and a series of searches commence. Although she is Martha's roommate, Betsy knows almost nothing definitive about her, from her camp year – 'Woodsprite, I *think*' – to the activities in which she was involved – 'Dramatics? I think she went to Dramatics'.[12] Betsy's relationship with Martha is marked by uncertainty and a lack of knowledge, two of the qualities which Peeren argues are generated by, and come to define, the figure of the missing person.[13]

However, Martha's absence is not the *cause* of this lack of knowledge, because it is only after her disappearance that it is discovered how little people know about her. This suggests that even before she goes missing, Martha is not a fully 'present' character to those around her. She does not disappear from a place in which she is a visible or perceptible presence, but from one in which she is already quasi-absent in terms of what people know about her. Betsy illustrates this particularly pointedly when she tries to recollect any useful details she can give to the chief of police:

Betsy thought again, remembering as well as she could the sleeping figure in the other bed, the soiled laundry on the floor, the open suitcase, the tin boxes of

---

11. Shirley Jackson, 'The Missing Girl', in *Just an Ordinary Day*, ed. Laurence Jackson Hyman and Sarah Hyman DeWitt (London: Penguin, 2017), pp. 373–85 (p. 373). All further references are to this edition.
12. Jackson, 'The Missing Girl', p. 375, p. 377.
13. Peeren, *The Spectral Metaphor*, p. 144.

cookies, the towels, the face cloths, the soap, the pencils. . . . 'She had her own clock,' Betsy volunteered.[14]

Despite her best efforts at remembering Martha, Betsy can only summon memories of her possessions, the material objects which attest to her one-time presence rather than any details about Martha or *her* materiality. What is striking about Betsy's attempted recollection is her fixation on the clock as an object she associates particularly with her missing roommate. Although it is a marker of Martha's presence that persists after her disappearance, the clock also serves to remind the reader of the amount of time she has been missing. It attests to her position between the 'here' and the 'not-here', between the visible and the invisible dimensions of being present and absent, and so, more than anything, the clock associates Martha with a dis-location which, in combination with her adolescence, is inexorably spectral.

Martha has moved outside the normal flow of time; she is not 'present' within the present but has become desynchronized, a condition that Derrida famously terms the '*non-contemporaneity with itself of the living present*'.[15] It is this quality of being out-of-time with herself that marks Martha as spectral, through her imperfect absence, since it is 'ghosts [that] invoke and perform this non-contemporaneity; they persist as an untimely time that destabilizes the order of things'.[16] Martha's compromised absence/imperfect presence destabilizes time as well as the clear distinction between 'presence' and 'absence', but it also draws attention to the way in which 'the present' is always in a state of 'untimeliness', since it is 'never constituted by being "in" the moment but rather being *undone* by the moment [. . .] never "now" but always "now" and "not now," or "now" and "other"'.[17] Martha is rendered ghostly by her disappearance, but this ghostliness in turn exposes the spectral (dis)arrangement of the present she leaves behind.

Martha's literal disappearance is further compounded by the partial or ineffective attempts at recording her presence in both writing and memory. When the search of her room yields no useful discoveries, an attempt is made to establish the pastimes in which she participated:

> A careful checkup of Recreational Activity lists showed that while she was listed for dramatics and nature study and swimming, her attendance at any of them was dubious; most of the counselors kept slipshod attendance records, and none

---

14. Jackson, 'The Missing Girl', p. 377.

15. Jacques Derrida, *Specters of Marx: The State of the Debt, the Work of Mourning, and the New International*, trans. by Peggy Kamuf (New York and London: Routledge, 1994), p. xix.

16. Patricia M. Keller, *Ghostly Landscapes: Film, Photography, and the Aesthetics of Haunting in Contemporary Spanish Culture* (Toronto: University of Toronto Press, 2016), p. 5.

17. Keller, *Ghostly Landscapes*, p. 5.

of them could remember whether any such girl could have come on any given day.[18]

Even in those places where Martha's name does appear, where an attempt is made to establish her past-presence, this merely demonstrates the problem of locating her. Her 'dubious' attendance at any of these activities does not suggest that she does *not* attend the sessions but, rather, that her doing so cannot be established definitively. Just as Martha is suspended between presence and absence by the material traces she leaves behind, the records which should establish her appearance unambiguously instead (dis)locate her between 'here' and 'not-here'. This administrative incompleteness is strangely reflected in the attitude the counsellors have towards their adolescent charges: 'one girl is much like another, at *this* age. Their unformed minds, their unformed bodies, their little mistakes.'[19] The girls themselves are viewed as only partial, as subjects-in-formation rather than fixed, readily identifiable individuals. There is an implied association between this incomplete registration and fledgling identity, as if these girls – and Martha in particular – are susceptible to disappearing because they are not fully 'present' as adult women.

As Deborah Martin argues, the female adolescent is 'an uncanny figure *par excellence*, on the border of personhood in more ways than one. As both female and child, she twice challenges categorization as a "proper" subject, embodying anxieties about categorization and posing a double threat to the power relations of patriarchy'.[20] Martha's adolescent liminality makes her predisposed to the same semantic slipperiness as the spectre, belonging to multiple categories without ever inhabiting any one in particular. Jackson replicates the female adolescent's doubled-experience of un/belonging (and the problem of categorization) in the way the adults, the invigilators of patriarchal standards of femininity, do (or, perhaps, choose) not to keep track of Martha in their records, and, moreover, use this as the basis for 'solving' the categorical difficulty she represents.

To the problem of her physical disappearance, the adults propose an administrative solution. Rather than continue the search, the authority figures – particularly Old Jane and Martha's uncle – conspire to erase Martha completely by suggesting that she was not, and never has been, 'present', and so cannot have disappeared at all. They literalize the conceptual non-position between presence and absence through which she has been defined during her time at the camp – to their minds, this denies the very possibility of her being missing, since there is no figure which presupposes the act of disappearance. The only response that denies her disappearance is an even more thorough erasure, one which writes her out of existence:

18. Jackson, 'The Missing Girl', p. 378.
19. Jackson, 'The Missing Girl', p. 379.
20. Deborah Martin, 'Feminine Adolescence as Uncanny: Masculinity, Haunting and Self-Estrangement', *Forum for Modern Language Studies* 49, no. 2 (February 2013): 135–44 (p. 138).

Old Jane nodded and shuffled the papers in her hand. 'I have all the records here,' she said. 'Although a girl named Martha Alexander applied for admission to the Phillips Educational Camp for Girls Twelve to Sixteen, her application was put into the file marked 'possibly undesirable' and there is no record of her ever having come to the camp. Although her name has been entered upon various class lists, she is not noted as having participated personally in any activity.'[21]

Peeren has noted the degree to which the missing person is dependent upon those who are left behind to formulate or put into effect the conditions through which they can remain 'present' after their disappearance: 'most missing persons [. . .] are incapable of engineering their own recognition; they, or rather, the void left by their unexplained removal, can be conjured only by others, on their terms.'[22] What Peeren does not account for in her theorization is the desire for *non*-conjuration which might motivate those who are left behind. Those in a position to decide whether the missing girl will be recognized propose instead a kind of double disappearance: a literal one overlain with an administrative erasure from records which establish her prior existence, however tentatively. In doing so, Jackson's story demonstrates the multivalence of apparitionality: it does not just involve the dimensions of (im)material presence but of social and interpersonal relationships – the way in which the ghost or ghosted figure is apprehended or directed by non-spectral characters. This exemplifies what Patricia Keller means when she observes that 'haunting [. . .] is always a form of social mediation'.[23] Despite its ability to disrupt order and convention, the 'ghostliness' of the ghost is not solely within its ability to control; as Peeren notes in *The Spectral Metaphor*, 'the ghost is a metaphor certain people (are made to) live *as*' – it is not a condition of their choosing.[24]

The quality of being 'possibly undesirable' is particularly significant in explicating the motivation for Martha's erasure. Her uncle reveals that he has been sent a letter from her mother (which the reader does not get to read in full), whose contents he summarizes for those present:

'What I *mean*,' he said, looking around again, 'she has three girls and a boy, my sister [. . .] The oldest girl, that's Helen, she's married and out in San Francisco, so that's *her*. And – I'll show you my sister's letter – the second girl, that's Jane, well, *she's* married and *she* lives in Texas somewhere, has a little boy about two years old. And then the third girl – well, *that's* Mabel, and she's right at home with her mother, around the house and whatnot. Well – you see what I mean?'[25]

---

21. Jackson, 'The Missing Girl', p. 384.
22. Peeren, *The Spectral Metaphor*, p. 146.
23. Keller, *Ghostly Landscapes*, p. 7.
24. Peeren, *The Spectral Metaphor*, p. 6.
25. Jackson, 'The Missing Girl', pp. 383–4.

Martha's uncle equivocates as to what exactly he means, but there are two principal ways to read his suggestion. The first is that the mother denies that Martha is her daughter at all – she has 'three girls and a boy', all of whom are accounted for within some form of domestic arrangement. The more nuanced reading suggests that Martha is rendered invisible or un-locatable within the family due to the conceptually problematic nature of her adolescence, what Martin terms 'the constitutive strangeness of this life-stage'.[26] The three daughters mentioned in the letter are all explicitly defined through their domestic status – the eldest two are both married, with families of their own, with the remaining one 'right at home with her mother, around the house and whatnot'. In other words, they represent a fixed version of femininity which is easily locatable, both conceptually and physically. As an adolescent girl, Martha's position outside some conception of 'home' makes her, as Old Jane says, 'undesirable'.

She is, then, a doubly liminal figure in her figuration as a missing teenage girl, the not-quite child/not-quite adult whose absence is indicated by the persistence of objects and items which indicate her presence. The double disappearance which is enforced upon Martha is a response to the categoric disruption she represents as a young girl outside the home who is not married or might never be married. Indeed, she might be 'undesirable' because she does not wish to define herself in relation to any kind of matrimonial-domestic arrangement, a flagrant rejection of feminine propriety that Lily Robert-Foley wryly parodies when she asks, 'what is more terrifying: a spinster or a ghost?'[27] If Martha is incommensurate with categories of domestic containment, and as such embodies a conceptual challenge to an associated configuration of femininity, her spectral erasure becomes the least 'terrifying' possibility to those charged with restoring normality. As Diane Long Hoeveler observes about Jackson's story, its significance can be found 'in the way a young life is thrown away, discarded, snuffed out with absolutely no consequences at all'.[28] To (be made to) disappear is more acceptable than being permitted to enact any kind of social disruption.

The logic of substitution is twofold in 'The Missing Girl'. Martha's problematic conceptual position is translated into a revoking of any notion of 'presence', thereby turning her, essentially, into a ghost whose uncertain location between life and death remains unresolved throughout the text and at its end. Although a body is found a little over a year after the disappearance, there is only the suggestion that it 'might have been Martha Alexander's'.[29] This uncertainty maintains the possibility

---

26. Martin, 'Feminine Adolescence as Uncanny', p. 135.

27. Lily Robert-Foley, 'Haunted Readings of Female Gothic Short Stories', *Short Fiction in Theory and Practice* 7, no. 2 (October 2017): 177–92 (p. 179).

28. Diane Long Hoeveler, 'Life Lessons in Shirley Jackson's Late Fiction: Ethics, Cosmology, Eschatology', in *Shirley Jackson: Essays on the Literary Legacy*, ed. Bernice M. Murphy (Jefferson: McFarland, 2005), pp. 267–80 (p. 269).

29. Jackson, 'The Missing Girl', p. 384.

of a future return, thereby perpetuating her spectral subjectivity.[30] At the same time, the story makes clear that Martha is in some sense synecdochical, an 'embodiment' of adolescent femininity in general and a prime candidate for spectralization. One of the principal reasons so little is known about Martha as an individual is that she cannot be easily distinguished from many of the other girls in the camp, particularly in terms of her appearance. As the narrator observes: 'It was not possible to get a picture of the girl; the picture on her camp application blank was so blurred that it resembled a hundred other girls in the camp'.[31] Martha's unclear identity is rendered photographically in her blurred features, but, perhaps counter-intuitively, this establishes a connection with the 'hundred other girls in the camp' to whom she bears a resemblance. This same association is made by the swimming counsellor, who asks police chief Hook, 'did you ever look at fifty girls all in white bathing caps?' - the suggestion being that it is impossible to differentiate between those who look so similar.[32] In the de-individuation associated with her spectrality, Martha functions as a representation for a broader conception of adolescent femininity, underlining the fact that the circumstances of her spectral erasure are by no means restricted to her alone. Martin Scofield argues that this encompassing of the personal/private with a wider social significance is particularly suited to short fiction because the short story 'is perhaps the exemplary form for the perception of crisis, crux, turning point; and as such it has proved ideal for recording decisive moments, intimately private but often with broad social resonances'.[33] In the account of one adolescent girl's disappearance, Jackson uses these conventions of the short story to dramatize, and take to their logical extremes, social and cultural attitudes towards certain forms of femininity – adolescent, transitory, disruptive – which are not confined to a domestic setting, a theme which she also explores in 'Nightmare'.

'X' and the City: 'Nightmare'

Where 'The Missing Girl' uses the conceptually disruptive force of spectrality to interrogate social responses to adolescence, 'Nightmare' takes as its focus the attenuation of individuality which women experience in urban spaces. Toni Morgan works as a secretary in an unspecified corporation, and the narrative

---

30. The narrative both sustains and is founded upon the ghostly possibilities of Martha making a ghostly return, but this is complicated by the fact that she may not be recognized or accepted in the process, given the degree and nature of her erasure. Under such circumstances, any possible reappearance would be decidedly Derridean, a '[r]epetition *and* first time' in which 'the spirit comes by *coming back* [revenant]'. See Derrida, *Specters of Marx*, p. 10.
31. Jackson, 'The Missing Girl', p. 380.
32. Jackson, 'The Missing Girl', p. 379.
33. Martin Scofield, *The Cambridge Introduction to the American Short Story* (Cambridge: Cambridge University Press, 2006), p. 238.

sees her being tasked to deliver a package across town for her boss, Mr Lang. As opposed to Martha and her sisters in 'The Missing Girl', Toni's professional identity affords her some freedom from the domestic sphere – her occupation seemingly allows her to move outside the home without conjuring the same anxieties about the propriety of her situation.[34] However, as William Chafe has argued, the distinction between the private/domestic and public/professional worlds is not as oppositional as might be supposed: 'If a woman worked in a secretarial position,' he points out, 'she was described as nurturant and "wifely" in the way she took care of her boss.'[35] Reviewing the position of the woman-worker in social and cultural discourses of the post-/war years, Chafe points out that women's visibility and presence within the workplace had to be rationalized and approved according to a predetermined metaphorical schema in which professional femininity was overlain with domestic attributes and characteristics. The working woman of this period was a figure suspended between 'the home' and 'the office' as sites of identity-production, and became part of a discursive formation which both raised and perpetuated anxieties about women outside the home. Toni's mobility is therefore 'permissible' because she carries the haunting trace of these domestic expectations into her secretarial work, in addition to the material package she is charged with delivering. Her freedom of movement is literally weighed down by this symbol of her male employer, one whose double meaning as 'slang for sexual parts' leads Hoeveler to read this task as a form of punishment and humiliation that is enacted against Toni 'for seeking employment outside of the home'.[36] While her venturing into the city might be read as an escape from this configuration, it is nonetheless significant that her license for doing so is not self-derived; although it is during her time out on the streets that the most explicit spectral components of the narrative are realized, Toni 'begins' the narrative as an already-haunted figure.

As her trip across town begins, Toni asks a newspaper vendor for directions, and in doing so, her attention is drawn to a poster on the inside of the newspaper stand:

---

34. Toni is also older than Martha, closer to the age of the latter's sisters, albeit without their maternal commitments. However, Hoeveler argues that the story 'is written from a dependent and frightened child's point of view, a child who is powerless to do anything other than obey commands and follow orders she does not understand'. This tension between her actual age and the child-like register of her narrative perspective suggests that Toni is more of an unsettled presence in her story than might initially be guessed, subject to a haunting reversion to immaturity as she moves throughout the city. This tendency to infantilize subjects who are haunted can be seen throughout Jackson's corpus, and finds its clearest expression in the characterization of Eleanor in *The Haunting of Hill House*. See Hoeveler, 'Life Lessons in Shirley Jackson's Late Fiction', p. 270.

35. William H. Chafe, *The Paradox of Change: American Women in the 20th Century* (Oxford: Oxford University Press, 1991), p. 124.

36. Hoeveler, 'Life Lessons in Shirley Jackson's Late Fiction', p. 271.

'Find Miss X,' the poster said in screaming red letters, 'Find Miss X. Find Miss X. Find Miss X.' The words were repeated over and over, each line smaller and in a different color; the bottom line was barely visible.[37]

Initially, Toni's interest in Miss X appears to be minimal, but this changes once a sound truck appears, offering advice for how passers-by might spot the mysterious figure: '"Miss X" is walking the streets of the city, completely alone. She is wearing a blue hat with a red feather, blue gloves, and dark blue shoes.'[38] These clothes are identical to the ones Toni is wearing, which are described extensively in the opening paragraph of the story. Toni's response is to try and alter her appearance, by removing some items – 'she slid off her blue gloves and rolled them up and put them in her pocketbook' – modifying others – '[s]he buttoned her coat to hide the blue suit' – or else substituting them for new ones – 'Put my old hat in a box and I'll wear this one.'[39] However, these attempts at instantiating her difference from 'Miss X' are unsuccessful because the advertisement acknowledges, and keeps pace with, the changes: 'Miss X has changed her clothes now, but she is still walking alone through the streets of the city, find Miss X! Miss X is now wearing a gray and red hat, and is carrying *two* packages; don't forget, *two* packages.'[40] All of this suggests an adaptive form of doubling, with 'Miss X' being figured as Toni's sartorial double, an unperceived or secret 'other' who nonetheless haunts Toni as a (self-)fashioned spectre for whom she could be substituted. In her work on Gothic fashion, Catherine Spooner argues that clothing has a particularly significant association with spectrality. It attests to the immanence of the body within both the culture of everyday life and critical/discursive accounts, because 'the body in Western culture is inarticulable except through clothes.'[41] At the same time, this 'fabric-ation' of the subject can lead to the 'erasure or effacement of the body beneath' the clothing, since these clothes which signify the body's presence can be taken off or exchanged, or the signification of the clothes themselves can overwrite the subject's own meaning – as Spooner puts it, 'the body is perpetually collapsing under its sartorial freight.'[42] Although 'Miss X' appears to exemplify this idea of bodily erasure through clothing – she has no 'form' other than what she wears – their shared sartorial situation invites a reading of Toni as an increasingly spectral figure as well.

Toni's haunting is inexorably linked to walking around the city; the further she moves away from the office, the more pronounced the resemblance between herself

---

37. Shirley Jackson, 'Nightmare', in *Just an Ordinary Day*, ed. Laurence Jackson Hyman and Sarah Hyman DeWitt (London: Penguin, 2017), pp. 42–58 (p. 44). All further references are to this edition.
38. Jackson, 'Nightmare', p. 46.
39. Jackson, 'Nightmare', pp. 48–51.
40. Jackson, 'Nightmare', p. 52.
41. Catherine Spooner, *Fashioning Gothic Bodies* (Manchester: Manchester University Press, 2012), p. 3.
42. Spooner, *Fashioning Gothic Bodies*, p. 6.

and Miss X becomes. It is perhaps no accident that it is within this urban landscape that Toni's individuality is put under pressure in this manner. Critics such as Janet Wolff have pointed out that the history of women walking in the city has been structured around a spectral conception of in/visibility. In the nineteenth century, women in public urban spaces were marked as being all-too-visible: 'The privilege of passing unnoticed in the city [...] was not accorded to women, whose presence on the streets would certainly be noticed.'[43] Conversely, the modern city works to etherealize the experiences of women who move within and through it: 'The lives of women in the modern city – in private as well as in public [...] are thus, as [Avery] Gordon puts it, "barely visible, or seemingly not there".'[44] Toni's negotiation of these streets is not a politically neutral act, but is overlain, palimpsestically, with these competing historical configurations of in/visible women operating in public spaces. The conceptual weight of these configurations threatens to desubstantialize Toni's subjectivity, which is why her increasing identification with the spectral 'Miss X' occurs out in the open streets of the city. Indeed, the problems of in/visibility are brought into tension with each other in the letter 'X'. X can be read as an entity in and of itself – a mark or 'character' in a text, for instance – as well as indicating the presence of something that is hidden, secret or even invisible – such as the archetypal use of X in 'X marks the spot', wherein X represents an entity which is simultaneously visible and invisible. At the same time, the 'X' of 'Miss X' is a negative formulation of identity – Miss X has no visible character behind the character, meaning that 'she' can resemble, or even become, anyone. 'Miss X' is a non-name, or a name without a referent, a name crossed-out – the 'invisibility of a visible X', to quote Derrida – and her simultaneous visible-invisibility is what comes to define Toni's experience of her situation.[45]

At the end of the text, Toni can no longer escape the inevitable end point of her identification with Miss X, and so she capitulates:

> [S]he heard a footstep, and looked up to see a man in a blue suit coming toward her.
> 'Are you Miss X?' the man in the blue suit asked her.
> Miss Morgan opened her mouth, and then said, 'Yes,' tiredly.[46]

---

43. Janet Wolff, 'Gender and the Haunting of Cities (or, the Retirement of the Flâneur)', in *The Invisible Flâneuse? Gender, Public Space, and Visual Culture in Nineteenth-Century Paris*, ed. Aruna D'Souza and Tom McDonough (Manchester: Manchester University Press, 2006), pp. 18–31 (p. 19).

44. Wolff, 'Gender and the Haunting of Cities', p. 27. For further work on women's transitory experience of the city (and the regulation of gendered movement in the urban environment more generally), see Deborah L. Rogers, *Streetwalking the Metropolis: Women, the City, and Modernity* (2000). In contrast, Elizabeth Wilson offers a more positive assessment of the city as a site of potential political and personal liberation in *The Sphinx in the City: Urban Life, the Control of Disorder, and Women* (1991).

45. Derrida, *Specters of Marx*, p. 7.

46. Jackson, 'Nightmare', p. 57.

Although this is the first time that someone has actually asked Toni whether she is this mysterious figure, her response indicates her assimilation with, or substitution by, Miss X. Toni is haunted by this feminized letter to such an extent that it ends up consuming her own name and identity, in a manner similar to the way in which the insistent 'R' of Rebecca de Winter overwhelms the nameless narrator in Daphne du Maurier's eponymous novel. In her reading of *Rebecca*, Dorothy Dodge Robbins argues that '[s]o impactful is the letter R on the narrator's psyche, it essentially consumes her own name'.[47] The 'consonant's powerful synecdochial forces' are similarly evident in Jackson's story, particularly in terms of the apparitional quality of the presence 'behind' the respective consonants.[48]

The story ends with Toni's disappearance from her former life, fully assuming the identity of 'Miss X' to travel to different cities, waiting for someone to recognize her, as they failed to do in New York. Yet the very fact that no one notices her similarity to 'Miss X' while she walks through the streets suggests that Toni is already 'missing' before this moment of elective substitution. As Wolff suggests about the current condition of urban femininity, Toni does not really seem to 'be there' in an unambiguous state of 'presence' because, despite the manifold instructions to identify and interact with the Miss X she so resembles, the only person to do so, the man in the blue suit, is part of the advertising campaign himself. Although this degree of collective disregard might be seen as purposeful – they actively choose *not* to notice her – the more mundane, yet unsettling, reality is that Toni is insufficiently present to register on the consciousness of her passers-by. As with 'The Missing Girl', Jackson uses the story of one woman's experience of dissociation to foreground the derealization of a form of femininity that operates outside the home. In coming to terms with the uncanny sensation of being/becoming Miss X, Toni announces herself as a spectralized figure, whose always-already invisibility is only revealed through this act of haunting. Jackson's story is a cautionary tale for mobile, urban and working women that freedom from the immediate constraints of domesticity is no utopian scheme of personal autonomy but is marked by its own dangers and forms of de-presencing. Ghosts can haunt street corners as effectively as they do suburban neighbourhoods.

The Living/Live-In Spectre: 'The Good Wife'

In both 'The Missing Girl' and 'Nightmare', the spectralization of femininity is tied to women's negotiation of spaces outside the home. However, this should not be taken to suggest that Jackson regards the house as a safe or stable locus for the consolidation of feminine identity. If Martha Alexander and Toni Morgan (are made to) disappear in response to their transgressive mobility, 'The Good Wife'

---

47. Dorothy Dodge Robbins, 'R Is for Rebecca: A Consonant and Consummate Haunting', *Names: A Journal of Onomastics* 64, no. 2 (May 2016): 69–77 (p. 70).
48. Robbins, 'R Is for Rebecca', p. 77.

(1996) presents the home itself as a site of entrapment and enforced submission which gradually attenuates female individuality. The house/family home, as Andrew Hock Soon Ng points out, is frequently depicted as a site of the Gothic 'unspeakable', such that characters in Gothic texts frequently fall victim to 'an excessive experience of derealization and immateriality' that the domestic interior engenders.[49] This Gothic tableau forms the backdrop for the action of 'The Good Wife'.

The 'good wife' in question is Helen Benjamin, who has recently married her husband James, from whose perspective the story is focalized. Suspecting an ongoing communication and possible assignation with a man named Ferguson, Mr Benjamin has confined his wife to her bedroom until she confesses to the nature of her indiscretion. Although the conception of femininity present in this narrative equates women's place with the domestic sphere (albeit as a negative synthesis), the story also demonstrates the extent to which the house, and particularly the marital home, is a negotiation between male possession and female habitation. Robert-Foley points out that '[t]he house, which is both female mind and body, lives in ambiguous real estate: it is both the "woman's sphere", yet the man's property'.[50] The husband's proprietorial prerogative over the domestic setting allows him to both define and confine the acceptable limits of women's behaviour and experience. If, as subjects, 'we are haunted by the inescapable recognition that the place to which we turn and return for the familiar comforts of home, the dwelling, are, equally, those which can estrange, dehumanize', then it becomes possible to see Helen's domestic (and textual) position as one under erasure, turning her into a living, or live-in, spectral presence.[51]

When Mr Benjamin visits his wife in her room, his description indicates the degree to which she is in the process of becoming this spectral figure:

> [O]nce he had looked at her, even without intending to, he found it not difficult; she was always the same, these mornings now, and it came as more of a shock to him daily to realize that although, throughout the rest of the house, she existed as a presence made up half of recollection, half of intention, here in her room she was the same as always, and not influential at all.[52]

Although Mr Benjamin has no desire even to look at his wife, he finds it easy to do so because she has become an immutable figure, one who is 'always the same'.

---

49. Andrew Hock Soon Ng, *Women and Domestic Space in Contemporary Gothic Narratives: The House as Subject* (New York: Palgrave Macmillan, 2015), p. 1, 10.

50. Robert-Foley, 'Haunted Readings of Female Gothic Short Stories', p. 183.

51. Julian Wolfreys, *Haunted Selves, Haunting Places in English Literature and Culture, 1800-Present* (Basingstoke: Palgrave Macmillan, 2018), p. 32.

52. Shirley Jackson, 'The Good Wife', in *Just an Ordinary Day*, ed. Laurence Jackson Hyman and Sarah Hyman DeWitt (London: Penguin, 2017), pp. 150–7 (p. 152). All further references are to this edition.

Helen appears to exist in a phantasmatic state, outside the normal flow of time, where she might or might not be perceived or acknowledged by her husband. This temporal disruption extends beyond her bedroom to the rest of the house, where she exists as a half-recollected presence, which indicates her material absence at the same time that she is physically confined. Helen's semi-existence in the rest of the house is not within her control, since it depends upon the recollections in the minds of others, namely her husband and the maid Genevieve, whose description as having 'incurious eyes' as well as being incapable of refusing Mr Benjamin's instructions, present her as lacking either the agency or the inclination to provide Helen with the means to make her presence more tangible.[53] Following Peeren's conceptualization, Helen can be identified as a 'missing figure'. Her 'spectral li[fe]' is marked 'not by difference, potentiality and becoming, but by sameness and preservation', despite the fact that she is not physically missing in the manner of Martha and Toni.[54]

At the same time, Jackson's text reconfigures another of Peeren's formulations. Instead of Helen's spectral condition deriving from the fact she 'cannot be seen' and yet 'remain[s] present', her position might best be defined as one wherein she *can* be seen, yet remains absent. She is a figure defined by her lack of influence, owing to the absence of both economic power and social visibility in comparison with her husband. The boundaries of her existence are both physical – the walls of her bedroom – and conceptual, a patriarchal construction which, in consolidating an acceptable version of femininity – being a 'good' wife – derealizes, or at the very least attenuates, her position. Living as a 'present' missing person in a house with which she is socially and culturally identified as a woman, and yet which is not hers, constitutes the spectral erasure of Helen's identity.

Spectral femininity in 'The Good Wife' also reflects anxieties around language – and, particularly, writing – as a means by which female characters can find themselves marginalized and even written-out of existence. Not only is Helen denied access to standard writing implements such as 'pencil and paper', but the narrator implies that Mr Benjamin has also confiscated her lipstick, lest she 'found it possible to scrawl with [it] upon a handkerchief'.[55] Helen's (in)ability to express herself in writing is bound up with markers of her femininity, both of which are negated by her husband's capacity to prevent her interacting with the world outside the home, not to mention communicating her femininity to her potential admirer (or anyone else). Moreover, this inability to fashion herself in writing – be it with pencil or lipstick – diminishes Helen's capacity to articulate a strong or 'influential' agency for herself:

> [S]he was not capable anymore of expressions such as 'I am kept prisoner by my husband, help me' or 'Save an unfortunate woman unjustly confined' or 'Get the

---

53. Jackson, 'The Good Wife', pp. 152–6.
54. Peeren, *The Spectral Metaphor*, p. 144.
55. Jackson, 'The Good Wife', p. 154.

police' or even 'Help' [. . .] He did not for a minute believe that she was crafty enough to be planning an escape, or to use this apparent resigned state of mind to deceive him into thinking she had accepted his authority.[56]

Her incarceration within the marital home directly affects Helen's self-configuration; she internalizes the material boundaries of her confinement and reconfigures them as the practices of an enforced self-regulation. Mr Benjamin's imprisonment of his wife is psychological as well as physical, erasing her ability to articulate a desire for freedom or self-preservation. The house becomes a correctional facility in which the husband invigilates and re-conditions the errant form of femininity he believes his wife to embody.[57] The marital home is clearly shown to be a site for the regulation of gender formations, which, as Alexis Shotwell observes about Jackson's fiction in general, are 'multiply and complexly co-emergent among selves, people, and houses'.[58] This co-emergence is particularly apparent in 'The Good Wife', since Mr Benjamin is able to imprison his wife through an implicit appeal to what Shotwell terms 'a social polity that emphasizes "proper womanliness"': Helen must be house-bound until she embodies and enacts the 'good wife' model of femininity the 'social polity' and her husband expect.[59]

Jackson pushes the patriarchal manipulation of women to a further extreme by having Mr Benjamin appropriate his wife's voice and hand – her language and her writing – to maintain the illusion of her freedom to the outside world, and thereby extend her domestic imprisonment indefinitely. This deception also represents the story's most overt example of spectral substitution. At the end of the text, Mr Benjamin writes two letters: one to Helen's mother (whose own letter arrives that morning), and another which the reader presumes is intended for Mr Ferguson. Significantly, Benjamin does not write these letters in his own voice or style, but imitates that of his wife: 'Dearest Mommy', he wrote, 'my mean old finger is still too painful to write with – James says he thinks I must have sprained it, but I think he is just tired of taking dictation from me – as if he had ever done anything else.'[60] Although presenting himself

---

56. Jackson, 'The Good Wife', p. 155.

57. It is never established definitively whether Helen is corresponding with another man, or, if she is, what she says/writes. The resultant ambiguity leaves the exact nature of her supposed transgression indistinct or phantasmatic, which in turn emphasizes the insidious nature of her imprisonment and treatment at the hands of her husband. The basis on which his programme of derealization rests might prove to be as insubstantial as the presence of his wife.

58. Alexis Shotwell, '"No Proper Feeling for Her House": The Relational Formation of White Womanliness in Shirley Jackson's Fiction', *Tulsa Studies in Women's Literature* 32, no. 1 (Spring 2013): 119–41 (p. 138).

59. Shotwell, '"No Proper Feeling for Her House"', p. 119.

60. Jackson, 'The Good Wife', p. 156.

as the mere transcriber of his wife's speech, Benjamin actually fashions an alternative version of Helen to use in the manner of a ventriloquist puppet – she 'speaks', but the words are his.

This process operates through a twin-effect: giving voice to an entity which does not exist by ventriloquizing it through the body, speech and style of his absent-present wife. For the letter to Ferguson, Benjamin swaps 'the sheet of [Helen's] monogrammed notepaper' for some 'cheap notepaper', and substitutes his own fountain pen for another one 'filled with brown ink', as well as switching from his right hand to his left. This change of writing apparatus indicates a concomitant change in the style of his substitution: 'My dearest, I have finally thought of a way to get around the jealous old fool.'⁶¹ The husband no longer obtrudes as the mediator of his wife's speech, but stands in as his wife *himself*, thereby completing the logic of spectral substitution he enacts against her. Helen is occluded from the narrative in this exchange of 'letters', both epistolary (her 'non-voice' is fabricated and substitutes her real voice) and alphabetical (Mr Benjamin becomes Mr(s) Benjamin, capable of assuming his wife's language to speak in 'her' voice and write in 'her' hand).⁶² The intricacy of this performance of substitution that is also a form of spectralization attests to Jackson's skill in using the compact form of the short story to explore the ghostliness of women's experiences, with a degree of sophistication equal to that seen in her novels.

This figuration of spectrality as a form of expropriation is articulated particularly cogently by Julian Wolfreys: 'The self is expropriated from itself, from within itself, the home becomes unhomely, a place of displacement and loss [. . .] when at home, in his or her home [. . .] this is when the subject discovers his own having-become-expropriated.'⁶³ The home is an important component in this realization of self-dislocation because of its association with the uncanny; as a space of familiarity and presumed safety; it is the site where the affective disruption of the unfamiliar is most perceptible. The 'disappearance' of Helen Benjamin is all the more unsettling because it happens in a place which has been discursively granted as one *of* or *for* women. Where Martha and Toni are erased because of their transgressive mobility beyond the domestic, Helen's spectralization results in her figurative disappearance *within* the domestic. This threatening configuration of the family home stands as Jackson's coded warning about the dangers for women's self-definition in relation to arrangements of domesticity more generally – as Daniel Miller points out, '[t]here are many conflicts between the agency expressed by individuals [. . .] that make the private more a turbulent sea of constant negotiation rather than simply

---

61. Jackson, 'The Good Wife', p. 157.

62. In the course of spectralizing his wife, he almost comes to be possessed *by* her (or, at least, his own construction/appropriation of her). He enacts a kind of self-possession – since his 'wife' is also himself – that underlines the complex (and strange) permutations of spectral identity that operate in Jackson's story.

63. Wolfreys, *Haunted Selves, Haunting Places*, pp. 3–4.

some haven for the self'.[64] These stories both extrapolate and refine this insight. For young women, there is no configuration of space which is a 'safe haven for the self', and they are continually haunted by the metaphorical or conceptual threat of erasure, and, occasionally, a literal disappearance.

This dynamic of in/security even comes back to Jackson's writing. Jackson creates and sustains these missing women in her stories, but, as 'The Good Wife' demonstrates, writing is no guarantee of a secure presence. Their (enforced) disappearance turns them into ghostly figures who are capable of haunting, which Keller characterizes as a 'phenomenon by which an unsettled, asymmetrical relation manifests itself and becomes known'.[65] In other words, haunting is the mechanism which makes a disequilibrium – such as the uneven power relations between a young girl and adults, or husband and wife – apprehensible, so that something might be done about it. However, as Jackson's stories demonstrate, haunting as a process of rendering-visible an asymmetry of power is only effective when someone is there to acknowledge and bear witness to it. In the case of 'The Good Wife', Helen Benjamin's spectralization is not an elective decision intended to draw attention to her situation but is, rather, the consequence of her domestic entrapment, unable to communicate in her own words while being simulated in the writing of her husband. The conditions of ghostly appearance and signification are not within her control, just as they are not within Martha's or Toni's. Whether it is administrative records, the insistence of an alphabetical character, or a malicious spouse's paper and pencil, writing that is performed by hands other than those of these missing women works to make them absent from their own lives.

Conclusion

The missing women of these stories encapsulate the contradictory conditions of figurative spectrality, particularly as this relates to gendered proscriptions of femininity and domesticity. Throughout her corpus, Jackson practises a complex, multifaceted derealization of women through their situations, and this variety is mostly clearly seen through a spectral reading of her short fiction.

The spectral logic of substitution is evident through its association with literal or figurative disappearance: in order for substitution to work, one element must be removed in order to be re-presented by that which takes its place. The spectral displacement enacted by these forms of substitution and erasure is explicitly tied to a recognition that conventional configurations of gender that were (re)asserted in the post-war period – such as domestic efficiency, marital submissiveness and limited personal and economic autonomy – provided an all-too-restricted basis for articulating identity. Invariably, these configurations were situational, with the

---

64. Daniel Miller, 'Behind Closed Doors', in *Home Possessions: Material Culture Behind Closed Doors*, ed. Daniel Miller (Oxford and New York: Berg, 2001), pp. 1–22 (p. 4).

65. Keller, *Ghostly Landscapes*, p. 7.

woman centred as homemaker and care-giver, which served as a legitimate, socially sanctioned basis on which to define the home as the woman's space (within which to confine her), and to punish any instance of mobility away from the home into public spaces of heightened visibility.

These stories of women who find their position and presence impossible to sustain reveal Jackson at her most nuanced, dexterously abrading the veneer of domestic(ated) life to reveal the enervating – and occasionally lethal – reality for white, middle-class women in mid-century America. That is, for women exactly like Shirley Jackson.

References

Anderson, Melanie R. (2020), 'Introduction', in Jill E. Anderson and Melanie R. Anderson (eds), *Shirley Jackson and Domesticity: Beyond the Haunted House*, 1–6, New York and London: Bloomsbury.

Chaffe, William H. (1991), *The Paradox of Change: American Women in the 20th Century*, New York and Oxford: Oxford University Press.

Derrida, Jacques ([1993] 1994), *Specters of Marx: The State of the Debt, the Work of Mourning, and the New International*, trans. Peggy Kamuf, New York and London: Routledge.

Hall, Joan Wylie (1993), *Shirley Jackson: A Study of the Short Fiction*, New York: Twayne.

Hoeveler, Diane Long (2005), 'Life Lessons in Shirley Jackson's Late Fiction: Ethics, Cosmology, Eschatology', in Bernice M. Murphy (ed.), *Shirley Jackson: Essays on the Literary Legacy*, 267–80, Jefferson and London: McFarland.

Jackson, Shirley (2017), 'The Good Wife', in Laurence Jackson Hyman and Sarah Hyman DeWitt (eds), *Just an Ordinary Day*, 150–7, London: Penguin.

Jackson, Shirley (2017), 'The Missing Girl', in Laurence Jackson Hyman and Sarah Hyman DeWitt (eds), *Just an Ordinary Day*, 373–85, London: Penguin.

Jackson, Shirley (2017), 'Nightmare', in Laurence Jackson Hyman and Sarah Hyman DeWitt (eds), *Just an Ordinary Day*, 42–58, London: Penguin.

Keller, Patricia M. (2016), *Ghostly Landscapes: Film, Photography, and the Aesthetics of Haunting in Contemporary Spanish Culture*, Toronto: University of Toronto Press.

Martin, Deborah (2013), 'Feminine Adolescence as Uncanny: Masculinity, Haunting and Self-Estrangement', *Forum for Modern Language Studies* 49, no. 2 (February): 135–44.

Miller, Daniel (2001), 'Behind Closed Doors', in Daniel Miller (ed.), *Home Possessions: Material Culture behind Closed Doors*, 1–22, Oxford and New York: Berg.

Ng, Andrew Hock Soon (2015), *Women and Domestic Space in Contemporary Gothic Narratives: The House as Subject*, New York: Palgrave Macmillan.

Peeren, Esther (2014), *The Spectral Metaphor: Living Ghosts and the Agency of Invisibility*, Basingstoke and New York: Palgrave Macmillan.

Robbins, Dorothy Dodge (2016), 'R Is for Rebecca: A Consonant and Consummate Haunting', *Names: A Journal of Onomastics* 64, no. 2 (May): 69–77.

Robert-Foley, Lily (2017), 'Haunted Readings of Female Gothic Short Stories', *Short Fiction in Theory and Practice* 7, no. 2 (October): 177–92.

Schofield, Martin (2006), *The Cambridge Introduction to the American Short Story*, Cambridge: Cambridge University Press.

Shotwell, Alexis (2013), '"No Proper Feeling for Her House": The Relational Formation of White Womanliness in Shirley Jackson's Fiction', *Tulsa Studies in Women's Literature* 32, no. 1 (Spring): 119–41.

Spooner, Catherine (2004), *Fashioning Gothic Bodies*, Manchester: Manchester University Press.

Wallace, Diana (2009), '"The Haunting Idea": Female Gothic Metaphors and Feminist Theory', in Diana Wallace and Andrew Smith (eds), *The Female Gothic: New Directions*, 26–41, Basingstoke: Palgrave Macmillan.

Wolff, Janet (2006), 'Gender and the Haunting of Cities (or, the Retirement of the Flâneur)', in Aruna D'Souza and Tom McDonough (eds), *The Invisible Flâneuse? Gender, Public Space, and Visual Culture in Nineteenth-Century Paris*, 18–31, Manchester: Manchester University Press.

Wolfreys, Julian (2018), *Haunted Selves, Haunted Places in English Literature and Culture, 1800-Present*, Basingstoke: Palgrave Macmillan.

III

SPACE AND PLACE

Chapter 8

INTO THE GOTHIC WILDERNESS

THE (UN)NATURAL WORLD IN 'MRS. SPENCER AND THE OBERONS' AND 'THE MAN IN THE WOODS'

Alissa Burger

Untamed nature and the forest specifically are staples of the Gothic tradition, from fairy tales like 'Hansel and Gretel' or 'Little Red Riding Hood' to the dark adventure of Stephen King's *Pet Sematary* (1983) and beyond. Nathaniel Hawthorne's classic short story 'Young Goodman Brown' (1835) is a particularly salient example, in which a young man from Salem Village, Massachusetts, ventures into the forest at night on a dark journey to meet with the devil himself. As Hawthorne describes Young Goodman Brown's walk, 'He had taken a dreary road, darkened by all the gloomiest trees of the forest, which barely stood aside to let the narrow path creep through, and closed immediately behind.'[1] Confronted in these shadowy woods with his pious-seeming fellow villagers, all of whom have sworn their allegiance to the devil and are congregating in the heart of the woods for a witch meeting, Brown's faith in humanity, his community and himself – as this was his purpose in venturing forth as well – is fundamentally compromised. This Gothic wilderness is a place where anything can happen, where the laws of reason and order governing communal 'civilized' society fall away, and the boundaries between the real and the fantastic become permeable and unfixed.

The Gothic wilderness is the antithesis of civilization: darkness countering light, fantasy challenging reason, secrets threatening to upend the appearance of order. As Elizabeth Parker explains in *The Forest and the EcoGothic: The Deep Dark Woods in the Popular Imagination*, 'When we imagine the forest, we tend toward extremes. The landscape is commonly read as a binary space – as either "good" or "bad". When it is "good", it is a remedial setting of wonder and enchantment; when it is "bad", it is a dangerous and terrifying wilderness.'[2] Defining her notion of the ecoGothic wilderness more specifically, Parker argues that

---

1. Nathaniel Hawthorne, 'Young Goodman Brown', in *American Gothic Tales*, ed. Joyce Carol Oates (New York: Plume), p. 53.
2. Elizabeth Parker, *The Forest and the EcoGothic: The Deep Dark Woods in the Popular Imagination* (Cham, Switzerland: Palgrave Macmillan, 2020), p. 1.

the ecoGothic is a flavoured mode through which we can examine our darker, more complicated cultural representations of the nonhuman world – which are all the more relevant in times of ecological crisis. It is concerned with texts with a pervasive sense of ecocentric ambience independent of human presence. Transhistorical in its approach, it explores our ecophobic anxieties, our fears of Nature which are so often tinged with desire. The primary and consistent concern of the ecoGothic is with the deliberate interrogation of the Gothic nature of Gothic Nature.[3]

In this Gothic wilderness, fairy-tale children who are cast out into the forest might encounter neglect, starvation, wild animals or the threat of cannibalism, while in Young Goodman Brown's Salem, the woods are the realm of infernal temptation, drawing the good people of Salem away from the community, the church, and one another. The Gothic wilderness is a liminal space, where anything can happen. As Heinrich Zimmer notes, 'The magic forest . . . is always full of adventures. No one can enter it without losing his way. The forest has always been a place of initiation[,] for there the demonic presences, the ancestral spirits, and the forces of nature reveal themselves.'[4] In addition to the physical and spiritual threats posed by the wilderness, it also reflects and interrogates the individual who dares to enter it, with Tony Magistrale arguing that 'Hawthorne's natural landscapes appear to be animated by subtle forces that ultimately invite his protagonists into a confrontation with ethical codes and principles', forcing them to decide what they believe and who they truly are.[5] Consequently, the Gothic wilderness is also often a reflection of the self, mirroring both the anxieties of individual identity and the larger mores and expectations of the community. Finally, as Parker notes, 'there is a common, if largely undiscussed tendency to talk about the Gothic forest in decidedly *vague* terms', making it difficult – if not impossible – to effectively define, respond to, or contain.[6] When the Gothic protagonist enters the woods, they are likely to become lost: in the wilderness, in the magical, and within themselves.

While the modern wilderness may seem more easily knowable and navigable, elements of mystery, danger and the supernatural linger. There are still plenty of shadows to be found beneath the trees and within the self, and much of Shirley Jackson's writing, from short stories like 'The Summer People' (1950) to her novel *Hangsaman* (1951), demonstrates what dark truths could be revealed if one strays from the beaten path and the well-lighted small town or suburban streets. Jackson's consideration of the Gothic wilderness brings this world into direct

---

3. Parker, *The Forest and the EcoGothic*, p. 36.
4. Quoted in Reginald Cook, 'The Forest of Goodman Brown's Night: A Reading of Hawthorne's "Young Goodman Brown"', *The New England Quarterly* 43, no. 3 (1970): 473.
5. Tony Magistrale, 'Stephen King's *Pet Sematary*: Hawthorne's Woods Revisited', in *The Gothic World of Stephen King*, ed. Gary Hoppenstand and Ray B. Browne (Bowling Green: Bowling Green State University Popular Press, 1987), p. 129.
6. Parker, *The Forest and the EcoGothic*, p. 3, emphasis original.

contact and comparison with the domestic, which was a frequent focus of her work, ranging across a broad spectrum of styles from horror to humour. Add to these considerations the blurring of lines between the real and the fantastic, as well as the interrogation of selfhood and identity, and Jackson's Gothic wilderness is a very dangerous place indeed.

Two of Shirley Jackson's posthumously published short stories that engage with this trope of the Gothic wilderness are 'Mrs. Spencer and the Oberons' (2013) and 'The Man in the Woods' (2014). Each of these stories foregrounds the protagonists' recognition of the wilderness as a space of both freedom and danger, as they negotiate interactions with others and their deepest sense of themselves through their isolation and engagement with the natural world around them, with the wilderness serving as a threshold of profound change and transformation. These two stories also both draw on classic narrative tropes, with the invocation of the medieval and Renaissance figure of Oberon, king of the fairies, in 'Mrs. Spencer and the Oberons' and the central negotiation of the Greek sorceress Circe, Green Man legends, and the figure of James George Frazer's 'King of the Wood' in 'The Man in the Woods'. Through Jackson's use of 'interactive narrative modes' in synthesizing elements of multiple genres, and her dynamic combination of classical and contemporary influences, the connections between past and present, the civilized and the wild, and perception and reality become impossible to disentangle with any degree of certainty.[7] Finally, intersecting with a theme that runs through much of Jackson's work, the domestic is of central importance in these two stories, through the entry into the wilderness which challenges the traditional domestic ideal and subverts the order it promises. A close consideration of these two stories offers the opportunity to explore the ways in which Jackson builds upon and subverts literary traditions from the classical to the Gothic, as well as the explicit contrast between civilization and the unnatural wilderness which threatens to disrupt the community, the family and the self.

Revelry and Resistance in 'Mrs. Spencer and the Oberons'

Mrs Margaret Spencer is a very particular woman, preoccupied with appearances, devoted to the pristine maintenance of her home and family, and driven by a need for order and respectability. She is a woman whose 'behavior is never anything other than correct'.[8] The day that she receives the Oberons' letter, in which they ask her to help them find a house in town for the summer, is filled with a litany of tasks that must be handled and which she repeats to herself almost like a talismanic mantra,

---

7. James Egan, 'Comic-Satiric-Fantastic-Gothic: Interactive Modes in Shirley Jackson's Narratives', in *Shirley Jackson: Essays on the Literary Legacy*, ed. Bernice M. Murphy (Jefferson: McFarland, 2005), p. 34.

8. Ruth Franklin, *Shirley Jackson: A Rather Haunted Life* (New York: Liveright, 2016), p. 267.

thinking 'lemon cream, silver, flowers' as she bustles about her day, maintaining an uneasy balance of efficiency and barely repressed hysteria.[9] The Oberons are friends of Mrs Spencer's sister Charlotte and a wrinkle in her otherwise well-ordered life. As far as Mrs Spencer is concerned, the Oberons are not the 'right' kind of people, so she simply refuses to know them, privately avoiding them and publicly shunning them to the extent that Mrs Spencer never actually meets them, hearing about them only through others. The Oberons are the very opposite of Mrs Spencer: open and gregarious where Mrs Spencer is reserved, fun and free-spirited where Mrs Spencer is rigid. The rest of the community is quickly taken by the Oberons, including Mrs Spencer's friends and even her own husband and children, and as Mrs Spencer remains intractable in her opinion of the family, she is the one who becomes seen as unreasonable and unkind, excluded from the larger social strata of which the Oberons are now the centre.

The Oberons' name is significant, evoking the fairy king of William Shakespeare's *A Midsummer Night's Dream*. Tracing this influence further back, Shakespeare himself drew on Oberon figures who had come before, including John Bourchier, Lord Berner's English translation of the French *Houn de Bordeaux* (1534) and Robert Greene's *The Scottish Historie of James the Fourth* (1594).[10] Laura Aydelotte explains that 'The fairy tale king of the sources is an often contradictory character, at once a beneficent guide and a darkly powerful threat; a meddlesome trickster and a haughtily detached observer of human affairs', a contradiction Shakespeare diffuses to some extent by separating these characteristics between Oberon and Puck.[11] The Oberons of Bourchier, Greene and Shakespeare hold tremendous power for both good and ill and are capable of having a profound impact on the humans whose paths they cross. Similarly, as in *A Midsummer Night's Dream*, the appearance of the Oberons in Jackson's 'Mrs. Spencer and the Oberons' is the catalyst for disruption, unpredictability and fun. While Shakespeare separated the contradictory elements of his source texts' Oberons between his own Oberon and Puck, Jackson instead reflects this division through the other characters' responses: the Oberons are a welcome change for everyone but Mrs Spencer, who sees them as an enemy and a threat.

Echoing the forest revelries of Shakespeare's *A Midsummer Night's Dream*, Mrs Spencer finds herself drawn to the wilderness to at last confront the mysterious Oberons, when she comes home to find that everyone in town, including her own family, has gone out to the Oberons' house for a picnic. While she can see the lights of the Oberons' house and hear the laughter of the party, however, Mrs Spencer

---

9. Shirley Jackson, 'Mrs. Spencer and the Oberons', in *Let Me Tell You: New Stories, Essays, and Other Writings*, ed. Lawrence Jackson Hyman and Sarah Hyman DeWitt (New York: Random House, 2015), p. 32.

10. Laura Aydelotte, '"A Local Habitation and a Name": The Origins of Shakespeare's Oberon', in *Shakespeare Survey 65: A Midsummer Night's Dream*, ed. Peter Holland (Cambridge: Cambridge University Press, 2012), p. 1.

11. Aydelotte, '"A Local Habitation and a Name"', p. 1.

cannot make her way there as she 'finds herself ostracized, wandering lost on a dark night, trying to follow the dreamlike sounds of laughter and singing that reach her from the Oberons' distant house'.[12] After driving the road a few times in both directions and finding herself unable to locate the Oberons' driveway,

> Beginning to feel frantic, she turned her car quickly and drove back along the road until she came to the other end . . . and turning again, back once more to the lighted highway. Once, she stopped, hearing first only silence and then, far away, the voices singing and the laughter. It seemed to her that she had spent hours, perhaps years, searching up and down a dark and empty road, following the distant merriment, never able to find a way to get closer to it.[13]

Even when she gets out and walks, sliding in wet leaves and tearing her stockings, with 'her hair . . . draggled and her lipstick worn away', she cannot find the entrance.[14] Following traditions of fairy stories and fantasy, Mrs Spencer has encountered a magical barrier, one through which she cannot pass. She is an inadmissible outsider, with an invisible blockade confining her to the Gothic wilderness, keeping her from her family and friends, and she is ultimately forced to turn back and go home alone.

Mrs Spencer's fruitless search echoes Hawthorne's journey into the Gothic wilderness. In order to see what is right in front of him, Hawthorne's Young Goodman Brown must change how he does his looking: he must accept the impossible, radically reframe the familiar faces he encounters in the woods and grasp the fallen nature of the human condition. Brown is completely transformed by this experience, his perspective is fundamentally shifted and he is never able to see his loved ones, his village or his fellow community members the same way again. In contrast, while Mrs Spencer's isolation echoes that of Brown's, her journey remains unsuccessful and incompletely achieved because she is unable to see the world around her in a new or different way. She refuses to be changed or to reconsider her perspective, and instead it is the world around her that is transformed. When she ventures into the woods, she does so with an iron-clad belief in the sanctity of well-ordered meals, cleanliness, and formality, and even as her shoes are muddied and her singing husband's voice echoes through the trees, these signs of disorder are aberrant to her, unequivocally wrong and in need of rectification. The others around her have proven themselves to be less rigid and more accepting, with her husband defending the Oberons, her son befriending one of the Oberons' children, and one of Mrs Spencer's friends chiding her with the admonition that 'I always knew you could carry a grudge . . . but I do think that in this case you're just carrying one too far'.[15] The previously reliable family babysitter

---

12. Franklin, *Shirley Jackson*, p. 267.
13. Jackson, 'Mrs. Spencer and the Oberons', p. 47.
14. Jackson, 'Mrs. Spencer and the Oberons', p. 46.
15. Jackson, 'Mrs. Spencer and the Oberons', p. 41.

tells Mrs Spencer that she will not be sitting for the children anymore and one of Mrs Spencer's friends admonishes her that 'maybe you don't have that many friends to spare'.[16] Mrs Finley, the woman who occasionally assists Mrs Spencer with the cleaning, tells her when the Oberons are moving in that 'Half the town's down there anyway [to help]. They likely don't need *you*', not just insulting Mrs Spencer's sense of her own essential nature but breaching the class stratification that would usually keep Mrs Finley quiet and deferential in Mrs Spencer's presence.[17] As she runs back and forth along the Oberons' road, searching fruitlessly for the entrance to their driveway, Mrs Spencer is lost in the wilderness and lacks the belief or true fellow feeling that would see her safely into the arms of her family and friends. As a result, she remains isolated and alone.

Mrs Spencer never gains entry to the Oberons' revelry. She does finally succeed in finding her way out of the woods and home again, though she discovers that everything has changed. There are almost no lights on in town and there is an oppressive silence, an absence of life. Mrs Spencer has constructed her understanding of the world, her worth within it and her own identity based almost entirely on the domestic sphere and her roles as a wife and mother: she can make a great lemon cream pie, network with the 'right sort' of ladies, and care for her home and family with efficiency and skill. Her children are well taken care of, well dressed, and trained with formal manners, and as a wife, she supports her husband's professional aspirations through her skill as a hostess and her social acumen in getting invited to join the most prestigious women's social groups. However, while she has dedicated her life, time and energy to these pursuits, they have proven fallible and offer no protection. This realization emphasizes and heightens the sense of beleaguered dissatisfaction that Mrs Spencer has felt regarding domestic and family chores throughout the story, though with those chores as the only defining drive in her life, she clings to them fiercely.

Where Young Goodman Brown's perspective is fundamentally changed by his journey into the Gothic wilderness, and he sees everyone and everything around him with new eyes, Mrs Spencer has maintained her own firmly held beliefs, while the rest of the world has shifted without her. Mrs Spencer has retreated to her home and the assumption of domestic safety and order, only to find that even that domestic space is not sacred. She initially looks forward to the return of her family, thinking that 'she must be neat and ready for them . . . [but then] she realized that they would be coming home dirty and sticky and perhaps wet from the river, perhaps tracking mud across the white doorsill, putting grimy hands on the stair rail, bringing their filthy shoes into the living room'.[18] The family's anticipated raucous return mirrors the influence of the Gothic wilderness: the barrier between order and chaos, between civilization and the wilderness that surrounds it, has been breached and can never be restored. The revelry in the woods is horrifying

16. Jackson, 'Mrs. Spencer and the Oberons', p. 41.
17. Jackson, 'Mrs. Spencer and the Oberons', p. 38, emphasis original.
18. Jackson, 'Mrs. Spencer and the Oberons', p. 48.

to Mrs Spencer and she sees the Oberons' influence as malicious and insidious, something that she cannot categorize, control or mitigate. Where others have heard laughter and seen lights in the trees, she has seen a threat to her well-ordered existence, a challenge to her supremacy in both her home and her community. The danger cannot be kept out, the fun cannot be forgotten, and while Mrs Spencer will certainly cling to any shred of control and propriety she can, Jackson makes it clear that she is fighting a losing battle, that one housewife is no match for the forces of fantasy, chaos and the Gothic wilderness that the Oberons represent.

Tradition and Change in 'The Man in the Woods'

In Jackson's 'The Man in the Woods', the Gothic wilderness is the destination and central setting, rather than the disruptive detour presented in 'Mrs. Spencer and the Oberons'. As Bernice M. Murphy explains, one common trope in the Gothic wilderness narrative is the story 'in which bad things happen to individuals or groups of individuals who decide to leave the community behind and venture into the wilderness, of their own free will.'[19] When 'The Man in the Woods' begins, the protagonist, Christopher, is walking, having just passed a crossroads and chosen to venture down the road that takes him further into the woods, though his free will seems somewhat suspect, with Christopher 'turning onto the forest road *as though he had a choice*, looking back once to see the other road, the one he had not chosen, going peacefully on through fields, in and out of town, perhaps even coming to an end somewhere beyond Christopher's sight.'[20] He does not seem pleased to be on this journey or by his surroundings, 'hating the trees that moved slowly against his progress, hating the dust beneath his feet, hating the sky, hating this road, all roads, everywhere.'[21] Where he has come from, where he is headed, and why he set out in the first place are details that remain enigmatic, noted only in 'the numberless line of walking days that dissolved, seemingly years ago, into the place he had left, once, before he started walking.'[22] While there is certainly an outside world from which Christopher has come, that world is inconsequential, remaining unseen and rarely acknowledged. Where Mrs Spencer followed in the footsteps of Hawthorne's Young Goodman Brown, Christopher is more akin to a fairy-tale hero, entering a world outside of the everyday, venturing into the wilderness to find a witch's cottage (of sorts) and the magical revelations that lie within. The path Christopher travels leads him to a house in the woods, 'a comfortable-looking, settled old house, made

---

19. Bernice M. Murphy, *The Rural Gothic in American Popular Culture* (New York: Palgrave Macmillan, 2013), p. 11.
20. Shirley Jackson, 'The Man in the Woods', in *Let Me Tell You: New Stories, Essays, and Other Writings*, ed. Lawrence Jackson Hyman and Sarah Hyman DeWitt (New York: Random House, 2015), p. 173, emphasis added.
21. Jackson, 'The Man in the Woods', p. 173.
22. Jackson, 'The Man in the Woods', p. 173.

of stone ... easily found in the pathless forest because it lay correctly, compactly, at the end of the road, which was not a road at all, of course, but merely a way to the house'.[23] Christopher knocks, is welcomed in by two sisters named Circe and Phyllis, and makes the acquaintance of the master of the house, Mr Oakes. All seems preordained and Christopher is invited in as though he had been expected. He is given dinner, a place to sleep and a cryptic overview of some of the house's most notable features, namely its records and its roses. In the story's final lines, Christopher seems poised to take over as the guardian of the records, heading out to challenge Mr Oakes and claim his position within this Gothic wilderness.

'The Man in the Woods' is a 'playful, appreciative remix of a handful of dark folkloric tropes', drawing on mythological and literary traditions of Circe and the Green Man, among others.[24] Though Circe's companion calls her 'Aunt Cissy', she herself is adamant in this naming, saying 'Circe I was born and Circe I will have for my name till I die'.[25] Her name signals to the reader that magic is afoot, drawing on the Greek narrative of Circe, a sorceress who turned Odysseus's men into swine and seduced Odysseus himself as 'he stayed as her lover, before she told him how to navigate through the waters of the Sirens and between Scylla, a monster, and Charybdis, a whirlpool'.[26] Circe is a figure of incredible power and potential destruction, which is mirrored in Jackson's 'The Man in the Woods'. She welcomes Christopher into their home and feeds him well, though what it is she is feeding him is a bit suspect, including the possibility that Circe and Phyllis are serving him the bodies of Mr Oakes's previous and unsuccessful challengers, that they have dosed the food with a potion to give Christopher strength or both. While less prominent in mythological narratives, Phyllis's name is significant as well, 'a name associated with someone left behind, someone who must acquiesce to men, given that the original Phyllis was a woman whom Demophon married on his way back from the Trojan War ... [but] left behind when he returned to Greece'.[27] Based on varying accounts, Phyllis either committed suicide or died of grief waiting for Demophon to return. In Jackson's 'The Man in the Woods' both of these women, like their mythological predecessors, find themselves linked to a specific place and relegated to waiting, powerful but contained. Circe and Phyllis combine elements of passivity and agency: this is likely the nexus of their existence, a place they will never leave, but they are the ones who endure, who make sure that the rituals

23. Jackson, 'The Man in the Woods', p. 174.
24. Emera, '"The Man in the Woods," by Shirley Jackson (2014)', *The Black Letters: A Literary Blog*, 18 April 2019, theblackletters.net/the-man-in-the-woods-by-shirley-jackson-2014-e.
25. Jackson, 'The Man in the Woods', p. 176.
26. Arthur Cotterell and Rachel Storm, *The Illustrated Encyclopedia of World Mythology* (New York: Metro Books, 2012), p. 34.
27. Betsy Pelz, 'Shirley Jackson: "The Man in the Woods"', *The Mookse and the Gripes*, 21 April 2014, https://mookesandgripes.com/review/2014/04/21/shirley-jackson-the-man-in-the-woods/.

follow their prescribed and proper course, and when Mr Oakes, Christopher and the other challengers have all gone, they will remain, tending the house in the woods, guiding and caring for the next champion who comes along.

Mr Oakes is a combination of the folkloric Green Man figure of nature and rebirth and the guardian described by James George Frazer in *The Golden Bough*. As Frazer writes, this guardian is always on alert for his inevitable challenger, in 'a custom . . . which seems to transport us at once from civilisation to savagery'.[28] Frazer explains:

> In the sacred grove there grew a certain tree round which at any time of the day and probably far into the night, a grim figure might be seen to prowl. In his hand he carried a drawn sword, and he kept peering warily about him as if at every instant he expected to be set upon by an enemy. He was a priest and a murderer; and the man for whom he looked was sooner or later to murder him and hold the priesthood in his stead. Such was the rule of the sanctuary. A candidate for the priesthood could only succeed to office by slaying the priest, and having slain him, he retained office till he was himself slain by a stronger or a craftier.[29]

Mr Oakes follows this tradition of Frazer's 'King of the Wood', a priest and protector, who is always in danger of being beset, murdered, and supplanted. Despite this adversarial existence, Mr Oakes is at one with nature, evidenced in the proliferation of his roses and his intimate understanding and acceptance of the cycles of life, death, and rebirth. He shows Christopher his roses with great pride, explaining that 'I planted them myself . . . I was the first one to ever clear away even this much of the forest. Because I wished to plant roses in the midst of this wilderness'.[30] Mr Oakes is even more firmly rooted in this one specific place than Circe and Phyllis, unable to leave his post unguarded, sending Circe to gather the roses he planted.[31] These roses also present a tension between the untamed wilderness and cultivated natural beauty: just as with the records he keeps, Mr Oakes's roses are a bulwark against the chaos, a means of imposing order and influence on the unpredictable Gothic wilderness and the ritual over which he has no control. The roses and the records will be his marker, what he leaves behind as proof that he existed and at least for a time, held power in these woods. He shares his instructions for the care of the roses with Christopher but also adjures the younger man to 'Remember who planted them', simultaneous instruction and preparation for his own potential usurpation and death.[32] Like the perennially 'drawn sword' of Frazer's guardian,

---

28. James George Frazer, *The Golden Bough: A Study of Magic and Religion, Volume 1: The Magic Art and the Evolution of Kings*, 3rd edn (New York: Macmillan and Co., 1935), p. 8.
29. Frazer, *The Golden Bough*, pp. 8–9.
30. Jackson, 'The Man in the Woods', p. 184.
31. Jackson, 'The Man in the Woods', p. 184.
32. Jackson, 'The Man in the Woods', p. 184.

Mr Oakes also takes up arms towards the story's conclusion, sharpening his knife and 'turning the edge little by little with infinite delicacy' as he continues to talk with Christopher, working to ascertain the worthiness of his potential successor.[33]

Jackson's story ends in the dark, tense moments leading up to this violent confrontation, as Mr Oakes walks out into the darkness and Christopher prepares to follow, armed with the women's advice, as with his back 'pressed . . . in terror against the door, he heard the voice calling from the direction of the river, so clear and ringing through the trees that he hardly knew it as Mr Oakes's: "Who is he dares enter these my woods?"'[34] In an interview with *The New Yorker*'s Cressida Leyshon, Jackson's son Laurence Jackson Hyman says that 'In "The Man in the Woods" [Jackson] has created a story grounded in mythology, told like a fairy tale, with her typical hanging ending, though in this case the clues suggest pretty clearly how it will end', with Christopher's own victory seemingly foreshadowed by his cat's earlier triumph over Mr Oakes's.[35] As with so many of Jackson's ambiguous conclusions, what this means remains uncertain: If Christopher succeeds in slaying his rival and wins this post, what will his life look like? What has brought him – or led him or compelled him – to this point and this place? How long will it be before another, younger man comes to challenge him as well? The path forward and the answers to these questions remain lost in the shadows of Jackson's Gothic wilderness.

As with 'Mrs. Spencer and the Oberons', the role of the domestic is central to 'The Man in the Woods', though this domesticity takes on a different cast, as it is both part of and counter to the wilderness that Christopher encounters in the forest. When Christopher first arrives at the house, 'Everything seems normal, but since nothing is normal about the situation, it's like looking at a warped version of a quaint visit'.[36] The house is a refuge in the wilderness, offering safety, warm food and a place to sleep, though the food may well be the bodies of the failed challengers and his bed is 'a stone bench . . . mattressed with leaves, and had for blankets heavy furs that looked like bearskins'.[37] The women are solicitous and welcoming, though cryptic; while they are in some ways the traditional heart of the home, they also exist on its periphery, described as 'handmaidens' and left to sleep on the kitchen floor.[38] In writing of Jackson's domestic horror, S. T. Joshi notes that 'The house controls the inhabitants, not the inhabitants the house' and

---

33. Jackson, 'The Man in the Woods', p. 186.
34. Jackson, 'The Man in the Woods', p. 187.
35. Quoted in Cressida Leyshon, 'The Week in Fiction: Shirley Jackson', *The New Yorker*, 21 April 2014, https://www.newyorker.com/books.page-turner/this-week-in-fiction-shirley-jackson/amp.
36. Trevor Berrett, 'Shirley Jackson: "The Man in the Woods"', *The Mookse and the Gripes*, 21 April 2014, https://mookesandgripes.com/review/2014/04/21/shirley-jackson-the-man-in-the-woods/.
37. Jackson, 'The Man in the Woods', p. 181.
38. Jackson, 'The Man in the Woods', p. 182.

this is undeniably true in 'The Man in the Woods'.[39] Mr Oakes is unable to leave his station, even temporarily. Circe and Phyllis serve Mr Oakes, but since guardians will come and go when challenged and bested in combat, their foremost loyalty is to the house and the Gothic wilderness which surrounds it, maintaining its order, welcoming its guests (whether well- or ill-fated) and keeping its secrets.

Like countless fairy-tale heroes before him, Christopher is entirely changed by his journey into the Gothic wilderness. However his confrontation with Mr Oakes turns out, Christopher will not be returning to the world beyond these woods. His life before venturing into forest remains largely unexamined: he tells Mr Oakes that he was a student, offering no further details or explanation. He walked away from his old life and he kept walking, in part, because 'he had nothing else to do'.[40] He may have been disaffected with his previous life and looking for a change. He may be on the run or he may have been expelled from his previous community for some undisclosed transgression. He may even have been inexplicably compelled to set out, since his appearance at the house in the woods seems expected and almost preordained, hearkening to a kind of otherworldly call to adventure or destiny. Christopher is not yet at home in the woods, 'looking with frightened eyes at the trees that reached for him on either side', but if he survives his combat with Mr Oakes, the Gothic wilderness is a place to which he will soon become accustomed, his new and permanent home, a space that is both threatening and full of unexpected promise – though only for the right challenger.[41]

Jackson's Gothic Wilderness

With 'Mrs. Spencer and the Oberons' and 'The Man in the Woods', Jackson builds on the larger Gothic tradition of the untamed wilderness, including the freedom and danger that can be found in its shadows. Both Mrs Spencer and Christopher set out from the known and civilized world and find an entirely new way of being in and seeing the world around them, though to different effect. Mrs Spencer turns back towards the well-lighted and predictable domestic space, even though the chaos of the wilderness will soon encroach there as well, with the return of her boisterous and unbound family, while Christopher has no choice but to embrace the wilderness in all of its terrible wonder and danger. Even the characters' names reflect their different experiences in the woods: Mrs Spencer is defined by her rigid formality and addressed throughout the story by her surname, with her first name (Margaret) only rarely mentioned, while Christopher's informality and lack of family name unfix him from the larger, ordered world beyond the forest. While the Gothic wilderness is adversarial in both stories, it is also a place of great

---

39. S. T. Joshi, 'Shirley Jackson: Domestic Horror', in *Shirley Jackson: Essays on the Literary Legacy*, ed. Bernice M. Murphy (Jefferson: McFarland, 2005), p. 191.
40. Jackson, 'The Man in the Woods', p. 173.
41. Jackson, 'The Man in the Woods', p. 187.

potential, with Mrs Spencer's family and friends sloughing off the strictures and stifling expectations of social propriety and the well-ordered life, and Christopher poised to become the lord of the manor if he is indeed successful in besting Mr Oakes in the coming combat. Either way, just as it was for Hawthorne's Young Goodman Brown and in the larger tradition of Parker's ecoGothic, Jackson's Gothic wilderness is transformative. Those who enter it, whether unwillingly or with enthusiasm, will never be the same again.

Combining elements of the established Gothic tradition with her own signature brand of horror, in 'Mrs. Spencer and the Oberons' and 'The Man in the Woods', Jackson synthesizes old and new, the traditional and the subversive, and the domestic and fantastic. Jackson's Gothic wilderness is simultaneously familiar and unpredictable, blazing new trails in these unmapped woods. In true Jackson fashion, she also leaves her readers with no certainty as to exactly where those trails will end or what will be waiting at their conclusion. Both Mrs Spencer and Christopher find themselves on the cusp of transformation in their respective stories' final lines. They have both been challenged by what they have seen and experienced in their journey into the Gothic wilderness, with Mrs Spencer refusing change, while Christopher embraces its inevitability. But what happens next hangs precariously in the balance, suspended in those moments before Mrs Spencer's family walks through the front door, or Christopher takes his first step away from the house and into the wilderness to fight Mr Oakes. Will Mrs Spencer's family be properly abashed in the face of her propriety, or does the Oberons' party mark a sea change in the lives of the family and the community, the embrace of a less structured and regimented way of living? Will Christopher best Mr Oakes and become the master of the house, or will he be one more defeated challenger, served up for dinner when the next one comes along? Jackson provides her readers with clues and possibilities but in the end, these woods are places of uncertainty and the reader is left with these mysteries, abiding and unanswered questions about where these characters' next steps into the Gothic wilderness will take them.

References

Aydelotte, Laura (2012), '"A Local Habitation and a Name": The Origins of Shakespeare's Oberon', in Peter Holland (ed.), *Shakespeare Survey 65: A Midsummer Night's Dream*, 1–11, Cambridge: Cambridge University Press.

Berrett, Trevor (2014), 'Shirley Jackson: "The Man in the Woods"', *The Mookse and the Gripes*, 21 April. https://mookesandgripes.com/review/2014/04/21/shirley-jackson-the-man-in-the-woods/.

Cook, Reginald (1970), 'The Forest of Goodman Brown's Night: A Reading of Hawthorne's "Young Goodman Brown"', *The New England Quarterly* 43 (3): 473–81.

Cotterell, Arthur and Rachel Storm (2012), *The Illustrated Encyclopedia of World Mythology*, New York: Metro Books.

Egan, James (2005), 'Comic-Satiric-Fantastic-Gothic: Interactive Modes in Shirley Jackson's Narratives', in Bernice M. Murphy (ed.), *Shirley Jackson: Essays on the Literary Legacy*, 34–51, Jefferson: McFarland.

Emera (2019), '"The Man in the Woods," by Shirley Jackson (2014)', *The Black Letters: A Literary Blog*, 18 April. theblackletters.net/the-man-in-the-woods-by-shirley-jackson-2014-e.
Franklin, Ruth (2016), *Shirley Jackson: A Rather Haunted Life*, New York: Liveright.
Frazer, James George (1935), *The Golden Bough: A Study in Magic and Religion, Vol. 1: The Magic Art and the Evolution of Kings*, 3rd edn, New York: Macmillan and Co.
Hawthorne, Nathaniel (1996), 'Young Goodman Brown', in Joyce Carol Oates (ed.), *American Gothic Tales*, 52–64, New York: Plume.
Jackson, Shirley (2015), 'The Man in the Woods', in Laurence Jackson Hyman and Sarah Hyman DeWitt (eds), *Let Me Tell You: New Stories, Essays, and Other Writings*, 173–87, New York: Random House.
Jackson, Shirley (2015), 'Mrs. Spencer and the Oberons', in Laurence Jackson Hyman and Sarah Hyman DeWitt (eds), *Let Me Tell You: New Stories, Essays, and Other Writings*, 29–49, New York: Random House.
Joshi, S. T. (2005), 'Shirley Jackson: Domestic Horror', in Bernice M. Murphy (ed.), *Shirley Jackson: Essays on the Literary Legacy*, 183–98, Jefferson: McFarland.
Leyshon, Cressida (2014), 'The Week in Fiction: Shirley Jackson', *The New Yorker*, 21 April. https://www.newyorker.com/books.page-turner/this-week-in-fiction-shirley-jackson/amp.
Magistrale, Tony (1987), 'Stephen King's *Pet Sematary*: Hawthorne's Woods Revisited', in Gary Hoppenstand and Ray B. Browne (eds), *The Gothic World of Stephen King*, 126–34, Bowling Green: Bowling Green State University Popular Press.
Murphy, Bernice M. (2013), *The Rural Gothic in American Popular Culture*, New York: Palgrave Macmillan.
Parker, Elizabeth (2020), *The Forest and the EcoGothic: The Deep Dark Woods in the Popular Imagination*, Palgrave Gothic Series, Cham, Switzerland: Palgrave Macmillan.
Pelz, Betsy (2014), 'Shirley Jackson: "The Man in the Woods"', *The Mookse and the Gripes*, 21 April. https://mookesandgripes.com/review/2014/04/21/shirley-jackson-the-man-in-the-woods/.

Chapter 9

THE ANXIOUS CITY IN SHIRLEY JACKSON'S 'PILLAR OF SALT' AND 'THE TOOTH'

A PHENOMENOLOGY OF THE UNCANNY

Luke Reid

About halfway through 'Pillar of Salt', Shirley Jackson's short story from 1948, a young couple on a two-week vacation to New York find a severed leg lying in the sand on the beach at Long Island. 'It's a leg all right', the husband, Brad, says matter-of-factly after taking a closer look, apparently unfazed by the horror of the scene.[1] His wife, Margaret, however, is shaken. For her, the leg is just the latest in a succession of frights and portents, her vacation increasingly eerie and unsettling. The couple have returned to New York for the first time since leaving one year earlier to start a family in small-town New Hampshire, and for Margaret the trip is meant to be a respite from the childcare and domestic duties of her new life back home, if not also an attempt to reclaim the faster-paced, metropolitan self she left behind. As the story's title suggests, that former self might not be so easy to glimpse anymore, let alone recapture. At every turn, she encounters a New York now alien to her, its near-constant stimuli an assault of bustle and cacophony, its grittier underside warping into a nightmarish space that first rattles and then unravels her. The story ends with her at a downtown intersection, struck by a paralyzing attack of agoraphobia and looking frantically at the other side of the street, unable to cross. As Jackson writes: 'she wondered, How do people ever manage to get there, and knew that by wondering, by admitting a doubt, she was lost.'[2]

Among other things, the scene dramatizes the difficulty of 'placemaking' in the modern metropolis, both as an effect of the post-war city in general, and, more pointedly, as an emblematic experience of women of the time, with Margaret's disorientation and paralysis serving as twin expressions of an anxious and gendered 'placelessness'.[3] As with Jackson's housebound fictions, the story on the

---

1. Shirley Jackson, 'Pillar of Salt', in *The Lottery and Other Stories*, 235–53 (New York: Farrar, Straus and Giroux, 2005), pp. 235–53 (p. 247).
2. Jackson, 'Pillar of Salt', p. 252.
3. Here, I am using Dylan Trigg's definition of 'placemaking' – a phenomenological concept in which the subject 'cultivat[es] a fundamental identification with place', such that

whole focuses on the rupture of the uncanny within the fabric of the everyday, particularly through a lens of spatiality and embodied subjectivity. Indeed, while Jackson's signal space is the home (the locus of her gothic poetics and the site where her depictions of women and the uncanny most fully come to life), her city stories develop a phenomenology of gender and space I see as apposite to her more involved examinations of domesticity and its psychic effects on the lived body. Here, I consider two of Jackson's city stories through this lens, 'Pillar of Salt' (1948) and 'The Tooth' (1948). In these stories, the city is an equally gendered and equally ambiguous foil to domestic space, the ambivalence of home as both refuge and prison called into relief by the city's own temptations and dangers. If New York offers up the lure of escape, then it also conjures the terror of the same. The city experience is then deeply unnerving, at times even horrific, and yet often for these same reasons, it is also revealing, if not instructive.[4] For both of Jackson's central characters, New York opens up a parallel reality that dramatizes the danger of escape as much as it illuminates the uncanny strangeness of their day-to-day lives back home. Does the city precipitate the respective breakdowns of these women or does it bring to the surface and reflect back this everyday estrangement, the alienating isolation through which they already live day in and day out?

One way to consider this question is through the specifically gendered urban subjectivity Jackson develops in these tales. In many respects, her portraits of urban space recall early twentieth-century theories of the city and its alienating effects – from Georg Simmel's 'The Metropolis and Mental Life' (1903) to Walter Benjamin's discussions of 'shock' and the *flâneur* (1939) to the Vienna Circle's discourse on 'derealization'.[5] But whereas these theories advance a one-way relation between cities and subjects (with the city acting *on* the subject as a force of alienation), I would argue that Jackson anticipates a co-relational notion of cities and bodies as mutually defining. Her stories depict an increasingly blurred line between subjects

---

'the self and world form a corresponding and synthetic relationship of resemblance' (2012: 170). I am also using it as it appears in phenomenological approaches to urban theory and design – for example, in Iris Aravot's article, 'Back to Phenomenological Placemaking', in which she argues that the outcome of post-war urban design was a sense of 'placelessness' that then required a redirection towards 'placemaking' (2010: 201–2).

4. In this particular context, I am borrowing the phrase 'the city experience' from Richard Pascal's article, '"Farther than Samarkand": The Escape Theme in Shirley Jackson's "The Tooth"', which has been instructive to my own consideration of the story (pp. 133–9). In what follows, I also considered Angela Hague's brief, but incisive, discussions of 'Pillar of Salt' and 'The Tooth' in her article, '"A Faithful Anatomy of Our Times": Reassessing Shirley Jackson' (pp. 77–9).

5. See Simmel, 'The Metropolis and Mental Life' (1903) in *The Sociology of Georg Simmel*, trans. K. Wolff; Benjamin, 'On Some Motifs in Baudelaire' (1939), in *Illuminations*, trans. H. Zohn; and Vidler, *Warped Space* (2000), in particular Chapter 1, 'Agoraphobia: Psychopathologies of Urban Space', in which he discusses the 1920s work of the Vienna Circle on 'derealization'.

and their environments, her characters in some sense dreaming the city and the city in turn dreaming them. Moreover, in a dynamic that also obtains in some of her later housebound novels, her city stories depict corporeality *as* subjectivity, breaking down many of the binary oppositions of the body and gesturing towards its social production as sexed and gendered.[6]

My reading of Jackson's city stories therefore relies on a phenomenological approach to her depictions of place, memory, and the embodied subject. In both 'Pillar of Salt' and 'The Tooth', place seems to enter the bodies of these women, inhabiting them, overlapping inside them, projecting outward and introjecting inward. The interactions of spatial memory, place and lived experience produce deep-seated feelings of unhomeliness, anxiety and even spectrality, revealing to these women the fundamental strangeness of their being-in-the-world. The result is akin to what Dylan Trigg terms 'a phenomenology of the uncanny', with Jackson's depictions of embodied subjectivity allowing her to explore the unsettling and yet, by the same token, generative subject position of women in the city – its vexations and impasses as well as its interventions and potentialities.[7] The anxious city and its phenomenality therefore produce an encounter with the uncanny which, while not necessarily beneficent, might nonetheless be read as critical and productive, even revelatory. As Trigg writes, a phenomenological approach to the unhomely enables us to see its potential 'for disturbing the familiarity of what has been taken-for-granted', such that 'strangeness and uncanniness become emblematic of second seeing'.[8]

In Jackson's city stories, it is precisely this type of strangeness that the urban experience provides, unsettling the taken-for-granted familiarity of these protagonists' daily existences. In 'Pillar of Salt', for example, Margaret's progressively disturbing vision of New York might indeed be read as a form of second sight, as if a rent in her reality were making visible some weird and eerie alternate world, allowing her to glimpse the living, festering ruin of New York that already exists just beyond its surface. This alternate world is directly tied to her embodied experience, in particular her growing feelings of invisibility and physical disintegration. When she first arrives, her own sense of reality appears diminished by what Jackson calls the 'blasting reality' of the metropolitan environment.[9] Moving through New York, watching its bewildering blur of action, it is almost as if Margaret, too, were blurring out of focus, losing contour and shape, transmuting into a spectral presence. At a party, when she tries to warn everyone about a possible fire in the building, no one listens or even seems to hear her, leaving her to think, 'I might as

---

6. I am relying here in part on Elizabeth Grosz's theories of urban space, gender and corporeality, particularly her paper 'Bodies—Cities', in *Space, Time, and Perversion* (pp. 103–10).

7. Dylan Trigg, *The Memory of Place: A Phenomenology of the Uncanny* (Athens: Ohio University Press, 2012), pp. 25–9.

8. Trigg, *The Memory of Place*, p. 25.

9. Jackson, 'Pillar of Salt', p. 237.

well not be here.'[10] In the street, carried by the jostling crowd, she is surrounded by people and yet totally invisible: 'No one even notice[s] me.'[11] These feelings bring to mind what Rebecca Munford, also in a discussion of Jackson's work, refers to as 'spectral femininity' – the representation of female 'social invisibility and historical dispossession' through ghostly representation, with the construction of feminine identity 'sharing the ghost's paradoxical position' as an absent presence and present absence.[12]

This sense of disappearance and erasure is mirrored in the city's own collapse and erosion. All around her the city is 'going to pieces', Margaret says, and yet no one else, not even Brad, seems to notice.[13] Her vision of New York all but realizes a prevalent figure associated with it in both the urban and popular discourses of Jackson's time – namely, that by mid-century the city had become a site of rapid and inexorable decay seemingly populated by the walking dead. As Brian L. Tochterman shows in his book *The Dying City*, as early as the 1930s and 1940s, city planners and social critics, from Lewis Mumford to Patrick Geddes, had started referring to New York as the 'Necropolis', the prevailing sentiment being that New York was too far gone to be saved, an urban wasteland stuck in irreversible cycles of poverty, alienation, material collapse and moral decline.[14] As Mumford put it, referring to New York: 'Make the patient as comfortable as possible; it's too late to operate.'[15] Indeed, through Margaret's eyes, the compulsions and repetitions of urban life are seen as a kind of death-drive spiral, the city's masses caught in what Jackson's narrator calls 'a voluntary neck-breaking speed, a deliberate whirling faster and faster to end in destruction'.[16] With everything moving so fast, the 'solid stuff' of the city simply falls apart 'under the strain', the buildings 'crumbling into fine dust', their 'cornices blowing off and windows caving in'.[17] In one of the nicer department stores, 'a great gaping hole in the tiled foyer' opens up at Margaret's feet.[18] The other shoppers just walk around it.

These images parallel Margaret's own sense of rupture and decay, the fault lines and voids splitting open within her psyche, as if New York were at once projecting and introjecting her anxious embodiment, the uncanny cityscape giving concrete shape to the vulnerability of her self-identity. Margaret's fixation on images of crumbling, for example, with the city dissolving into 'fine dust' or 'sand', gives

---

10. Jackson, 'Pillar of Salt', p. 241.
11. Jackson, 'Pillar of Salt', p. 250.
12. Rebecca Munford, 'Spectral Femininity', in *Women and the Gothic*, ed. Avril Horner and Sue Zlosknik (Edinburgh: Edinburgh University Press, 2016), pp. 120–34 (p. 121).
13. Jackson, 'Pillar of Salt', p. 244.
14. Brian Tochterman, *The Dying City: Postwar New York and the Ideology of Fear* (Chapel Hill: University of North Carolina Press, 2017), pp. 2–8.
15. Quoted in Tochterman, *The Dying City*, p. 3.
16. Jackson, 'Pillar of Salt', p. 244.
17. Jackson, 'Pillar of Salt', pp. 243–4.
18. Jackson, 'Pillar of Salt', p. 243.

material form to what she later describes as her own feeling of 'com[ing] apart', just as it gestures to the story's title and its implicit image of Margaret herself dissolving into particles – in her case, granules of salt.[19] Significantly, Jackson links this process to Margaret's life back home, the city not simply imposing this breakdown *on* her or even initiating it, but instead somehow melding with her consciousness and calling to the surface a previously repressed emotional reality which is now given shape and meaning.

This is most apparent on the beach at Long Island, an eerie, dream-like sequence in which Margaret experiences what Jackson describes as a 'double recollection'.[20] Looking out at the grey sky and water, moments before she and Brad discover the severed leg, Margaret suddenly recognizes the beach, remembering it, strangely, from her own imagination; at the same time, she finally identifies the tune that has been stuck in her head, nagging her ever since the train ride into the city. Jackson writes:

> The beach was the one where she had lived in imagination, writing for herself dreary love-broken stories where the heroine walked beside the wild waves; the little tune was the symbol of the golden world she escaped into to avoid the everyday dreariness that drove her into writing depressing stories about the beach.[21]

This 'double recollection' confronts Margaret with the distressingly circular nature of her own escape fantasies, her 'dreary love-broken stories' and 'everyday dreariness' leading her back, elliptically, to the beach, which, impossibly, now spreads out before her in reality. Here, the memory of an imagined place overlaps with the place itself, producing a deeply uncanny moment of recognition in which the boundaries between subjectivity and external reality blur and bleed into one another.

More specifically, the disturbing nature of the scene, coupled with its overt symbolism, speaks to what Dylan Trigg calls 'alien flesh', when places and memories overlap within the body, producing a phenomenological experience that is viscerally uncanny and self-alienating. As Trigg argues, spatial memory is at the crux of the relation between uncanniness and phenomenality, for, as he asks, what could be more intensely strange than the memory of a place suddenly obtruding into the 'still-unfolding present', such that the subject re-experiences a place, real or imagined, as a near-spectral return, 'in the process splitting identity into several often conflicting fractions?'[22] '[A]lien flesh', concludes Trigg, 'is the recognition of the body as the host for th[is] overlapping', and the result is 'a primal experience

---

19. Jackson, 'Pillar of Salt', p. 243, p. 249, p. 248.
20. Jackson, 'Pillar of Salt', p. 246.
21. Jackson, 'Pillar of Salt', p. 246.
22. Trigg, *The Memory of Place*, p. 33.

of uncanniness'.[23] For Margaret, this experience entails the realization that the beach, which at first was 'oddly familiar and reassuring' to her, is in fact the dead-end of all her fantasies back home.[24] Indeed, the scene suggests the beach itself is uncannily 'double' given that it is at once the source of an optative fantasy and, in the present, a reminder of that fantasy's impossibility. If, at home, the imagined beach in some sense renders Margaret 'double' – insofar as her daydreams of it conjure a kind of second self – then here, as she confronts the actual beach in reality, such doubleness now overlaps inside her body, just as Trigg describes, defamiliarizing both place and self, leaving Margaret disjointed and stuck.

As if giving grotesque form to these twin feelings of fragmentation and paralysis, the severed leg, which appears immediately after Margaret's 'double recollection', literalizes and reflects back this experience of 'alien flesh'. The suddenness of its appearance, along with the obscurity of its origins, even makes the leg seem like a projection of Margaret's psyche, conjured in response to her uncanny recognition only moments earlier. The eerie atmosphere of the scene contributes to this ambiguity. With grey fog moving in over the water and the beach all but abandoned save for a lone man in a lunch stand eyeing Margaret and Brad, the leg, in its oddly immaculate state – stark white, cleanly severed, sitting *on top* of the sand – seems to have washed ashore, not from the murky depths of the East River, but from Margaret's own unconscious, a nightmarish object that externalizes her equally nightmarish feelings of fracture and disunity. Lying on the sand 'like part of a wax dummy', it also foreshadows the story's climax and conclusion, with Margaret at the crosswalk unable to move, a premonitory symbol for physical immobility that also represents the affective impasse occasioned by her trip and its revelations.[25]

Following the Long Island section of the story, Margaret's anxiety becomes acute. Back in her friend's apartment, she is beset by a neurosis without object: 'I'm not going to worry about it', she tells herself.[26] 'No sense worrying', she repeats several times.[27] '[P]eople get ideas like that and then worry about them.'[28] Like the unidentified tune from earlier, circling in her head over and over again, these repetitions revolve around the negative space of an avoidance. What is Margaret worrying about (or trying not to worry about) in these passages? What does the 'it' or 'that' replace and elide? On the one hand, she appears to be struggling with the frenetic stresses and grotesque shocks of the modern city; on the other, her urban phobias and obsessions seem more like symptoms constructed to avoid a more penetrating anxiety about her life back home. Which is to say, while the story might simply be a very dark and at times macabre comedy about post-war city life, it more pointedly excavates a truth about a young housewife's domestic

---

23. Trigg, *The Memory of Place*, p. 163, 166.
24. Jackson, 'Pillar of Salt', p. 245.
25. Jackson, 'Pillar of Salt', p. 247.
26. Jackson, 'Pillar of Salt', p. 248.
27. Jackson, 'Pillar of Salt', pp. 248–50.
28. Jackson, 'Pillar of Salt', p. 248.

unhappiness (the 'everyday dreariness', the 'love-broken stories'), a truth so long ignored and so deeply repressed that, here, coming to the surface, it unleashes a paralysing crisis of anxiety and self-doubt.

But this crisis also unleashes a hidden reservoir of anger and imagination, the story gesturing (as so many of Jackson's stories do) to the destructive power of stifled female creativity. In this regard, the story's penultimate sequence, with Margaret alone in the apartment, is revealing. Sitting by the window trying to calm her thoughts, she traces her sightline along the windows and ledges of the buildings across the way, only to find, as she does so, that they begin to collapse and disintegrate before her eyes, 'soundlessly crumpl[ing] and fall[ing] into fine sand'.[29] These visions frighten her, driving her into the bedroom, where, in a telling reflex meant to restore equilibrium through domestic routine, she remakes the bed, as the narrator puts it, 'like any good housewife'.[30] It does not work; the visions return. When she looks out the window, the houses and tenements, one by one, are all 'dissolving'; when she reaches out to touch her own windowsill, the stone disintegrates into 'crumbs'.[31] Thinking a nap might quell the destructive images in her head, she lies down. The whole building begins to shake.[32]

To my mind, the sequence speaks less to the city's agency as a force of delusion and destruction and more to Margaret's own repressed rage and imaginative power. The city's fault lines have opened something up within her, its landscape of collapse providing a canvas of neglect and ruin upon which she now imagines and expresses her own lived experience, the anger and frustration which, otherwise, might not have taken shape or been given form. That her visions terrify her only testifies to how deep-seated and repressed the feelings that inspire them are. That the story culminates in a textbook example of agoraphobia might suggest the way in which Margaret's psyche refuses any further confrontation with these same feelings and the fracturing unhappiness they intimate.

In *The Interpretation of Dreams*, for instance, Freud takes up an identical example in order to show how a phobia might be used to conceal an anxiety greater than that occasioned by the phobia itself:

> Let us suppose that a neurotic patient is unable to cross the street alone – a condition which we rightly regard as a 'symptom.' If we remove this symptom by compelling him to carry out the act of which he believes himself incapable, the consequence will be an attack of anxiety. . . . We see, therefore, that the symptom has been constructed in order to avoid an outbreak of anxiety; the phobia is erected like a frontier fortification against the anxiety.[33]

---

29. Jackson, 'Pillar of Salt', p. 248.
30. Jackson, 'Pillar of Salt', p. 248.
31. Jackson, 'Pillar of Salt', p. 248.
32. Jackson, 'Pillar of Salt', p. 248.
33. Sigmund Freud, *The Interpretation of Dreams*, trans. J. Strachey (New York: Basic Books, 2010), p. 546. In part, I am also relying here on Trigg's discussion of this passage in

In 'Pillar of Salt', New York becomes entangled with Margaret's embodiment and subjectivity. As her latent anxieties threaten to come to the surface, the city's own 'corporeality' at once projects and introjects her escalating sense of fissure, producing an uncanny experience of both place and self. In the end, however, rather than suggesting her ultimate collapse, her attack of agoraphobia might instead suggest a 'fortification' against such a collapse. The story's final moments see Margaret calling her husband and begging him to come rescue her. The scene is a further testament to the impossible impasse of her situation. On the one hand, to continue in the city would be to exacerbate the mental collapse she is already experiencing. On the other, to return to her husband would be to return to the deep-seated unhappiness which her urban dissolution is desperately trying to call to the surface. Paralyzed at the crosswalk, Margaret's immobility perfectly encapsulates the standstill between her repressed fears and the 'fortifications' which prevent her from confronting them, between the true source of her distress and its symptom.

A very different conclusion awaits Clara Spencer, the protagonist of 'The Tooth', also from 1948 and often considered alongside 'Pillar of Salt' and another story, 'A Day in the Jungle' (1952), as part of a trilogy. Like Margaret, Clara is a young suburban housewife whose journey into New York is an increasingly dream-like and even nightmarish exploration of her own feelings of uncanny identity. But unlike Margaret, Clara ventures into the city alone, going in to have an abscessed tooth extracted, and her oneiric experience of New York is at least in part the result of the whiskey, codeine and sleeping pills she takes to blunt the pain before boarding an overnight bus, leaving her dizzy and light-headed. Clara's hallucinatory state proves revealing: As she slips in and out of consciousness, her dreams and visions finally give shape to her long-ignored feelings of domestic entrapment and marital ennui.

If not exactly a representation of these feelings, the tooth stands in for their root causes (so to speak), suggesting how deeply embedded, or internalized, Clara's domesticated role has become, both in her psyche and in her body. As Clara makes explicit, the tooth and what it represents have all but taken her place. Before leaving, she tells her husband she is 'all tooth. Nothing else', its throbbing pain blotting out her sense of identity.[34] The now-constant ache (a *double entendre* for Clara's frustrated desire) has therefore become a physical as well as ontological state. As

---

his book *Topophobia* (2017), particularly pp. xxv–xvii. It might also be worth noting that Jackson herself would later suffer from agoraphobia, her case becoming particularly acute in the final years of her life. In an unfortunate echo of 'Pillar of Salt', Jackson describes similar phobias in a letter dated July 1963 to her friend Carol Brandt: 'My two big difficulties [...] are a reluctance to be packed in tightly anywhere (as in cocktail parties or traffic jams!) and a reluctance to go alone across open spaces (like walking down a street)' (qtd. in Ruth Franklin, *Shirley Jackson: A Rather Haunted Life* [New York: W. W. Norton, 2016], p. 473).

34. Shirley Jackson, 'The Tooth', in *The Lottery and Other Stories* (New York: Farrar, Straus and Giroux, 2005), pp. 265–86 (p. 266).

her husband unwittingly reminds her, this aching began, not so coincidentally, right after their wedding night: 'You had a toothache on our honeymoon', he says.[35] The tooth, in these multiple senses, defines Clara's bodily self, her life-world, interweaving external reality, proprioception, orientation, embodiment and identity. On the road, its pulse of pain 'mingle[s] with the movement of the bus, a steady beat like her heartbeat . . . going on through the night.'[36] Later, in New York, Clara believes it is the tooth that has led her 'unerringly' to the dentist's office, as if it were a homing device or navigation system steering her through the city, directing her every step and movement.[37] As she puts it, she might simply be the tooth's 'unwilling vehicle' and nothing more.[38] When the dentist X-rays her mouth, she wonders if the tooth has just had 'its picture taken without her', if it were now 'the only part of her to have any identity'.[39] 'How far down do the roots go?' she asks in a panic.[40]

It is a question posed, in various forms, by many of Jackson's characters, insofar as her depictions of uncanny identity involve the recognition that, for many of these women, their self-identity is defined almost exclusively by a domestic existence which is both deeply constitutive and deeply alienating, often at one and the same time. Here, this uncanniness is depicted phenomenologically, as rooted in place and the body. If the home is the context for this lived experience, then the city, as itself an unsettling and mutually defining space, offers up the potentiality for different forms of embodied selfhood at once alluring and unnerving.

For Clara, this potentiality presents itself before she even arrives in the city, in the form of Jim, the strange man who mysteriously appears next to her at a rest stop and then boards the bus with her, whispering in her ear poetic fragments about a faraway neverland: 'Even farther than Samarkand . . . and the waves ringing on the shore like bells. . . . The flutes play all night . . . and the stars are as big as the moon.'[41] An iteration of Jackson's folkloric James Harris character, Jim lulls and entices Clara, coaxing and shuttling her from place to place – 'Come along', he whispers.[42] Jackson never resolves whether or not Jim is an actual person or a figment of Clara's imagination. The ambiguity is suggestive: As a projection of Clara's unconscious mind, Jim is a seductive, dashing figure who steps in to help her in her disorientation, seemingly embodying her fantasies of escape; as an actual person, he seems much more sinister or at least suspect, a shadowy creep potentially preying on Clara's drugged state. In this sense, Jim is an ambiguous figure who exists 'in between', an ambiguity Jackson echoes in her symbolic use

35. Jackson, 'The Tooth', p. 267.
36. Jackson, 'The Tooth', p. 269.
37. Jackson, 'The Tooth', p. 276.
38. Jackson, 'The Tooth', p. 276.
39. Jackson, 'The Tooth', p. 276.
40. Jackson, 'The Tooth', p. 276.
41. Jackson, 'The Tooth', pp. 270–1.
42. Jackson, 'The Tooth', p. 271.

of space and place. Repeatedly, Clara wakes up in one rest stop after another with Jim at her side, each roadside restaurant only slightly different than the last, as if she were trapped in a time loop of transitional space.[43] And indeed, in a jarring and even comedic juxtaposition with Jim's exotic Shangri-La, the story purposely foregrounds the repetitive and inescapable nature of such liminal 'non-places', themselves sites of unsettling 'in-between' power.

In New York, for example, Clara's bodily experience of the city is almost entirely defined by transitional space. Still dazed and confused, she moves from one bus to the next, from one diner to another.[44] She kills time in a seemingly endless succession of waiting rooms – at the bus depot, at Penn Station, at the first dentist's office and then again at a second dentist's office.[45] The story's most revealing passages take place on escalators and in elevators, in hallways and corridors, in lobbies and in washrooms.[46] Jackson therefore thematizes the transitional and the interstitial, with Clara's experience of New York confined to the in-between, the city's threshold areas and liminal zones. Accumulating and overlapping within her body, these zones produce a widening disjunct between place and self, an increasingly unhomely sense of her being-in-the-world. In these respects, the story's depiction of transitional space recalls, once more, Trigg's 'alien flesh'. More specifically, it brings to mind his related concept of *'un-place'*, whereby 'the involuntary absorption of liminal and transitional places saturates the self with the otherness of place', such that the body all but mutates into a host for this 'otherness', the subject transformed into a site of strange and disturbing (dis)locations.[47] As Trigg writes, the result is a phenomenological experience of the uncanny, in which '[d]oubling, (un)familiarity, and strangeness conspire to create an experience that refuses to fit into the notion of place and identity as forming a continuous duration'.[48] Like the tooth and its throbbing reminder of the feelings Clara has left too-long ignored, the liminal places of the city embed themselves within her body, at once constitutive and foreign, disrupting the continuity between self and place, between Clara and her environment.

In their liminality, these places mirror Clara's drugged and half-conscious state, and, similarly, they seem to shake loose a previously inaccessible emotional reality, one she desperately tries to suppress. At the dentist's, she makes her way through a series of corridors and rooms that transform into a series of 'labyrinths and passages, seeming to lead into the heart of the office building', as if she were penetrating, not merely the generic space of the office, but also the inmost chambers of the psyche.[49] When she finally enters the examination room, her

---

43. Jackson, 'The Tooth', pp. 270–3.
44. Jackson, 'The Tooth', pp. 273–4.
45. Jackson, 'The Tooth', pp. 273–9.
46. Jackson, 'The Tooth', pp. 274–86.
47. Trigg, *The Memory of Place*, p. 155.
48. Trigg, *The Memory of Place*, p. 163.
49. Jackson, 'The Tooth', p. 279.

fear and anxiety make explicit the Freudian symbolism of the scene. In her mind, the extraction of the tooth has become an excavation of the unconscious. First, the X-rays turn her inside out, making blindingly clear what should have stayed hidden and private; next, the operating theatre transmutes into what Clara thinks of as 'the vault', the dentist inadvertently articulating her implicit fears: 'All you've got to worry about', he says, 'is telling us all your secrets while you're asleep.'[50] Under anaesthesia, she returns to the office hallway in a frenetic dream of warped space and thwarted escape, the corridor now 'horribly clear' and Jim 'holding out his hands and laughing' at the other end of it, saying something she cannot hear.[51] She wakes in a panic, repeating: 'Did I talk? . . . Did I say anything? . . . Did I *say* anything?'[52]

As it happens, both in her dream and out loud, Clara *does* say something: 'I'm not afraid.'[53] Ironically, despite her fear that the removal of the tooth would be a symbolic act of disclosure and revelation, the extraction instead roots out Clara's fear itself. As she leaves the dentist's office, she steps back into the hallway from her nightmare, recognizing it in waking life. This time, however, she makes an escape of sorts, stepping through a side-door into the ladies' room, where, in a moment of anxious (mis)recognition, she strangely glimpses her true self. At the sink, she looks up into the mirror and cannot find her own face in among a group of women:

> She looked into the mirror as though into a group of strangers, all staring at her or around her; no one was familiar in the group, no one smiled at her or looked at her with recognition; you'd think my own face would know me, she thought, with a queer numbness in her throat. . . . Perhaps it's not a mirror, she thought, maybe it's a window and I'm looking straight through at these women waiting on the other side.[54]

Without the tooth, Clara becomes a kind of absent presence, her face somehow vanishing from the mirror in front of her. And yet, in her case, such 'ghostliness' reveals, rather than effectuates, the social invisibility of female dispossession. Placed in phenomenological terms, the scene and its uncanniness might be read as a critical engagement with gender, lived experience and the social production of the sexed body. Having shed the tooth and the domesticated role it represented, Clara is no longer visible to the world as it is, the world that makes her presence and even her reality contingent on that role and its circumscription. What she glimpses in the mirror is the presence of her own absence. It is a moment of unhomely anxiety, in the phenomenological sense (*Angst*), in that the world, and

---

50. Jackson, 'The Tooth', pp. 279–80.
51. Jackson, 'The Tooth', p. 280.
52. Jackson, 'The Tooth', p. 281.
53. Jackson, 'The Tooth', pp. 280–1.
54. Jackson, 'The Tooth', p. 283.

what Heidegger calls the 'groundless floating' of its inauthentic life, have been stripped away, leaving Clara alone with her own radical distinction from this world, seeing her authentic self perhaps for the first time in years.[55]

The moment, in short, provides an opportunity for reinvention, and Clara seizes it, as if the mirror were indeed a window and she were stepping through it to claim a new identity 'on the other side'.[56] Quickly, she sheds any identifying reminders of her former self – the 'Clara' of a previous existence and reality – dropping a silver barrette inscribed with her name and a pin with her initials on it into the metal ashstand by her side, each item making its own 'satisfactory clang' as it hits the bottom.[57] Like the 'waves ringing on the shore like bells' from Jim's first description of his neverland beach, these clangs signal the opening of a new world for her.[58] When she exits the washroom, she walks 'purposefully' down the hall, a stark contrast to her earlier trudging from place to place in a fog, whisked and shuttled, guided and directed by others.[59] When she steps out of the lobby and into the city, she steps out into a New York now profoundly altered. If, earlier, Jim appeared unbidden, now he is summoned, Clara conjuring his presence from a nearby crowd, taking his hand, and walking with him down the street, which, underfoot, has already transformed into 'hot sand'.[60]

These final moments could not be more different from those in 'Pillar of Salt' – in their disavowal and even abandonment of the rescuing husband; in their commitment to the female imagination and its transformative power; in their depiction of mobility rather than paralysis; in their fulfilment of desire rather than stasis. To read the scene as simply an effect of Clara's 'disordered' mind – in short, as an hallucination – seems only to pessimistically reinforce the historical pathologization of women as 'an irruption in the city, a symptom of disorder, and a problem'.[61] A far more interesting reading, to my mind, sees the scene as realizing the outsider perspective of women in the city, what Deborah Nord describes as 'a consciousness of transgression and trespassing', imposing this consciousness on the urban environment as a new reality, no longer suppressed nor relegated either to the 'outside' or the unconscious.[62] In this sense, 'The Tooth' seems to finish something that 'Pillar of Salt' starts – whereas Margaret's inexpressible feelings are channelled into visions of terrifying rage and destruction, here, Clara's encounter

---

55. Martin Heidegger, *Being and Time*, trans. J. Stambaugh (New York: State University of New York Press, 1996), p. 165.
56. Jackson, 'The Tooth', p. 283.
57. Jackson, 'The Tooth', p. 284, 285.
58. Jackson, 'The Tooth', p. 270.
59. Jackson, 'The Tooth', p. 286.
60. Jackson, 'The Tooth', p. 286.
61. Elizabeth Wilson, *The Sphinx in the City: Urban Life, the Control of Disorder, and Women* (Berkeley: University of California Press, 1991), p. 9.
62. Deborah Nord, *Walking the Victorian Streets: Women, Representation, and the City* (New York: Cornell University Press, 1995), p. 12.

with the anxious uncanny leads to the fulfilment of her latent desire, the realization of her fantasies.

As a brief foray into a possible line of enquiry, I have tried in this chapter to orient the phenomenality of anxiety and unhomeliness towards a different consideration of Jackson's uncanny, what I see as a potential approach to a writer who so often uses embodied experience and spatiality to realize her modality of the Gothic as a means to excavating the subject position of women at the mid-century. While so much of Jackson's work uses the Gothic and the uncanny to explore and process traumatic pasts (as well as present realities), her poetics of haunting often complicates this schematic, positing different expressions of unhomeliness and spectrality. In particular, for a writer who claimed that all of her books, when laid end to end, would form 'one long documentation of anxiety', her depictions of the anxious body, as well as those of anxious space, seem impossibly entangled with her depictions of haunting, in a way that still seems relatively unexplored.[63] A phenomenological approach to these depictions – of anxiety, of lived experience, of placemaking and placelessness, as well as haunting and uncanny identity – might help to further illuminate the ways in which Jackson's critical examinations of female subjecthood and its social production are, in more than one sense, rooted in the lived body and its phenomenal experience of place. In 'Pillar of Salt' and 'The Tooth', it is the anxious city that brings about such encounters, but we could easily imagine how a phenomenology of unsettled place might be applied to Jackson's other settings as well, from the home to the small town, calling to the surface the often-overlooked realities of women and their embodied experience.

References

Aravot, Iris (2010), 'Back to Phenomenological Placemaking', *Journal of Urban Design* 7 (2): 201–12.

Benjamin, Walter (1939; 1969), 'On Some Motifs in Baudelaire', in *Illuminations*, trans. Henry Zohn, ed. Hannah Arendt, 155–200, New York: Shocken Books.

Franklin, Ruth (2016), *Shirley Jackson: A Rather Haunted Life*, New York: W.W. Norton.

Freud, Sigmund (2010), *The Interpretation of Dreams*, trans. J. Strachey, New York: Basic Books.

Grosz, Elizabeth (1995), 'Bodies—Cities', in Elizabeth Grosz (ed.), *Space, Time, and Perversion*, 103–10, New York: Routledge.

Hague, Angela (2005), '"A Faithful Anatomy of Our Times": Reassessing Shirley Jackson', *Frontiers: A Journal of Women's Studies* 26 (2): 73–96.

Heidegger, Martin (1996), *Being and Time*, trans. Joan Stambaugh, New York: State University of New York Press.

Jackson, Shirley (1948a; 2005), 'Pillar of Salt', in *The Lottery and Other Stories*, 235–53, New York: Farrar, Straus and Giroux.

63. Quoted in Franklin, *Shirley Jackson*, p. 477.

Jackson, Shirley (1948b; 2005), 'The Tooth', in *The Lottery and Other Stories*, 265–86, New York: Farrar, Straus and Giroux.
Munford, Rebecca (2016), 'Spectral Femininity', in Avril Horner and Sue Zlosnik (eds), *Women and the Gothic*, 120–34, Edinburgh: Edinburgh University Press.
Nord, Deborah (1995), *Walking the Victorian Streets: Women, Representation, and the City*, New York: Cornell University Press.
Pascal, Richard (1982), '"Farther than Samarkand": The Escape Theme in Shirley Jackson's "The Tooth"', *Studies in Short Fiction* 19, no. 2 (Spring): 133–9.
Simmel, Georg (1950), 'The Metropolis and Mental Life', in *The Sociology of Georg Simmel*, ed. and trans. Kurt Wolff, 409–26, New York: The Free Press.
Tochterman, Brian L. (2017), *The Dying City: Postwar New York and the Ideology of Fear*, Chapel Hill: The University of North Carolina Press.
Trigg, Dylan (2012), *The Memory of Place: A Phenomenology of the Uncanny*, Athens: Ohio University Press.
Trigg, Dylan (2017), *Topophobia: A Phenomenology of Anxiety*, New York: Bloomsbury Academic.
Vidler, Anthony (2000), *Warped Space: Art, Architecture, and Anxiety in Modern Culture*, Cambridge, MA: The MIT Press.
Wilson, Elizabeth (1991), *The Sphinx in the City: Urban Life, the Control of Disorder, and Women*, Berkeley: University of California Press.

Chapter 10

ON HER WAY TO THE GROCERY STORE

SHOPPING, ALIENATION AND THE LOST HOUSEWIFE IN SHIRLEY JACKSON'S SHORT STORIES

Emma Liggins

Many of Shirley Jackson's short stories trace a disturbing path from the unhomely suburban home to the grocery store (and back again). It is usually, but not exclusively, the falsely bright housewife, overly invested in the delights of the domestic, who treads this path of doom. By the 1950s, according to Betty Friedan's narrative of suburban hell in *The Feminine Mystique* (1963), 'many women no longer left their homes, except to shop, chauffeur their children, or attend a social engagement with their husbands'.[1] The problem of going out shopping is the forced return to an 'empty' home space, what Friedan singles out as 'the dullness of domestic routine'.[2] Buying goods, particularly food, hardware and kitchen equipment, is one of the everyday activities of Jackson's female characters; immersed in consumer culture, they pop out to buy ingredients to make cakes and pies, to procure food for their children and husbands or to acquire items to facilitate domestic duties. Men sometimes return to the home from the drugstore, bearing gifts of candy to appease their restless wives, but the women recognize that purchasing and performing in the store, before carrying packages back to their gleaming kitchens, is an inescapable part of their lives. It is also a potent source of alienation. As Angelica Michelis has argued, despite being essential to the formation of modern subjectivities in the newly accessible public sphere, by the 1940s entering shops and exchanging money had become tainted and demoralizing,[3] as the familiar became strange.

The ritual of dropping into the store and its dark aftermath has so far gone relatively unnoticed in Jackson studies. While grocery shopping does feature in her novels – *The Road through the Wall* (1948) includes a biting exchange between a newcomer and local residents about where the nearest store is, resulting in

---

1. Betty Friedan, *The Feminine Mystique* (Harmondsworth: Penguin, 1963), p. 13, 15.
2. Friedan, *Feminine Mystique*, p. 44.
3. Angelica Michelis, 'Visual and Literary Representations of Shopping', in *A Cultural History of Shopping in the Modern Age*, ed. Vicki Howard (London: Bloomsbury, 2022), p. 129.

their thinly veiled antagonism to her newness and social awkwardness – it is in her short fiction that movements between commercial and domestic space often structure the narrative of housewife as alienated outsider. Early reviewers admired the only short story collection published in her lifetime, *The Lottery and Other Stories* (1949), for its originality and 'deadly accuracy', with Jackson saluted as 'the most exciting short-story writer who has appeared for years'.[4] Her gifts for creating tension and suggesting 'intangible terrors' are also astutely identified as 'deriv[ing] directly from her power to see and describe *objects*',[5] with domestic settings privileged over commercial realms. Bernice M. Murphy has argued that, in suburban Gothic, rather than being threatened by a monstrous 'Other', 'one is almost always more in danger from the people in the house next door, or one's own family... [or] one's fellow suburbanites',[6] and this is certainly borne out in many of these dark tales, most of which have a suburban or rural setting and a threat from within. While Jackson's short fiction has more recently been considered in relation to ideas of fragile domesticities, the invasion of domestic space and the lost girl, the connections between shopping, loss and the disorientating unhomeliness of home have not been fully investigated. Roberta Rubinstein has identified the tension between 'home/lost' as a key one in Jackson's oeuvre, suggesting that the home as an 'emotional space' is threatened by images of homelessness and 'the loss of the self'.[7] Yet, contrary to Rubinstein's arguments about Female Gothic, domestic spaces are not *always* maternal in these stories, as precarious husband/wife and mistress/servant relations, and beyond the home, storekeeper/housewife relations, are also significant to the potential alienation of the lost female protagonist. Michael J. Dalpe Jr has argued that Jackson's women lose control of their own narratives when they are outside the home, using the grocery store as an example of a public space governed by rules about 'polite performances'.[8] Uncomfortable confrontations between neighbours, Dalpe contends, are linked in Jackson's stories to 'expectations of gender performance' and a dangerous 'normalcy'; the stories then set out to challenge and undermine the performance of domesticity and the hegemonic systems it upholds.[9] In this chapter I will shift the focus to the strange relationship between spaces of consumption and the suburban/rural home

4. L. A. G. Strong, 'Fiction', *The Spectator*, 30 June 1950, pp. 905–6 (p. 906).

5. L. A. G. Strong, 'Fiction', *The Spectator*, 5 October 1951, pp. 451–2 (p. 451). This is from a review of *Hangsaman*, which compares it unfavourably to the exceptional power of her short stories.

6. Bernice M. Murphy, *The Suburban Gothic in American Popular Culture* (Basingstoke: Palgrave, 2009), p. 2.

7. Roberta Rubinstein, 'House Mothers and Haunted Daughters: Shirley Jackson and Female Gothic', *Tulsa Studies in Women's Literature* 15, no. 2 (1996): 309–31 (p. 317).

8. Michael Dalpe, Jr, '"You Didn't Look Like You Belonged in This House": Shirley Jackson's Fragile Domesticities' in *Shirley Jackson and Domesticity: Beyond the Haunted House*, ed. Jill E. Anderson and Melanie R. Anderson (London: Bloomsbury, 2020), p. 44.

9. Dalpe, Jr, 'You Didn't Look Like', p. 44.

in Jackson's short fiction, in the context of the history of shopping, the alienation of everyday life and the politics of the grocery store between the late 1940s and 1960s.

Trapped by the restrictive identity forced upon her by the ominous and suspicious storekeepers, the American housewife is then rendered vulnerable to the lurking strangeness of her home, often a newly rented property in an alien environment. With the rise of chain store groceries, argues Tracy Deutsch, 'women's use of consumption as a realm in which to challenge the political and social order, and especially to challenge conventional gender norms, had come to seem an eminently modern thing to do'.[10] Yet rather than offering a modern means of challenging convention, shopping in Jackson's writing seems to reinforce a harshly conformist gender normativity, which makes the return to the unhomely home much darker. If consumer culture 'lends itself to images of unconscious imprisonment', as Rachel Bowlby argues in *Carried Away: The Invention of Modern Shopping* (2000), then 'dark pictures' of the shopping world may emerge in contrast to the view of the delights and freedoms of consuming.[11] In stories such as 'Men with their Big Shoes' (1947), 'The Honeymoon of Mrs Smith' and 'The Summer People' (1950), and the more supernatural 'Home' (1965), grocers exercise an ominous control over city people at the mercy of the rules and rituals of suburban/rural life. This chapter explores the ways in which female identity becomes controlled by the storekeepers, drawing both on Henri Lefebvre's theories of space and on the cultural history of shopping to reappraise the disturbing dynamics of the store in relation to the housewife's feelings of alienation and loss in her new home.

Shopping, Alienation and the Rise of Consumer Society

By the 1940s the grocery store held a significant importance in the middle-class American woman's daily life. With the growth of local stores across the United States, particularly positioned in the suburban outskirts and before the widespread use of refrigerators, the expectation was that food for the family would be bought on a daily basis, while children were out at school. The ritual of leaving the home to go to the store meant that American women were often positioned in a transitional space, either going or returning. En route they also had to perform their femininities before the neighbours. Krista Lysack has highlighted the in-betweenness of going to the store and 'the ways in which the practice of shopping mediated between women's traditional domestic sphere and a public one . . . [mapping] the continuity

---

10. Tracy Deutsch, *Building a Housewife's Paradise: Gender, Politics, and American Grocery Stores in the Twentieth Century* (Chapel Hill: University of North Carolina Press, 2010), p. 45.

11. Rachel Bowlby, *Carried Away: The Invention of Modern Shopping* (New York: Columbia University Press, 2000), p. 3, 11.

between home and marketplace'.[12] While Jackson did write about disorientating experiences in urban department stores in stories such as 'My Life with R.H. Macy' (1942) and the shopping episode in *Life among the Savages* (1953), a more typical scenario is the repeated visit to the smaller suburban or rural store where disturbing encounters seem difficult to avoid. Jackson's characters look forward to consuming circulars from department stores that arrive in the post, but are less likely to visit. Women's entrance into the marketplace as consumers could certainly grant them new kinds of freedom, authority and agency. However, as post-1940s fiction indicates, the occupation of spaces of consumption involved particular exchanges with retailers and other customers that could also threaten their already fragile gender and class identities.

Historians of consumption have identified the post–Second World War retail landscape as dominated by the emergence of the supermarket and a new mass-consuming society, signifying 'an enormous transformation in the ways in which women sought to feed their families'.[13] According to Rachel Bowlby, the new American consumer society not only put 'an unremitting pressure on people to consume' but also forced them into the 'community space' of the supermarket, an unsettling arena often represented in fiction as one of 'exploitation or opportunity'.[14] The spatial theorist Henri Lefebvre has highlighted the ways in which space is ritualized, remarking that 'accessible space for normal use' is governed by 'established rules and practical procedures'.[15] The codes of social space are historically specific, requiring 'a level of performance' from those who enter,[16] which has interesting repercussions in terms of spaces of consumption and exchange. The grocery store, with its hierarchies and mix of classes, has its own unspoken rules: newcomers or transgressors of social etiquette will be the subject of gossip or confrontation; judgements will be passed on both purchases and performances. According to Tracy Deutsch, these were 'spaces where ethnic loyalties, gender identities and race relations were negotiated, reconfigured, and troubled', key to our understanding of survival and consumption in twentieth-century urban America.[17] Before the relative anonymity of the supermarket, stores were permeated by 'messy' social tensions and discord, as well as friendship and community, 'shaped by grocers' expectations that women customers would demand significant authority over the terms of purchase'.[18] In Jackson's stories, the

---

12. Krista Lysack, *Come Buy, Come Buy: Shopping and the Culture of Consumption in Victorian Women's Writing* (Ohio: Ohio University Press, 2008), p. 25.

13. Deutsch, *Housewife's Paradise*, p. 1. The emergence and embellishment of an ideology of the conservative female shopper in the 1940s and 1950s.

14. Bowlby, *Carried Away*, p. 155, p. 206, p. 188.

15. Henri Lefebvre, *The Production of Space*, trans. Donald Nicholson Smith (Oxford: Blackwell, 1991), p. 193.

16. Lefebvre, *Production of Space*, p. 33.

17. Deutsch, *Housewife's Paradise*, p. 3.

18. Deutsch, *Housewife's Paradise*, p. 14.

store-owner is almost universally presented as an ominous figure who regards the customer with suspicion or exposes secrets about their private lives, taking delight in intensifying social tensions or puncturing female authority.

Consumerism underpins the American housewife's problem with no name in *The Feminine Mystique*, in which social conformity breeds sadness and emptiness, the 'terrible boredom' of suburbia.[19] Shopping for groceries is the second in the damning list of conformist rituals in the first paragraph of Friedan's polemic about the 'strange stirring' and 'dissatisfaction' of women taught to 'glory in their own femininity'.[20] Desperation is linked to 'the enormous demands of her role as modern housewife: wife, mistress, mother, nurse, consumer, cook, chauffeur'.[21] This combination of wife and consumer is linked to susceptibility to advertising and the regressive 'happy housewife heroine' visible in the pages of popular women's magazines, the shrinking of 'woman's world to the home'.[22] The 'mindless conformity', materialism and zombie-like denizens, trying to live up to these unachievable ideals, argues Murphy, are suggestive of suburbia's 'social and gothic possibilities', inherent in 'the mores and anxieties of the modern age'.[23]

The mundanity of modernity finds its expression in the uncanny repetitions of the daily shop, where the bourgeois housewife is forced into a commercialized encounter with sellers who behave like friends but may be feigning intimacy and connection. Writing in *Critique of Everyday Life* (1947), Lefebvre identifies the links between consumption and estrangement as characteristic of modern newly urbanized society and of 'bourgeois everyday life'. He defines alienation in terms of the strangeness and disorientation of the modern world, where role-playing and fakery are essential, 'precious' aspects of a contradictory familiarity.[24] Whereas Karl Marx had associated alienation with the experience of the objectified proletariat workforce and their mechanized labour in industrial capitalism,[25] by the early twentieth century the concept can be used to describe the estrangement of the bourgeoisie, particularly women, who find themselves ill at ease, disorientated in the maelstroms of commercial exchange in the new consumer society. For Lefebvre, both financial transactions and commercial space invite estrangement, which becomes inherent in social relations: 'Alienation – I know it is there whenever I handle a banknote or enter a shop'.[26] In a postmodern society of mass consumption, argues Lauren Langman, the site of alienation 'in a fragmented world

---

19. Friedan, *Feminine Mystique*, p. 49.
20. Friedan, *Feminine Mystique*, p. 13.
21. Friedan, *Feminine Mystique*, p. 27.
22. Friedan, *Feminine Mystique*, p. 58.
23. Murphy, *Suburban Gothic*, p. 16, 17.
24. Henri Lefebvre, *Critique of Everyday Life, Volume 1* (1947), second edition, trans. John Moore (London and New York: Verso, 2008), 'Foreword' (1956–7), p. 5, 15.
25. See Lefebvre, *Critique of Everyday Life*, pp. 58–63, for his analysis of Marx's theories of alienation and exploitation.
26. Lefebvre, *Critique of Everyday Life*, p. 183.

of everyday life ... situated in consumption-based routines and lifestyles' becomes the shopping centre.[27] Friedan also notes that the housewife's 'fragmented' day, with never more than fifteen minutes on one thing, leads to a 'terrible tiredness'.[28] While Jackson's grocers are not anonymized purveyors of mass-produced goods, but pass requested items across the counter to customers whose names they usually remember, the shops certainly reproduce and reinforce these alienated interactions in which the buyer seems to be crushed by consumerist rituals.

Stories of the 1940s and 1950s: The Housewife as Outsider

In her autobiography *Dust Tracks on a Road* (1942), the African American writer Zora Neale Hurston records her bewilderment as a child at listening in on cryptic conversations in her local Florida store, unable to fully comprehend the 'double talk', the 'scrap[s] of gossip' that synchronize with the everyday transactions.[29] This 'double talk' permeates the store scenes of Jackson's fiction, where enquiries about health and family as well as the products bought and sold are coupled with hostile laughter, fake niceties and often a masked malevolence and danger. Despite finding *The Lottery and Other Stories* (1949) rather formulaic and a little monotonous, the *New York Times* reviewer noted the 'precise dexterity' achieved within 'a narrowly restricted range'. He admired the ways in which 'with a few lines of casual dialogue and a typical gesture or two, [the stories] draw blood ... an ironic or savage point is made through a seemingly unimportant incident, or through the establishment of a mood or prevailing atmosphere'.[30] This savagery of the trivial and the supposedly unimportant are now recognized as fundamental to suburban Gothic and its domestic terrors, its preoccupation with the sinister underside to the ordinary.[31] Subject to a cruel conversation in the grocery store about how to treat dogs who kill chickens, Mrs Walpole in 'The Renegade' (reprinted in *The Lottery* collection) feels faint and leaves without her shopping. By the end of the story she fearfully imagines the suggested spiked collar as her own punishment, 'the sharp points closing in on her throat'.[32] This is precisely because this cryptic advice makes her feel not only compromised but tortured for her lack of control over her own dog, and therefore for her less than perfect performance of the role of housewife. Perhaps she, and not her misbehaving pet, is the real renegade. The

---

27. Lauren Langman, 'Alienation and Everyday Life: Goffman Meets Marx at the Shopping Mall', *International Journal of Sociology and Social Policy* 11, no. 6/7/8 (1991): 107–24 (p. 108).
28. Friedan, *Feminine Mystique*, p. 27.
29. Zora Neale Hurston, *Dust Tracks on a Road* (1942; London: Virago, 1986), p. 62.
30. Orville Prescott, 'Books of the Times', *New York Times*, 15 April 1949, p. 21.
31. Murphy, *Suburban Gothic*, p. 2.
32. Shirley Jackson, 'The Renegade', in *The Lottery and Other Stories* (Harmondsworth: Penguin, 2009), pp. 69–83 (p. 83).

logic of Jackson's stories of the 1940s and 1950s is that women are doomed to remain outsiders in their suburban communities, subject to gossip and suspicion as they try to negotiate their roles as consumers within an economy of exchange balanced in favour of the collective power of the storekeepers.

In the early story 'Men with their Big Shoes' (*Yale Review*, 1947), a newly married and pregnant wife finds herself trapped in her new home with her red-faced and overpowering maid, Mrs Anderson. Warning signs are set off from the opening paragraph as Mrs Hart congratulates herself on her good fortune, admiring 'the quiet street' and the 'kind people who smiled at her as they passed' as she rests in her chintzy living room. 'It was a real house', Jackson's sly narrator confides, 'the milkman left milk there every morning ... you could cook on the real stove in the kitchen'.[33] As Deborah Sugg Ryan has argued, the twentieth-century suburban home mediates oppositions between 'modernity and nostalgia, urban and rural, past and future' which render the domestic space unsettling and sometimes unsafe;[34] in her desire to be modern, and her transition from urban to suburban, Mrs Hart exposes herself to danger. The dirty marks supposedly made by big-shoed men on the clean floor can also be attributed to both maid (thumbprints on the windows, marking the space) and the inquisitive absent-present storekeeper who conspire to deprive the nervous mistress of agency and choice. The maid has apparently shared confidences with the grocer Mrs Martin about the misdeeds of Mr Hart, presumably in the public space of the store, and Mrs Hart's desire that her maid convey to the storekeeper that she finds her 'such a nice person'[35] show the position of power held by this figure. The mistress's unreasonable fear of the 'belligerent authority'[36] of her maid fits with the magazine narratives about domestic intimidation; her 'timid uneasiness' is produced by the maid's superior knowledge of cooking and cleaning, despite never getting anything 'quite clean'.[37] The 'sickening conviction'[38] that her maid is in control means that Mrs Hart is deprived of a space of freedom in the realm where it should be most possible. The maid's worship of ritual is comically apparent in the repeated references to the morning cup of tea, and then her barely concealed anger when Mrs Hart varies the number of cups. By the end of the story the maid is constantly interrupting her mistress with accusations of her husband's infidelity before commandeering the spare room for herself. Meanwhile, the neighbours regard them with 'frozen faces',[39] the frozenness behind the façade of satisfying domesticity evocative of the housewives-turned-automatons in Ira Levin's satirical novel *The Stepford Wives* (1972).

33. Shirley Jackson, 'Men with their Big Shoes', in *The Lottery and Other Stories* (Harmondsworth: Penguin, 2009), pp. 255–64 (p. 255).
34. Deborah Sugg Ryan, *Ideal Homes: Domestic Design and Suburban Modernism, 1918-1939* (Manchester: Manchester University Press, 2018), p. 60.
35. Jackson, 'Men with their Big Shoes', p. 262.
36. Jackson, 'Men with their Big Shoes', p. 256.
37. Jackson, 'Men with their Big Shoes', p. 256.
38. Jackson, 'Men with their Big Shoes', p. 256.
39. Jackson, 'Men with their Big Shoes', p. 264.

Terrifying in her non-appearance, the absent grocer haunts the conversation between the housewife and her domineering 'real maid', joining forces with the help to deny the mistress any power in her 'real house'. Described as 'keen-eyed and shrill, watching other people's groceries',[40] the storekeeper, her stories and her surveillance exacerbate the housewife's sense of isolation. The bracketed question, '("Two loaves of whole wheat today, Mrs Hart? Company tonight, maybe?")'[41] indicates the quick assumptions made about the consumption of food. After this exchange, Mrs Hart speaks out against gossip, and feels 'a quick fear touching her; her kind neighbours watching her beneath their friendliness, looking out quietly from behind curtains'.[42] The maid's advice that she shouldn't let anything scare her during her pregnancy suggests that the store and all it stands for is definitely something to be afraid of. Like many of Jackson's early stories, the narrative ends with the housewife's 'sudden unalterable conviction that she was lost',[43] a motif of loss and alienation common across her first collection, according to Franklin.[44] Yet Franklin's view that this conviction is attributable to the men who drive women insane is not the full story; the 'knowing smile' of the help who now has her feet firmly under the table of Mrs Hart's insecure home is inextricably linked to 'the quick picture of Mrs Martin, leaning comfortably across the counter' and her imagined bracketed response: '("I see that you've got a new star boarder, Mrs Hart. Mrs Anderson'll see that you're taken good care of!")'.[45] Here the dangerous conspiracy is between the maid and the absent grocery clerk. Both lower-class women join forces to demonstrate their authority over the helpless housewife, who becomes vulnerable once she pays for services, suggesting that the dynamics of local hostility are not as simple as patriarchal control.

'The Summer People' (*Charm*, 1950), a dark tale of the consequences of outstaying your welcome, shows the store-owners of a small town closing ranks on the owners of a country cottage without heat or electricity. As New Yorkers Janet and Robert Allison have always relished their summers in the cottage and 'hated to leave in the fall', one year they decide 'with a slight feeling of adventure'[46] to stay beyond Labor Day into the autumn. Such capriciousness is punished by the retailers' communal refusal to supply food or fuel after the usual date, leaving the Allisons terrified of an impending storm at the end of the story, their phone line cut, their radio batteries fading and their car out of use. Darryl Hattenhauer reads this as a postmodern narrative of paranoia exposing 'bourgeois anxiety about the

---

40. Jackson, 'Men with their Big Shoes', p. 262.
41. Jackson, 'Men with their Big Shoes', p. 262.
42. Jackson, 'Men with their Big Shoes', p. 262.
43. Jackson, 'Men with their Big Shoes', p. 264.
44. Ruth Franklin, *Shirley Jackson: A Rather Haunted Life* (New York: Liveright, 2016), p. 254.
45. Jackson, 'Men with their Big Shoes', p. 254.
46. Shirley Jackson, 'The Summer People', in *Dark Tales* (Harmondsworth: Penguin, 2017), p. 182.

underclass'.[47] Rejecting the sinister undertones to the confrontations in the shops, he sees it as a narrative 'ultimately unsympathetic to the Allisons' hypocritical devaluing of the locals for their lack of urbanity'.[48] In the narrative, a ritualistic shopping trip precedes a series of unsuccessful phone calls to local stores, before the breakdown of the car and the damaged phone line cut off communication with the local community. The final trip to 'their village', 'their big trip into town'[49] is punctuated by increasingly hostile encounters with 'those natives with whom [Mrs Allison] had dealings',[50] as her sense of ownership disintegrates in line with their diminished bargaining power.

Positioning the female shopper within a number of stores in the confines of the short narrative increases the uncanniness of the encounters, as the impossibly shared information between store-owners and clerks in the community means that they repeat the same phrases, automaton-like, in order to challenge the authority of the customer. This technique for representing 'the strangeness of shopping and consuming'[51] is evident in other stories such as 'The Daemon Lover' (1947), structured around the frantic female protagonist's search for her lost/imagined husband on her wedding day. Entering a series of suburban stores, she is confronted by the increasing hostility of the 'knowing'[52] staff with their confusing responses. Their uncannily repeated replies are partly attributed to her breaking of commercial rituals by asking questions rather than buying anything. What Deutsch refers to as 'the centrality of gender relations to grocery stores' is always in evidence in the dynamics between buyers and sellers, with lone women buyers often humiliated or mocked by dismissive male sellers.[53] Entering the stores without her husband in 'The Summer People', Mrs Allison's negotiations are marked by her casual references to the city she has left, prompting fake smiles from the store-owners no longer hiding their antagonism to her outsider status. Mr Babcock, 'her grocer', looks reflectively into a bag of cookies as he intones, 'Nobody ever stayed at the lake past Labor Day'.[54] It is significant that Mrs Allison reads these 'inconclusive conversations with Mr Babcock'[55] in relation to her belief in his mental degeneration; yet the 'irritating native tricks' she identifies in his repetitive, 'trite' speech hold more power in the community than the city-dwellers imagine. As this line about 'summer people' not staying on after Labor

47. Darryl Hattenhauer, *Shirley Jackson's American Gothic* (New York: State University of New York Press, 2003), p. 51.
48. Hattenhauer, *Shirley Jackson's American Gothic*, p. 53.
49. Jackson, 'The Summer People', p. 182, p. 183.
50. Jackson, 'The Summer People', p. 182.
51. Bowlby, *Carried Away*, p. 11.
52. Shirley Jackson, 'The Daemon Lover', in *The Lottery and Other Stories* (Harmondsworth: Penguin, 2009), pp. 9–28 (p. 19).
53. Deutsch, *Housewife's Paradise*, p. 40.
54. Jackson, 'The Summer People', p. 182.
55. Jackson, 'The Summer People', p. 183.

Day is uncannily repeated by all four of the store-owners, the Allisons' sense of ownership and enjoyment of the 'personal' transactions in the town rings hollow. Mrs Allison is unable to join the local women in the hardware store in their 'acute' discussions of the prices of house dresses, nor can she look Mr Walpole in the face as he winds string around her new baking dishes before he 'shoved the package ... across the counter'.[56] These foreboding transactions taint the ride home after their 'day of what seemed whirlwind shopping'[57]: the autumn sky is darkening and the dirt road is rough and difficult to navigate so that 'their cottage, silhouetted against the sky'[58] looks more hostile than homely.

Wartime rationing and the sellers' resistance to new technologies are also key contexts. In the 1940s women could use price control and rationing programs 'to report violations and to threaten uncooperative grocers'.[59] The final news broadcast heard by the Allisons on their fading radio includes 'the estimated rise in food prices during the coming week'.[60] The city people's modern use of the telephone to order deliveries is also seen to put them at a disadvantage, missing out on goods sold temporarily: 'she was never able to form any accurate idea of Mr Babcock's current stock by telephone'.[61] The unnamed kerosene man withholds his supply as 'about now it's starting to get pretty short',[62] interrupting the housewife's falsely bright cajoling as if to prove her bargaining power is running low, setting the failed transaction alongside her strategies for overruling 'when in disagreement with her neighbours'.[63] The housewife's anger and thoughts about retaliatory withholding of her custom is ineffective, as is her attempt to order kerosene by phone from her grocer, whose voice indicates 'suspicion of anyone who tried to communicate with him by means of this unreliable instrument'.[64] Her husband, 'duly armed with a list of groceries',[65] is unable to go into battle once the car refuses to start, enhancing the sense of helplessness in the house and the 'state of tension that preceded a thunderstorm', 'the room seemed unexpectedly dark'.[66] The 'inhuman' voices from the radio, the New York dance band and the advertising of razor blades, echo eerily across the lake, as the couple come to the realization that the car had been 'tampered with' and that their neighbours, the Halls, suppliers of eggs and butter, have ostensibly left town but still have a light on in their house. Failure to shop leaves the summer people stranded and 'huddled together' against the 'black

---

56. Jackson, 'The Summer People', p. 184
57. Jackson, 'The Summer People', p. 185.
58. Jackson, 'The Summer People', p. 186.
59. Deutsch, *Housewife's Paradise*, p. 8.
60. Jackson, 'The Summer People', p. 194.
61. Jackson, 'The Summer People', p. 183.
62. Jackson, 'The Summer People', p. 187.
63. Jackson, 'The Summer People', p. 187.
64. Jackson, 'The Summer People', p. 189.
65. Jackson, 'The Summer People', p. 190.
66. Jackson, 'The Summer People', p. 191.

masses of the trees',[67] uneasily awaiting what now seems an unimaginable return to normality. The desires of the 'city folk' have to be rationed and their bargaining power diminished, as Jackson portrays the hidden sentiments of the store-owners, whose 'native tricks' seem to be not only the denial of goods but a more sinister malevolence which renders the enjoyment of home an impossibility.

In a retrospective detailing Jackson's penchant for themes of isolation and psychological distress, Joyce Carol Oates notes the ways in which she draws readers of her disturbing 'eerie tales' into 'the emotional maelstroms of the young women protagonists'. She singles out 'The Honeymoon of Mrs Smith' as a 'fabulist revision of the Bluebeard legend in which the murderer's seventh wife is maddeningly complicit with her potential killer'.[68] A chilling variation on the 'demon lover' story, it shows store staff, customers and neighbours conspiring to warn the female character (though not too emphatically) that she has married a serial killer. Hattenhauer links it to other unpublished stories such as 'What a Thought', probably rejected by publishers in the 1950s and 1960s, because they address the disturbing homicidal thoughts of husbands and wives.[69] This story opens in the grocery store in a town organized around surveillance, where any 'deviation from the normal . . . was noted and passed from gossip to gossip'.[70] The newcomer Mrs Smith has only recently occupied the 'shabby apartment house', a 'tawdry' place where she silently submits to her new husband's 'routine of economy'.[71] Sensing from the eye-signals of the grocer and other customers that she has interrupted a conversation about herself and her husband, Mrs Smith experiences the store as an overcrowded, claustrophobic space, its occupants dangerously desperate for gossip: 'she had a clear sense of people moving closer, as though the dozen other customers, the grocer, the butcher, the clerks, were pressing against her, listening avidly'.[72] Her reading out of the grocery list is punctuated by ambiguous responses and glances, by the butcher's pretence of indifference and the grocer's hesitation. Requests for bread, milk and 'the smallest possible can of peas', as she may be 'going away over the weekend', are met with the grocer's 'satisfaction', as this ambiguous 'going away' is coupled with the possibility that over-purchasing may result in 'all that food in the kitchen [. . .] just rotting there while . . . '.[73] The rot in the kitchen is a metaphor for the decay at the heart of her sham marriage, anticipating the husband's later remark that he is not hungry, a moment of realization when 'each

---

67. Jackson, 'The Summer People', p. 194.
68. Joyce Carol Oates, 'Distress Signals', *New York Times*, 29 December 1996, BR10.
69. Hattenhauer, *Shirley Jackson's American Gothic*, p. 76. It was published for the first time in the anthology *Just an Ordinary Day* (1996).
70. Shirley Jackson, 'The Honeymoon of Mrs Smith', in *Dark Tales* (Harmondsworth: Penguin, 2017), p. 45.
71. Jackson, 'The Honeymoon of Mrs Smith', p. 44.
72. Jackson, 'The Honeymoon of Mrs Smith', p. 41.
73. Jackson, 'The Honeymoon of Mrs Smith', p. 41.

of them knew now that the other knew'.[74] The darkly comic conversation with her neighbour Mrs Jones – with her repeated mantra 'All you have to do is scream'[75] – precedes her retreat to her 'bleak little kitchen' to numbly 'see to her groceries' before desperately drinking four cups of coffee. The clear-eyed realization of the 'tawdry' nature of her unsustainable domestic set-up suggests she has deviated too far from the normal.

The menacing atmosphere of the story builds, as the reader tries to find an explanation for why the community has taken against the new husband. Details about his role of murderer are only gradually revealed. Even though they recognize it is not 'their business', 'it all looks mighty suspicious . . . we all got talking, and we figured – well, we figured someone ought to say something to you about it'.[76] This sense of a sinister collective of storekeepers is very much to the fore in a striking sequence suggesting their ghoulish enjoyment of her impending death:

> The man in the liquor store had said substantially that to her, fumbling and letting his voice die away under her cool, inquiring glance. The man in the drugstore had begun to say it, and then, blushing, had concluded, 'Well, it's not *my* business, anyway'. The woman in the lending library, the landlady, had given her the nervous appraising look, wondering if she knew, if anyone had told her, wondered if they dared. . . . She was different in their eyes, she was marked; if the dreadful fact were not true (and they all hoped it was), she was in a position of such incredible, extreme embarrassment that their solicitude was even more deserved. If the dreadful fact *were* true (and they all hoped it was), they had none of them, the landlady, the grocer, the clerks, the druggist, lived in vain, gone through their days without the supreme excitement of being close to and yet secure from an unbearable situation. If the dreadful fact *were* true (and they all hoped it was), Mrs Smith was, for them, a salvation and a heroine, a fragile, lovely creature whose preservation was in hands other than theirs.[77]

Realizing that she is going to be murdered by the end of the story, the store-owners try to warn her but also relish the scandal, the best piece of gossip they have ever encountered; but for this, they had 'lived in vain'. The female customer's 'cool, enquiring glance' initially suggests her superiority, but the collective power of the store-owners, of the repetitive 'they' signals her doom, 'she was marked'. The signature use of brackets here to suggest unspoken or imagined thoughts in the repeated phrase, 'If the dreadful fact *were* true (and they all hoped it was)' betrays their control within the community, their imagining of her violent sacrifice. In her reading of *The Road through the Wall*, Murphy describes a group of locals horrifically enjoying their own safety after the announcement of the death of a

---

74. Jackson, 'The Honeymoon of Mrs Smith', p. 52.
75. Jackson, 'The Honeymoon of Mrs Smith', p. 49.
76. Jackson, 'The Honeymoon of Mrs Smith', p. 42.
77. Jackson, 'The Honeymoon of Mrs Smith', pp. 42–3.

child as 'connoisseurs of other people's misery',[78] and this is entirely apposite to the savagely gloating warnings of the sellers in this story. If, as Deutsch argues, 'grocery stores were as much about capitalism as they were about gender',[79] then the consumer society also seems to share in the responsibility for Mrs Smith's horrific honeymoon, 'pressing against her' so she has no choice but to capitulate.

Stories of the 1960s: Strangeness and the Supernatural

In a review of the posthumous collection *Come Along with Me* (1968), Guy Davenport astutely commented on Jackson's dark predilection for the ways in which 'the familiar can become alien'.[80] If 'it was in plain old clapboard and potted geranium reality that Shirley Jackson recognized the strange discontinuousness of things', then her half-hysterical heroines become alienated and haunted by the warped mundanity of the contemporary. In contrast to her 1940s reviewers, this framing of her writing easily identifies the strangeness at the heart of the familiar, noting significantly that the settings 'carr[y] the meaning'. There is an increased tendency for her later stories to begin either in, or *en route* to, commercial spaces, placing the American housewife in awkward encounters with both storekeepers and the local community. One response to the rapid expansion of the suburban population throughout the 1950s was, argues Megan Behrent, the proliferation of 'suburban captivity narratives', defamiliarizing the domestic and 'subverting ... the ubiquitous narrative of the smiling housewife',[81] a subversion increasingly linked to notions of evil and the supernatural in Jackson's short fiction of the 1960s.

As a number of Jackson critics have noted, her stories are often less overtly supernatural than uncanny, bordering on the weird tale. S. T Joshi notes her 'utterly refreshing glee at the exhibition of human greed, misery, and evil', suggesting that her 'constant reworking of the interlocking themes of domesticity and loneliness' does not 'require the supernatural to arouse fear and horror'.[82] 'The Possibility of Evil' (1965) opens with the paradigmatic line: 'Miss Adela Strangeworth stepped daintily along Main Street on her way to the grocery'.[83] The twist in this tale is that the malevolent presence in the store is the female protagonist who generates evil in the community. Its ageing central character reminisces about the opening

---

78. Murphy, *Suburban Gothic*, p. 24.
79. Deutsch, *Housewife's Paradise*, p. 10.
80. Guy Davenport, 'Dark Psychological Weather', *New York Times*, 15 September 1968, BR4.
81. Megan Behrent, 'Suburban Captivity Narratives: Feminism, Domesticity and the Liberation of the American Housewife', *Journal of Narrative Theory* 49, no. 2 (2019): 247–86 (p. 260).
82. S. T. Joshi, *The Modern Weird Tale* (Jefferson: McFarland and Co, 2001), p. 49.
83. Shirley Jackson, 'The Possibility of Evil', in *Dark Tales* (Harmondsworth: Penguin, 2017), p. 1.

of the store as a crucial moment in the history of her unnamed little town. The polite conversations around the counter mix Miss Strangeworth's food order with her enquiries about her neighbours' tiredness and ill health. The reader only later learns that the disturbances of the town are partly attributable to the poison pen letters sent from the rose-perfumed Strangeworth House. Although the female character here is a generator of malicious gossip rather than subject to it, the story still ends with the threat to the domestic: the final destruction of the roses outside her sparkling house on Pleasant Street reiterates that both store and home, insecure spaces, have a hidden malevolence that leaves women vulnerable.

In an illuminating discussion of the ways in which anxiety becomes Gothic in Jackson's writing, Wyatt Bonikowski has highlighted the 'psychological experience of insecurity' which manifests itself in haunted houses, spectral presences and demonic visitation, arguing that 'readers of Jackson's work are led into a world in which no space is secure'.[84] The evocatively titled 'Home' (1964) is one of her few overtly supernatural stories, in which the hostility of the local storekeepers is the necessary prelude to the invasion of Ethel Sloane's car by desolate ghosts trying to gain access to her newly acquired country property. Acknowledging the darker tone of some of her late ghost stories, Franklin sees it as a variation on 'the theme of homes that have been corrupted', as 'places that seem secure become suddenly dangerous; the familiar turns menacing'.[85] The spectral old woman and child who accept a lift up the Sanderson road in the heavy rain almost seem to be conjured up by the storekeepers' antagonism, breaking down the misplaced assertiveness of the outsider and making it impossible for her to enjoy her new home. Structurally, the story is similar to 'The Possibility of Evil', opening with the housewife entering the hardware store, before returning to her home, though the menace is increased by the circular return to the store in the final paragraphs. The repeated trips in this story to the hardware store are explained in terms of the need for 'so many odd things you never expect you're going to need in an old house',[86] from closet hooks to clothespins. The housewife's need for the oddity of the store and the uncanny repetitions of the conversations about the treacherous road recall the ominous warnings heralding female sacrifice in 'The Honeymoon of Mrs Smith'.

The storekeepers, the keepers of stories, are again identified as a threatening group, hostile to outsiders and mocking consumer confidence. Ethel addresses the hardware clerk 'confidently' in the first paragraph, gaining a 'tactful' response,[87] and continues laughing and whistling in the course of her shopping trip. By the end of the story, the frowning clerk is very much in charge of the conversation, his

---

84. Wyatt Bonikowski, '"Only One Antagonist": The Demon Lover and the Feminine Experience in the Work of Shirley Jackson', *Gothic Studies* 15, no. 2 (2013): 66–88 (p. 66, p. 67).
85. Franklin, *A Rather Haunted Life*, p. 480.
86. Shirley Jackson, 'Home', in *Dark Tales* (Harmondsworth: Penguin, 2017), p. 171.
87. Jackson, 'Home', p. 171.

hands 'very still on the counter', repeating the mantra that 'we don't use that road much'[88] before securing her assent to attending a PTA social as he passes her a box of clothespins. Within the nexus of 'buyer-seller' relations, commercial encounters with strangers in public places produce a kind of 'alienated interaction' typical of the 'emergence of consumer society'.[89] Ethel enjoys them knowing 'who she was' and that she is the bestower of business, having made it clear that all the Sloane grocery business was going to come their way'.[90] Her thought, 'always tell them your business . . . then they don't have to ask'[91] sounds like the kind of advice shared among consumers eager to establish their authority. Yet there is a veiled menace in the storekeepers watching her drive away, with their ominous warning to 'stay careful . . . no matter what you see'.[92] Ethel's wish that 'the store-keepers in the village' might remember her name in exchange for her bringing 'more business' is based on the false assumption that the customer is always powerful; her confident assertion that 'they make you feel at home right away, as though you were born not half a mile from here'[93] in fact highlights the opposite, the difficulties of ever feeling 'at home' in the stores.

The haunted route to the store signals the fraught relations between domestic and public spheres, the dangers of consuming. The Sanderson house, 'so proud and remote, waiting for me to come home'[94] seems to be positioned down a steep and treacherous road that no-one else uses. The despairing ghosts, with their 'disgusting wet cold',[95] materialize in the moment Ethel is congratulating herself on the privacy of the road and the vision of 'my very own house',[96] as if to mock her sense of ownership with their weariness and reminder of the house's undisclosed past. Her loss of control as she 'navigat[es] the sharp curves'[97] symbolizes her powerlessness within the community. Like the dripping, despairing ghosts, she will remain an outsider. The spectral child, shivering barefoot in the rain, is described as 'a little Sanderson boy stolen or lost or something',[98] figuratively associated with the 'lost' housewife, his 'horrible laughter' as the car skids towards the creek eerily echoing her own laughter throughout the story. The ghosts want to get back because there were 'strangers in the house',[99] a phrase repeated twice

88. Jackson, 'Home', p. 179.
89. Langman, 'Alienation', p. 113, 114.
90. Jackson, 'Home', p. 171.
91. Jackson, 'Home', p. 172.
92. Jackson, 'Home', p. 173.
93. Jackson, 'Home', p. 171.
94. Jackson, 'Home', p. 173.
95. Jackson, 'Home', p. 178.
96. Jackson, 'Home', p. 174.
97. Jackson, 'Home', p. 176.
98. Jackson, 'Home', p. 177.
99. Jackson, 'Home', p. 178.

– 'When the strangers are gone, we can go home',[100] reinforcing the strangeness of inhabiting a new community. Although the excited Ethel is looking forward to talking about her 'very own' ghosts in the village, she is unable to tell her story to the store staff, a silencing of the housewife's anxiety signifying that her public performances are controlled by others. To the 1960s readers of the *Ladies' Home Journal*, a publication packed with adverts of domestic appliances and advice on home-making, the deceptively titled 'Home' may have reiterated not domestic bliss, but the loss and alienation of inhabitation.

If successful home-making could not be separated from the ritualistic daily purchasing of food and household items, Jackson's twist in the tale of suburban unease is to persistently render the store a place of fear, alienation and surveillance. The early stories 'Men with their Big Shoes' and 'The Summer People' foreground the storekeepers with their uncanny repetitions and knowing interruptions as complicit in the sense of loss experienced by the housewife. Later stories emphasize the active malevolence of the shopping space, with storekeepers in 'The Honeymoon of Mrs Smith' and 'Home' heralding doom, calling up ghosts and cruelly relishing domestic violence. Trapped between the sinister store and the emptiness of home, the housewife is figured as a constructed figure whose performance is constantly scrutinized in public. Deutsch writes of 'the enormous importance of an ordinary trip to the grocery store';[101] these ordinary trips prefigure darkness and anxiety for the Jackson housewife crushed by the numbing routines of the new consumer society.

References

Behrent, Megan (2019), 'Suburban Captivity Narratives: Feminism, Domesticity and the liberation of the American Housewife', *Journal of Narrative Theory* 49 (2): 247–86.
Bonikowski, Wyatt (2013), '"Only One Antagonist": The Demon Lover and the Feminine Experience in the Work of Shirley Jackson', *Gothic Studies* 15 (2): 66–88.
Bowlby, Rachel (2000), *Carried Away: The Invention of Modern Shopping*, New York: Columbia University Press.
Dalpe, Jr, Michael (2020), '"You Didn't Look Like You Belonged in This House": Shirley Jackson's Fragile Domesticities', in Jill E. Anderson and Melanie R. Anderson (eds), *Shirley Jackson and Domesticity: Beyond the Haunted House*, 43–58, London: Bloomsbury.
Davenport, Guy (1968), 'Dark Psychological Weather', *New York Times*, 15 September, BR4.
Deutsch, Tracy (2010), *Building a Housewife's Paradise: Gender, Politics, and American Grocery Stores in the Twentieth Century*, Chapel Hill: University of North Carolina Press.
Franklin, Ruth (2016), *Shirley Jackson: A Rather Haunted Life*, New York: Liveright Press.

---

100. Jackson, 'Home', p. 179.
101. Deutsch, *Housewife's Paradise*, p. 12.

Friedan, Betty (1963), *The Feminine Mystique*, Harmondsworth: Penguin.
Hattenhauer, Darryl (2003), *Shirley Jackson's American Gothic*. Albany: State University of New York Press.
Hurston, Zora Neale (1986), *Dust Tracks on a Road*, 1942; London: Virago.
Jackson, Shirley (2009), *The Lottery and other Stories*, 1949; Harmondsworth: Penguin.
Jackson, Shirley (2009), *The Road through the Wall*, 1947; Harmondsworth: Penguin.
Jackson, Shirley (2016), *Dark Tales*, Harmondsworth: Penguin.
Joshi, S. T. (2001), *The Modern Weird Tale*, Jefferson: McFarland and Co.
Langman, Lauren (1991), 'Alienation and Everyday Life: Goffman meets Marx at the Shopping Mall', *International Journal of Sociology and Social Policy* 11 (6/7/8): 107–24.
Lefebvre, Henri (1991), *The Production of Space*, trans. Donald Nicholson-Smith, Oxford: Blackwell.
Lefebvre, Henri (2008), *Critique of Everyday Life, Volume 1*, trans. John Moore, 1947/1957 second edition; London and New York: Verso.
Lysack, Krista (2008), *Come Buy, Come Buy: Shopping and the Culture of Consumption in Victorian Women's Writing*, Ohio: Ohio University Press.
Michelis, Angelica (2022), 'Visual and Literary Representations of Shopping', in Vicki Howard (ed.), *The Cultural History of Shopping: The Modern Age*, 129–52, London: Bloomsbury.
Murphy, Bernice M. (2009), *Suburban Gothic in American Popular Culture*, Basingstoke: Palgrave.
Oates, Joyce Carol (1996), 'Distress Signals', *New York Times*, 29 December, BR10.
Prescott, Orville (1949), 'Books of the Times', *New York Times*, 15 April, 21.
Rubinstein, Roberta (1996), 'House Mothers and Haunted Daughters: Shirley Jackson and Female Gothic', *Tulsa Studies in Women's Literature* 15 (2): 309–31.
Strong, L. A. G. (1950), 'Fiction', *The Spectator*, 30 June, 905–06.
Strong, L. A. G. (1951), 'Fiction', *The Spectator*, 5 October, 451–2.
Sugg Ryan, Deborah (2018), *Ideal Homes: Domestic Design and Suburban Modernism, 1918–1939*, Manchester: Manchester University Press.

IV

GENRE AND FORM

Chapter 11

'I COULD DO WITH A CHANGE'

SHIRLEY JACKSON'S ENGAGEMENT WITH
POST-WAR SCIENCE FICTION

Janice Lynne Deitner

Though in recent years more attention has been paid to Shirley Jackson's generic innovations and 'how expertly she manipulates rhetorical and genre conventions to achieve rich thematic permutations and tonal effects', most writers and critics who discuss Jackson and genre usually still do so through the conventions of Horror or the Gothic.[1] Only a few have discussed her engagement with Science Fiction (SF). Ruth Franklin's 2016 Jackson biography includes only one mention of SF; referring to 1954's 'Bulletin', Franklin expresses surprise that '[d]espite the popularity of this genre in the 1950s, Jackson wrote only one published story that truly qualifies as science fiction'.[2] Yet, Science Fiction writer and critic Damon Knight asserts that Jackson's 'stories don't and can't follow the rules', including the rules of genre, and this rule-breaking allows Jackson's work to be read as Science Fiction.[3] For example, a 2020 Popular Mechanics article lists Jackson's story 'The Lottery' (1948) as one of 'The Best Sci-Fi Stories Everyone Should Read'.[4] *The Encyclopedia of Science Fiction* (*SFE*) sees one possible setting of 'The Lottery' as a post-apocalyptic New England, even though Jackson does not specify a post-disaster or even a New England

---

1. James Egan, 'Comic-Satiric-Fantastic-Gothic: Interactive Modes in Shirley Jackson's Narratives', in *Shirley Jackson: Essays on the Literary Legacy*, ed. Bernice M. Murphy (Jefferson and London: McFarland & Company, Inc., 2005), p. 34.

2. Ruth Franklin, *Shirley Jackson: A Rather Haunted Life* (New York and London: Liveright Publishing Corporation, 2016), p. 384.

3. Damon Knight, *In Search of Wonder: Essays on Modern Science Fiction*, revised and enlarged edition (Chicago: Advent Publishers, 1967), p. 226.

4. Editors, 'The Best Sci-Fi Stories Everyone Should Read', *Popular Mechanics*, 2020, https://www.popularmechanics.com/culture/g1622/the-30-sci-fi-stories-everyone-should-read/?slide=14 (accessed 13 October 2022). Additionally, the *Internet Speculative Fiction Database* divides Jackson's work into 'Non-Genre Titles' and an unlabelled section, ostensibly 'Speculative Fiction.' 'The Lottery' and all other stories I discuss here, aside from 'Paranoia,' are in the unlabelled 'speculative' section.

setting.⁵ In a 1950 issue of *The Magazine of Fantasy and Science Fiction* (*F&SF*), a review of *The Lottery* (1949) calls it 'a brilliant collection of naturalistic glimpses of a world with terrifying holes in it'.⁶ A post-disaster reading of 'The Lottery' extrapolates from these holes, or blank spaces, that Jackson deliberately constructs into her texts. In a similar way, Jackson's son Laurence Jackson Hyman says of 'The Beautiful Stranger' (1968) that a husband who seems strange and unfamiliar to his wife 'may have experienced an alien abduction'.⁷ Again, the words 'may have' point to possible readings based on what Jackson does not say. Speaking of her Gothic work, Jack Sullivan evokes M. R. James's theory that 'a supernatural tale should leave a narrow "loophole" for a natural explanation', arguing that Jackson instead 'leav[es] a loophole for a *supernatural* explanation'.⁸ The same holds for Jackson's SF, where she carefully constructs blank spaces where genre conventions *could* be. The SFE claims that 'none of [Jackson's fiction] is SF in any orthodox sense'.⁹ In this chapter, I will argue that they are in an unorthodox sense, but an unorthodox sense that both corresponded with the changing generic boundaries of her time and presaged generic innovations to come.

Shirley Jackson published five stories in magazines dedicated to Science Fiction: 'Root of Evil' (1953) in *Fantastic* and 'Bulletin' (1954), 'One Ordinary Day, With Peanuts' (1955), 'The Missing Girl' (1957) and 'The Omen' (1958) in *F&SF*.¹⁰

---

5. John Clute, 'Jackson, Shirley', in *The Encyclopedia of Science Fiction*, ed. John Clute et al. (London: Gollancz, 2022), http://www.sf-encyclopedia.com/entry/jackson_shirley (accessed 20 March 2021).

6. Editors, 'Recommended Reading', *The Magazine of Fantasy & Science Fiction*, Winter/Spring 1950, p. 107.

7. Cressida Leyshon, 'This Week in Fiction: Shirley Jackson: "Paranoia"', *The New Yorker*, 2013, https://www.newyorker.com/books/page-turner/this-week-in-fiction-shirley-jackson-2 (accessed 16 April 2021). There are numerous other Jackson stories that engage with SF conventions. For example, 'All She Said Was Yes' (1962) features a teenage girl who can seemingly read minds, and 'Showdown' (2015) is about a small town caught in a time loop. Unfortunately, there is not enough space to include them here. This chapter is merely an introduction to and overview of Jackson in post-war Science Fiction. More work is needed to delve more deeply into Jackson's SF, particularly which other work may have been composed for SF magazines and rejected, and which other works incorporate or gesture towards SF conventions.

8. Jack Sullivan, 'The Haunted Mind of Shirley Jackson', *Rod Serling's The Twilight Zone Magazine*, August 1984, p. 72, Original emphasis. Sullivan made this observation in a piece accompanying a reprinting of 'One Ordinary Day with Peanuts,' one of the SF stories discussed in this chapter. On the same page Sullivan noted that Jackson's 'work became increasingly more open-ended and ambiguous, not only in its implications, but in its plotting' (72), another way to refer to what I call constructed blanks in Jackson's work.

9. Clute, 'Jackson, Shirley'.

10. Where possible, I use the original periodical versions of all short fiction, within the context of each issue. Additionally, for clarity I refer to the five stories published in SF

Focusing on these works of short fiction, I will explore three areas of Jackson's engagement with SF. The first is the changing state of SF, particularly regarding short fiction and periodical culture, and Jackson's place within the genre as an 'outsider'.[11] Second, I will compare the posthumously published story 'Paranoia' (2013) with Philip K. Dick's 'The Hanging Stranger' (1953) to demonstrate how Jackson's story bypasses any SF elements that Dick clearly employs and that would firmly anchor the story in the genre. This comparison will then frame my exploration of Jackson's SF stories and their blank spots from which genre conventions can be extrapolated, which will become visible when compared to contemporary SF stories by other authors.[12] SF author and critic Samuel R. Delany argues that SF readers must 'create for themselves the alternate world . . . that gives the story incidents their sense'.[13] Comparing Jackson with other SF writers gives generic 'sense' to what Jackson does not say. Finally, I discuss Jackson's SF story 'The Missing Girl', which anticipated feminist forms of SF that would come into being years after her death, a connection which becomes clear when compared with James Tiptree, Jr.'s 'The Women Men Don't See' (1973). These explorations will situate Jackson's short work as key texts within a changing genre.

First, however, it is necessary to briefly discuss SF history and the shifting conventions within which Jackson wrote.[14] Franklin's assertion, that only one story 'truly qualifies' as SF, raises the question of what those qualifications are.[15] In 1976, SF fan and feminist critic Jeanne Gomoll claimed that 'sf is definable . . . ONLY in terms of a certain time period', a useful delineation as Jackson's SF writing

magazines as Jackson's 'SF stories,' though, as mentioned, other Jackson texts can be read as SF. Additionally, as discussed later in this chapter, these magazines embraced a hybrid form of SF and Fantasy, yet they are predominately referred to as Science Fiction magazines.

11. R. A. Lupoff, *What If?: Stories That Should have Won the Hugo* (New York: Pocket Books, 1981), p. 166.

12. As many historians note, 'Science fiction was birthed in the short form' (Andrew Liptak, 'A New Golden Age of Short SFF: How Genre's Earliest Days Are Informing Its Future', *B&N Reads*, 29 March 2016. https://www.barnesandnoble.com/blog/sci-fi-fantasy/the-golden-age-of-short-sff-how-genres-earliest-days-are-informing-its-future/ (accessed 9 October 2022).), yet many of the stories by other authors that I discuss here are longer forms, novelettes or novellas, that further allow for detailed SF extrapolation. By comparison, Jackson's short fiction further truncates the short SF story by only gesturing towards conventions.

13. S. R. Delany, 'Reading Modern American Science Fiction', in *American Writing Today*, ed. R. Kostelanetz (Troy: Whitston Publishing Company, 1991), p. 521.

14. By necessity this is a brief overview of the genre, though most definitions of SF are highly contested (as is already evident from the opening paragraphs of this chapter). Even the capitalization of 'SF' in both the shortened form and the words 'Science Fiction' is a point of contention. For clarity and readability, I capitalize S and F throughout.

15. Franklin, *Shirley Jackson*, p. 384.

was published in the 1950s.[16] SF historian Rob Latham calls the 1950s 'the most significant transitional decade' in American SF, defining the period here by what came before and after, not by its own innovations.[17] Yet, SF in the post-war era was pushing back against earlier constraints. In 1926, *Amazing Stories* became the first magazine dedicated to 'scientifiction' or 'scientific fact' mixed with 'prophetic vision'.[18] From then until around the Second World War, the genre was firmly under the 'dominance' of one magazine, *Astounding,* and its editor John W. Campbell,[19] who believed that 'even the most speculative of science fiction stories ought to be founded on a clear understanding of real-world science and human psychology'.[20] In 1939, Campbell 'purified science fiction and fantasy' into distinct genres by founding a second magazine, called Unknown.[21] In the inaugural editor's note, Campbell claimed that 'Unknown is both our title and our only classification' for content.[22] Jackson discussed *Unknown* with penpal Jeanne Beatty and appears to have been a fan of Campbell's less strictly defined fare.[23] Campbell's 'prescriptions' and strict delineations were viewed 'as the unbreakable laws of the genre'.[24]

Between 1945 and 1950 cultural forces, particularly the diversification and expansion of the magazine market, began breaking Campbell's 'laws'; 'new magazines in effect smashed the fetters from the writers' wrists'.[25] Additionally, these magazines acted as 'vehicles for a new kind of SF committed to understanding the genre as a mode of social criticism', a trend made clear in the close reading of Jackson's SF below.[26] Founded in 1949, *The Magazine of Fantasy and Science Fiction* 'was light, playful, experimental', a perfect home for four out

16. Jeanne Gomoll, 'To Define SF – Impossible?', *Janus* 03 (March 1976): 34.
17. Rob Latham, 'A Genre Comes of Age: The Maturation of Science Fiction in the 1950s', in *American Literature in Transition*, ed. Steven Belletto (Cambridge: Cambridge University Press, 2018), p. 326.
18. Hugo Gernsback, 'A New Sort of Magazine', *Amazing Stories*, April 1926, p. 1.
19. James Gunn, 'Introduction', in *The Road to Science Fiction #3: From Heinlein to Here*, ed. James Gunn (New York: New American Library, 1979), p. 2.
20. Robert Silverberg, 'Science Fiction in the Fifties: The Real Golden Age', in *Nebula Awards Showcase 2010*, ed. B. Fawcett (New York: ROC, 2010), p. 165. Silverberg, a science fiction author who was first published in 1955, argues that contrary to previous consensus that claims the Campbell years as a '"golden age" . . . it was more like a false dawn. The real golden age arrived a decade later' in the 1950s (p. 163).
21. Alec Nevala-Lee, *Astounding: John W. Campbell, Isaac Asimov, Robert A. Heinlein, L. Ron Hubbard, and the Golden Age of Science Fiction* (New York: HarperCollins Publishers, 2018), p. 121.
22. John W. Campbell, 'Unknown', *Unknown*, March 1939, p. 5.
23. Shirey Jackson, 'Letter to Jeanne Beatty, a Fan', in *The Letters of Shirley Jackson*, ed. Laurence Jackson Hyman (New York: Random House, 2021), pp. 411–12, (p. 412); SJP Box 4.
24. Gunn, 'Introduction', p. 3.
25. Lupoff, *What If?*, p. 4.
26. Roger Luckhurst, *Science Fiction* (Cambridge: Polity, 2005), p. 109.

of Jackson's five SF stories.[27] In the first issue, publisher Lawrence E. Spivak issued a call to action: 'To authors who have . . . found the usual markets closed to . . . experiments, let me assure you that the latch string is out and the welcome-mat freshly dusted'.[28] Originally entitled *The Magazine of Fantasy*, Science Fiction was added in the second issue. This openness, combined with the magazine's penchant for calling the genre 'science-fantasy', further collapsed Campbell's strict delineations.[29] Jackson was a fan, having 'rea[d] that magazine since its first issue'.[30]

In 1952 Damon Knight crafted a definition that captured the era's shifting, democratizing parameters: simply put, SF 'means what we point to when we say it'.[31] Yet, it is illustrative of the era's ambiguity that elsewhere Knight implements strict generic definitions.[32] This ambivalence greeted Jackson's foray into the genre. Arguing that 'One Ordinary Day, with Peanuts', discussed herein, was 'the most overlooked story of 1955', Richard A. Lupoff speculates that 'Shirley Jackson . . . wasn't one of the gang. . . . She was resented as an outsider, an interloper'.[33] Jackson's name appeared on the cover of three out of the four issues of *F&SF* (and on the back cover of *Fantastic*). The editors included Jackson in ads for *F&SF*, listing her name with stars of the genre like Robert Heinlein, Richard Matheson and Ray Bradbury. Yet, as Lupoff indicates, she was 'an outsider'.

Regardless, much of her work, particularly the short fiction, embraces Knight's definition and gestures towards SF tropes, even if these gestures are not immediately apparent. Comparing Jackson's story 'Paranoia' with 'The Hanging Stranger' by Philip K. Dick, we can see how Jackson creates blanks in the narrative where Dick clearly places Science Fiction elements.[34] Both stories also demonstrate

27. Silverberg, 'Science Fiction in the Fifties', p. 166.
28. Lawrence E. Spivak, 'Introduction', *The Magazine of Fantasy*, Fall 1949, p. 5.
29. See also Michael Ashley, *Transformations: The Story of Science-Fiction Magazines from 1950-1970* (Liverpool: Liverpool University Press, 2005), especially volume two, pp. 20–24 for more on *F&SF's* impact on the genre, including its change of name.
30. Shirley Jackson, *The Letters of Shirley Jackson*, ed. L. J. Hyman (New York: Random House, 2021). Jackson also notes that she 'long ago wrote them a plug which they used for quite a while.' On the same page, a footnote indicates that 'payment for 'Bulletin' included a lifetime subscription', which further demonstrates Jackson's interest in the magazine and the genre (255).
31. Damon Knight, 'Book Reviews: The Dissecting Table', *Science Fiction Adventures*, November 1952, p. 122.
32. See, for example, his review of Ray Bradbury's collection *The Golden Apples of the Sun*: 'Book Reviews: The Dissecting Table', *Science Fiction Adventures*, December 1953, pp. 117–20. Here he breaks down Bradbury's book into categories such as 'mainstream', 'Science fiction', 'Watered down science fiction', 'Anti-science fiction' and 'Fantasy' (pp. 117–18).
33. Lupoff, *What If?*, p. 166.
34. Laurence Jackson Hyman estimates that 'Paranoia' was written in the early 1940s, no later than 1948 (Leyshon, 'This Week in Fiction'), which means that it predates Dick's

post-war SF's engagement with cultural anxieties, which will be evident through the rest of this chapter. Dick's story opens as storeowner Ed Loyce heads to his store after a day spent working on his house: 'he like[s] the idea of repairing the foundations himself', hinting at his status as a self-made man.[35] He owns a house, two cars, a business, all signs of middle-class male success in the 1950s. The setting is described as 'a small town',[36] but Ed looks on 'the flow of people moving along the sidewalk' from the comfort of his car; commuters imply commerce, business, modernity, but also an undifferentiated mass from which Loyce stands out.[37] By contrast, Jackson's main character, Mr Beresford, is not an individual. 'There were twenty small-size gray suits like Mr. Beresford's on every New York block, fifty men still clean-shaven and pressed after a day in an air-cooled office, a hundred small men.'[38] Regarding the ubiquity of grey suits, one 1955 newspaper article noted that 'the standard gray flannel suit of commerce' is 'a habiliment supposed to betoken solidity of character'.[39] Instead, Jackson diminishes these suits to an undifferentiated mass of 'small men' who, unlike Loyce, do not work hard enough to get dirty.[40]

Regardless of their differences, both men encounter strange things in familiar settings, invasions that put them at odds with the crowds around them. On a light post near his store Loyce encounters a 'shapeless dark bundle, swinging a little with the wind'.[41] At first he thinks it must be a commercial 'displa[y]' put up by 'the Chamber of Commerce'.[42] Eventually, however, he recognizes it as a human body, wearing a grey suit that echoes Beresford's garb. Dick stresses that this is a stranger, not 'a local man',[43] in opposition to the people that Loyce *does* know, all of whom ignore it as if it were nothing, all offering some variation on, '[t]here must be a good reason, or it wouldn't be there'.[44] Loyce's vague insistence, that

---

1953 story while engaging in many of the same themes. Both stories also contain themes found in one of the most well-known pieces of post-war paranoid SF, Jack Finney's *The Body Snatchers* (1955).

35. Philip K. Dick, 'The Hanging Stranger', *Science Fiction Adventures*, December 1953, p. 122.

36. Dick, 'The Hanging Stranger', p. 127.

37. Dick, 'The Hanging Stranger', p. 124.

38. Shirley Jackson, 'Paranoia', in *Let Me Tell You*, ed. Laurence Jackson Hyman and Sarah Hyman Dewitt (London: Penguin Books, 2015), p. 3.

39. John McNulty, 'Tom Rath, Commuter', *New York Times*, 17 July 1955, BR18. This is a review for the 1955 novel *The Man in the Gray Flannel Suit* by Sloan Wilson, which deals with issues of conformity and commercial culture in post-war America. Wilson's novel is a critique of such conformity but is often read as upholding the very values it targets.

40. Jackson, 'Paranoia', p. 3.

41. Dick, 'The Hanging Stranger', p. 122.

42. Dick, 'The Hanging Stranger', p. 124.

43. Dick, 'The Hanging Stranger', p. 125, 135.

44. Dick, 'The Hanging Stranger', p. 125.

'[s]omething's happened! Things are going on!',[45] also describes the elusiveness of Beresford's decidedly more vague experience, when a man 'in a light hat' with 'a small mustache' stops and stares at him 'in the middle of the crowd'.[46] According to the 'masculine code' of the post-war era 'a clean-shaven man was sociable and reliable. A mustached man . . . demonstrated a willful independence'.[47] Inversely, however, this mustachioed man is part of a growing collective that terrorizes Beresford, beginning when the man refuses Beresford entry to a bus with the help of 'the packed crowd' inside.[48] Loyce also encounters a man with 'a small mustache', also on a bus, shortly after he uncovers the cause for the blasé reaction to the hanging body: an alien invasion of '[p]seudo-men. Imitation men'.[49] The language here reinforces Loyce as a *real* man, in opposition to the man on the bus: a 'slender man', coded as effeminate by the 'book between his small hands'.[50] Aaron S. Lecklider writes of post-war anxieties about intellectuals as 'queerly feminine'[51] and 'whose bodily signifiers reflected a dangerously subversive disposition'.[52] Unable to tell if this man is an 'imitation man', or just panicked by his unmanliness, Loyce attacks him.

Both characters eventually seek comfort and safety in the feminized domestic sphere and find instead that home is a centre for their respective invasions. In Dick's story Loyce *sees* the invading force and describes them as 'alien – from some other world'.[53] Before this reveal, Dick's narration conflates these aliens with 'the scurrying commuters' mentioned above;[54] 'the swarming crowds' are like the '[t]hings descending from the sky . . . in a dense swarm'.[55] In this way, the story structure continuously forecasts the reveal of the invasion. By contrast, Jackson never explains the man in the light hat and his growing number of supposed accomplices. Moving inhumanly quickly through the streets, they could be alien, supernatural, using scientific gadgets like teleportation or, as the title implies, a figment of Beresford's paranoid imagination.[56] Dick reveals every detail of the

---

45. Dick, 'The Hanging Stranger', p. 126.
46. Jackson, 'Paranoia', p. 4.
47. Christopher Oldstone-Moore, 'Mustaches and Masculine Codes in Early Twentieth-Century America', *Journal of Social History* 45, no. 1 (2011): 47.
48. Jackson, 'Paranoia', p. 4.
49. Dick, 'The Hanging Stranger', p. 129.
50. Dick, 'The Hanging Stranger', p. 130.
51. Aaron S. Lecklider, 'Inventing the Egghead: The Paradoxes of Brainpower in Cold War American Culture', *Journal of American Studies* 45, no. 2 (2011): 250.
52. Lecklider, 'Inventing the Egghead', p. 249.
53. Dick, 'The Hanging Stranger', p. 128.
54. Dick, 'The Hanging Stranger', p. 122.
55. Dick, 'The Hanging Stranger', p. 127, 128.
56. Because of the overwhelming focus on masculinity and the recurring imagery of an effeminate man with a moustache as threat, both stories could easily be read as queer panic stories which reflect anxieties about masculinity that are present in much post-war SF and

threat, including the identity of the stranger and some history of the aliens, setting up a seemingly realistic situation and slowly introducing Science Fiction elements. In Jackson's story, nothing is settled or explained, as she sets up a seemingly realistic situation and slowly bores unexplained holes in it, allowing the reader the freedom to extrapolate in any direction they choose. In stories like this one, Jackson engages with the era's erosion of generic consensus.

Unfortunately, though it is the story that Franklin says 'truly qualifies' as SF, 1954's 'Bulletin' does not foreground this innovative extrapolation.[57] The editor's introduction instead highlights its generic clarity: 'There can . . . be no question as to classifying Miss Jackson's first story for *F&SF* – a pure science-fiction fantasy of time travel'.[58] Jackson's stories for *F&SF* get less and less 'pure', which we will see later, yet this one does engage most directly with Science Fiction tropes. Jackson said of the story that it 'may be the result of reading too much science fiction', which demonstrates her interest in the genre and apparently an attempt to directly apply generic conventions.[59] Yet there are still elements of uncertainty. The story starts with an unnamed editor's note, neither publication nor year specified aside from reference to 'this university',[60] omissions that de-anchor the starting point: a 'time travel machine . . . has returned' from 2123 without its time traveller, but did it go forward or backward in time?[61] The word 'machine' quickly disappears, as the editor refers to documents that returned in the 'time travel element', a vagueness that places Jackson's story somewhere in the tradition of *The Time Machine* (1895), where H. G. Wells barely describes the details of the titular machine, and *Kindred* (1979), where Octavia Butler does not bother with a device or explanation for time travel.[62] The mechanics of Jackson's 'element' go undivulged; even in a 'pure science-fiction fantasy', Jackson has no need for pure science.

The bulk of the story comprises pieces of the documents that have returned, though their fragmentary nature impedes understanding. Centred in these fragments is a 2123 American History Exam containing such statements as 'Currency was originally used as a medium of exchange',[63] which hint at a very different way of life from ours in which such statements are true. Statements referring to 'Throat-scratch, the disease which swept through twentieth-century

---

the wider culture. I have touched upon these anxieties here, but a closer comparison would be useful to shed light on Jackson's critique, and Dick's reinforcement, of gender norms.

57. Franklin, *Shirley Jackson*, p. 384.
58. Editor, 'Editor's Introduction: Bulletin', *The Magazine of Fantasy and Science Fiction* 46 (March 1954): 46. Editor introductions are an important part of periodical SF, as they situate the writer in the history of the genre and the magazine, as well as commenting on the story they introduce.
59. Jackson, *Letters*, p. 249.
60. Shirley Jackson, 'Bulletin', *The Magazine of Fantasy & Science Fiction*, 1954, p. 46.
61. Jackson, 'Bulletin', p. 46.
62. Jackson, 'Bulletin', p. 46.
63. Jackson, 'Bulletin', p. 47.

life',[64] and 'aboriginal Americans liv[ing] above-ground and dr[inking] water'[65] hint at dark apocalyptic events in our future. These hints are then called into doubt by their possible falseness, as they are part of a True or False section. Another part instructs students to identify certain historical figures. The list includes real women: Suffragist Carrie Chapman Catt, Health Secretary Oveta Culp Hobby and actress Edna Wallace Hopper, and their inclusion betrays a hope that the future will recognize women's historical contributions. There are also many telling mistakes, such as conflation of author and boxer in the name 'Sinclair (Joe) Louis' and the misspelled 'George Washingham'.[66]

Even without knowing the time machine's starting point, 2123 is less than two hundred years from the story's publication date, an insufficient amount of time to have history become so muddled. This discrepancy evokes Isaac Asimov's story 'Nightfall' (1941), in which a planet with many suns only experiences darkness every 2,050 years. One scientist explains that with '*total darkness* . . . they say, things called Stars appeared, which robbed men of their souls and left them unreasoning brutes, so that they destroyed the civilization they themselves had built up'.[67] The terror caused by unforeseen darkness leads to the destruction of all civilizing institutions and scientific records, requiring society to start anew. Asimov chose a long enough period that living memory is useless in preparing society for the next darkness; all warnings become legend. Jackson's choice of two hundred years is not as effective. Furthermore, the documents contain references to Jackson's present of the 1950s, which fossilize the narrative and disallow much speculation or extrapolation. Though 'Bulletin' *is* Jackson's most straightforward example of what people think of as Science Fiction, her most compelling SF stories allow more extrapolation within the text itself.

Like *Bulletin*, 1953's 'Root of Evil' has a fragmentary structure, this time a 'roving camera' format. It is Jackson's only story published in *Fantastic Magazine*, a venue focused on 'nonscientific or supernatural fantasy'.[68] Instead of science, there is uniformity in the theme of economic anxiety: a poor woodchopper, a journalist who exposes financial corruption, a down-on-his-luck PR man, and so on. Jackson's story about how money can't buy happiness fits right into these themes while also pushing against them. The story approaches this theme satirically and thus fits under Kingsley Amis's term 'comic inferno', coined in 1960 to describe a type of SF 'which cheerfully extracts Satire . . . from a scenario rooted in Dystopia',[69] making

64. Jackson, 'Bulletin', pp. 47–48
65. Jackson, 'Bulletin', p. 48.
66. Jackson, 'Bulletin', p. 47.
67. Isaac Asimov, 'Nightfall', in *Nightfall, and Other Stories* (Garden City: Doubleday, 1969), p. 19. Original emphasis.
68. Paul A. Carter, *The Creation of Tomorrow: Fifty Years of Magazine Science Fiction* (New York: Columbia University Press, 1977), p. 28.
69. David Langford, 'Comic Inferno', in *The Encyclopedia of Science Fiction*, ed. John Clute and David Langford (London and Reading: SFE Ltd and Ansible Editions, 2021).

it a 'suitab[le]' tool for 'satire on aspects of modern consumer-society'.[70] Amis used the work of Frederik Pohl as a central example, particularly 1954's 'The Midas Plague', a story in which the plenty of the 1950s is extrapolated to an extreme degree: the poorer you are, the more you must consume to balance the economy. Pohl describes his protagonist, Morey Field, as a 'blessed economic consuming unit . . . striving manfully to eat and drink and wear out his share of the ceaseless tide of wealth'.[71] 'Root of Evil' contains a similar comic critique, namely the impossible task of giving away money in the paranoid 1950s. The roving narration highlights various people reacting to a classified ad for free money, many who pronounce it a hoax, or a test, but never think of writing and asking for money even while bemoaning their need. Each reaction to the ad explores stereotyped 1950s gender roles. For example, a daughter's desire for a store-bought dress prompts the threat, 'I'll get married or something. . . . Then I can have dresses'.[72] Her mother breaks into performative tears, which quickly disappear with her daughter's acquiescence to her wishes. Elsewhere, a young couple argues over money, the man's financial instability becoming a critique of his masculinity, as his girlfriend complains, 'Some men are making good money at twenty-four'.[73] Finally, we see a mother and her sons react with paranoia and fear when the youngest son writes for money and receives it, his brother nonsensically commenting, 'look what you got us into'.[74] When the roving camera finally lands on the man with the money, his apartment is stuffed with bills. The satire then turns on his failure of imagination, as 'looking with desperation and frustration at the stacks of money' he bemoans: 'In the name of heaven . . . what am I going to *do* with it all.'[75] Conversely, Pohl's Morey starts by believing '[i]t wasn't so hard to be a proper, industrious consumer if you *worked* at it'.[76] He ends the story by reprogramming society's many robots, one of Pohl's overt SF conventions, to consume and discard society's excess. Morey also installs 'satisfaction circuits . . . Adjustable circuits, of course', so that the robots get satisfaction from making things and, more importantly, possessing them.[77] Amis claims that 'a delight in consistent and concrete elaboration . . . typifies the comic inferno', but Jackson's story instead presents snapshots with no elaboration, unlike Pohl's detailed exploration that celebrates the innovative man.[78]

Published one year after 'Midas', Jackson's 'One Ordinary Day, With Peanuts' also contains extended critiques of consumption society. A highly anthologized

---

70. Kingsley Amis, *New Maps of Hell: A Survey of Science Fiction* (New York: Arno Press, 1975), p. 118.
71. Frederick Pohl, 'The Midas Plague', *Galaxy Magazine*, April 1954, p. 12.
72. Shirley Jackson, 'Root of Evil', *Fantastic*, April 1952, p. 127.
73. Jackson, 'Root of Evil', pp. 126–7.
74. Jackson, 'Root of Evil', p. 129.
75. Jackson, 'Root of Evil', p. 162. Original emphasis.
76. Pohl, 'The Midas Plague', p. 14. Original emphasis.
77. Pohl, 'The Midas Plague', p. 56.
78. Amis, *New Maps of Hell*, p. 118.

story, in both genre and non-genre collections, it still prompts commentary on categorization in the editor's introduction: 'I don't know a better writer of unexpected and *unclassifiable* fiction than Shirley Jackson'; he also calls it 'delightfully unconventional'.[79] The story begins with Mr John Philip Johnson 'irradiat[ing]' a 'feeling of well-being' as he randomly travels through the city 'in wide detours, more like a puppy than a man intent on business'.[80] This randomness removes him from the many scenes of focused commerce that he both encounters and undermines: '[m]oving with comparative laziness', he obstructs the crowds, like those in 'The Hanging Stranger', who are 'clattering along to get somewhere quickly'.[81] He is thus defined as a force outside of modern urban life. Like his name, the story is almost palindromic as Johnson moves out from his home and back, spreading good deeds, goodwill and peanuts. At the centre of his journey Mr Johnson pairs up two strangers who both reduce his matchmaking to a commercial transaction. The woman refuses to give him her time until he offers to 'pay for it';[82] she then calculates her price. The man that Mr Johnson chooses insists, 'I got to see it first, what I'm buying.'[83] Young love portrayed as a commercial interaction seems to indicate merely a realistic satire on post-war consumerism.

Yet there are hints at something beyond the everyday, obvious in Mr Johnson's 'peculiar convincing emphasis' as he offers to buy the woman's time, or the way he chooses the young man, '[s]electing and considering' the possibilities with an undefined ability.[84] Later, a taxi 'seem[s] to draw in towards Mr. Johnson against its own will'.[85] Mr Johnson then gives the driver gambling advice that hints at arcane knowledge, perhaps even some form of witchcraft, that requires something beyond regular human perception. Again, Jackson holds back any explanation. In his defence of the story, Lupoff admits that 'it isn't quite science fiction, as we usually think of science fiction. There's no *hardware* in it, there are no *aliens* in it (or are there?). . . . It's a totally unclassifiable story, with implications of – what? Fantasy? Science fiction? Paranoia? Hmm'.[86] That 'hmm' speaks for all possible extrapolations from the little information Jackson gives. The unspoken blanks in the story allow Mr Johnson to be both quotidian and otherworldly, possibly godlike, at the same time.

---

79. Editor, 'Editor's Introduction: One Ordinary Day, With Peanuts', *The Magazine of Fantasy & Science Fiction*, January 1955, p. 53. Emphasis added.
80. Shirley Jackson, 'One Ordinary Day, With Peanuts', *The Magazine of Fantasy & Science Fiction*, January 1955, p. 53.
81. Jackson, 'One Ordinary Day, With Peanuts', p. 55.
82. Jackson, 'One Ordinary Day, With Peanuts', p. 56.
83. Jackson, 'One Ordinary Day, With Peanuts', p. 57.
84. Jackson, 'One Ordinary Day, With Peanuts', p. 56, 57.
85. Jackson, 'One Ordinary Day, With Peanuts', pp. 59–60.
86. Lupoff, *What If?*, p. 166. Original emphasis.

John Clute reads 'Godgame implications' here,[87] referring to a type of SF or fantasy story where an all-powerful 'god-like figure' controls others' lives.[88] One example is 'Microcosmic God' (1941), by Theodore Sturgeon, 'a story about a man who had too much power'.[89] Sturgeon's story self-consciously refers to the way its godlike scientist character, Kidder, is unlike the mad scientist of SF tropes; he is 'apparently unconscious of the fact that he held power enough ... to become master of the world' through his inventions.[90] Instead, Kidder builds 'a new world, to which he [is] god'[91] inventing a race of creatures called Neoterics, who are 'completely in Kidder's power'.[92] Jackson's 'god' is never so clearly delineated. The closest the story gets is when Mr Johnson returns home to 'his double'.[93] Mrs Johnson is 'a comfortable woman ... smiling as Mr. Johnson smile[s]', a description that highlights their interchangeability.[94] Mrs Johnson recounts her day of petty bad deeds, some cancelling out Mr Johnson's good deeds. They do create a balance, but when Mr Johnson offers to switch places tomorrow, his good humour is revealed to contain cold indifference; his wife's assertion, 'I could do with a change', is met only with 'Right ... What's for dinner?'[95] The title reinforces the ordinariness of this interchangeability, normalizing their behaviour. Conversely, Sturgeon's 'god' acts out of a drive to invent, and eventually an interest in '[his] little people'.[96] Sturgeon states this clearly, often addressing the reader directly, as if he is talking about a real historical figure. Jackson's arbitrary 'gods' give no reason or rationale for their actions, demanding the reader extrapolate meaning from what remains unspoken.

By the time of Jackson's last story for *F&SF*, 'The Omen' from March 1958, the genre was entering what Robert Silverberg calls 'the dull and gray late-fifties doldrums'.[97] The editor's introduction again references genre, calling the story 'a simple warm fantasy on the unexpected nature of omens'.[98] The story starts as

---

87. Clute, 'Jackson, Shirley'.

88. John Clute and David Langford, 'Godgame', in *The Encyclopedia of Science Fiction*, ed. John Clute and David Langford (London and Reading: SFE Ltd and Ansible Editions, 2019).

89. Theodore Sturgeon, 'Microcosmic God', *Astounding*, April 1941.

90. Sturgeon, 'Microcosmic God', p. 48.

91. Sturgeon, 'Microcosmic God', p. 54.

92. Sturgeon, 'Microcosmic God', p. 51.

93. Diane Long Hoeveler, 'Life Lessons in Shirley Jackson's Late Fiction: Ethics, Cosmology, Eschatology', in *Shirley Jackson: Essays on the Literary Legacy*, ed. Bernice M. Murphy (Jefferson and London: McFarland & Company, Inc., 2005), p. 277.

94. Jackson, 'One Ordinary Day, With Peanuts', p. 60.

95. Jackson, 'One Ordinary Day, With Peanuts', p. 61.

96. Sturgeon, 'Microcosmic God', p. 66.

97. Silverberg, 'Science Fiction in the Fifties', p. 171.

98. Editor, 'Editor's Introduction: The Omen', *The Magazine of Fantasy & Science Fiction*, March 1958, p. 118.

Grandma Williams, about to embark on a shopping trip, makes a list of presents for her family.[99] She translates their desires into nonsensical shorthand: perfume is reduced to a brand name, 'Carnation', cigars from the Spanish brand name 'El Signo' to 'the sign'. The list goes on: '*Blue cat. Telephone*'.[100] However, Granny's story is only the frame narrative, her list merely a catalyst for the voyage of Miss Edith Webster. Edith resembles the girl in 'Root of Evil' with a manipulative and controlling mother. Subsequently, marriage is Edith's only idea of freedom. Unable to decide between her mother and marriage, Edith wishes for an omen. The narrator calls this 'a most dangerous way of thinking', presaging Edith's impending capitulation of agency.[101] She almost immediately ends up on the wrong bus, where she finds Granny's dropped list. She picks it up 'without thinking any more about it', claiming it as her omen while relieving herself of thought and agency.[102]

When Edith gets off the bus in a completely strange neighbourhood, the narration draws attention to a shift. '*Now at this point* begins the series of events which might easily have been a dream',[103] the language signalling the beginning of a Fantastic Voyage, a common plot structure in SF and fantasy.[104] Edith's urban adventure is like Mr Beresford's in 'Paranoia', and also like that of young Miss Morgan in Jackson's posthumously published story 'Nightmare' (1996), who starts out 'for a street she had never heard of', journeying through urban liminal space.[105] It also resembles Robert Abernathy's 1955 story 'Single Combat', in which a man journeys through a city that has become 'whole, immense, living', having 'evolved' into 'a higher creature' with 'will and purpose'.[106] Granny's list leads Edith into the path of a similar urban 'creature', here created by a commercial gimmick, to 'find Miss Murrain' somewhere in the city for 'ONE HUNDRED DOLLARS' in free groceries.[107] Members of an ever-growing crowd continuously ask if Edith is Miss Murrain. The word 'murrain', though obsolete, means '[d]eath, mortality, esp. by infectious disease' ('murrain'), a meaning hinted at in infectious need of the crowd, 'mostly women, housewives . . . several pushing baby carriages . . . all of them . . .

---

99. Shirley Jackson, 'The Omen', *The Magazine of Fantasy & Science Fiction*, March 1958.
100. Jackson, 'The Omen', p. 120.
101. Jackson, 'The Omen', p. 122.
102. Jackson, 'The Omen', p. 123.
103. Jackson, 'The Omen', p. 123. Emphasis added.
104. Brian M. Stableford, 'Fantastic Voyages', in *The Encyclopedia of Science Fiction*, ed. John Clute and David Langford (London and Reading: SFE Ltd and Ansible Editions, 2022).
105. Shirley Jackson, 'Nightmare', in *Just an Ordinary Day: Stories*, ed. Laurence Jackson Hyman and S. H. DeWitt (New York: Bantam Books, 1996), p. 36.
106. Robert Abernathy, 'Single Combat', *The Magazine of Fantasy & Science Fiction*, January 1955, p. 67, 68. Similar to the aliens in 'The Hanging Stranger', in Abernathy's story, the 'people swar[m] like moths', p. 65.
107. Jackson, 'The Omen', p. 125. A similar gimmick is central to 'Nightmare'. The protagonists in both stories are targeted by the gimmick, and both start to doubt their own identity as a result.

staring at her'.[108] This vision of domesticity surrounds her like a zombie horde or alien swarm, similar to Abernathy's 'blind passersby, the walking dead'.[109] The crowd, like her mother, will not listen to her assertions of identity. 'Not bothering to try to think any more', Edith follows the rest of the omen to what 'had become inevitable', her acceptance of marriage, as she becomes 'infected' with hegemonic delimitations of womanhood.[110]

Here and elsewhere, Jackson's 'science fantasy' concerns itself with internal, domestically focused journeys, often centring the plight of women. It also anticipates the SF of the 1960s, when authors 'reinterpret[ed] science fiction in personal terms . . . protest[ing] the established order and even the traditional way of perceiving reality'.[111] This revolutionary aspect of what is often called 'New Wave' SF was a perfect tool for feminist authors. In 1971, SF author Joanna Russ declared that women cannot write using existing cultural myths. New myths are necessary, and SF provides the space to create those myths.[112] Feminist historian Luise White noted that Jackson was 'a woman who must have felt the pain of living all the mythologies' to which Russ refers,[113] and though Jackson did not live to see it, her play with generic boundaries foresees these developments. Russ would write in 1980 that 'a good case can be made for Jackson as a proto-feminist writer'.[114] Reading her work alongside Russ's contemporaries reveals a proto-feminist *Science Fiction* writer. Jackson's story 'The Missing Girl' is such a proto-feminist SF story.[115] The *F&SF* introduction again stresses Jackson's lack of generic decidability, noting that the magazine 'can – perhaps even should – once in a while break away from precisely defined categories to publish a story that can be described only as "strange" and "good", and that is so commercially unclassifiable as to be anathema to more rigid magazines'.[116] Critic Diane Hoeveler also addresses genre, arguing

108. Jackson, 'The Omen, p. 126.
109. Abernathy, 'Single Combat', p. 63.
110. Jackson, 'The Omen', p. 128.
111. Gunn, 'Introduction', p. 16.
112. Joanna Russ, 'What Can a Heroine Do? or Why Women Can't Write', in *To Write Like a Woman: Essays in Feminism and Science Fiction*, ed. Joanna Russ (Bloomington: Indiana University Press, 1995), pp. 79–93.
113. Jeffrey D. Smith and Jeanne Gomoll, *Khatru 3 & 4: Symposium: Women in Science Fiction* (Madison: The James Tiptree Literary Award Council, 2009), p. 73.
114. Joanna Russ, 'On the Fascination of Horror Stories, Including Lovecraft's', in *To Write Like a Woman: Essays in Feminism and Science Fiction*, ed. Joanna Russ (Bloomington: Indiana University Press, 1995), p. 64.
115. Another good example is 1949's 'The Intoxicated', which explores ideas that are common in Feminist SF, of the end of the world as a chance to rebuild society. Though there is not enough space to include it here, I touch on this aspect in my PhD thesis, '"There's a Terrible Difference": Bodies of Knowledge in Shirley Jackson's America', to be submitted October 2023.
116. Editor, 'Editor's Introduction: The Missing Girl', *The Magazine of Fantasy & Science Fiction*, December 1957, p. 42.

that the story 'is neither science fiction, nor ... fantasy, except in the most perverse use of the terms'.[117] However, reading this story alongside other works of feminist SF makes clear Jackson's engagement with feminist generic innovation.

'The Missing Girl' of the title, Martha, disappears from summer camp, leading Hoeveler to claim that she is 'lonely, ignored, and victimized'.[118] However, this reading merely extrapolates from the sparse information Jackson provides; because of blanks built into the story, it is possible to extrapolate in other ways. The story starts from the point of view of Martha's roommate, Betsy, as she tries to ignore Martha's 'humming ... always humming'. Though the story is named after Martha's *missingness*, Betsy registers and very much feels her presence and can 'describe[e] every movement' she makes. Additionally, Martha's final words imply agency: 'I'm going out ... I've got something to do.'[119] The very real fear of violence towards women haunts the text, especially in the possibly imagined stories told about Martha after her disappearance, but her words here centre her and her needs. Later, the police ask Betsy, 'She sound happy?' Betsy responds, 'Very happy'.[120] Jackson offers nothing but a happily humming, very present girl who chooses to leave. It is as much of an extrapolation to read her end as violent as to decide she chooses not to come back.[121]

The police also analyse every possible reading of Martha's final words, asking 'How did she say it? As though she meant it? Or do you think she was lying?'[122] Tellingly Chief Hook, the ineffectual authority figure investigating the disappearance, thinks Martha might be lying as she asserts her agency. He is part of an old boys' network that includes the newspaper owner's son who is 'given first chance' to tell Martha's story.[123] Martha's disappearance is not within their understanding. They construct explanations and, by the authority of Martha's uncle, retroactively rewrite Martha's story for society's consumption. Her uncle describes Martha's three sisters, two married and one 'right at home with her mother ... Well – you see what I mean'.[124] He does not need to elaborate; Martha, neither married nor at home with her mother, is 'marked "possibly undesirable" and erased from the camp records.[125] No futuristic device is needed to rewrite history or erase memory, but it does not matter because Martha has long ago walked out of the narrative.

---

117. Hoeveler, 'Life Lessons in Shirley Jackson's Late Fiction', p. 269.
118. Hoeveler, 'Life Lessons in Shirley Jackson's Late Fiction', p. 269.
119. Shirley Jackson, 'The Missing Girl', *The Magazine of Fantasy & Science Fiction*, December 1957, p. 42.
120. Jackson, 'The Missing Girl', p. 45.
121. Jackson's story 'Louisa, Please Come Home' (1960) provides another view of a 'missing' girl who chooses to walk out of her family's very domestic life. A comparison of these two stories can be found in my PhD thesis.
122. Jackson, 'The Missing Girl', p. 45.
123. Jackson, 'The Missing Girl', p. 49.
124. Jackson, 'The Missing Girl', pp. 50–51.
125. Jackson, 'The Missing Girl', p. 51.

Comparing 'The Missing Girl' with James Tiptree, Jr.'s feminist SF story 'The Women Men Don't See' (1973), published in *F&SF* exactly sixteen years later to the month, reinforces this reading.[126] Like Chief Hook, Tiptree's narrator Don Felton is a representative of the patriarchal order, a federal agent. He encounters two women, Ruth and Althea Parsons, who, because they are 'small, plain and neutral-colored', he sees as only 'a double female blur'.[127] Because he refuses to see them as they are, Don consistently misreads them according to his preconceptions; because they will not conform, he must continually reassess and reclaim dominant understanding, incorrectly claiming, 'I have Mrs. Parsons figured now', or '[o]f course, I know her now'.[128] When Don tries to label Ruth a man-hater, she refuses the description and responds, mysteriously, 'Sometimes I think I'd like to go . . . really far away.'[129] In a key passage, Ruth tells Don that women 'live by ones and twos in the chinks of your world-machine',[130] protected only by slipping through the cracks. In her world, escaping into invisibility is safety, unless, as Ruth reiterates, she can fulfil her 'dream . . . of going away'.[131]

In 'The Missing Girl', despite the stories made up to give meaning to her disappearance, Martha's lack of presence will not be decided. In the end of Tiptree's story, Don finally realizes that 'Mrs. Ruth Parsons isn't even living in the same world with me',[132] and when Ruth and Althea run away with aliens, he declares that Ruth is 'as alien as they'.[133] Just as in 'The Hanging Stranger', aliens are central and could just as easily be placed in many of Jackson's stories, but they were not. Yet, Ruth's choice to leave a broken system for the unknown combined with Jackson's undecidable story allows for the possibility that Martha made a similar choice. Both Martha and Ruth choose to walk out of a world that attempts to circumscribe and define their reality. By reading Jackson's story alongside Tiptree's, where missing women choose to disappear on their own terms, the blanks in Jackson's story become filled with possibility. Yet, Jackson's blank spaces still contain room for a multitude of readings.

126. 'Tiptree' was the pen name of Alice Sheldon, who kept her real identity hidden until she was outed in late 1976. I have no evidence that Sheldon read Jackson, though she often admitted that she read a lot of periodical SF without paying attention to the authors' names (see, for example, Smith and Gomoll, *Khatru 3 & 4*, p. 108). It is possible she read 'The Missing Girl' or other Jackson stories, but more research is needed.

127. James Tiptree, Jr, 'The Women Men Don't See', *The Magazine of Fantasy & Science Fiction*, December 1973, p. 5, p. 4.

128. Tiptree, 'The Women Men Don't See', p. 9.

129. Tiptree, 'The Women Men Don't See', p. 20.

130. Tiptree, 'The Women Men Don't See', p. 21.

131. Tiptree, 'The Women Men Don't See', p. 22.

132. Tiptree, 'The Women Men Don't See', p. 22.

133. Tiptree, 'The Women Men Don't See', p. 25.

If, as Tom Shippey argues, 'the assertion that science fiction insistently conveys' is that '*[t]hings do not have to be the way they are*',[134] Shirley Jackson's engagement with Science Fiction extends this assertion to the genre itself, just as Mrs Johnson's words in 'One Ordinary Day', 'I could do with a change',[135] echo the changing state of SF in the post-war years. Jackson's very deliberate blank spaces, where things go undefined, both allow for contextual SF readings and anticipate the way SF would be used over a decade later by 'New Wave' and feminist writers deconstructing and reconstructing the possibilities available outside of a patriarchal society. Additionally, by closely reading Jackson's stories *as* Science Fiction, her commentary on gender norms, economic anxiety and the status of women becomes clear. Jackson's fiction in general, and short fiction in particular, opens multiple possibilities for transformative change, no technological gadgets required.

References

Abernathy, Robert (1955), 'Single Combat', *The Magazine of Fantasy & Science Fiction*, January, 62–70.

Amis, Kingsley (1975), *New Maps of Hell: A Survey of Science Fiction*, New York: Arno Press.

Ashley, Mike (2005), *Transformations: The Story of Science-Fiction Magazines from 1950–1970*, Liverpool: Liverpool University Press.

Asimov, Isaac (1969), 'Nightfall', in *Nightfall, and Other Stories*, 9–54, Garden City: Doubleday.

Campbell, John W. (1939), 'Unknown', *Unknown*, March, 5.

Carter, Paul Allen (1977), *The Creation of Tomorrow: Fifty Years of Magazine Science Fiction*, New York: Columbia University Press.

Clute, John (2022), 'Jackson, Shirley', in John Clute et al. (eds), *The Encyclopedia of Science Fiction*, London: Gollancz. http://www.sf-encyclopedia.com/entry/jackson_shirley (accessed 20 March 2021).

Clute, John and David Langford (2019), 'Godgame', in John Clute and David Langford (eds), *The Encyclopedia of Science Fiction*, London and Reading: SFE Ltd and Ansible Editions. http://www.sf-encyclopedia.com/entry/godgame (accessed 22 April 2021).

Delany, Savid R. (1991), 'Reading Modern American Science Fiction', in Richard Kostelanetz (ed.) *American Writing Today*, 517–28, Troy: Whitston Publishing Company.

Dick, Philip K. (1953), 'The Hanging Stranger', *Science Fiction Adventures*, December, 122–36.

Editor (1954), 'Editor's Introduction: Bulletin', *The Magazine of Fantasy & Science Fiction*, March, 46.

---

134. Tom Shippey, 'Hard Reading: The Challenges of Science Fiction', in *A Companion to Science Fiction*, ed. D. Seed (Malden: Blackwell, 2005), pp. 16–17. Original emphasis.

135. Jackson, 'One Ordinary Day, With Peanuts', p. 67.

Editor (1955), 'Editor's Introduction: One Ordinary Day, With Peanuts', *The Magazine of Fantasy & Science Fiction*, January, 53.

Editor (1957), 'Editor's Introduction: The Missing Girl', *The Magazine of Fantasy & Science Fiction*, December, 42.

Editor (1958), 'Editor's Introduction: The Omen', *The Magazine of Fantasy & Science Fiction*, March, 118.

Editors (1950), 'Recommended Reading', *The Magazine of Fantasy & Science Fiction*, Winter/Spring, 105–7.

Editors (2020), *The Best Sci-Fi Stories Everyone Should Read, Popular Mechanics*. https://www.popularmechanics.com/culture/g1622/the-30-sci-fi-stories-everyone-should-read/?slide=14 (accessed 13 October 2022).

Egan, J.ames (2005), 'Comic-Satiric-Fantastic-Gothic: Interactive Modes in Shirley Jackson's Narratives', in Bernice M. Murphy (ed.), *Shirley Jackson: Essays on the Literary Legacy*, 34–51, Jefferson and London: McFarland & Company, Inc.

Franklin, Ruth (2016), *Shirley Jackson: A Rather Haunted Life*, New York and London: Liveright Publishing Corporation.

Gernsback, Hugo (1926), 'A New Sort of Magazine', *Amazing Stories*, April, 3.

Gomoll, Jeanne (1976), 'To Define SF – Impossible?', *Janus 03*, March, 3–4, 34.

Gunn, James (1979), 'Introduction', in James Gunn (ed.), *The Road to Science Fiction #3: From Heinlein to Here*, 1–22, New York: New American Library.

Hoeveler, Diane Long (2005), 'Life Lessons in Shirley Jackson's Late Fiction: Ethics, Cosmology, Eschatology', in Bernice M. Murphy (ed.), *Shirley Jackson: Essays on the Literary Legacy*, 267–80, Jefferson and London: McFarland & Company, Inc.

Jackson, Shirley (1953), 'Root of Evil', *Fantastic*, April, 124–9, 162.

Jackson, Shirley (1954), 'Bulletin', *The Magazine of Fantasy & Science Fiction*, 46–8.

Jackson, Shirley (1955), 'One Ordinary Day, With Peanuts', *The Magazine of Fantasy & Science Fiction*, January, 53–61.

Jackson, Shirley (1957), 'The Missing Girl', *The Magazine of Fantasy & Science Fiction*, December, 42–52.

Jackson, Shirley (1958), 'The Omen', *The Magazine of Fantasy & Science Fiction*, March, 118–30.

Jackson, Shirley (1996), 'Nightmare', in Laurence Jackson Hyman and Sarah Hyman DeWitt (eds), *Just an Ordinary Day: Stories*, 34–46, New York: Bantam Books.

Jackson, Shirley (2015), 'Paranoia', in Laurence Jackson Hyman and Sarah Hyman DeWitt (eds), *Let Me Tell You*, 3–14, London: Penguin Books.

Jackson, Shirley (2021), *The Letters of Shirley Jackson*, ed. Laurence Jackson Hyman, New York: Random House.

Knight, Damon (1952), 'Book Reviews: The Dissecting Table (November 1952)', *Science Fiction Adventures*, November, 122–5.

Knight, Damon (1953), 'Book Reviews: The Dissecting Table (December 1953)', *Science Fiction Adventures*, December, 117–21.

Knight, Damon (1967), *In Search of Wonder: Essays on Modern Science Fiction*, revised and enlarged edition, Chicago: Advent Publishers.

Langford, David (2021), 'Comic Inferno', in John Clute and David Langford (eds), *The Encyclopedia of Science Fiction*, London and Reading: SFE Ltd and Ansible Editions. https://sf-encyclopedia.com/entry/comic_inferno (accessed 8 October 2022).

Latham, Rob (2018), 'A Genre Comes of Age: The Maturation of Science Fiction in the 1950s', in Steven Belletto (ed.), *American Literature in Transition, 1950–1960*, 326–37, Cambridge: Cambridge University Press.

Lecklider, Aaron S. (2011), 'Inventing the Egghead: The Paradoxes of Brainpower in Cold War American Culture', *Journal of American Studies* 45 (2): 245–65.
Leyshon, Cressida (2013), 'This Week in Fiction: Shirley Jackson: "Paranoia"', *The New Yorker*. https://www.newyorker.com/books/page-turner/this-week-in-fiction-shirley-jackson-2 (accessed 16 April 2021).
Liptak, Andrew (2016), 'A New Golden Age of Short SFF: How Genre's Earliest Days Are Informing Its Future', *B&N Reads*, 29 March. https://www.barnesandnoble.com/blog/sci-fi-fantasy/the-golden-age-of-short-sff-how-genres-earliest-days-are-informing-its-future/ (accessed 9 October 2022).
Luckhurst, Roger (2005), *Science Fiction*, Cambridge: Polity.
Lupoff, Richard A. (1981), *What If?: Stories That Should have Won the Hugo*, VOLUME 1, New York: Pocket Books.
McNulty, John (1955), 'Tom Rath, Commuter', *New York Times*, 17 July, BR18.
'murrain, n., adj., and adv.' (March 2023), *OED Online*, Oxford University Press. http://www.oed.com/view/Entry/123953 (accessed 9 July 2023).
Nevala-Lee, Alec (2018), *Astounding: John W. Campbell, Isaac Asimov, Robert A. Heinlein, L. Ron Hubbard, and the Golden Age of Science Fiction*, New York: HarperCollins Publishers.
Oldstone-Moore, Christopher (2011), 'Mustaches and Masculine Codes in Early Twentieth-Century America', *Journal of Social History* 45 (1): 47–60. https://doi.org/10.1093/jsh/shr002 (accessed 18 April 2021).
Pohl, Frederik (1954), 'The Midas Plague', *Galaxy Magazine*, April, 6–58.
Russ, Joanna (1995a), 'What Can a Heroine Do? or Why Women Can't Write', in Joanna Russ (ed.), *To Write Like a Woman: Essays in Feminism and Science Fiction*, 79–93, Bloomington: Indiana University Press.
Russ, Joanna (1995b), 'On the Fascination of Horror Stories, Including Lovecraft's', in Joanna Russ (ed.), *To Write Like a Woman: Essays in Feminism and Science Fiction*, 60–4, Bloomington: Indiana University Press.
Shippey, Tom (2005), 'Hard Reading: The Challenges of Science Fiction', in David Seed (ed.), *A Companion to Science Fiction*, 11–26, Malden: Blackwell.
Shirley Jackson Papers (SJP), Manuscript Division, Library of Congress, Washington, DC.
Silverberg, Robert (2010), 'Science Fiction in the Fifties: The Real Golden Age', in Bill Fawcett (ed.), *Nebula Awards Showcase 2010*, 163–72, New York: ROC.
Smith, Jeffrey D. and Jeanne Gomoll, eds (2009), *Khatru 3 & 4: Symposium: Women in Science Fiction*, Madison: The James Tiptree Literary Award Council.
Spivak, Lawrence E. (1949), 'Introduction', *The Magazine of Fantasy*, Fall, 3–5.
Stableford, Brian M. (2022), 'Fantastic Voyages', in John Clute and David Langford (eds), *The Encyclopedia of Science Fiction*, London and Reading: SFE Ltd and Ansible Editions. http://www.sf-encyclopedia.com/entry/fantastic_voyages (accessed 12 October 2022).
Sturgeon, Theodore (1941), 'Microcosmic God', *Astounding*, April, 46–68.
Sullivan, Jack (1984), 'The Haunted Mind of Shirley Jackson', *Rod Serling's The Twilight Zone Magazine*, August, 71–4.
Tiptree, Jr, James (1973), 'The Women Men Don't See', *The Magazine of Fantasy & Science Fiction*, December, 4–29.

Chapter 12

'THIS GLOOMY KIND OF STORY'

SHIRLEY JACKSON'S *CONTE CRUELS* AND THE HORROR TALE IN THE POST-PULP ERA

Kevin Knott

'The shining example from the early years was Shirley Jackson' is how Michael Ashley wrote of Jackson's work in *The Magazine of Fantasy and Science Fiction* (*F&SF*) in his 1997 entry for John Clute and John Grant's *The Encyclopedia of Fantasy*.[1] Ashley's praise is extraordinary for a magazine which attracted so many notable writers, including Ray Bradbury, Isaac Asimov and Robert Bloch. As Michael Ashley notes, the editors of *F&SF* desired to compete with the 'slicks' in terms of overall literary quality,[2] and Jackson's stories helped elevate the literary bona fides of an emerging genre publication. In the 1950s when pulp publications were in decline, they were physically replaced with the cheaper digest-sized magazines that became synonymous with the ascendance of literary science fiction during the era, especially the decade's early years.[3] However the format change did not mean 'pulp fiction' had ceased being published or that the well-documented literary ambitions of the publishers and editors of the new magazines had foreclosed on the pulp tradition entirely. More than a few pulp writers were able to successfully make the transition to other media, including these new genre magazines that replaced old pulps, and so first-time contributors to these magazines had clear antecedents for guidance. But while Shirley Jackson was celebrated in one of the most important speculative fiction publications of the last seventy-five years, understanding her contributions to the development of the field was continually obscured by the changing state of genre marketing in these magazines and the scholarly response to these unstable genre definitions.

In the 1988 biography *Private Demons: The Life of Shirley Jackson*, Judy Oppenheimer explained how Jackson consciously chose to submit new work to

---

1. Michael Ashley, 'The Magazine of Fantasy and Science Fiction', in *The Encyclopedia of Fantasy*, ed. John Clute and John Grant (New York: Palgrave MacMillan, 1997), p. 150.
2. Ashley, 'The Magazine of Fantasy and Science Fiction', p. 150.
3. Michael Ashley and Peter Nicholls, 'Digest', *The Encyclopedia of Science Fiction*, 2 April 2015, http://www.sf-encyclopedia.com/1295.aspx.

these publications because editors would be more willing to take on experimental work.[4] Jackson was not alone as many established and emerging US writers would turn to the late pulp magazines and those early speculative fiction magazines as publishing venues where writers could gather an audience more interested in unconventional fiction.[5] Nevertheless, Jackson's reputation as a writer, for good and ill, had been established already with the 1948 publication of 'The Lottery' in *The New Yorker*, and one year later the publication of her collection *The Lottery and Other Stories*. Choosing to publish in pulp magazines, even those with more cultivated literary ambitions like *F&SF*, was not a motivation for financial success since they held little mainstream appeal. In these magazines, Jackson could experiment, pushing the boundaries of modernism and blending the sensationalism of pulp fiction with the grim philosophical cynicism of mid-century U.S. storytelling, leading to her adoption of the *conte cruel* form as the synthesis of these two threads of compositional philosophy.[6]

After 'The Lottery', Shirley Jackson's mother, Geraldine, discouraged her daughter from writing more macabre stories, which she described in a letter to her daughter as 'this gloomy kind of story'.[7] Since the aforementioned letter is included in Jackson's own origin story for 'The Lottery', scholars must be suspicious of the claim, though *Washington Post* columnist and reviewer Michael Dirda noted the letter's inclusion in Jackson's account as evidence of her intention to continue in this mode.[8] Jackson would further experiment with the genre in the pages of *F&SF*. H. P. Lovecraft has long been credited with first identifying the *conte cruel* for English-speaking audiences; however, US literary critics James Gibbons Huneker (in 1917) and Edgar Saltus (in 1919) had a decade before discussed the *conte cruel* and its popularization by Auguste Villiers de l'Isle-Adam in the 1883 collection of the same name.[9] In appropriating European folk tales, Villiers had modernized

---

4. Judy Oppenheimer, *Private Demons: The Life of Shirley Jackson* (New York: Ballantine Books, 1988), p. 150.

5. David M. Earle, *Re-Covering Modernism: Pulps, Paperbacks, and the Prejudice of Form* (New York: Routledge, 2009). Earle outlines how this high versus low modernism divide was often blurred by authors who crossed this imaginary boundary.

6. Various definitions exist for the *conte cruel*, including H. P. Lovecraft's pithy summarization in 'Supernatural Horror in Literature' (1927), 'in which the wrenching of the emotions is accomplished through dramatic tantalisations, frustrations, and gruesome physical horrors', p. 53.

7. Shirley Jackson, 'Biography of a Story', in *Shirley Jackson: A Study of the Short Fiction*, ed. Joan Wylie Hall (New York: Twayne Publishers, 1993), p. 125.

8. Michael Dirda, 'Shirley Jackson: Let Me Tell You (Review)', *Washington Post*, 29 July 2015, https://www.washingtonpost.com/entertainment/books/new-collection-of-shirley-jackson-writings-best-left-to-devoted-fans/2015/07/29/8ae21996-308a-11e5-8353-1215475949f4_story.html.

9. James Gibbons Huneker, 'The French Poe', in *For France*, ed. Charles Hanson Towne (Garden City: Doubleday, Page and Company, 1917), pp. 401–7.

the French conte to reflect his scepticism of European modernism and its faith in technology and social improvement, which Jackson would mirror in her own writing over fifty years later. Villiers experimented with fantasy and science fiction as well, and he depicted in his writing what Saltus describes in *The Philosophy of Disenchantment* as the folly of seeking happiness when the goal in life should be 'to avert as many pains as possible'.[10] The *conte cruel* as practiced by Villiers demonstrated, fundamentally, a protagonist caught in the tension between seeking happiness and the impending pain engendered by that pursuit, often with tragically ironic results.

For Lovecraft, defining the *conte cruel* was complicated by his desire to see it as a style distinctly apart from the Gothic. Still, Lovecraft's definition proffered three vague characteristics 'in which the wrenching of the emotions is accomplished through dramatic tantalisations, frustrations, and gruesome physical horrors'.[11] Within that scope virtually any horror story might fit his definition of the '*conte cruel*', and Lovecraft's characterization of the genre is further problematized by his own example, Villiers's 'The Torture by Hope' (1883, English trans. 1891). The story focuses on the struggle to achieve the protagonist's goal of freedom, eschewing any of the overtly gruesome physical horrors identified by Lovecraft, despite being a tale pitting the imprisoned Rabbi Aser Abarbanel of Aragon against his inquisitor captor Pedro Arbuez d'Espila. What the story does depict is the anticipatory anxiety of pursuing one's goals and the moral confusion which arises when the desired outcome is contradicted by the circumstances. In this case, the rabbi discovers his escape to freedom is an orchestrated test authored by his principal torturer to prolong his psychological torment.[12] As demonstrated in Villiers' stories, the *conte cruel* operated as an early form of social science fiction,[13] an attempt to probe and critique human behaviour and institutions on the cusp of modernism's birth. His goal was not the ambient dread that defined the early Gothic and Weird writing of the twentieth century and that Lovecraft had sought to classify. Rather, Villiers's fiction offered a sharp critique of modern optimism by depicting episodes of human frailty, rather than the inherent violence of much nineteenth-[h] and early twentieth-century horror. The stories are then 'cruel' in the

---

10. Edgar Saltus, *The Philosophy of Disenchantment* (Boston: Houghton, Mifflin and Company, 1885/1887), Project Gutenberg ebook.

11. H. P. Lovecraft, 'The Supernatural Horror in Literature', in *The Annotated Supernatural Horror in Literature: Revised and Updated*, ed. S. T. Joshi (New York: Hippocampus Press, 2012), p. 53.

12. Villiers de l'Isle-Adam, 'A Torture by Hope', in *The Strand*, trans. M. P. Shiel (London, June 1891), pp. 559–62.

13. Donald F. Theall's coined the term 'social science fiction' in his 1975 study of Ursula Le Guin's fiction, especially 'The Ones Who Walk Away from Omelas' (1973). Theall connects the storytelling of Le Guin to the critical and transformative modelling of existing social structures and institutions.

way they demonstrate the inevitability of suffering as a vain conflict with reality, underscoring the shocking pessimism common in the *conte cruel*.

Such is the experience with Shirley Jackson's befuddling time-travelling story 'The Bulletin' (1954), her first story published in the pages of *F&SF*. By 1954 then editor Anthony Boucher was in complete control of the direction of the magazine, now no longer co-editing with its other founder, J. Francis McComas, and Boucher had greater literary aspirations for not only the publication but also the collective fields of fantasy and science fiction. And so, Boucher's headnote to 'The Bulletin' illustrates something of his own internal debate about how to classify Jackson's body of short fiction to date:

> There has been some argument as to whether the title story and other items in Shirley Jackson's splendid collection *The Lottery* (Farrar, Straus, 1949) can be strictly classed as fantasy fiction; they are intensely disquieting stories of an uncertain and terrifying world . . . but is this anything other than a realistic depiction of the world we live in? There can, however, be no question as to classifying Miss Jackson's first story for F&SF – a pure science-fantasy of time travel, and as tantalizingly provocative a fragment as we've seen in years.[14]

Boucher may have been the first, and perhaps the only person, to raise the question of whether Jackson's first short story collection represented fantasy fiction or not, but he understates the provocative nature of 'The Bulletin'. The narrative begins with a sort of prologue, an editor's note about the time travelling experiment undertaken by Professor Browning on behalf of the University Space Department. Jackson never details in the story what the device or vehicle may be. Instead, what follows are a series of distinctly separate documents collected from Professor Browning's briefcase and curated in this report by the unnamed editor on behalf of the Department. These documents are the only items that return with the *time travel element*. 'It is assumed by members of the Space Department', the editor's note in the story reads, 'that these following papers were to serve as the basis for notes for the expected lecture by Professor Browning, which will now, of course, be indefinitely postponed.'[15] The documents contain on the surface virtually no direct information revealing what may have transpired during Browning's journey to the future, and even less about why he did not return. The opening document, for example, is a news clipping from 8 May 2123, which describes in the broadest terms possible a 'distressing' incident that has occurred – Jackson never clarifies if Browning went back or forward in time. Parsing the language, the newspaper story indicates an 'act' took place sometime prior to 2123, arising due to a lack of intelligent planning on the government's part.[16] And then the documents become

---

14. Shirley Jackson, 'Bulletin', *The Magazine of Fantasy and Science Fiction*, March 1954, p. 46.
15. Jackson, 'Bulletin', p. 46.
16. Jackson, 'Bulletin', p. 46.

even more peculiar. A letter from Jerry, a young boy away at camp, dated June 4 requests 'cake and some cokies [sic] and candy' from his parents,[17] and next a college mid-term exam for American History 102.

The exam comprises the bulk of the short story, although with only five questions excerpted. The first entails a simple identification assignment from a list of nineteen US historical figures, ranging in significance from presidents to capitalists like R. H. Macy – a coy reference to 'My Life with R. H. Macy' (1941), Jackson's story about an unnamed narrator's experiences working at the Macy's department store. The second question asks students to respond to the following prompt: 'The historian Roosevelt-san has observed that 'Twentieth-century man had both intelligence and instinct; he chose, unfortunately, to rely upon intelligence.' Discuss.'[18] The deployment of the Japanese honorific '-san' along with the familiar US presidential name raises some curiosity about what has taken place in US history that would have led to the adoption of Japanese naming practices, though the implication is a counterfactual version of twentieth-century history in which the United States has become subject to Japanese authority. The mystery is further complicated by the true or false questions that follow:

> Currency was originally used as a medium of exchange.
> The aboriginal Americans lived above-ground and drank water.
> The first American settlers rebelled against the rule of Churchill III and set up their own government because of the price of tea.
> Throat-scratch, the disease which swept through twentieth-century life, was introduced to this country by Sir Walter Raleigh.
> The hero Jackie Robinson is chiefly known for his voyage to obtain the golden fleece.
> Working was the principal occupation of twentieth-century humanity.
> The first king in American, George Washingham, refused the crown three times.
> The cat was at one time tame, and used in domestic service.[19]

Jackson is being playful in distorting US history while also filling in perceived gaps in her hypothetical version of twentieth-century history. In fact, the questions seem to be a comical jab about what American life after 1954 would be like based on a wry interpretation of apocalyptic science fiction. The exam underscores this point in the last two questions: one about twentieth-century people's daily lives ('eating, entertainment, and mating habits'), and the other asking, 'In what sense did ancient Americans contribute to our world today? Can we learn anything of value by studying them?'[20] Again, Jackson's use of the word 'ancient' strongly suggests, finally, that the country no longer exists in the way that Browning's

17. Jackson, 'Bulletin', p. 47.
18. Jackson, 'Bulletin', p. 47.
19. Jackson, 'Bulletin', pp. 47–8.
20. Jackson, 'Bulletin', p. 48.

colleagues might recognize, assuming they are from some version of the United States.

The final document makes clear the criticism implicit in the story. A small card from a fortune-telling machine indicates Professor Browning now weighs 186, and the breezy fortune encourages him to 'Try not to dwell on the past'.[21] The scholars at the University Space Department are most interested in the last document, perhaps to the detriment of the larger question of what happened to the United States in the twentieth century. The editor's final note informs the reader that Professor Browning was 200 pounds when he left, suggesting that

> The evidence loss of weight shown indicates clearly the changes incident to time travel, and points, perhaps, to some of its perils; there is possibly a hint here of an entirely different system of weights and measures than that currently in use. We anticipate that several learned and informed papers on this subject are already in preparation.[22]

Jackson was likely hoping audiences would be familiar with Jonathan Swift's *Gulliver's Travels* (1726), especially its third book, wherein the pedantic scholars of Laputa's scientific pursuits blinded them to the impracticality of their learning. Similarly, in focusing so exclusively on the minutiae, the Space Department researchers miss the distressing unwillingness of Professor Browning to return to the present time in their collective celebration of the device's successful time travel.[23] The scholars of the University Space Department have what they desired, proof of time travel, even at the cost of the glum certainty they will suffer and die in this unidentified future tragedy.

Here, Jackson deploys the crucial elements of the *conte cruel* – the tantalizing pursuit of a desired outcome ('tantalizations'), the dramatic irony of the protagonist's lack of awareness ('frustrations') and the macabre inevitability of the protagonist's fate ('gruesome physical horrors'), while also deconstructing the narrative expectations of storytelling itself. In this way she lays out only the necessary clues and foregoes any characterization or plot, pushing the definition of a classic pulp mystery, to force the audience to literally detect what has happened, and thus manufacture their own narrative based on those clues. The stakes are then raised to a *conte cruel*, albeit not in the way that Villiers may have imagined. In Jackson's *conte cruel*, she assumes that people cannot be shaken out of their habits of being, whether evidence is precedented to the contrary, and so warning Professor Browning's colleagues is immaterial. Like Villiers's tormented

---

21. Jackson, 'Bulletin', p. 48.
22. Jackson, 'Bulletin', p. 48.
23. In the Shirley Jackson seminar I had taught in spring 2022, the class determined that Jerry was most certainly Professor Browning's child and the exam was probably taken from the son's history course, a playful mystery that unfolds as a series of clues revealing Browning's new life in the future (or potentially a past disrupted by his time travel).

rabbi, they have become conditioned to see only what they want to see, failing to have the necessary objectivity that will enable them to fully comprehend their circumstances. And so, Jackson raises a surprising question about the audience's own sympathies even while mocking the researchers for being so tunnel-blind in their pursuits, which once more harkens back to Swift's *Gulliver's Travels*. The satire, for Jackson, is not the absurdity of the researchers' rigid focus but the fatalism of being unable to change the course of human actions. These researchers cannot, for whatever undefined reason, make the changes necessary to avoid this critical moment in their future. Even so, Jackson leaves the audience with the knowledge that Professor Browning saw no reason to return, acting in his own best interest rather than heroically attempting to change the future. The question hauntingly lingers: What would the audience have done in the same situation?

In her most renowned work published in *F&SF*, 'One Ordinary Day, With Peanuts' (1955), Jackson introduces a frightening but plausible hypothetical: if some people are altruistically driven to do good in the world, then presumably someone else might be malevolently driven to do evil as well. The story received little fanfare on its first publication, introduced with a simple headnote that read: 'I don't know a better writer of unexpected and unclassifiable fiction that Shirley Jackson, who offers us this time a story as delightfully unconventional as its title.'[24] Otherwise, the narrative begins innocently enough with Mr John Philip Johnson leaving his home for a pleasant stroll. In the first of many altruistic moments, he volunteers to attend to a young boy while his mother supervises furniture movers.[25] Later, a woman rushing to work knocks into Mr Johnson, sending him sprawling to the ground. In this scene Mr Johnson was bent over to pet a kitten; Jackson layers the sentimentality on thickly to drive home Mr Johnson's extraordinary kindness. So kind is Mr Johnson that the rushed woman agrees to pay him for any damages, but Mr Johnson not only reassures her that no harm has been done, but he also insists on paying her for making her late to work.[26] Mr Johnson later employs this accidental strategy to create an opportunity for more philanthropy as he intentionally collides with a rushing man, Arthur Adams, whose immediate suspicions are aroused when Mr Johnson asks about Adams's hourly pay. Accusing him of being a communist,[27] Mr Johnson allays Adams's fears by handing him money from his wallet, enough to cover an entire day's wage and then some. He does the same for the woman, Mildred Kent, and then adds to the previous amount with the suggestion that Arthur and Mildred spend the day at Coney Island, the movies, or eating a nice lunch together. In the exchange that follows, Jackson provides a fascinating rehearsal of their incredulousness:

---

24. Shirley Jackson, 'One Ordinary Day, With Peanuts', *F&SF*, January 1955, p. 53.
25. Jackson, 'One Ordinary Day, With Peanuts', p. 53.
26. Jackson, 'One Ordinary Day, With Peanuts', pp. 55–6.
27. Jackson, 'One Ordinary Day, With Peanuts', p. 57.

As he started to move away Arthur Adams, breaking from his dumfounded stare, said, 'But see here, mister, you *can't* do this. Why – how do you know – I mean, *we* don't even know – I mean, how do you know we won't just take the money and not do what you said?'

'You've taken the money,' Mr. Johnson said. 'You don't have to follow any of my suggestions. You may know something you prefer to do – perhaps a museum, or something.'

'But suppose I just run away with it and leave her here?'

'I know you won't,' said Mr. Johnson gently. 'Because you remembered to ask *me* that. Goodbye,' he added, and went on.[28]

Mr Johnson is delighted by his own benevolence and the ways in which he can influence human action through it, particularly the matchmaking of Arthur and Mildred. Nevertheless, his sensitivity borders on the fanciful. Subsequently, Johnson demonstrates an implausible insight when he encourages his taxi driver to bet on a different horse, insisting that the driver's previous 'hot tip' must be wrong because one should not bet on a horse whose name is a fire sign on Wednesday.[29] Mr Johnson persuades the driver to wait; to bet instead on a horse whose name suggests a grain, before going further and specifically telling him: 'Or, as a matter of fact, to make it even easier, any horse whose name includes the letters C, R. L.'[30]

Either way, Jackson has conditioned the audience until this point to see Mr Johnson as a strange, but otherwise genial, character whose generosity is his defining characteristic. Thus, the gut punch reversal at the end is indeed shocking. Returning home, Mr Johnson's wife and he swap stories, enquiring tenderly about each other's day. Mrs Johnson has for her part accused a woman of shoplifting and sent three dogs to the pound, but the critical twist occurs in the final paragraphs:

'Well,' she said, 'I got onto a bus and asked the driver for a transfer, and when he helped someone else first I said that he was impertinent, and quarrelled with him. And then I said why wasn't he in the army, and I said it loud enough for everyone to hear, and I took his number and I turned in a complaint. Probably got him fired.'

'Fine,' said Mr. Johnson, 'But you do look tired. Want to change over tomorrow?'

'I would like to,' she said. 'I could do with a change.'[31]

The conversation ends with the couple discussing dinner plans, highlighting the utter banality of their prior compact. Mr and Mrs Johnson must switch prescribed roles regularly, one performing acts of humiliation and cruelty and the other acts

28. Jackson, 'One Ordinary Day, With Peanuts', p. 58.
29. Jackson, 'One Ordinary Day, With Peanuts', p. 60.
30. Jackson, 'One Ordinary Day, With Peanuts', p. 60.
31. Jackson, 'One Ordinary Day, With Peanuts', p. 61.

of veneration and charity. Worse, that these roles are planned, even exchanged as chores, indicates a provocative rationality at work. What each character gains is left for the reader to determine, but Jackson still plants the audience with the horrifying knowledge that someone in the world may be knowingly making their lives better or worse, with the chance of meeting either person being entirely and frighteningly random.

Thinking about this story as a *conte cruel* like 'The Bulletin' before it, it is important to see how literary historian and contemporary writer of the *conte cruel* Brian Stableford has expanded upon the definition that Lovecraft established nearly a century ago. Stableford's characterization displays a greater respect for the French folk traditions that informed the nineteenth-century form than prior definitions:

> A *conte cruel* reverts to a demonstrative rather than an inquisitive function but it seeks to demonstrate exactly what the conservative moral fable tried heroically to deny: that life is a bitch and there's no hope of compensation in this world or any other. The *conte cruel* is, in a sense, a kind of 'amoral fable,' but its inherent cruelty is partly derived from the fact that the nullity it seeks to demonstrate is an aching void rather than a mere circumstantial absence.[32]

Stableford's demarcation between the fable and the *conte cruel* is the key to understanding the moral register represented by this mode of storytelling. The *conte cruel* has no message, no lesson to be learned from the described experience. Instead, this mode of storytelling punctures the appropriated delusions, the various myths about human kindness, the positive arc of history, or the presence of benevolent deities, that enables human beings to live comfortably in an irrational and amoral existence. The 'aching void' is the emptiness, the nullity to use Stableford's word, for the moral absence around which human institutions and society is built, like a paper mâché figure. And so, while the characters may suffer, it is the audience who experiences the prick of spiritual or moral crisis as the narrative of the *conte cruel* makes visible the 'aching void' at the centre of human existence. Yet, these stories can only successfully affect the audience if one genuinely identifies with the circumstances. The characters are sometimes so morally reprehensible that whatever existential crisis they may be suffering is overshadowed by their unpleasantness.

In the most disturbing of the *F&SF* stories, 'The Missing Girl', Shirley Jackson returns to the familiar theme of the forgotten individual, one that began in *Hangsaman* (1951) and beautifully, if somberly perfected in the short story 'Louisa, Please Come Home' (1960). 'The Missing Girl' opens with Betsy, a teenager away at camp, earnestly attempting to ignore her roommate, Martha Alexander. The exposition establishes that Betsy is then unmoved by her missing roommate until

---

32. Brian Stableford, *The A to Z of Fantasy Literature* (Lanham: Scarecrow Press, 2009), p. 85.

prompted by a fellow camper to report the incident to the Camp Mother, or else 'You know, it might mean trouble for *you* if she's really missing.'[33] Betsy is only stirred to action after acknowledging that she may suffer negative repercussions for whatever accident might have befallen Martha, but she is slow to act because she is free from her roommate. A prosaic inquest follows into Martha Alexander's time at the camp, which reveals that no one has any record or knowledge of the young girl. Hilda Scarlett, teasingly known as Will, has never seen Martha in the infirmary, and the Camp Mother, Old Jane, knows only what Betsy can impart to her – in time, this institutional incompetence will help protect the camp legally and ethically. And so, the Camp Mother calls in Chief Hook, the local chief of policy, who has gained his position through nepotism and mild charm. From the outset, he is poorly prepared for detecting her whereabouts, though the obvious choice of starting with her interests leads the party to the unsatisfactory knowledge that Martha was 'happy', not a senior, and perhaps interested in drama. When pressed by Chief Hook, Betsy admits the two girls had roomed together for a year and a half, but she knew almost nothing about the roommate, resulting in an investigation of the room they shared.[34] And while the room reveals a plethora of 'clues', none lead the investigators any closer to the girl. Instead, they interview the other camp counsellors, who each in turn confess they had taken no notice of the girl and their memory of her activities are suspect at best. No further in the investigation than before they started, Chief Hook recalls, apropos of nothing, having lost a hunter on Bad Mountain, and that is where the investigation will continue.[35]

The confusion is compounded as Chief Hook interviews people about the area around Bad Mountain. People report having seen someone, maybe, ducking behind trees or walking along the road, but without a clear picture – Martha's camp photo is blurry – they have no way to compare whomever they saw to Martha.[36] As the camp leadership succumbs to the growing pressure to find the girl, sometimes literally hiding in their offices, the stories of the girl's potential demise grow further. Speculation in the town and camp indicates the strong belief that the girl is already dead, buried somewhere in the woods or on the mountain. So frustrated is Chief Hook that he organizes a meeting between the girl's uncle and the camp staff on the eleventh day, and here Jackson delivers her shocking twist. Speaking on behalf of the mother, the Martha's uncle stumbles through a story of his sister's many children, three girls and a boy, and each are doing well for themselves, except for Martha. As he cannot bring himself to say what he means aloud, Old Jane understands completely. Since the camp has no official record of her making use of the camp's services, Martha most likely has never attended the

---

33. 'The Missing Girl', December 1957, p. 43.
34. 'The Missing Girl', December 1957, p. 46.
35. 'The Missing Girl', December 1957, p. 48.
36. 'The Missing Girl', December 1957, p. 48.

camp, and the group can collectively call off the search as a case of a dissatisfied runaway.

The story's coda is two short paragraphs. The first paragraph reveals that Martha Alexander's body was eventually found among thorn bushes that no one had bothered to check, and the few witnesses who had come forward had not described accurately what Martha was wearing.[37] The final paragraph is the most damning, however, choosing to focus on the two people who should have best known the teenager:

> She was buried quietly in the local cemetery; Betsy, a senior huntsman the past summer but rooming alone, stood for a moment by the grave but was unable to recognize any aspect of the clothes or the body. Old Jane attended the funeral, as befitted the head of the camp, and she and Betsy stood alone in the cemetery by the grave. Although she did not cry over her lost girl, Old Jane touched her eyes occasionally with a plain white handkerchief, since she had come up from New York particularly for the services. (p. 52)

Jackson's conclusion unfolds the moral incongruity of the *conte cruel* in the 'The Missing Girl'. In this version of the universe, Betsy gets what she wants – to room alone in her senior year where she would be untroubled by the weird girl, Martha – and for her part, Old Jane is untroubled by the events, losing nothing in status or reputation from the event. She attends the graveside services out of obligation and nothing more; she is unable to even summon a tear for the dead girl. No one, not Chief Hook, Hilda 'Will' Scarlett, or even the girl's uncle, genuinely cared for her well-being. Nowhere was a sincere attempt made to find the girl, nor did the characters make any effort to pretend, buffooning their way through an investigation that included the insistence that Martha's copy of *Gulliver's Travels* from the camp library was an essential clue.[38]

The inclusion of the novel is one of Jackson's sly winks to the reader that the tale shares the same satirical lineage as *Gulliver's Travels*. Jackson, inspired by the former novel, insists that social institutions fail us when they are needed most, but they also fail when they are presumed to be working as intended. The most significant absurdity of the story is, undoubtedly, how none of the camp counsellors, attendees or even the camp's nurse have any recollection of a girl who had been attending the camp through one full summer and a half. The authorities simply trust that the system of the summer camp will foster the security necessary to protect the campers and insulate the counsellors from fault, while also presumably performing the necessary tasks of nurturing and improving the young girls as promised to their parents. Martha's utter invisibility would never have been made known unless she had gone missing, and the camp staff, Martha's family and the community at large would continue, erroneously, believing that the

---

37. 'The Missing Girl', December 1957, p. 52.
38. 'The Missing Girl', December 1957, p. 46.

camp had been successful in its intended goals. In such a world where only crisis reveals systemic failure, Jackson's cynical interpretation of even the nostalgic and deeply sentimental summer camp experience of so many middle-class Americans provokes her audience's sense of decency, and in so doing, she underscores how the characters in the story are allowed to be so insensitive, so untrammelled by their cruelty. They did no more or no less than was required of them.

Which is why the final story submitted to F&SF in March 1958, 'The Omen', is so important for reflecting on the fatalism common in Jackson's *conte cruels*. This time Boucher writes in the headnote a bit of puffery to sell the story to readers: 'This time, however, she uses her spellweaving powers to create a simple warm fantasy on the unexpected nature of omens – tender, funny and wholly delightful.'[39] The story more accurately resembles a frightening fairy tale that ends 'happily ever after' only through the anxious travails of the main character, but Boucher's light sales pitch is not unwarranted. Here, Jackson most explicitly employs magical elements. Introduced with the framing narrative of Grandma Williams, whom the reader is told, 'It would be pushing truth too far to say that Grandma Williams was the finest person in the world to live with.'[40] Her family continues to humour but grow intolerant of the elderly woman's refusal to accept her diminished role in life; as an aging woman, she can no longer help physically, and appears to be slipping mentally, yet she attempts to overcome this inadequacy by being generous. When she receives an unexpected sum of money, she solicits wish lists from the family to help her gather surprise gifts for them all. Writing on a slip of paper the words 'Carnation', 'The sign', 'Blue cat' and 'Telephone', her shorthand for the gifts becomes the omen that leads Edith Webster on her circuitous adventure to matrimony.

Jackson continues the fairy tale mode in the story of Edith Webster, contrasting Granny's life and family with the domestic troubles bedevilling Edith. 'Edith loved her mother quite as much as Granny's daughter loved Granny', Jackson writes, 'but Edith's mother was perhaps a shade more selfish than Granny – Granny, as Edith would have point out if she had known about it, had at least allowed her daughter to get married.'[41] Edith's mother fears she will be abandoned if the young woman marries, and Edith, for her part, worries that her mother will never grant permission for Edith to make her own choices. Neither woman is wrong, the narration indicates, on this point. Both possess valid reasons and are otherwise 'good' people as fairy-tale characters go. Among Jackson's many stories this one most explicitly breaks the fourth wall and communicates directly with the reader through editorial asides and omniscient jokes that tease at the fabricated reality of the story. For example, as Edith is walking, she wonders to herself how much easier life would be if she had some external force guiding her, giving her the titular

---

39. 'The Omen', March 1958, p. 118.
40. 'The Omen', March 1958, p. 118.
41. 'The Omen', March 1958, p. 121.

omen, to which Jackson quips, 'All of which is, of course, a most dangerous way of thinking.'[42]

Edith finds Granny Williams's list of gifts, and sensing that the paper was put in her path by an external, benevolent source, Edith makes her way through the town by following the 'clues'. However, Edith's magical thinking guides her to be pursued by an angry mob of shoppers who are convinced by the carnation that she wears and her loitering on the street that she is the advertised 'Miss Murrain' from a radio contest who will grant them a $100 in grocery shopping, if they bring her to the store.[43] Edith later escapes into a restaurant, Kitty's Lunch, where she gathers the courage to telephone Jerry she will accept his marriage proposal in defiance of her mother and in completion of all four listed items.[44] The scene is set up comically to exemplify what a fool Edith has been all this time, waiting three years to accept a marriage proposal out of fear for her mother's disapproval. However, the return to the framing narrative at the end in which Granny returns home with the 'wrong' gifts indicates that Jackson has more in mind than a romantic conclusion.

Granny details her encounter with Jerry, the soon-to-be fiancé, rushing to the restaurant to meet Edith, though neither was aware of their entanglement in each other's stories. Jerry takes a moment to narrate his long-awaited rendezvous to the elderly woman, and Granny nearly swoons over the romantic narrative, with the final line being the cryptic ' "It was positively *sentimental*', said Granny happily."'[45] The emphasis on the sentimentality of the story highlights the irony Jackson has constructed in which Edith's dehumanization, wherein the mob's fighting over her as if she were an actual lottery ticket, is part of her wish-fulfilment. Meanwhile, like 'One Fine Day, With Peanuts', Granny is privy to only one side of the overall story. From her perspective the matrimonial conclusion of the story is sentimental, happily so, yet unbeknownst to her, the otherwise innocent list of gifts set off a bewildering and unnerving chase through the city streets that preceded Edith's surrender to both marriage and the rupture between she and her mother's relationship. Granny cannot know that the story that warms her heart is also born of cruelty and irreparable dissolution. As with any story, Granny can only react to the narrative as presented to her.

Jackson sets her *conte cruel* stories in moments of crisis where the uncertainty of how to proceed or to resolve the crisis in which the characters, and the reader by extension, are subject. Here, no abject horror awaits at the end of the story, at least nothing terrifying in the conventional sense. The monsters are not tentacled, and the villains are not maniacal; what does remain of the pulp-weird is the profound alienation of the protagonist who must confront his or her own aching void, to paraphrase Brian Stableford. The *conte cruel* personalizes the Weird, threading the existential dread through the mundane desires of individuals who manifest

---

42. 'The Omen', March 1958, p. 122.
43. 'The Omen', March 1958, pp. 125–7.
44. 'The Omen', March 1958, pp. 128–9.
45. 'The Omen', March 1958, p. 130.

their own sense of the unknowable, the all-consuming or the peculiarly weird fragmentation of reality. As the characters achieve their desired goals, they are untethered from the larger reality that grounds them in the 'real world', forcing them to see it for the unfamiliar, uncanny place they have always been a partner, or just as disturbingly, the audience is made aware of the same by virtue of reading the tragic events of the characters. Thus, Professor Browning's journey into the future in 'The Bulletin' highlights the narrowness of vision and the scholastic indifference of himself and his cohorts, even as they achieve their greatest success. Mr Johnson in 'One Ordinary Day, with Peanuts' eagerly wants to share his generosity of spirit, unmoved by the knowledge that he also shares in bringing suffering that negates that generosity. And while 'The Missing Girl' begins with Betsy receiving her wish to be freed of Martha's distracting presence, it is the collective delusion of middle-class families wanting to provide happy memories for their sons and daughters that is weirdly undone in the end. Finally, the mild 'The Omen' stakes a wayward Edith against the tumults of lost agency as she is tormented until she finally accepts that she alone must make her own choices, even if the reader is left to wonder if Edith ever knew what she wanted or was even capable of articulating that desire.

Placing Jackson, even her *conte cruel* stories, within the larger historical framework of the Weird's development is not without problems. S. T. Joshi has said of Jackson's role as a Weird writer, 'her work only borders upon the weird by any conventional standard',[46] and since the conventional standard is the 'cosmic horror' that fell out of fashion after the 1950s, he is correct. Yet, the *conte cruel* does prefigure the kinds of narratives told during the era of the 'Weird transition', which Benjamin Noys and Timothy S. Murphy describes as the years between the Old Weird pre-1950s and the New Weird of the 1980s.[47] Like Rod Serling's *The Twilight Zone* (1959–64), Shirley Jackson's select stories in *F&SF* help scholars reconsider the overall evolution of the Weird, tying it more firmly to its pulp roots while allowing readers to explore its various iterations across multiple mediums. What role the *conte cruel* has played in the development of the Weird remains a thorny question. The *conte cruel* need not be 'Weird', 'Gothic' or 'Horror', remaining as a mode apart but sharing in the same literary genealogy of these other forms. What may be useful for scholars to consider instead is how authors like Shirley Jackson appropriated the form and why then these exercises in literary experimentation failed to take root with mainstream audiences (and overlooked by literary historians). Was the fatalism demonstrated in Jackson's stories too 'gloomy' for audiences who disliked the abject despair, and perhaps for other authors of the form? The history of the *conte cruel* can aid in this conversation by completing the picture of pulp modernist horror and the evolution of Shirley Jackson's own short fiction as she experimented with new forms in the pages of *F&SF*.

---

46. S. T. Joshi, *The Modern Weird Tale* (Jefferson: McFarland and Company, 2001), p. 4.
47. Benjamin Noys and Timothy S. Murphy, 'Introduction: Old and New Weird', *Genre* 49 (2016): 123.

References

Ashley, Michael (1997), 'The Magazine of Fantasy and Science Fiction', in John Clute and John Grant (eds), *The Encyclopedia of Fantasy*, 153, New York: Palgrave MacMillan.
Ashley, Michael and Peter Nicholls (2015), 'Digest', *The Encyclopedia of Science Fiction*, 2 April. http://www.sf-encyclopedia.com/1295.aspx.
Dirda, Michael (2015), 'Shirley Jackson: Let Me Tell You (Review)', *Washington Post*, 29 July. https://www.washingtonpost.com/entertainment/books/new-collection-of-shirley-jackson-writings-best-left-to-devoted-fans/2015/07/29/8ae21996-308a-11e5-8353-1215475949f4_story.html.
Earle, David M. (2009), *Re-Covering Modernism: Pulps, Paperbacks, and the Prejudice of Form*, New York: Routledge.
Huneker, James Gibbons (1917), 'The French Poe', in Charles Hanson Towne (ed.), *For France*, 401–7, Garden City: Doubleday, Page and Company.
Jackson, Shirley (1954), 'Bulletin', *The Magazine of Fantasy and Science Fiction*, March, 46–8.
Jackson, Shirley (1955), 'One Ordinary Day, With Peanuts', January, 53–61.
Jackson, Shirley (1957), 'The Missing Girl', December, 42–52.
Jackson, Shirley (1958), 'The Omen', March, 118–30.
Jackson, Shirley (1993), 'Biography of a Story', in Joan Wylie Hall (ed.), *Shirley Jackson: A Study of the Short Fiction*, 125, New York: Twayne Publishers.
Joshi, S. T. (2001), *The Modern Weird Tale*, Jefferson: McFarland and Company.
Lovecraft, H. P. (2012), 'The Supernatural Horror in Literature', in S. T. Joshi (ed.), *The Annotated Supernatural Horror in Literature: Revised and Updated*, 53, New York: Hippocampus Press.
Noys, Benjamin and Timothy S. Murphy (2016), 'Introduction: Old and New Weird', *Genre* 49: 117–34. https://doi.org/10.1215/00166928-3512285.
Oppenheimer, Judy (1988), *Private Demons: The Life of Shirley Jackson*, New York: Ballantine Books.
Saltus, Edgar (1885/1887), *The Philosophy of Disenchantment*, Boston: Houghton, Mifflin and Company, Project Gutenberg ebook
Stableford, Brian (2009), *The A to Z of Fantasy Literature*, Lanham: Scarecrow Press.
Swift, Jonathan(1726), *Gulliver's Travels*.
Theall, Donald F. (1975), 'The Art of Social Science Fiction: The Ambiguous Utopian Dialectics of Ursula K. Le Guin', *Science-Fiction Studies* 2 (3): 256–64.
Villiers de l'Isle-Adam (1891), 'A Torture by Hope', trans. M. P. Shiel, *The Strand*, 559–62, London, June.

Chapter 13

MYTH AND RITUAL IN SHIRLEY JACKSON'S SHORT FICTION

Samantha Landau

Introduction[1]

'Who is he dares enter these my woods?' Jackson writes, concluding her short story 'The Man in the Woods' with a lethal challenge that recalls folktales of death and rebirth.[2] Though the story ends before the killing takes place, it is strongly implied. Ruth Franklin has said that this story is 'a fable incorporating different strands of mythology'.[3] Taking a closer look at Jackson's short fiction, however, reveals that many of her stories fall under that description to a large extent. Whether encountered in an isolated village, as in 'The Lottery', on the edge of a lake, as in 'The Summer People', or in the forest, as in 'The Man in the Woods', the uncanny spaces in Shirley Jackson's stories take on a mythic quality. They lose something of the supernatural – her ghosts and demons are all in human form and face human trials and tribulations. Disturbances to the social order and attempts to resolve them recall seminal texts on ritual such as James G. Frazer's *The Golden Bough*, Jane Harrison's *Themis*, Mircae Eliade's *The Sacred and the Profane*, and, of course, her husband Stanley Edgar Hyman's essays and lectures. Indeed, some characters and symbolism in Jackson's fiction can be traced to Hyman's source materials,

---

1. Funding for the research that buttresses this chapter was generously provided by a JSPS Kakenhi grant for the project 'Domestic Spaces in Gothic Literature [17K02518]' and by the University of Tokyo English Department and Center for Global Communication Strategies. I express my sincere gratitude to Ruth Franklin for discussing the archival materials with me, especially the contents of the Jackson-Hyman, Hyman-Burke and Hyman-Ellison letters. Thank you to Barnaby Ralph for his encouragement and assistance in editing this chapter.
2. Shirley Jackson, 'The Man in the Woods', in *Let Me Tell You* (New York: Random House, 2015), p. 187.
3. Ruth Franklin, 'Forward', in *Let Me Tell You* (New York: Random House, 2015), p. xxii.

including Child Ballad 243, which is the origin of *The Lottery*'s mysterious James Harris.[4]

Jackson's interpretation of the fantastic aspects of folklore is something more uncanny and less marvellous than in the theories presented by the Cambridge Ritualists, by Burke or even by Hyman. Instead of reporting on the *meaning* of the ritual, for Jackson, it often has none beyond the necessity of its repetition.[5] Further, her fiction seems to insist that only the sensitive are able to notice more than hints of the real meaning of the ritual until it is too late. Her use of ritual and folkloric references thus provides an updated version of the threat that looms over the main characters in folk literature: they will be forced to confront the possibility of their inner demons, and they will likely discover that said demons are real. Jackson uses the framework of symbolic action, the literary version of myth, to show how literature is buttressed by myth and that literature itself is a ritualistic act. In other words, in her works, symbolic acts have a ritual rather than a cathartic meaning, just as myth does not always have a deeper symbolic meaning but is, instead, a by-product of ritual.[6] The process of a hollow ritual creating myth is best seen in Jackson's work in the forms of the ritual of the scapegoat and the ritual that Frazer termed 'killing the god'.[7]

---

4. For a lengthier discussion of the importance of this folktale and its variants to Jackson's interpretation of the supernatural, myth and ritual, see Samantha Landau, 'Occult Influences in Shirley Jackson's *The Lottery*', *Gakuen* 936 (2018): 11–21.

5. The lack of meaning in the ritual probably shows Jackson's works in affinity with other twentieth century writers, such as W. H. Auden and Ted Hughes. See Matthew Kane Sterenberg, 'Myth and the Modern Problem: Mythic Thinking in Twentieth Century Britain' (unpublished doctoral dissertation, Northwestern University, 2007). For an analysis of how historians have overlooked this issue, see Sterenberg, 'Myth and the Modern Problem', pp. 9–11 and pp. 20–1.

6. This is also Hyman's assertion about myth – that ritual creates it, rather than the myth creating the ritual, and as a consequence, later interpretations of the ritual are bound to misinterpret its symbolic significance: 'Basic to this view, as Harrison makes clear, is a dynamic or evolutionary concept of process, in which rites die out, and myths continue in religion, literature, art, and various symbolic forms with increased misunderstanding of the ancient rite, and a compensatory transformation for intelligibility in new terms.' See Stanley Edgar Hyman, 'The Ritual View of Myth and the Mythic', in *The Promised End: Essays and Reviews, 1942-1962* (Cleveland: The World Publishing Company, 1963), pp. 280–1.

7. The concept behind killing the god, Frazer claims, is that by his death, those who worshipped him could catch his soul and relocate it to his successor and could take his energy before the decay of his body to prevent the decay of his godliness. For examples of Frazer's interpretation of god-killing rituals and their associated myths, see James George Frazer, *The Golden Bough: A New Abridgment* (Oxford: Oxford University Press, 2009), pp. 228–53.

Ritual in/and Fiction

I take the position that Jackson's work may be read as the enactment of some of Hyman's theories. However, previous research on the topic of myth and ritual in Jackson's works reveals a schism in the scholarship. For example, while Darryl Hattenhauer has argued that Jackson's use of myth in her works functions in opposition to Hyman's theories and criticism, Shelley Ingram has asserted that Jackson's works are far more 'sophisticated'. Ingram states: 'she was not simply subverting or undercutting Hyman's views; she was dynamically interacting with them'.[8] Moreover, Hyman's ideas on myth can be seen in Jackson's oeuvre. For example, Jackson makes use of Hyman's concept that 'literature is analogous to myth' but it is not myth itself because no one person can create myths.[9] These common influences and affinities arose naturally – Jackson and Hyman lived in the same house, shared a vast home library and socialized with the same group of people who were working with and around the same ideas on myth, ritual and folklore.

Jackson wrote fiction at the same time as Hyman was working on lectures and essays – most famously for his college course 'Myth, Ritual, and Literature'. Though they worked in the same room for years, they eventually separated their writing spaces. Jackson wrote, humorously, to Jeanne Beatty about the separation:

> it is so quiet without stanley's typewriter going downstairs. he has a downstairs study, see, and i have an <u>upstairs</u> study because if you must know the disagreeable truth he kicked me out of the downstairs study because my desk was a mess and i never covered my typewriter . . . so i raided the house for everything i liked best and brought it all up to my study and shut the door and i live in here.[10]

This letter, written in February of 1960, indicates that Jackson and Hyman shared writing space in their home for many years (perhaps two decades or more) before separating themselves. All four of their children were involved in the incident, so it could not have taken place before the late 1950s.

However, more than physical proximity and in-person intellectual discourse, Jackson imbued views on ritual and myth like those held by Hyman into her oeuvre. Ingram maintains that 'Jackson consciously and playfully manipulates myth,

---

8. This opposition is pointed out by Ingram. See Shelley Ingram, 'Speaking of Magic: Folk Narrative in *Hangsaman* and *We Have Always Lived in the Castle*', in *Shirley Jackson: Influences and Confluences*, ed. Melanie R. Anderson and Lisa Kroger (New York: Routledge, 2016), p. 54.

9. Hyman, 'The Ritual View of Myth and the Mythic', p. 293. He also explains that modern writers can use symbolic action to create the 'equivalent . . . [of] . . . the myth's expression of a public rite'.

10. Shirley Jackson, *The Letters of Shirley Jackson*, ed. Laurence Jackson Hyman (New York: Random House, 2021), p. 423.

ritual, fairy tale, legend, and other folk narrative forms, wrenching them from their myriad "traditional" contexts and reconstituting them in the text'.[11] Ingram calls this an 'estrangement' – a step sideways from a folktale, with the meaning of the ritual forgotten but its communal origins still intact. It is here that Ingram and I diverge in our analysis. Rather than stepping sideways, I argue that Jackson stepped *towards* reading and writing about ritual as a symbolic act, in the style of Burkean literary analysis, the kind of analysis that fascinated Hyman. According to Burke, practical actions, like rowing a boat, take place in reality. Writing about rowing a boat would be, then, a symbolic act. The acts of writing fiction and poetry are also symbolic acts to Burke, acts that help form ritual behaviours and contribute to the creation of myths. He specifically mentions the role of magic and religion as important to 'verbal coercion' or 'establishment by decree' (as in the creation story from Genesis, for example), thereby indicating the power of language in specific contexts.[12] These contexts become important to Jackson and her milieu in the ways that they treat language and its function in fiction.

Sidestepping the endpoint is an important part of Kenneth Burke's framework of symbolism and symbolic action (what Burke termed the 'individual symbolic equivalent for the ancient collective ritual').[13] Symbolic action, as a theory, influenced Stanley Hyman's foundational approaches to literature and folklore; Jackson was not only present in the room for this but also assisted him in parsing his thoughts over many years.[14] Jackson was probably first exposed to Burke's ideas while at Syracuse University via Hyman and her English professor Leonard Brown.[15] According to John Crowley, Jackson's term paper on Ernest Hemingway for Leonard Brown's class contained elements of Burkean literary analysis, such as the use of a terministic screen, a phenomenological approach to literature best described in his book *Language as Symbolic Action*.[16] In his analysis of Jackson's term paper, Crowley asserts that it cannot be proven Jackson was exposed to Burke's

11. Ingram, 'Speaking of Magic', p. 54.
12. See Kenneth Burke, *The Philosophy of Literary Form: Studies in Symbolic Action*, 3rd edn (Berkeley: University of California Press, 1973), pp. 3–33.
13. Hyman, 'The Ritual View of Myth and the Mythic', p. 286.
14. Starting in their undergraduate days, Jackson and Hyman's vibrant intellectual exchange illustrates how their dialogues were foundational to each other's work. See, for example, Ruth Franklin, pp. 105–6, on rituals to invoke ghosts, 115–16 on encounters with Kenneth Burke and 123–6 on their work on the student magazine *Spectre*. As Franklin points out, the intellectual frenzy of their early relationship provided a basis for some of the motifs of Jackson's later works, as well as foreshadowing the deep problems of their marital relationship.
15. Ruth Franklin, *Shirley Jackson: A Rather Haunted Life* (New York: Liveright, 2016), pp. 115–16. See also John W. Crowley and Shirley Jackson, 'Ernest Hemingway by Shirley Jackson; Introduction: Shirley Jackson on Ernest Hemingway: A Recovered Term Paper', *Syracuse University Library Associates Courier* 21 (1996): 35.
16. While Burke's terministic screen theory is from a little over twenty years after 'The Lottery' was published, many of the ideas contained in that volume were related to

theories in Brown's class. However, he says her paper used phenomenological techniques to explore psychology, rather than the reverse: 'The method was somewhat phenomenological in aim, seeking to get at the psychological depth of a work through the sheer comparison of its surfaces.'[17] Crowley's assertion that Jackson's focus was phenomenological is buttressed by notes for this same paper in Jackson's notebooks in the Library of Congress archive, and by the following page of notes on Burke's theories.[18]

developments in theory that took place over the course of that twenty years. These ideas were later to find concrete form in Burke's 1966 book *Language as Symbolic Action*.

17. Crowley and Jackson, 'Ernest Hemingway by Shirley Jackson; Introduction: Shirley Jackson on Ernest Hemingway: A Recovered Term Paper', p. 35.

18. Shirley Jackson Papers, 'College Notebooks', *The Library of Congress*, Box 37.

Notable here are the references to 'the problem of evil', 'actions: words', and 'rebirth – old not filling the need', all of which are central themes in Jackson's works.[19] These are important to Burke's and Hyman's work as well. Like other scholars of myth and ritual, such as Jane Harrison and Frye Northop, Burke subscribes to a tripartite meta-narratological process – that is, pollution, purification and redemption. Jackson's notebook confirms that by 1939 she was, at least, aware of Burke's theories on symbol and ritual and their applications to literature.

These early hints of Jackson's encounters with ritual and symbolic action in literature are later cemented by letters between Burke and Hyman from 1964 and 1965 supporting the notion that Jackson was involved in the development of their theoretical approaches to literature. The most obvious of these is the condolence letter that Burke sent to Hyman on Jackson's death in August 1965, in which he states their work would not have been possible without Jackson.[20] In another letter around the same time, Burke wrote: 'I realize more and more how essential a part Shily [sic] played in our scheme.'[21] While it is unclear what Hyman replied to these letters, the subject of the conversation, their 'scheme', and the fact that Burke called Jackson 'essential' signal how vital her role was to their works.

Jackson and Hyman seem mainly interested in the way Burke approached the construction of reality: that it is formed through symbolic action, and shared among people, groups and societies, and that reality is not an absolute but based on context. Jackson and Hyman also subscribe to the idea that the symbolic can manifest as the physical. In this, they are certainly proto-Foucauldian, and follow Plato's idea that language is a persuasive act, and that reality is created through actions and language represents these actions with the symbolic. Moreover, language does not only represent actions; it can motivate them and create reality that way. Burke does not agree with Plato's aversion to the consequences of language and the symbolic.

The debate on the importance of myth and ritual to literature and literary studies was of great concern not only to Jackson's husband but also among their intellectual milieu, including writers and academics that were members of their close-knit group of friends, such as Ralph Ellison and Kenneth Burke.[22] Crable asserts that as early as 1945, Hyman encouraged Ellison to 'deepen his

---

19. Shirley Jackson Papers, 'College Notebooks', *The Library of Congress*, Box 37.

20. While *Language as Symbolic Action* was published in 1966, the year following Jackson's death, it is likely that Jackson was present to hear conversations between Hyman and Burke that lead to the writing of the book. It is also likely that Jackson engaged directly with Burke about these theories, considering the topics of conversation among their group of friends. See Stanley Edgar Hyman Papers, 'Burke, Kenneth, 1952-1970, undated', *The Library of Congress*, Box 5.

21. Stanley Edgar Hyman Papers, 'Burke, Kenneth, 1952-1970, undated', *The Library of Congress*, Box 5.

22. For an analysis of the myth and ritual debate between Ralph Ellison and Stanley Edgar Hyman, see Bryan Crable, '"The Myth and Ritual Business": Ralph Ellison, Stanley

understanding of myth and ritual' by reading works by the Cambridge Ritualists.[23] This should not come as a surprise, since Hyman was already interested in myth, ritual and symbolic action during his undergraduate years at Syracuse. Among other references to their conversations on the topic, Ellison wrote to Hyman: 'I am not at all surprised that Kenneth Burke rates highz [sic] with you, having noticed similarities in your approaches to art. But, perhaps, most of all because he is also a hero of my own . . . and I'm never able to understand critics who don't admire him.'[24]

In addition to the dialogue between Hyman and Jackson's works, hollow rituals and symbolic action were important to other authors that Jackson had close friendships with, such as Ralph Ellison. Ellison even commented in a letter to Hyman that Jackson's work bore similarities to his own regarding the use of symbolic action and ritual:

> My other object is over the understatement, for while I believe that the ritual may be understated (providing the reader understands and makes the willing suspension of skepticism that marks belief) the tragic action ne ercan [sic] be. As Old man Aristotle points out in the Poetics, one requirement of tragic action is that it be of a certain proportion [. . .] What do you think? It is a rich story and perhaps it success [sic] exactly because of the incongruity to which I am objecting. I'd like to see Shirley present the same rite in terms of its contemporary equivalent. Let me know if she's done anything else of the kind; we're beginning to work the same vein.[25]

Ellison not only recognized that he and Jackson were 'beginning to work in the same vein' but also wrote encouragingly of Jackson's work and wanted her to explore symbolic action further in her writing. He felt that her use of ritual was too nuanced and ought to be teased out further, made plainer to the reader. This is perhaps a fair criticism, as Jackson's use of rituals remained somewhat ambiguous; this ambiguity probably contributed to scholarship overlooking the influence of ritual theory in her works. Moreover, Ellison's recognition of their use of the same theories on ritual also refers to 'tragic action', which is related not only to the classical literature he mentions but also to Burkean theory. Such comments indicate an ongoing intellectual dialogue on the subjects of ritual and myth between Ellison, Hyman, Jackson and perhaps other friends as well.

Edgar Hyman, and American Sacrementalism', *African American Review* 53, no. 2 (2020): 111–26.

   23. Crable, '"The Myth and Ritual Business"', p. 116.

   24. Stanley Edgar Hyman Papers, 'Correspondence: Ellison, Ralph and Fanny 1942-1970', *The Library of Congress*, Box 6.

   25. Stanley Edgar Hyman Papers, 'Correspondence: Ellison, Ralph and Fanny 1942-1970', *The Library of Congress*, Box 6.

Hollow Rituals, Symbolic Meaning

As previously explained, allusions to ritual in Jackson's oeuvre draw on Hyman's critical work on the Myth and Ritual School and from Burke's theories on literature as symbolic action. In practice, Jackson uses the theory of symbolic action as a kind of mythmaking motif in her fiction, which enacts a hollow rhetoric. Not all myths have a deeper symbolic meaning all the time. Sometimes the text is about a rhetoric of reception and response. For example, in Frazer's *Golden Bough*, the scapegoat ritual is said to exist for purification purposes. But if the ritual of the scapegoat has lost its origins, then it might be considered a hollow ritual – that is, a ritual with a symbolic function but no deeper meaning.[26] The scapegoat as a hollow ritual is central to Jackson's 'The Lottery' (1948) but, as previously mentioned, can be found in other parts of her work as well. There is no catharsis in these tales; the ritual is repeated, but the meaning is lost. It is, in essence, performativity and repetition without transformation.

Jackson uses these repetitions on common themes where individuals are threatened by a group or a supernatural being, such as figures of the demonic, like James Harris (from *The Lottery*), or communal acts of transgression. For example, the short stories 'The Rock' and 'The Summer People' focus both on isolation and on seemingly ritualistic behaviours enacted in rural, natural spaces – a lakeside, forested area, and a hotel literally built into an island cave. In 'The Summer People', an older couple, the Allisons, have spent seventeen summers at their lake house; they decide to stay past Labor Day instead of returning home to the city. In a series of subsequent disturbing events, they realize that by staying they have committed an unnatural act, which the villagers of the town near the lake, and even the lake itself, seem to condemn. The story ends ambiguously with the power blown out in their cottage and a squall howling across the lake, as the couple wait in the dark for whatever seems to be menacing them. In 'The Rock', a young couple, the Ellisons, and the husband's sister, Paula, have come for a vacation in an isolated island hotel, which is built straight into the rock of the island. As the husband is recovering from illness, the couple isolate themselves, and Paula is encouraged to explore. She meets another guest, a 'little man' named Mr Johnson, with whom she has disturbing conversations that play on her anxieties about her relationship with her brother and his wife. In the end it is revealed that Mr Johnson wishes to do *something* to Paula, *something* that the landlady tries to protect her from.

Both stories make clear Jackson's technique of using symbolic action via ritual while almost never referring to any event or person directly, and instead making them ambiguous. This is especially true of the endpoints of this type of story for Jackson – neither 'The Rock' nor 'The Summer People' reveals what the ritual's purpose is intended to be. If the Allisons survive the storm, what would their interactions be with the villagers? Or with the lake? If Paula is forced to stay at

---

26. Burke sometimes also refers to this as a 'hollow rhetoric', echoing the 'rhetoric of reception and response' that underpins his theories.

the black island hotel, what does Mr Johnson intend to do with her? Reading this technique as one of inspiring terror in the reader is more than possible – many who have written on Jackson have done so, including myself. But if instead we read this technique through the lens of Hyman's and Burke's work, then we may also consider how 'myth tells a story sanctioning a rite,' and that 'neither means or explains anything'.[27] The ambiguity of the symbolic action in these two stories reminds us that myth itself does not exist to explicate historic persons or events (which Hyman terms 'euhemerist'); neither does it arise from concepts like a 'quest for knowledge' or to explain nature (which Hyman terms 'cognitionist').

As the Allisons stubbornly disobey the ritual of return to the city (for city people must return to the city before Labor Day), the lake people do everything in their power to force them to carry it out, but to what end? The Allisons are harassed by the villagers and are alarmed by weird phenomena that seem supernatural or demonic: no one will deliver groceries or gas for the stove; the phone wires are cut; the car dies; a letter arrives from their son with strange fingerprints smeared all over it; a storm comes up over the lake. Despite these odd occurrences, the Allisons still do not begin their journey home to the city and the consequences seem dire. Without grocery deliveries and gas, their electricity and radio out, the couple is left in the darkness: 'while the lightning flashed outside, and the radio faded and sputtered, the two old people huddled together in their summer cottage and waited'.[28] They 'waited', but it is unclear what they are waiting for. The Allisons are on the edge of a sinister something, invoked by a suddenly unfamiliar and unfriendly community and landscape, which reminds that Jackson's rituals are a hollow act. Hollow acts sidestep the endpoint, an essential part of symbolic action.

Unlike 'The Rock', which features the ritual of choosing a victim, 'The Summer People' echoes *The Lottery* through attachment to the landscape and the passage of time. While the season of summer recalls ancient ritual from 'The Lottery', the similarities end there; savage potential and consistent symbolism release the repressed, cruel ambitions of the lake people against the perceived intrusion of the outsiders instead of focusing on the choice of one victim from within the community. In 'The Summer People', outsiders are easily identifiable vacationers who want to stay past the appointed time for vacationing: Labor Day. The Allisons are able to actualize their exclusion by rejecting the commonly accepted flow of time. The country people are focused on their environment through a resistance to change. They had an 'instinctive distrust of anything that did not look as permanent as trees and rocks and sky'.[29] That resistance to change is the main reason why the Allisons' continued presence at the lake threatens the balance, endangering the lake peoples' ritualistic behaviours that determine their perception of time. Since the foundation of their idea of continuity within the community relies on such

---

27. Hyman, 'The Ritual View of Myth and the Mythic', p. 287.
28. Shirley Jackson, 'The Summer People', in *Shirley Jackson: Novels and Stories*, ed. Joyce Carol Oates (New York: Library of America, 2010), p. 607.
29. Jackson, 'The Summer People', p. 596.

a lack of change, the lake people are highly perturbed by the Allisons' desires. The lake people consider time truly sacred: those who come in the summer must return to their own homes before Labor Day.

To Kill the God

In Jackson's posthumously collected short fiction, analysis of the motif of myth and ritual can become more flexible in scope and depth. The outsized influence and presence of *The Lottery*, with its laser focus on the scapegoat and its variants, makes it possible for scholarship to widen its lens to include more communal behaviours, isolationism and cycles of rebirth. For example, between the isolation of the family in 'The Rock' and 'The Summer People' is the 'The Man in the Woods', a story based on the ritual of killing the god.[30] This short story stands out as exemplary of the wilderness/forest as a nexus of ritual and myth – but like the other two stories, part of its focus is on the placement and habitation of a temporary, uncanny home that dislocates the main character from reality and places him in a fantasy. The main character, Christopher, leaves civilization (the city) behind and enters the forest; the reader is never told the reason why. In the woods, he meets a nameless cat (later called Grimalkin)[31] and comes upon a strange house with a doorway covered in roses. There is a mysterious group of people living in that house: two women, Sibyl and Circe (named from Greek myth), and Mr Oakes (named from myth and folklore on 'The King of the Wood'). The reader is unclear of their relationship – they are not family but are clearly living as a family unit might. Although Christopher is welcomed into the house with food and a bed for the night, a sense of foreboding permeates the dwelling. At the end of the story, Christopher is lured into the forest to fight Mr Oakes; it is implied that Christopher should murder Mr Oakes to remain at the house as its owner.

'The Man in the Woods' is a rare example of Jackson's use of the forest as a locus of ritual. The forest is a representation of a delineation between the seemingly logical world, where symbols and social order make sense to the reader, and the space of the illogical, in which a new symbology overthrows or replaces the old. First, the trees themselves create an atmosphere of fear, which Christopher notices

---

30. Unlike most of her other posthumously published short fiction, the location of 'The Man in the Woods' (2015; date written unknown) in the Library of Congress archive is muddled; the title of the story is written in brown crayon, though the draft is clearly a fair copy. It is mixed in with other papers and, unlike most of her other stories, does not have its own folder or even a line in the finding aid.

31. Curiously, Grimalkin is a nickname Jackson used for herself in several early letters to Hyman. She wrote that it means 'old she-cat' and even signs one of the letters 'Grimalkin'. Though it might be overreaching, mention of Grimalkin might be some self-insertion of the author into the story. See Stanley Edgar Hyman Papers, 'Family Papers: Jackson, Shirley, letters to Stanley Hyman September 1938-July 1939', *The Library of Congress*, Box 2.

almost immediately: 'He glanced apprehensively at the trees so close to him, irritated by the sound of his own voice in the silence, as though the trees were listening to him and, listening, had nodded solemnly to one another.'[32] The forest is anthropomorphic, 'listening' and possibly leading Christopher to the house. It seems that only the river 'knew a way out of the forest', which implies that both Christopher and his feline companion will not leave.[33] Second, Mr Oakes urges Christopher to eat the food (a risky act in many folktales), which also implies that Christopher will become a permanent inhabitant of the forest. Finally, Mr Oakes asks Christopher to care for his roses and to remember who planted them, indicating that Christopher may receive both Mr Oakes's place and property.

Jackson's ritual in the woods lends potential to the idea that destructive forces are already lurking inside us, waiting for the right environment to emerge. Christopher has entered a space where the social rules are foreign to him: that he imagines the woods are closing behind him as he walks forward, that both cats and men can steal an identity through duelling. Within the house in the woods, Christopher's propensity for participation in the ritual emerges – he does not hesitate to follow Mr Oakes to the stream, even knowing that he is meant to kill the older man. Mr Oakes also embodies a patriarchal order that involves itself in violence, and Circe and Sybil represent the women who perpetuate it; it is Sybil who gives the knife to Christopher, but Mr Oakes who sharpens it. Thus, the forest in 'The Man in the Woods' is a locus of ritual (sacrifice), and a representation of the continuation of the ritual through violence and transference of name and power.

Mr Oakes, by his very name, reminds us of Frazer's writing on the rituals of killing the god known as 'King of the Wood'. By his name, by the location of the fight between Mr Oakes and Christopher, and by the words that he utters as Christopher comes to fight him, he identifies himself thus. Frazer's description of the battle seems to closely match Jackson's writing as well:

> The rule that he held office till a stronger should slay him might suppose to secure both the preservation of his divine life in full vigour and its transference to a suitable successor as soon as that vigour began to be impaired. For so long as he could maintain his position by the strong hand, it might be inferred that his natural force was not abated; whereas his defeat and death at the hands of another proved that his strength was beginning to fail and that it was time his divine life should be lodged in a less dilapidated tabernacle.[34]

As Mr Oakes is aging, and Christopher is young, the story's foreshadowing of this fight appears through the symbolism of the caretaker role that Mr Oakes performs. He tells Christopher about how he was 'the first one to clear away even this much

---

32. Jackson, 'The Man in the Woods', p. 174.
33. Jackson, 'The Man in the Woods', p. 174.
34. Frazer, *The Golden Bough*, p. 273.

of the forest' so that he could plant roses.[35] When Christopher projects that the roses would grow big enough to 'cover the house', Mr Oakes seems pleased that they would be his legacy; instead of saying he would be there to see them, he tells Christopher to 'remember who planted them'.[36] Before their fight, Mr Oakes again says that he wants Christopher to care for the roses.[37] The roses will not grow for Mr Oakes anymore; having received 'King of the Wood' energy from Mr Oakes, it will be up to Christopher to take care of them. The fight with Mr Oakes will allow him to pass through his violent initiation and take his place in the patriarchal order.

Conclusion

More work must be done to elucidate the connections between Jackson's practical applications of myth and ritual theory, and the critics and theorists whose work she was inspired by and interacted with. Alongside such vital research, new writing on Jackson should concern itself with extant scholarship on the intellectual dialogues between Ellison, Burke, Hyman and others of their milieu to make clear how Jackson's interpretation of ritual and myth may have contributed to said dialogue. By doing so, we will have a clearer picture of Jackson's importance to twentieth-century literature and criticism, as well as a better understanding of the long-lasting appeal of her works.

In Jackson's oeuvre, rituals and strange interactions take place in uncanny landscapes, and the characters find reality shift from under their feet. Christopher in 'The Man in the Woods' participates in the ritual and thus demonstrates his potential to become a monster himself through a process akin to 'killing the god'. Christopher knows that just as Grimalkin's name and power were transferable, so is Mr Oakes'. In 'The Summer People', the Allisons refuse their usual ritual of return to the city and seem to fall victim to *new* rituals carried out against them as the locals try to force them to leave. For Jackson, these types of stories connect with folkloric rituals related to death and rebirth described in texts like Frazer's *Golden Bough* and discussed in letters between Hyman, Burke and Ellison.

Hollow rituals that buttress evocations of terror, the uncanny and the irrational become symbolic action in her fiction. 'There are *practical* acts, and there are symbolic acts,' as Kenneth Burke wrote – there is a difference between a house built in fiction and one built in reality.[38] There is a difference between the construction of a scapegoating ritual in a folk ballad and the image of that ritual that each reader of *The Lottery* forms for themselves as they read. Reading Shirley Jackson, too, becomes a symbolic act.

35. Jackson, 'The Man in the Woods', p. 184.
36. Jackson, 'The Man in the Woods', p. 184.
37. Jackson, 'The Man in the Woods', p. 186.
38. Burke, *The Philosophy of Literary Form*, pp. 8–9.

References

Burke, Kenneth (1966), *Language as Symbolic Action: Essays on Life, Literature, and Method*, Berkeley: University of California Press.

Burke, Kenneth (1973), *The Philosophy of Literary Form: Studies in Symbolic Action*, 3rd edn, Berkeley: University of California Press.

Coupe, Laurence (2005), *Kenneth Burke on Myth: An Introduction*, New York: Routledge.

Crable, Bryan (2020), '"The Myth and Ritual Business": Ralph Ellison, Stanley Edgar Hyman, and American Sacrementalism', *African American Review* 53 (2): 111–26.

Crowley, John W. and Shirley Jackson (1996), 'Ernest Hemingway by Shirley Jackson; Introduction: Shirley Jackson on Ernest Hemingway: A Recovered Term Paper', *Syracuse University Library Associates Courier* 21: 33–50. https://surface.syr.edu/cgi/viewcontent.cgi?article=1051&context=libassoc (accessed 15 April 2021).

Downey, Dara (2011), '"Reading Her Difficult Riddle": Shirley Jackson and Late 1950s' Anthropology', in Darryl Jones, Elizabeth McCarthy and Bernice M. Murphy (eds), *It Came from the 1950s!: Popular Culture, Popular Anxieties*, 176–97, Hampshire: Palgrave.

Eliade, Mircae (1959), *The Sacred and the Profane: The Nature of Religion*, trans. Willard R. Trask, New York: Harcourt Brace Jovanovich.

Fergusson, Francis (1998), 'The Idea of a Theater', in Robert A. Segal (ed.), *The Myth and Ritual Theory*, 245–66, Malden: Blackwell.

Franklin, Ruth (2016), *Shirley Jackson: A Rather Haunted Life*, New York: Liveright.

Frazer, James George (2009), *The Golden Bough: A New Abridgment*, Oxford: Oxford University Press.

Hyman, Stanley Edgar, Stanley Hyman Papers, Manuscript Division, United States Library of Congress, https://hdl.loc.gov/loc.mss/eadmss.ms997001.

Hyman, Stanley Edgar (1963), 'The Ritual View of Myth and the Mythic' (1955), in Stanley Edgar Hyman (ed.), *The Promised End: Essays and Reviews, 1942-1962*, 278–94, Cleveland: The World Publishing Company.

Hyman, Stanley Edgar (1978), 'The Critic's Credentials', in Phoebe Pettingell (ed.), *The Critic's Credentials: Essays and Reviews by Stanley Edgar Hyman*, 3–20, New York: Antheneum.

Ingram, Shelly (2016), 'Speaking of Magic: Folk Narrative in *Hangsaman* and *We Have Always Lived in the Castle*', in Melanie R. Anderson and Lisa Kroger (eds), *Shirley Jackson: Influences and Confluences*, 54–75, New York: Routledge.

Jackson, Shirley, Shirley Jackson Papers, 1932–1991, Manuscript Division, United States Library of Congress. https://hdl.loc.gov/loc.mss/eadmss.ms996001.

Jackson, Shirley (2010), 'The Rock', in Joyce Carol Oates (ed.), *Novels and Stories*, 753–71, New York: The Library of America.

Jackson, Shirley (2010), 'The Summer People', in Joyce Carol Oates (ed.), *Novels and Stories*, 594–607, New York: The Library of America.

Jackson, Shirley (2015), 'The Man in the Woods', in Laurence Jackson Hyman and Sarah Hyman Dewitt (eds), *Let Me Tell You: New Stories, Essays, and Other Writings*, 276–89, New York: Random House.

Landau, Samantha (2018), 'Occult Influences in Shirley Jackson's *The Lottery*', *Gakuen* 936: 11–21. http://dx.doi.org/10.17613/4zbs-7b59 (accessed 25 July 2022).

Murphy, Bernice M. (2005), '"The People of the Village Have Always Hated Us": Shirley Jackson's New England Gothic', in Bernice M. Murphy (ed.), *Shirley Jackson: Essays on the Literary Legacy*, 104–26, Jefferson: McFarland and Company.

Sterenberg, Matthew Kane (2007), 'Myth and the Modern Problem: Mythic Thinking in Twentieth Century Britain', unpublished doctoral dissertation, Northwestern University. https://www.proquest.com/openview/45fb5d8bebdaae6e50355393e4cd2d3e/1?pq-origsite=gscholar&cbl=18750 (accessed 15 August 2022).

Vickery, John B. (1957), 'The Golden Bough and Modern Poetry', *The Journal of Aesthetics and Art Criticism* 15 (3): 271–88. https://www.jstor.org/stable/427292 (accessed 21 April 2021).

INDEX

Abernathy, Robert   193
adolescence   40, 116, 120–1, see also childhood
'Adventure on a Bad Night'   2
'The Adventures of James Harris'   13, 97, see also Harris, James (and variants)
ageing   16, 24, 41, 174, 211
agoraphobia   148, 154–5
alcohol   35, 41, 155
alienation   25, 101–4, 149–56, 162–6, 169
aliens   187–8, 191, 196
American Dream   27–43, 90
Amis, Kingsley   189–90
Anderson, Melanie R.   9, 17
apocalyptic/apocalypse   38, 169–70, 181, 189, 204, see also dystopia
architecture, buildings   23, 154, see also houses
Aristotle   221
Ashley, Michael   200
Asimov, Isaac   189, 200, see also science fiction

ballads   13–14, 46, 109, 215–16, see also 'The Daemon Lover' (ballad); 'The Daemon Lover' (story)
beach   148, 152–3
Beatty, Jeanne   184, 217
'The Beautiful Stranger'   25, 182
Benjamin, Walter   149
Berner (Lord)   138
Bewitched (TV show)   72
The Bible   98
Bloch, Robert   200
Bluebeard   46, 54, see also fairy tales; folklore
Bonikowski, Wyatt   175
Boucher, Anthony   203, 211
Bourchier, John   138
bourgeois   76, 166, 169, see also class; economics

Bowen, Elizabeth   49, 52
Bradbury, Ray   185, 200, see also science fiction
'The Bulletin'   181, 188–9, 203, 213
Burke, Kenneth   218, 220–3
'The Bus'   10, 34, 40, 50
buses (transport)   157, 187, 193
Butler, Octavia E.   188, see also science fiction

Calvin, John   102
Cambridge Ritualists   216, 221
Campbell, John W.   184
Campbell, Ramsey   29
cannibalism   136, 142
capitalism   39–41, 67, 166, 174, see also class; consumerism; economics; middle class
'Charlie Roberts'   2
Child, Francis James   14, 46
childhood   11, 39, 60, 136, 140, 164, 173–5
children's literature   11
Christianity   98
Circe   142, see also Greek myth; The Odyssey
cities   148, 172, 223, see also urban
civilisation   143
class   42, 140, 169, 186, see also consumerism; economics; middle class
clothes   84, 123, 139, 186
Clute, John   200
'Colloquy'   82, 94–5
colonialism   35, 43
colour   83–4, 123
Come Along with Me   174
comedy, the comic   168, 173
consumerism   86, 90, 151, 140–6, 162–5, 186, 190, see also class; economics; middle class

conte cruel   201
Cosmopolitan (magazine)   90

'The Daemon Lover' (ballad)   13–14, 24, 46, 73
'The Daemon Lover' (story)   14, 50, 87, 97, 102, 170
Dahl, Roald   56
Dark Tales   27, 36
Datlow, Ellen   3
'A Day in the Jungle'   155
death drive   151, *see also* Freud, Sigmund; uncanny
Delany, Samuel R.   183
de l'Isle-Adam, Auguste Villiers   201–2
Derrida, Jacques   117, 124
'Devil of a Tale'   17–20
the Devil/Satan   17–18, 98, 135
Dick, Philip K.   182, 185–6
'Dinner for a Gentleman'   25
Dirda, Michael   201
domesticity   31, 64–5, 120, 137–40, 144–8, 153–4, 162, 187, 194
dreams/dreaming   82, 155, *see also* sleep
drugs/pharmacology   90, 155, *see also* medicine
du Maurier, Daphne   125
dystopia   39, 189–90, *see also* apocalypse; science fiction

early modern   9–12
ecocriticism   136
ecogothic   135, *see also* Gothic
economics   162, *see also* class; consumerism; middle class
Eliade, Mircae   215
'Elizabeth'   53, 97, 102
Ellison, Ralph   220, 221
embodiment   114, 121, 150–1, 156
epigraphs   15–17, 34, 97, 99

fables   208, 215, *see also* fairy tales; folklore
fairy tales   135, 137, 211, 218
fantastic   24, 216
Fantastic Magazine   189
Female Gothic   163, *see also* Gothic
feminist   31–3, 43, 54, 68, 114, 183, 194
film   65, 71–2

flâneur   149, *see also* urban
folk horror   29
folklore   13–14, 46–8, 67, 142, 201, 208, 216, 225, *see also* ballads; fables; fairy tales
food   16–17, 142, 162, 168–9, 171, 192, 206
forest   135–6, *see also* ecocriticism; ecogothic
Foucault, Michel   82, 220
Franklin, Ruth   32, 85, 89, 91, 99, 169, 181
Frazer, James George   137, 143, 215, 225
Freud, Sigmund   82–4, 154, 158, *see also* death drive; uncanny
The Interpretation of Dreams   83, 154
Friedan, Betty   162, 166–7
Fromm, Erich   89

Geddes, Patrick   151
ghosts   13, 85, 114, 175–7
Gibson, Marion   72
Glanvill, Joseph   11, 97
God/gods   15, 20, 101, 192, *see also* Protestantism; Puritanism; religion
Gomoll, Jeanne   183
'The Good Wife'   115, 125
Gothic   35–6, 43, 123, 126, 135, 145, 166, 175, 181, 213
Graves, Robert   71
Greek myth   70, 137, 142, 224
Greene, Robert   138
the Green Man   143

Hall, Joan Wylie   3, 30, 47, 87, 108, 113
'The Hanging Stranger'   191
Hangsaman   114, 136, 208
Harris, James (and variants)   23, 46–7, 87–8, 97, 156, 216, 222, *see* 'The Daemon Lover' (ballad); 'The Daemon Lover' (story)
Harrison, Jane   215
Hattenhauer, Darryl   11, 30, 93, 169–70, 172, 217
haunted house   175
The Haunting of Hill House (Netflix)   3
The Haunting of Hill House (novel)   1, 13, 34, 49, 83
Hawthorne, Nathaniel   30, 103, 107, 135–6, 139, 141

Heinlein, Robert   185
Hemingway, Ernest   218
Hoeveler, Diane Long   194–5
'Home'   30, 34, 36, 164, 175
'The Honeymoon of Mrs Smith'   53, 55, 164, 175
'The House-Carpenter,' see 'The Daemon Lover' (ballad)
houses   33, 37, 128, 144, 169, 224
housewife   25, 65, 154–5, 163, 166, 174
'How I Write'   83
Huneker, James Gibbons   201
Hurston, Zora Neale   167
Hyman, Laurence Jackson   144, 182
Hyman, Stanley Edgar   2, 11, 29–30, 65, 89, 215, 217, 220–3
hysteria   138, 174

'The Intoxicated'   40, 49–50

Jackson, Geraldine   201
James, M. R.   41, 182
James Harris, see Harris, James (and variants)
Jim Harris, see Harris, James (and variants)
Joshi, S. T.   174, 213
Just an Ordinary Day   18, 56, 114

Kafka, Franz   30
King, Stephen   3, 135
Knight, Damon   181, 184

labour (work)   66, 94, 122
Lacan, Jacques   47
Ladies' Home Journal   36, 177
Lefebvre, Henri   164–5
Let Me Tell You   2, 27
letters
    letters about Jackson   220–1
    letters as motif   87, 129, 137, 204
    letters by Jackson   201, 217
Levin, Ira   168
Library of Congress   2, 219
Life among the Savages   165
'Like Mother Used to Make'   53, 97, 102
'Little Red Riding Hood'   135, see also fairy tales; folklore

'Lord of the Castle'   17, 64, 74
'The Lottery'   3, 29, 181, 201, 215, 223
The Lottery and Other Stories   97, 163, 167, 201
'Louisa, Please Come Home'   10, 23, 208
Lovecraft, H. P.   28, 34, 38, 201
'The Lovely House,' see 'A Visit'

Machado, Carmen Maria   46
The Magazine of Fantasy and Science Fiction   116, 184, 200
'The Man in the Woods'   64, 137, 141, 215, 224
Marlowe, Christopher   110
marriage   56, 65, 89, 92, 103, 128, 140, 155, 162–8, 170, 182, 194
Marx, Karl   166
Matheson, Richard   185
May, Rollo   86
medicine   81, 90, 156
'Men with their Big Shoes'   164, 168
middle class   32, 87, 164, 186
Midsommar (film)   3
'The Missing Girl'   115, 182, 195, 208–10, 213
More, Henry   12
motherhood   94, 140, 148, 162, 166–8, 193–4
Mr Harris, see Harris, James (and variants)
'Mrs Spencer and the Oberons'   25, 137–40
Mumford, Lewis   151
murder   56, 173
Murphy, Bernice M.   47, 72, 141, 163, 166, 173
'My Life with R. H. Macy'   165, 204
mythology   194, 215

naming   142, 189, 207, 224
nature   137, 222, see also beach; ecocriticism; ecogothic
neighbourhood   193
    neighbours   154
New England   28, 98, 181
New Jersey   41–2
New Weird   43
New York   106–7, 148, 151, 155, 169, 186
The New Yorker   144, 201

New York Times 167
'Nightmare' 10, 22, 83–4, 114, 121, 193
Nord, Deborah 159
nostalgia 168

Oates, Joyce Carol 27, 172
The Odyssey 142
'The Omen' 182, 192–3, 213
'One Ordinary Day, With Peanuts' 182, 190–2, 197, 206, 212–13
'Only Stand and Wait' 2
Oppenheimer, Judy 200–1

'Paranoia' 53, 183, 185–6, 193
'The Phantom Lover' 50, *see also* 'The Daemon Lover' (ballad); 'The Daemon Lover' (story)
phenomenology 150, 156
'Pillar of Salt' 148
Plath, Sylvia 30
Plato 220
Poe, Edgar Allan 28
Pohl, Fredrik 190
poison 142
'The Possibility of Evil' 30, 34, 37, 174
postmodernism 169–70
post-war era 148, 165, 171, 184, 191
pregnancy 168–9
Protestantism 97
psychiatry 184, 219
    psychological illness 15–16, 85, 90–5
    psychosurgery 92
psychoanalysis 65, 81, 89
pulp fiction 200
Puritanism 98

race 35, 40–1, 165
religion 67–8, 109, 143, 218
'The Renegade' 14
reviews (of Jackson) 174, 181
ritual 165, 168, 177, 216, 222
The Road Through the Wall 11, 162–3, 173
'The Rock' 222
'Root of Evil' 182, 189–90, 193
Russ, Joanna 194

Salem 99, 135–6
Saltus, Edgar 201–2

San Francisco 32
satire 189–90, 210
science fiction 181, 202
servants 168–9
sex 20–1, 58, 103, 156
Shakespeare, William 138
Shirley Jackson Awards 3
Simmel, Georg 149
sleep 52, 70, 81–2, 85, 144, 158
'The Smoking Room' 17–20
Southern Gothic 31
spectral 150–1, 175
speculative fiction 200
Sturgeon, Theodore 192
suburban 162–3, 167, 174
'The Summer People' 29, 34, 40, 136, 164, 169, 215, 222
supernatural 9–11, 76, 174, 215
superstition 10, 13, 25, 36
surveillance 21, 92, 169, 172, 177
Swift, Jonathan 205–6, 210
Syracuse 29, 218, 221

Theroux, Paul 1
Tiptree Jr., James 183, 196
Tochterman, Brian L. 151
Todorov, Tzvetan 9, 24
'The Tooth' 14, 50–3, 82, 91, 97, 102, 150, 155
Trump, Donald 27, 41, 43
The Twilight Zone 213

uncanny 31, 113, 118, 129, 149, 155, 213, 215
urban (spaces) 121, 168–70, 193
urban legends 59

vacations 148, 169, 222
Vandermeer, Jeff 28
Vermont 33
'The Very Strange House Next Door' 67
Vienna Circle 149
'The Villager' 103
'A Visit' 23, 30, 64, 72

'A Warning to Married Women,' *see* 'The Daemon Lover' (ballad)
Washington Post 201

We Have Always Lived in the Castle 1, 16–17, 34, 100
Weird fiction 27, 213
Weird Realism 42
Weird Tales 28
Wells, H. G. 188
'What a Thought' 172

The Wicker Man 3
wilderness 135–6
witchcraft, witches 12–16, 64, 97, 99, 127, 141
The Witchcraft of Salem Village 99
World War II 81, 86, 94, 114, 165, 171, 184

www.ingramcontent.com/pod-product-compliance
Lightning Source LLC
Chambersburg PA
CBHW071829300426
44116CB00009B/1490